Elementary School Counseling in a Changing World

Editors:
Edwin R. Gerler, Jr.
Joseph C. Ciechalski
Larry D. Parker

ERIC Counseling and Personnel Services Clearinghouse
2108 School of Education
The University of Michigan
Ann Arbor, Michigan 48109-1259

and

The American School Counselor Association
a division of the
American Association for Counseling and Development
5999 Stevenson Avenue
Alexandria, Virginia 22304

ERIC Counseling and Personnel Services Clearinghouse
2108 School of Education
The University of Michigan
Ann Arbor, MI 48109-1259

ISBN 1-56109-000-X

This publication was prepared with partial funding from the Office of Educational Research and Improvement, U.S. Department of Education under contract no. R188062011. The opinions expressed in this report do not necessarily reflect the positions or policies of OERI, the Department of Education, or ERIC/CAPS.

CONTENTS

INTRODUCTION

This monograph is one expression of the expanded collaboration that has developed between the American School Counselor Association (ASCA) and ERIC/CAPS. Under the thoughtful leadership of ASCA President Jim Whitledge, numerous joint activities have been initiated with collaboration on publications being one of the most notable. Working closely with the ASCA Publication Committee and the Chair, Norm Gysbers, it was decided that Edwin Gerler's proposal for a volume on elementary counseling was an ideal publication to inaugurate the "new look" in joint publications. The completed manuscript is outstanding in its coverage and focuses on topics of critical concern to elementary school counselors and those associated with elementary guidance. It should prove to be a book of both immediate interest and long time usefulness for all school counselors. The editors, Edwin R. Gerler, Jr., Joseph C. Ciechalski, and Larry D. Parker, are to be congratulated for their skill in assembling such a timely and relevant book.

We look forward to many new products and publications which will grow out of this collaboration.

Garry R. Walz
Director, ERIC/CAPS

FOREWORD

In the past two decades there have been an enormous number of changes in our society that have impacted the lives of children, their parents, and teachers. Professional counselors have drawn upon their best resources to meet the problems created by an increasingly stressful world. Counselors have experienced both the joy of success and the sting of defeat. Now, as we look to the next decade, it is obvious that societal changes will continue at a rapid pace making the work of counselors even more complex and difficult.

What have we learned? What must we continue to do? What new initiatives must be taken? What new roles and interventions must be emphasized for developmental guidance and counseling programs?

There is considerable diversity among young people and their opportunities. We sometimes lose sight of the social and cultural forces which are part of the daily lives of children and their families. We sometimes fail to understand how certain environmental factors affect the ways in which children think about school, learn, and respond to counseling. Too often differences are forgotten when children are seated together in a classroom, or grouped by age, or described in terms of developmental stages. Helping all children to achieve academically and personally requires a knowledge of their changing world.

This book is designed to help increase one's awareness of the cultural and social issues which face children and their counselors. It draws attention to environmental factors which impinge on both teaching and counseling techniques. It encourages counselors to re-examine their roles and interventions as they meet the counseling and guidance challenges of the 1990s.

Robert D. Myrick
University of Florida

PREFACE

In his classic book, *The Counselor in a Changing World*, G. Gilbert Wrenn wrote:

> We must understand the new social forces that are influencing young people, as well as the rest of us—and we must learn to apply new psychological insights into the nature of the individual. . . . Counselors must anticipate social change, not necessarily its rate and magnitude, but at least its direction. It is difficult to appreciate how swiftly things are changing. Perhaps the estimate that the sum total of human knowledge doubles every ten or fifteen years may provide some idea of what is going on. We must move fast merely to keep up with our students.

What Wrenn stated in the early 1960s continues to be true; counselors "must anticipate social change" as they plan programs to promote child development. This book of readings is to help counselors in elementary schools use the perspective of the 1980s to prepare for the changes of a new decade and for the beginning of a new century. The book shows how counselors help children grow and develop in a changing world shaped by cultural diversity, new family structures, rampant substance abuse, and by various other social, economic, and political forces.

Each chapter of the book contains articles that have been published in a variety of counseling journals during the 1980s. The journals included are: *Elementary School Guidance and Counseling*, *The School Counselor*, *Journal of Counseling and Development*, *Counselor Education and Supervision*, *Journal of Multicultural Counseling and Development*, *Journal of Humanistic Education and Development*, *Journal for Specialists in Group Work*, *Vocational Guidance Quarterly*, and *Career Development Quarterly*. The book contains articles by recognized authorities, including, Paul Pedersen on multicultural issues, Norman Gysbers and Ken Hoyt on career development, Garry Walz on the influence of computers, Norman Sprinthall and John Horan on substance abuse, and articles by noted experts in child counseling, Bob Myrick, Don Keat, and Dick Nelson. The book also contains articles by well established practitioners and new scholars in the area of elementary school counseling. The book thus affords practicing counselors and future counselors an opportunity to examine varying perspectives on elementary school counseling.

Because of space limitations, we have had to make difficult choices about which articles to use in each chapter. The book includes articles that discuss practical programs and strategies as well as theory and research. Each chapter begins with an introduction by the editors and concludes with a set of issues and questions for discussion. The issues and questions presented are designed to stimulate thinking about the current status of elementary school counseling in preparation for innovative counseling services and strategies for the 1990s and beyond.

As is true of virtually all publications, this book contains material that is already out of date. The articles on technology, for example, contain information about computer software and hardware that is changing rapidly. The perspective of the authors of these articles, however, is valuable and illustrates how difficult it is for elementary school counselors to stay current with technological advances.

Elementary school counseling is experiencing varied patterns of growth in the United States. The increasing numbers of elementary school counselors in some states is exciting. We hope this book of readings will show educators throughout the nation the value of establishing elementary school counseling programs and will challenge coordinators of existing programs to improve the services they offer. We also hope that this book will serve as a valuable resource for graduate students who are preparing themselves to work as elementary school counselors.

Editors:
Edwin R. Gerler, Jr.
Joseph C. Ciechalski
Larry D. Parker

ABOUT THE EDITORS

Edwin R. Gerler, Jr. is a Professor in the Department of Counselor Education at North Carolina State University in Raleigh. He has written extensively, including the book, *Counseling the Young Learner*, published by Prentice-Hall. He has co-produced a film on elementary school counseling that is marketed by AACD. He has been the editor of two AACD journals in addition to serving on several editorial boards. He is presently the editor of *Elementary School Guidance and Counseling*. He has also been an elementary school counselor and teacher.

Joseph C. Ciechalski is an Assistant Professor in the Department of Counselor Education at East Carolina University in Greenville, North Carolina. He has coauthored the book, *Psychological Techniques for Teachers*, published by Accelerated Development. He has written numerous articles and reviews. He currently serves on the editorial board of *Elementary School Guidance and Counseling*. He has had extensive public school counseling and teaching experience.

Larry D. Parker is a doctoral student in the Department of Counselor Education at North Carolina State University in Raleigh. He is currently an editorial assistant for *Elementary School Guidance and Counseling*. He has special expertise in cross-cultural counseling and in working with exceptional children. He has been an elementary school counselor and teacher.

Correspondence about this manuscript should be sent to:

Edwin R. Gerler, Jr.
520 Poe Hall
Department of Counselor Education
North Carolina State University
Raleigh, North Carolina 27695-7801

Phone: (919) 737-2244

CONTRIBUTORS

Pat Alford, Director, Call Rape, Tulsa, Oklahoma

H. A. Altmann, Professor, Department of Educational Psychology, University of Calgary, Alberta, Canada

Ronald F. Anderson, Director, Student Services, Wake County Public Schools, Raleigh, North Carolina

Carolyn J. Bauer, Associate Professor, Department of Curriculum & Instruction, Oklahoma State University, Stillwater

David L. Beck, Family Consultant, Southeast Wyoming Mental Health Center, Torrington

Judy O. Berry, Associate Professor of Communicative Disorders, University of Tulsa

Alex Bettesworth, Master's Degree Student in Counseling Psychology and Children's Group Facilitator, Community Center for Family Counseling, University of Oregon, Eugene

Jerry Bockoven, Doctoral Student in Counseling Psychology and Director of a Social Skills Program for Children, Community Center for Family Counseling, University of Oregon, Eugene

Judith Boser, Educational Researcher, Bureau of Educational Research and Service, University of Tennessee, Knoxville

Joe H. Brown, Professor, Department of Educational Psychology and Counseling, School of Education, University of Louisville

Michael L. Bundy, Counselor, Willow Brook Elementary School, Oak Ridge, Tennessee

Chari Campbell, Elementary School Counselor, M. K. Rawlings Elementary School, Gainesville, Florida

Jon Carlson, Psychologist, Wellness Clinic, Lake Geneva, Wisconsin

Harriet C. Cobb, Assistant Professor, Psychology Department, James Madison University, Harrisonburg, Virginia

Elizabeth H. Conroy, Doctoral Student, Department of Counselor Education, North Carolina State University, Raleigh, and Elementary School Counselor, Durham County Schools, Durham, North Carolina

Margaret Crosbie-Burnett, Assistant Professor, Department of Counseling Psychology and Counselor Education, University of Wisconsin—Madison

Nancy J. Cunningham, Associate Professor, Department of Educational Psychology and Counseling, School of Education, University of Louisville

Ruth B. Davis, Assistant Director, CASPAR (Cambridge and Somerville Program for Alcoholism Rehabilitation) Alcohol Education Program, Somerville, Massachusetts

Lena DiCicco, Director, CASPAR (Cambridge and Somerville Program for Alcoholism Rehabilitation) Alcohol Education Program, Somerville, Massachusetts

Don Dinkmeyer, Jr., Editor, CMTI Press, Coral Springs, Florida

R. Wiley Dixon, Guidance Supervisor, Alachua County Schools, Gainesville, Florida

Alan G. Downe, Regional Manager of Programs, McMan Youth Services, Edmonton, Alberta, Canada

C. Jerry Downing, Professor of Counseling and Personnel Services, College of Education, University of Nevada, Reno

Kevin Duncan, Counselor and Consultant, Colorado Springs, Colorado

Lynn W. England, Sex Abuse Specialist, Plateau Mental Health Center, Cookeville, Tennessee

Edwin R. Gerler, Jr., Associate Professor, Department of Counselor Education, North Carolina State University, Raleigh

Samuel T. Gladding, Assistant Professor of Counseling, Fairfield University, Fairfield, Connecticut

Richard A. Granum, Pupil Services Consultant, Wyoming Department of Education, Cheyenne

Norman C. Gysbers, Professor, Department of Educational and Counseling Psychology, University of Missouri—Columbia

Mary Bowe Hageman, Art Teacher, Stratford Public Schools, Stratford, Connecticut

JoAnn Harris-Bowlsbey, Assistant Vice-President, American College Testing Program, Hunt Valley, Maryland

Jill Hay, Elementary School Counselor, Central Elementary School, Belle Plaine, Iowa

John Horan, Professor and Director, Counseling Psychology, Arizona State University, Tempe

Kenneth B. Hoyt, University Distinguished Professor, College of Education, Kansas State University, Manhattan

Charles W. Humes, Associate Professor, Counselor Education, Virginia Polytechnic Institute and State University, Northern Virginia Graduate Center, Falls Church

Patricia D. Johnston, Resource Room/Behavioral Needs Specialist, Somerville Public Schools, Somerville, Massachusetts

Donald B. Keat II, Professor, Division of Counseling and Educational Psychology, Pennsylvania State University, University Park

Andres Kerns, Doctoral Student, Arizona State University, Tempe

Gerald H. Krockover, Professor of Education and Geosciences, and Director of Undergraduate Studies and Field Experiences, Purdue University, West Lafayette, Indiana

Wade Lewis, Director of Clinical Services, Middle Peninsula—Northern Neck Counseling Center, Gloucester, Virginia

Don C. Locke, Professor and Department Head, Department of Counselor Education, North Carolina State University, Raleigh

John N. Mangieri, Dean, School of Education, Texas Christian University, Fort Worth

Don Martin, Assistant Professor, Department of Counseling Education, Western Illinois University, Macomb

Maggie Martin, Counseling Psychologist, Counseling Center, Western Illinois University, Macomb

James McDonald, Elementary Counselor, Bellefonte Area School District, Bellefonte, Pennsylvania

Kathy L. Metzgar, Intern, Bellefonte Area School District, Bellefonte, Pennsylvania

Phyllis H. Mohr, Graduate Student, Department of Counselor Education, North Carolina State University, Raleigh

Carol Lynn Morse, Assistant Professor of Counseling Psychology and Coordinator, Community Center for Family Counseling, University of Oregon, Eugene

Linda A. Morse, Counselor, Cumberland Elementary School, West Lafayette, Indiana

Robert D. Myrick, Professor, Counselor Education Department, College of Education, University of Florida, Gainesville

Richard C. Nelson, Professor, Counseling and Personnel Services, Purdue University, West Lafayette, Indiana

Laurel L. Newcomer, School Counselor, Delavan School District, Delavan, Wisconsin

Ione Nysetvoid, Graduate Student, Counseling Psychology, University of Calgary, Alberta, Canada

Christine Olson, Doctoral Student, Arizona State University, Tempe

Alan Orenstein, Program Evaluator, CASPAR (Cambridge and Somerville Program for Alcoholism Rehabilitation) Alcohol Education Program, Somerville, Massachusetts

Larry D. Parker, Doctoral Student, Counselor Education, North Carolina State University, Raleigh

Paul Pedersen, Professor of Education and Chairman of Counseling and Guidance, Syracuse University, Syracuse, New York

Deborah Raykovitz, Elementary School Counselor, Bellefonte Area School District, Bellefonte, Pennsylvania

Hank Resnik, Senior Writer, Quest International, Granville, Ohio

Herbert C. Richards, Associate Professor, Foundations Department, School of Education, University of Virginia, Charlottesville

Jane A. Romatowski, Associate Professor, Division of Education, University of Michigan—Dearborn

Robert P. Sanche, Head of the Department for the Education of Exceptional Children, University of Saskatchewan, Saskatoon, Saskatchewan, Canada

Barbara J. Shade, Associate Professor of Educational Psychology, Division of Education, University of Wisconsin—Parkside, Kenosha

Sandra N. Sorsdahl, Research Associate, Department for the Education of Exceptional Children, University of Saskatchewan, Saskatoon, Saskatchewan, Canada

Norman A. Sprinthall, Professor, Department of Counselor Education, North Carolina State University, Raleigh

Nancy K. Staley, Associate Professor of Education, University of South Carolina, Aiken

Charles L. Thompson, Professor of Educational and Counseling Psychology, University of Tennessee, Knoxville

Mary L. Trepanier, Assistant Professor, Division of Education, University of Michigan—Dearborn

Ann Vernon, Associate Professor and Coordinator of Counseling, Department of Educational Administration and Counseling, University of Northern Iowa, Cedar Falls

Garry R. Walz, Director, ERIC Counseling and Personnel Services Clearinghouse and Professor of Education, School of Education, University of Michigan, Ann Arbor

CHAPTER 1

A CULTURALLY DIVERSE WORLD

Our society faces challenges in accepting and benefitting from cultural diversity. Problems emanating from racism exist despite efforts aimed at educational reform. Counselors must be aware of transmitting their own cultural values to clients and of drawing erroneous conclusions about clients' emotional and social well-being based on cultural differences. Moreover, because counseling theories and techniques are not always applicable across cultures, counselors must often look to new and creative ways to work effectively in multicultural settings. Chapter 1 offers elementary school counselors help in understanding cultural bias and provides practical strategies to promote child development in a multicultural society.

The tone for the chapter is set by Paul Pedersen's important article, "Ten Frequent Assumptions of Cultural Bias in Counseling." This article will help elementary school counselors challenge culturally based assumptions about what constitutes normal behavior on the part of individuals, what importance individuals place on independence, and what requirements should be placed on individuals to adapt to institutions. Don Locke's article, "Fostering the Self-Esteem of African-American Children" gives counselors practical ideas for implementing multicultural programs with elementary school children and their parents. Barbara Shade's provocative article examines how environmental conditions at school may have negative effects on children from various cultures. Finally, Larry Parker's extensive annotated bibliography provides elementary school counselors with resources for improving cultural awareness and understanding.

The intent of Chapter 1 is to help elementary school counselors challenge their cultural assumptions and in so doing to learn about themselves and the children they serve. As Pedersen observes,

> All counseling is, to a greater or lesser extent, cross-cultural. As counselors increase their contact with other countries and other cultures they can expect to learn a great deal about themselves. They can expect to challenge more of their unexamined assumptions about themselves and the world about them. They can expect to move beyond the parochial concerns and perspectives of a culturally limited perspective to look at the world in a new, more comprehensive perspective.

The 1990s will be a decade of increasing cultural change. Elementary school counselors should be leaders in helping children to learn from this change.

Ten Frequent Assumptions of Cultural Bias in Counseling

Paul Pedersen

It is time that we as counselors in the United States recognize that the Western cultural biases in our conventional thinking have little to do with geography and much to do with social, economic, and political perceptions. Just as there are many "Western" thinkers in non-Western parts of the world, there are also many "non-Western" thinkers in the Western hemisphere. In strictly numerical terms it is increasingly true that the Western viewpoint is the more exotic: The majority of people in the world accept a non-Western perspective. Despite that numerical reality, many social scientists, including psychologists, depend on textbooks, research findings, and implicit psychological theory based almost entirely on assumptions specific to European and American culture. These assumptions are usually so implicit and so taken for granted that they are not challenged even by broad-minded and insightful psychologists. The consequences of these unexamined assumptions are institutionalized racism, ageism, sexism, and other forms of cultural bias.

In this article I attempt to identify 10 of the most frequently encountered examples of cultural bias that consistently emerge in the literature about multicultural counseling and development. In educating counselors, it is important for educators to examine their own culturally biased assumptions. Teachers seldom, if ever, look at the assumptions behind their theories and research about counseling, but rather seek to establish whether or not the logical and reasonable directions of their arguments follow a straight line from one premise to the next.

It is likely, even probable, that two individuals with different assumptions will disagree without one of those persons being right and the other being wrong. If neither individual examines the assumptions underlying one or both viewpoints, they may never learn how and why the disagreement between them occurred. They will each misunderstand the other's viewpoint and proceed on the assumption that one of the two was right and the other was wrong, when, in fact they may both have been right (or possibly both wrong) according to their own assumptions. The examination of culturally learned assumptions must become a more important part of the curriculum in the development of counselors for a world that includes many cultures.

Assumptions Reflecting Cultural Bias

Assumptions Regarding Normal Behavior

The first such frequent assumption is the assumption that people all share a common measure of "normal" behavior. People frequently presume that when I describe a person's behavior as "normal," this judgment is meaningful and implies a particular pattern of behaviors by the normal person. There is an implicit assumption that the definition of *normal* is more or less universal across social, cultural, and economic or political backgrounds. If the label *normal* is challenged in a particular instance, the variation can frequently be explained as a deviation from otherwise normal behavior because of sociocultural differences from the norms of society. People feel a need to explain variations in normality in ways that protect the status quo of normality, even if this requires elegant and elaborate rationalizations.

Arguments against the established norm as a universal standard of measurement for normal behavior are usually criticized as potentially destructive of the social fabric and subject to the weaknesses of relativism, in which anything can be right or normal if judged entirely by its own idiosyncratic standard. As Kuhn (1962) pointed out, when a principle of scientific theory has become accepted by society, it functions as a selective screen for defining problems and evidence that coincidentally fit with the scientific principle. Evidence that does not fit the expected pattern is rejected as irrelevant or too chaotic to consider. To the extent that an accepted principle or perception does not accurately describe reality, society is insulated from contact with reality by the fixed form of abstract principles. Research data itself becomes something used to defend abstractions that promote stereotypes and inaccurate generalizations about normality.

What is considered normal behavior will change according to the situation, the cultural background of a person or persons being judged, and the time during which a behavior is being displayed or observed. Many psychological research projects are based on experimenters' backgrounds that may have influenced the definition of normality used in the research. These complex but not chaotic cultural patterns describe the experimenter's own personal cultural orientation. The possibility of error in a diagnosis, for example, is evident in the application of a definition of normal behavior based on one culture to a culturally diverse population without regard for variations in social, cultural, economic, or political background.

Emphasis on Individualism

A second frequent assumption is that individuals are the basic building blocks of society. Many counselors in the United States presume that counseling is primarily directed toward the development of individuals rather than units of individuals or groups such as the family, organizations, or society. If one examines the jargon used in counseling, the preference of Western counselors for the welfare of individuals becomes quickly evident. The criteria of self-awareness, self-fulfillment, and self-discovery are important measures of success in most counseling in Western society. The constructs of person in personality, of individuality in measuring achievement and aptitude, and of separation from the group in developing abilities all presume that a counselor's task is to change the individual in a positive direction, even, perhaps, at the expense of the group in which that individual has a role. In some cases the welfare of an individual client is seen to be frustrated by the conflicting agenda of a group in which that individual is a member.

While teaching English as a second language (ESL) in Indonesia I was asked why English speakers always capitalize the first person singular (*I*) in writing English. I confessed that, because I was not an expert in ESL, I really had no idea why the letter *I* was capitalized when referring to the first person singular. The students smiled at me and said knowingly that they already knew why. It was, they presumed, because English speakers are so thoroughly individualistic that the capitalization of the first person singular comes naturally to them.

In Chinese culture it would be normal and natural to put the welfare of the family before the welfare of any individual member of that family. To speak of an individual's health and welfare independent of the health and welfare of the family unit would not make sense in that context. Individual counseling has even been described as destructive of society because it promotes the personal benefits of individuals at the expense of the social community (Kleinman, 1979). The criticism of "romantic love" by members of many non-Western cultures is based on romantic love's emphasis on the welfare of individuals over the welfare of family units. In these cultures, the decision of whom to marry is recognized as uniquely important to the larger family, which exercises an influence in the matching of couples and in the preservation of marriage alliances in the name of the family. It is important for counselors to work comfortably and skillfully both in cultures that primarily emphasize the welfare of the individual and in cultures that emphasize the value of the unit.

Fragmentation by Academic Disciplines

A third frequent assumption is the definition of problems from a framework limited by academic discipline boundaries. There is a tendency to separate the identity of counselor from that of psychologist, sociologist, anthropologist, theologian, or medical doctor. Unfortunately, the problems a client is facing are not inhibited by any of these artificial boundaries. The research literature in various disciplines frequently overlaps, but counselors do not exchange questions and insights between disciplines, as they should. Wrenn (1962) spoke of counselors becoming culturally encapsulated, substituting symbiotic stereotypes for reality, disregarding cultural variations among clients, and accepting as dogma a technique-oriented definition of the counseling process.

In many cultures, for example, the really important mental health questions are related to questions about life (or before life) and death (or after death). If a client believes in reincarnation, then which person does a counselor consider—the person the client was, the person the client is, or the person the client will become? Each of these aspects of the person may be a legitimate focus of the conversation if, indeed, it is possible to separate these identities at all. Once again, it is important for counselors to become skilled in going beyond the boundaries of their own self-reference criteria to examine the problem or issue from the client's cultural perspective. Kleinman (1979) described how frequently a medical doctor may take the limited "disease" perspective in dealing with a patient as a "malfunctioning unit," whereas the patient is more likely to take the broadly defined "illness" perspective when a particular problem has a systemic impact on the patient's family, friends, and total surrounding context. The self-imposed boundaries counselors in the United States place on their description of counseling are themselves culturally learned and must be relearned as counselors move from one culture to another.

A fourth assumption is based on Western cultures' dependence on abstract words and the assumption of counselors in the United States that others will understand these abstractions in the same way as they intend. Hall (1976) differentiated high-context from low-context cultures. High-context cultures require reference to a context to give a concept meaning and low-context cultures are less dependent on context and more likely to presume that abstract concepts carry their own meaning with them from one context to another. Concepts such as *good* or *bad* have little meaning without putting the concept in a contextual setting for much, if not most, of the world's population. Because the dominant culture in this century has tended to be a low-context culture there is a dependence in counseling on abstract concepts such as *fairness* or *humane*, which, outside of a particular context, are difficult to understand.

With increased attention in Western cultures being given to interactionalism, in which knowledge of both the person and the environment are necessary for an accurate interpretation of an event, the emphasis on contextualism has increased. The popularity of systems theory has likewise encouraged many counselors to move away from abstractions out of context. Even when dealing with a low context culture it is frequently useful to attach abstract concepts to a particular context to make sure that the concept is understood as intended.

Although low-context abstractions are useful short cuts in conveying an idea, they may foster misunderstandings and inaccuracies if their intended meaning is not verified.

Overemphasis on Independence

A fifth assumption is that independence is valuable and dependencies are undesirable. As part of the Western emphasis on individualism there is a presumption that an individual should not be dependent on others; nor should the individual allow others to be dependent on them. If a counselor encounters "excessive" dependency in a client, he or she is likely to see the elimination of that dependency as a desirable outcome for counseling. Yet, there are many cultures in which dependencies are described as not only healthy but absolutely necessary. One example would be the Japanese concept of *amae*. Doi (1974) described this concept as technically referring to the relationship between a mother and her eldest son. While the son is young and dependent he is being prepared for the time when his mother will be old and dependent. Significantly, this concept of amae is widely used as the criteria for evaluating relationships between employer and employees, a teacher and a student, or many other relationships in society in which dependency is considered a healthy and normal aspect of relationships.

The counselor needs to consider a client's cultural perspective in determining the extent to which dependency might or might not be excessive. Because most counselors have been trained in a cultural context in which dependency is devalued, it is even more important to consider the function a particular dependency might have in the client's cultural context. It might easily be possible for a Western-trained counselor and a non-Western counselor to be working with the same client with the Western counselor attempting to lead the client to greater independence while the other counselor is attempting to help the client be more comfortable in the context of a necessary dependency.

Neglect of Client's Support Systems

A sixth assumption relates to the perceived importance of natural support systems surrounding a client. Counselors need to endorse the potential effectiveness of family and peer support to a client. What happens more frequently in Western society is that counselors erode the natural support systems by substituting the "purchase of friendship" through professional counseling services in formal contexts. In many cultures the notion of formal counseling is less preferred than nonformal or informal alternatives available to a client (Pedersen, 1986). The idea of telling intimate family secrets to a stranger is not allowed in many, if not most, of the world's cultures. These problems are dealt with inside the family or group context with little or no outside involvement. Wherever possible, the natural support systems surrounding a client should be mobilized as a valuable ally rather than as an assumed rival for the client's attention. If a client has to choose between the support system and the counselor, there is a strong likelihood that the client will choose the support system. Pearson (1985) has written extensively on how those natural support systems can be identified and used in a counseling context.

In some cases the counselor will no doubt find the natural support systems surrounding a client to add to the client's problem, and a successful outcome will depend on replacing those systems with alternatives. If, however, the system is removed without recognizing how important that support is for a client, then a new support system will be sought out by the client independently. The health of the individual is tied in many ways to the health of the supporting unit surrounding that individual. The counselor needs to include consideration of a client's natural support system in an effective treatment plan for counseling.

Dependence on Linear Thinking

A seventh assumption is that everyone depends on linear thinking—wherein each cause has an effect and each effect is tied to a cause—to understand the world around them. This kind of linear thinking is most evident in the dependence on measures of things. The use of measures for describing the goodness, badness, appropriateness, or inappropriateness of a construct is an almost unquestioned necessity for good counseling. The use of tests in counseling requires these measures, and any evaluation of counseling would be stated in measured degrees. How then can counselors adapt counseling to a cultural context where the cause and the effect are seen as two aspects of the same undifferentiated reality (as in the concept of *Yin* and *Yang*) with neither cause nor effect being separate from the other? In some cultures constructs lend themselves less to quantification than in others. The way of thinking in these cultures is likely to be nonlinear: An event is described independent of its relationship to surrounding, preceding, or consequent events. Nonlinear thinking presents some unique problems to counselors whose training presumes the universal appropriateness of linear thinking.

Counseling has frequently erred in assuming that if a test, book, or concept is accurately translated in terms of its content, the translated tool will be effective and appropriate. Not all persons from all cultures are socialized to think in the same way. Consequently, in translating, it is important to change not just the content of a message for counseling but also the way of thinking through which that message is being expressed. Although counselors spend considerable time making sure that the content of their message is culturally appropriate, they spend less time adapting the underlying way of thinking behind the translated message.

Focus on Changing Individual, Not System

The eighth assumption is that counselors need to change individuals to fit the system and are not intended to change the system to fit the individual. Counselors need to recognize when counseling should be more activistic and change the system to fit the individual rather than trying to change the individual to fit the system. In many minority groups counseling has a bad reputation as a source of help for taking the side of the status quo in forcing individuals to adjust or adapt to the institutions of society. Counselors are sometimes seen as agents of the status quo, whose primary task it is to protect social institutions, even though those same institutions may be exploiting individuals such as the client.

It is important for counselors to differentiate between the best interests of the client and the best interests of the surrounding social institutions. Frequently, the counselor assumes that it is much more difficult to change the social institutions than to help the individual adapt to conditions as they are. Counselors who do not at least question whether the best interests of the client are being served by existing social institutions and whether those social institutions can be changed, at least in small ways, are failing in professional obligations. There is an ethical obligation to the client that requires counselors to protect the client's best interests even at the risk of offending social institutions. If a counselor's effectiveness is judged by his or her ability to protect the system from attack, then that counselor is merely an agent of the prevailing social system and institutions.

Neglect of History

The ninth assumption relates to the relevance of history for a proper understanding of contemporary events. Counselors are more likely to focus on the immediate events that created a crisis, and if clients begin talking about their own history or the history of their "people" the counselor is likely to stop listening and wait for clients to "catch up" to current events, which the counselor considers more salient than past history. The client's perspective may require historical background knowledge that the client feels is relevant to the complete description of his or her problem from his or her point of view. In many cultures the connection between past and present history makes it necessary for counselors to clearly understand a client's historical context to understand his or her present behavior.

Counseling in the United States is a young profession in a young country, in comparison to other nations and professions of the world, and is therefore perhaps less conscious of history than are professions in cultures and nations with a longer tradition. Counselors lack a sufficient awareness of the ways in which people solved their psychological problems in the past thousands of years. They lack the patience for a longer perspective in which the current situation may be transitional. They are perceived to lack respect for traditional time-tested ways in which a particular culture has dealt with personal problems, and to prefer the latest trend or fad in counseling to traditional methods.

Dangers of Cultural Encapsulation

The tenth assumption is the assumption that counselors already know all of their assumptions. In an era of diminishing resources counselors need to recognize the dangers of a closed, biased, and culturally encapsulated system that promotes domination by an elitist group, whatever its origin or special point of view. If counselors are unwilling or unable to challenge their own assumptions, they will be less likely to communicate effectively with persons from other cultures.

Cross-cultural counseling is an attempt to integrate our assumptions with and coordinate them among contrasting assumptions of other persons from different cultures. In this way, culture complicates counselors' lives, but it brings counselors closer to culturally defined reality.

All counseling is, to a greater or lesser extent, cross-cultural. As counselors increase their contact with other countries and other cultures they can expect to learn a great deal about themselves. They can expect to challenge more of their unexamined assumptions about themselves and the world about them. They can expect to move beyond the parochial concerns and perspectives of a culturally limited perspective to look at the world in a new, more comprehensive perspective. The primary argument for cross-cultural awareness in counseling has less to do with the ethical imperative of how counselors should relate to others and more to do with the accuracy and effectiveness of counseling as an international professional activity.

References

Doi, T. (1974). Amae: A key concept for understanding Japanese personality structure. In T. Lebra & W. Lebra (Eds.), *Japanese culture and behavior.* Honolulu: University of Hawaii Press.

Hall, E. T. (1976). *Beyond culture.* Garden City, NY: Anchor Books.

Kleinman, A. (1979). *Patients and healers in the context of culture.* Berkeley: University of California Press.
Kuhn, T. (1962). *The structure of scientific revolutions.* Chicago: University of Chicago Press.
Pearson, R. (1985). The recognition and use of natural support systems in cross cultural counseling. In P. Pedersen (Ed.), *Handbook of cross cultural counseling and therapy* (pp. 299–306). Westport, CT: Greenwood Press.
Pedersen, P. (1986). The cultural role of conceptual and contextual support systems in counseling. *Journal of the American Mental Health Counselors Association, 8,* 35–42.
Wrenn, C. G. (1962). The culturally encapsulated counselor. *Harvard Educational Review, 32,* 444–449.

Fostering the Self-Esteem of African-American Children

Don C. Locke

The needs of African-American students have received much attention in the last decade. The attention has shifted from a "culturally deprived" orientation to one focused on providing for "culturally different" needs. One can find numerous publications advocating biculturalism or multiculturalism in the counseling and education literature (Saville-Troike, 1978; Allan & Narine, 1981; Locke & Hardaway, 1981; McNeely & Parker, 1983; Locke & Ciechalski, 1985). The consequences of multiculturalism are sufficiently clear to warrant the adoption of theoretical models in cross-cultural or multicultural situations. Locke (1988) has advocated the inclusion of relevant experiences in the education of all culturally different students. Such activities should be person-centered rather than problem-centered and should break from traditional techniques and restrictive thinking in guidance. Activities should include methods and techniques that contribute to the maximum psychological growth and development of African-American children. It is commonly accepted today that one's ability to cope with adversity is a function of a positive self-concept. Those who feel good about themselves are more likely to become happy, healthy citizens.

Elementary school counselors must seek to develop empathy with African-American children. Terry (1970) challenged Whites to avoid being "color blind." His challenge requires that attention focus on the unique cultural needs of all students. Such an effort requires elementary school counselors to learn as much as possible about the African-American cultural experience. Counselors may take courses in cross-cultural education or counseling, may participate in relevant in-service activities focused on multiculturalism, or may become self-educated in this area. The goal of such a learning experience is to accomplish what Wrenn (1962) identified as a measure to avoid cultural encapsulation:

> We should persist in a regime of unlearning something each day. We should check items of information to be given to students in terms of the direction and rate of change, not just the accuracy of information for now. We should accept as an obligation the encouragement of students who think differently from us. We must batter down our tendency to be self-righteous. (pp. 448–449)

General Guidelines

Some specific guidelines for elementary school counselors are provided as necessary attitudes or behaviors that will help foster multiculturalism in general, and positive images for African-American children in particular.

1. Plan to be open and honest in relationships with African-American children. Leave yourself open to culturally different attitudes and encourage African-American children to be open and honest with you about issues related to their culture.
2. Learn as much as possible about your own culture. One can appreciate another culture much more if there is first an appreciation of one's own culture.
3. Seek to genuinely respect and appreciate culturally different attitudes and behaviors. Demonstrate that you both recognize and value the African-American culture.
4. Take advantage of all available opportunities to participate in activities in the African-American community. Invite persons from the African-American community to your school throughout the school year.
5. Keep in mind that African-American children are both members of their unique cultural group and are unique individuals as well. Strive to keep a healthy balance between your view of students as cultural beings and as unique beings.
6. Eliminate all your behaviors that suggest prejudice or racism and do not tolerate such behaviors from your colleagues or from children themselves.
7. Encourage teachers and administrators in your school to institutionalize practices that acknowledge the African-American culture. Such activities should go beyond the celebration of Black History Month.
8. Hold high expectations of African-American children and encourage all who work with African-American children to do likewise. Remember that the self-fulfilling prophesy has much to do with the performance of young children.
9. Ask questions about the African-American culture. Learn as much as possible about the African-American culture and share what you learn with your colleagues and students in your school.
10. Develop culturally specific strategies, mechanisms, techniques, and programs to foster the psychological development of African-American children. Such efforts should be developed using the following principles:

a. Programs should be interdisciplinary in nature, drawing from social sciences, language arts, music, humanities, and other subjects.
b. Programs should be an integral part of the curriculum. The counselor and teachers should develop mutually agreeable methods of program delivery.
c. Guidance materials and the approach used should be appropriate to the maturity level of the students. At the early primary level, activities should deal more with the immediate experiences of the child (home and school). At the upper primary level, activities may focus on the community.
d. Program objectives should help students develop both cognitive skills and affective learning. The self-concept should be enriched as a result of any skill mastery.
e. Programs should take advantage of opportunities within the school and community populations. Persons from the community should be perceived as primary resources.

Specific Guidance Activities

The following lessons or activities are designed for use by teachers or counselors in entire-classroom groups. Although the primary objective of each activity centers on African-American children, all children in a classroom may benefit from participation; counselors or teachers may adapt the activities for use with small groups. These activities are designed to help the counselor or teacher put into operation the guidelines presented earlier in this article. Those guidelines should be the foundation for these activities.

For each activity, the following information is presented: name of activity, suggested grade level, general objective for activity, and a brief description of the activity.

Activity 1: Same or Different
Grade Level: Kindergarten–First
Objective: To have each child recognize physical similarities and differences between children of similar or different racial groups.
Description: The counselor will discuss physical attributes of people in general. Children will look at themselves in mirrors and tell what they see. Children will look at neighboring children and take turns describing each other. Children will draw or paint pictures of themselves and a neighbor, paying attention to details already discussed.

Activity 2: All About Me Booklet
Grade Level: Second
Objective: To help students develop good self-concepts through analysis of self, family, and friends.
Description: Each student will develop a booklet containing a drawing or photograph of himself or herself, family, home, pets, and friends. Students will list three things they like about themselves, three things they would like to change about themselves, and three things they like about their best friends.

Activity 3: African-American People
Grade Level: Third
Objective: To introduce young children to noted personalities in the African and African-American culture.
Description: The counselor will collect photographs of famous African-American people and talk with students about what made them famous. Students will research and add other famous African-American people to the collection. The counselor and students will develop a "Win, Lose, or Draw" game using information already presented.

Activity 4: Appreciation of Speech Patterns
Grade Level: Fourth
Objective: To get students to understand and appreciate cultural differences in speech patterns.
Description: The counselor will have students read the poem "In the Morning" by Paul Lawrence Dunbar. The counselor will lead a discussion of the words in dialect in the poem and compare the dialect with the same words in "standard English." Counselor will relate the words in the poem to "Black English." Counselors may refer to Smitherman (1977) or Baugh (1983) for background on "Black English."

Activity 5: Where Did We Come From?
Grade Level: Fifth–Sixth
Objective: To have students demonstrate an understanding of the geographical location from which their ancestors came.
Description: Students will select three families in their neighborhood and interview them. They will also interview an adult in their immediate family. Students will use the following questions in their interviews: What is the family name? From what countries did they or their ancestors come? Why did they come to the United

States of America? What special customs or traditions from their home country do they still observe?

Activity 6: Appreciating Cultural Feelings
Grade Level: Seventh–Eighth
Objective: To have students learn to express feelings in general and ethnic or racial feelings in particular.
Description: Students will play the "I Think, I Feel, I Want Game" (Palmer, 1977). Each student will select a partner and sit facing each other. They will begin each sentence with one of the following statements: "I think," "I feel," or "I want." To help students get started, counselors may ask how students would feel if a snake slithered into the classroom. How would they feel if everyone were invited to a party except them? How would they feel if an African-American student invited them to a party. How would they feel if a White student invited them to a party? How would they feel if someone called them a name? How would they feel if someone used an undesirable racial designation in addressing them?

Activity 7: Kwanzaa Celebration
Grade Level: Kindergarten–Eighth
Objective: To familiarize students with the African-American celebration of Kwanzaa.
Description: Kwanzaa, a holiday celebrated by more than 13 million African-Americans in 1984, is a unique American holiday that pays tribute to the cultural roots of Americans who are of African ancestry. (In this article, the terms *America* and *American* refer to the United States and those individuals residing in the United States respectively.) The counselor should coordinate the activity for the school by helping teachers get sufficient information on the seven principles of Kwanzaa (Nguzo Saba) and the Kwanzaa symbols (Mazao, Mkeka, Kinara, Vibunzi, Zawadi, Kikombe Cha Umoja, and Mishumaa Saba). Teachers will plan specific activities for each classroom. Counselors may refer to McClester (1985) for information on Kwanzaa and specific ideas for planning a celebration.

Evaluation

The implementation of programs designed to foster the self-esteem of African-American children must also include provisions for the evaluation of such effort. The success of such programs can best be determined by observing how students behave. Affective behavioral outcomes are crucial to any program designed to foster development of self-esteem. Counselors should identify the specific student outcomes desired and the observable behavioral indicators of such outcomes.

Some of the specific student outcomes might include the following: The student

1. participates voluntarily in many activities.
2. interacts positively with members of his or her own racial group and with groups different from himself or herself.
3. freely selects partners on other than racial factors.
4. avoids name-calling or ridiculing of others.
5. exhibits courteous behaviors by listening to the ideas and feelings of others.
6. avoids personally destructive behaviors and attempts to prevent such actions by others.
7. describes verbally and in writing his or her cultural and individual unique qualities by enumerating characteristics, abilities, and skills.
8. strives to be worthy of the respect of others.
9. shares information about himself or herself, family, peer group, and community.
10. speaks out to defend self, asks for help when needed, and disagrees with others in an appropriate manner.

Summary

The implementation of some of these activities may challenge the professional skills of the elementary school counselor. The demands of a multicultural process may be new to many. The acquisition of new knowledge and skills may be necessary to work effectively with students from culturally different backgrounds. A coordinated, planned program is recommended and encouraged if the needs of all students' needs are to be met. In multicultural education it is essential that activities strengthen the self-esteem, identity, and mutual respect of the participants, both students and adults.

Every child enters a multicultural world when he or she leaves home and enters school. Vonnegut (1974) expressed the need of elementary school children to learn their cultural nature as follows:

> A first grader should understand that his or her culture isn't a rational invention; that there are thousands of other cultures and they all work pretty well; that all cultures function on faith rather than truth; that there

are lots of alternatives to our own society. Cultural relativity is desirable and attractive. (p. 139)

Such is the aim of multicultural education for minority children. Classroom guidance offers the school counselor a variety of opportunities not only to deal directly with cultural diversity, but also to foster the self-esteem of children by focusing on that diversity.

References

Allan, J., & Narine, J. (1981). Racial prejudice in the classroom: A developmental counseling approach. *Canadian Counsellor, 15*, 162–167.

Baugh, J. (1983). *Black street speech: Its history, structure, and survival.* Austin: University of Texas Press.

Locke, D. C. (1988). Teaching culturally different students: Growing pine trees or bonsai trees. *Contemporary Education, 9*, 130–133.

Locke, D. C., & Ciechalski, J. C. (1985). *Psychological techniques for teachers.* Muncie, IN: Accelerated Development, Inc.

Locke, D. C., & Hardaway, Y. V. (1981). Moral education in multicultural settings. *The Humanist Educator, 4*, 193–200.

McClester, C. (1985). *Kwanzaa: Everything you always wanted to know but didn't know where to ask.* New York: Gumbs and Thomas.

McNeely, S. N., & Parker, W. M. (1983). Exploring cultural awareness in schools: Four strategies. *Journal of Non-White Concerns in Personnel and Guidance, 12*, 2–6.

Palmer, P. (1977). *Liking myself.* San Luis Obispo, CA: Impact Publishers.

Saville-Troike, M. (1978). *A guide to culture in the classroom.* Rosslyn, VA: National Clearinghouse for Bilingual Education.

Smitherman, G. (1977). *Talkin and testifyin: The language of Black America.* Boston: Houghton Mifflin.

Terry, R. W. (1970). *For Whites only.* Grand Rapids: William B. Eeerdmans.

Vonnegut, K., Jr. (1974). Afterword. In F. Klagsbrun (Ed.), *Free to be—You and me* (pp. 139–141). New York: McGraw Hill.

Wrenn, C. G. (1962). The culturally encapsulated counselor. *Harvard Educational Review, 32*, 444–449.

Cultural Diversity and the School Environment

Barbara J. Shade

If a man does not keep pace
With his companions
Perhaps it is because he
Hears a different drummer . . .
—Thoreau

It was absolutely unbelievable! A group of my students in an inner-city junior high school invited me to attend services at their church. It was Youth Day and they were to appear on the program. Because I believed it important to be involved in the community in which I taught, I decided to go. I was absolutely dumbfounded!

There in the midst of this program was Tyrone. Instead of the shy, noncommunicative adolescent I knew, he was an expressive, reasonably articulate youth. Instead of the student who could not remember his multiplication tables, here was a youth who could sing and recite the words to many songs from memory without help. Instead of the young man who would not write a theme because he "couldn't think of anything," this young man could deliver an extemporaneous and comprehensive prayer. But, most astonishing, a highly distractable young man who usually could not sit still for 2 minutes remained quiet and attentive for 2 long hours.

What did this church have that school did not? Why could he perform here and not in the classroom? Why was he a pleasant participant here, but withdrawn, moody, and uncooperative at school?

Many scholars have tried to account for such inconsistency by suggesting that students like Tyrone do not have the ability to handle school work; therefore, they avoid it by being inattentive and uncooperative (Eisenberg, 1967). Others suggest that Tyrone's home and community environment have not conditioned him to be successful in school (Reissman, 1962). These, like most explanations, seem to concentrate on the deficiencies of the individual student. Recently, however, more attention is being given to the major proposition of environmental psychologists, which suggests that the performance of an individual is dependent not only on the student's traits but also on the congruency between the individual and the environment in which he or she is asked to perform (Mehrabian, 1976).

Could the classroom environment have a significant impact on Tyrone's academic performance? The possibility was one I had not considered as a teacher but was obviously one that needed further examination.

Each environment, be it a school, a classroom, a church, or a community, has a culture (Gump & Ross, 1977). This culture determines various patterns of behavior, rules of interaction, spatial arrangements, methods of communication, and procedures for information transmittal to make learning easier. Because each environment has its own psychological as well as physical requirements, it can be perceived as a socialization agent (Levy-Leboyer, 1979/1982). How individuals function within a particular milieu depends on their familiarity with the environment and its expectations, their perceptions and evaluation of physical and psychological factors, and the extent to which the environment can satisfy each individual's basic needs. The interpretation given to this information and subsequent behavior produced depends upon what some scholars have come to refer to as *cognitive style*.

Cognitive style is a psychological concept that represents the manner in which an individual's personality influences the way the person gathers, absorbs, and uses information. Guilford (1983) labeled it as the executive control mechanism of the intellect. Stanfield (1985) referred to it as collective consciousness or social knowledge that facilitates knowing the world, and Vernon (1973) suggested that it is a filter that mediates the interaction between the person and the environment.

It is this filter that accompanies Tyrone to church and to school and determines both his interpretation of the situations and the extent to which he is motivated to participate. Although there are different dimensions of cognitive style, the three that seem to have the most influence on my interaction with Tyrone are the information load within the environment, the communication patterns, and his social interaction preferences. In examining these three areas, I found some significant differences between the church and school environment, which might account for the behavioral patterns observed.

Environmental Style

The physical environment in which any human interaction occurs affects the degree and intensity of the social interaction, the level of behavioral control the person in charge must execute, and the degree of intrinsic motivation exhibited by the inhabitants. Probst (1974) pointed out that each time an individual enters a setting, he or she assesses it from the perspective of "Can this place be mine or adjusted to me?" "Can I produce results here?" "Can I relate to others in the environment?" If Moos (1979) is correct, students are more likely to answer these questions affirmatively if the environment is moderately arousing, pleasant, has sufficient information load to be stimulating, and is arranged to allow easy movement.

Businesses have known for some time that color, physical arrangement of space, lighting, and sound influence the reactions and productivity of their employees (Birren, 1978; Mehrabian, 1976). Because of this, they invest considerable time and study developing settings that perpetuate participation and performance. Brophy (1983) noted that the classroom is just as much of a workplace as are factories, offices, banks, and corporations. Children are required to arrive on time daily and perform tasks with a preconceived degree of competence. The results have a significant impact on their future life-styles and quality of life. Logic suggests, therefore, that the school workplace requires as much attention to increasing productivity through environmental design as does the business world.

Studies of the effect of the physical environment on academic achievement are limited. Those reviewed by King and Marans (1979), however, indicate that attention needs to be given to the color, temperature, spatial arrangements, and lighting to determine their effect on learning. Loughlin and Suina (1982) pointed out that concerns about a learning environment generally end with the development of the architectural design and the basic furnishings. Because the classroom environment offers information, engages interest, stimulates the use of skills, communicates limits and expectations, and promotes self-direction and movement, more attention should be given to the way that information is sent and received. An examination of the differences between the church and school suggests that how information is transmitted is a major source of concern for Tyrone.

Tyrone, like all of us, is confronted constantly with multiple bits of information that come from either the physical setting, surrounding objects, or persons within the environment. How one handles these stimuli depends largely on the individual's particular cognitive style. Some people are what Mehrabian (1976) called screeners, or what Witkin, Moore, Goodenough, and Cox (1977) referred to as field independent individuals; others are nonscreeners, or field dependent persons. Regardless of the particular stylistic label, some people tend to screen out irrelevant data or impose a pattern on the stimuli, whereas others seem to be sensitive to all of the cues. The latter type of individuals find themselves easily distracted. Mehrabian (1976) suggested that they reach their emotional tolerance level rather quickly and become hyperactive. Individuals who are screeners have few problems with environments that present a high level of information. For individuals who are nonscreeners, however, a high level of information may be stressful.

Tyrone is probably a nonscreener. Boykin (1978) would refer to him as having "behavioral verve." Tyrone learned to pay attention to a multiplicity of stimuli in an attempt to assess each for approach or avoidance behavior. He developed an attentional style that helped him cope with a highly stimulating urban environment. This multi-attentional style is obviously at work in the classroom, although it does not serve him as well there as it does in other settings.

I was trained as a teacher to provide students with a highly stimulating environment. Bulletin boards are up, learning centers are operating, and I am constantly moving around and talking. In addition, there are 30 very interesting people in the class who serve as rich sources of information and stimulation. Unknowingly, I create an arousing situation by sending complex information from many sources, and Tyrone pays attention to each and every cue.

The church, on the other hand, although stimulating, focuses on basically one set of stimuli at a time. The very nature of the arrangement and structure focuses attention on the singers, who maintain that attention by body movements and brightly colored robes as well as by their singing. The minister maintains involvement and attention with vocal tones, metaphors, and meaningful analogies. Screening is not necessary; the presenters and the situation do it for Tyrone. Clearly, the presenters cater to communication patterns that differ greatly from those I use in teaching.

Communication Style

Transmission of ideas and information between teachers and learners is the fundamental process in school interaction. Not only does it require a common language but it also requires common perceptions for gathering information (Marx, 1983).

Perception is the cornerstone of learning. Students must be able to gather information and assess it if they are to use the ideas effectively. Not all learners prefer the print and visual media that is dominant in the presentation of information in schools (*visuoprint learner*). Nor are all individuals particularly adept at gathering and integrating information that comes through listening (*aural learner*). Some individuals acquire information when presented in concrete forms, which can be touched; others learn better if they can convert material to sensitonic stimuli (*haptic-kinesthetic learners*). Some learners prefer to convert material to images that relate to the physical environment in some way (*visuospatial learners*); others prefer to relate to the social environment and find ways in which information can be translated to more interactive symbols (*interactive learners*) (James & Galbraith, 1985). The particular perceptual strength may be one that is unitary or, as Barsch (1971) pointed out, may be arranged in a preference hierarchy.

Teaching in my classroom is definitely a print and auditory experience. I talk; students listen or they read and write. I expect Tyrone to wait his turn and be acknowledged before speaking. I also expect him to speak in a rather structured language pattern using words that are literal, abstract, and verbatim. This is a very different communication pattern from the one promoted in Tyrone's church.

The church uses both verbal and nonverbal communication strategies (White, 1984). The words used are imaginative, figurative, and colorful, and participants often respond to the presentation with verbal outcries to denote approval. Those in the podium or choir loft often emphasize their meaning with gestures or changes in vocal inflection. Judging by the dimensions of the interchange, one might also conclude that Tyrone is exposed more often to the oral interactive mode of information presentation than to the print mode that dominates my classroom. This particular modality preference influences Tyrone's perceptions of the situation, as well as his social interaction preference.

Interactional Style

Social cognition involves focusing individual thoughts on the human interactions that occur in a particular situation (Roloff & Berger, 1982). This focus is particularly important for those individuals who tend to behave in ways that ease their adaptation to the situation in which they find themselves. Others determine their behavior based on their particular values and attitudes rather than on the situation.

Tyrone's interaction with me as a teacher suggests that he is more concerned about the interpersonal relationships involved in learning than about the completion of the tasks assigned. He needs my attention on a regular basis, he prefers to know more about me as a person, and he is constantly seeking attention to verify whether or not he is completing the task according to my wishes. If I do not respond to this need, Tyrone sits gloomily at his desk or tries to interact with his neighbors. This is a particularly annoying situation for me, because I expect Tyrone to work independently and complete his tasks when all he seems to want is social interaction.

At church Tyrone is a very gregarious individual. His affiliation with the choir and other groups suggests that he likes being around people, and he is quite responsive to the positive reinforcement received from others. Both his behaviors and communication patterns would tend to identify him as an extrovert (Morris, 1979). In a school setting where autonomy, independence, and individualism are valued, Tyrone's more personal affiliative needs seem out of place.

Zeichner (1978) pointed out that the social conditions of a classroom are important to academic performance. McDermott (1977) suggested that the interaction that occurs depends on behavioral values. My value for autonomy seems to be in direct conflict with Tyrone's need for affiliation and personal attention. Finding a way to accommodate both values seems to be an important concern.

In studies of teaching strategies that appealed to students who prefer a more personal approach, researchers found that peer-centered teaching was just as effective as teacher-directed instruction (Mevarech, 1985; Sharan, 1980). In addition, Johnson and Johnson (1983) suggested that cooperative learning is an effective strategy for students with a sociocentric learning style. They found that minority students, primarily Blacks, had particularly positive reactions to the supportive environment that was generated by using cooperative techniques. The use of such techniques would not only modify the environment for Tyrone, but could enhance my classroom management skills.

Summary

Teacher training programs emphasize the need to accommodate individual differences. Strategies suggested include using individualized instructional packets, variation in seating arrangements, or grouping according to perceived ability. Although these may be effective for some students, other adaptations are needed to accommodate students with other learning preferences (Glaser, 1977).

To equalize learning opportunities and allow each student to achieve maximum potential, educators need to develop environments that encourage academic performance rather than inhibit it. Much more attention must be given to the impact of the classroom physical environment on student behavior, attitudes, and achievement (Weinstein, 1979). Equal attention must be given to the role of verbal and nonverbal communication in teaching and learning, and to the importance of social relationships. These aspects of the teaching-learning process are as important as the tasks and materials used.

Churches, businesses, and other social systems spend an enormous amount of money and time in their attempts to develop settings that attract consumers. Perhaps schools should function in the same manner to promote a product that is important to the development and maintenance of society. Until this is done, students like Tyrone will choose to disengage from the formal learning process in a tragedy that can multiply to monumental proportions.

References

Barsch, R. (1971). The processing mode hierarchy as a potential deterrent to cognitive efficiency. In J. Hellmuth (Ed.), *Cognitive studies II: Deficits in cognition* (pp. 206–230). New York: Brunner/Mazel.

Birren, F. (1978). *Color and human response*. New York: Van Nostrand Reinhold.
Boykin, A. W. (1978). Psychological/behavioral verve in academic task performance. *Journal of Negro Education, 48*, 343–354.
Brophy, J. (1983). Conceptualizing student motivation. *Educational Psychologist, 18*, 200–215.
Eisenberg, L. (1967). Strengths of the inner city child. In A. H. Passow, M. Golberg, & A. J. Tannebaum (Eds.), *Education of the disadvantaged* (pp. 78–88). New York: Holt, Rinehart and Winston.
Glaser, R. (1977). *Adaptive education: Individual diversity and learning*. New York: Holt, Rinehart and Winston.
Guilford, J. P. (1983). Cognitive styles: What are they? *Educational and Psychological Measurement, 40*, 715–735.
Gump, P. V., & Ross, R. (1977). The fit of milieu and programme in school environments. In H. McGurk (Ed.), *Ecological factors in human development* (pp. 77–89). Amsterdam: North-Holland.
James, W. B., & Galbraith, M. W. (1985). Perceptual learning styles: Implications and techniques for the practitioner. *Lifelong Learning, 8*, 20–23.
Johnson, D. W., & Johnson, R. (1983). The socialization and achievement crises: Are co-operating learning experiences the solution? In L. Bickman (Ed.), *Applied social psychology manual 4* (pp. 119–164). Beverly Hills, CA: Sage.
King, J., & Marans, R. W. (1979). *The physical environment and the learning process*. Ann Arbor, MI: Architectural Research Laboratory and Institute for Social Research.
Levy-Leboyer, C. (1982). *Psychology and the environment* (D. Canter & E. E. Griffiths, Trans.). Beverly Hills, CA: Sage. (Original work published 1979)
Loughlin, C., & Suina, J. (1982). *The learning environment: An instructional strategy.* New York: Teachers College Press.
Marx, R. W. (1983). Student perception in classroom. *Educational Psychologist, 18*, 145–164.
McDermott, R. P. (1977). Social relations as contexts for learning in school. *Harvard Educational Review, 47*, 198–213.
Mehrabian, A. (1976). *Public places and private spaces*. New York: Basic Books.
Mevarech, Z. R. (1985). The effects of cooperative mastery learning strategies on mathematics achievement. *Journal of Educational Research, 78*, 372–377.
Moos, R. H. (1979). *Evaluating educational environments*. San Francisco: Jossey-Bass.
Morris, L. W. (1979). *Extraversion and introversion*. New York: Halsted Press.
Probst, R. (1974). Human needs and working places. *School Review, 82*, 617–620.
Reissman, F. (1962). *The culturally deprived child*. New York: Harper & Row.

Roloff, M. E., & Berger, C. R. (1982). *Social cognition and communication.* Beverly Hills, CA: Sage.

Sharan, S. (1980). Cooperative learning in small groups: Recent methods and effects on achievement, attitudes and ethnic relations. *Review of Educational Research, 50,* 241–271.

Stanfield, J. A. (1985). The ethnocentric basis of social science knowledge production. *Review of Research in Education, 12,* 387–415.

Vernon, P. E. (1973). Multivariate approaches to the study of cognitive styles. In J. R. Royce (Ed.), *Multivariate analysis of psychological theory* (pp. 125–147). New York: Academic Press.

Weinstein, C. S. (1979). The physical environment of the school: A review of the research. *Review of Educational Research, 49,* 577–610.

White, J. L. (1984). *The psychology of Blacks: An Afro-American perspective.* Englewood Cliffs, NJ: Prentice-Hall.

Witkin, H. A., Moore, C. A., Goodenough, D. R., & Cox, P. W. (1977). Field-dependent and field-independent cognitive styles and their educational implications. *Review of Educational Research, 47,* 1–64.

Zeichner, K. M. (1978). Group membership in the elementary school classroom. *Journal of Educational Psychology, 70,* 554–564.

An Annotated Bibliography in Cross-Cultural Counseling for Elementary and Middle School Counselors

Larry D. Parker

Elementary and middle school counselors do not choose their clients nor do they have the option to limit their efforts to one area of interest or expertise. Rather, we as counselors are charged with the responsibility of meeting the counseling needs of a total school population. Counselors work with students regardless of background, age, sex, or presenting problem. "If a child is enrolled in my school, he [or she] is potentially my client."

School counselors are there to "help" as well as advocate for children. How well counselors do this depends upon many variables. With an increasing emphasis placed upon "effectiveness" and a sincere desire to provide counseling services that are beneficial to all, there is an ever-increasing need to be able to communicate with and understand students from diverse backgrounds.

There is evidence that counseling needs of various racial and ethnic groups have not been met in the past and an indication that mental health services are under-used by subgroups (Jones & Korchin, 1982; Sue, 1981; Pedersen, 1985). A Delphi poll conducted by Heath, Neimeyer, and Pederson (1988) identified areas within counseling that are likely to be developed in a manner reflective of and sensitive to cross-cultural issues: theory and research, training and preparation, and social organization.

Professional journals in the counseling field frequently present articles and studies related to the issue of counseling clients from racial and ethnic groups. Departments of counselor education across the nation have reported cross-cultural counseling courses that have been added to their curriculum or fused into all courses where applicable (Hollis & Wantz, 1986). Clearly, the trend is toward the development of cross-cultural counseling skills rather than toward the application of one theory or one set of theories to all populations.

For those counselors who completed counselor preparation programs before the availability of courses in cross-cultural counseling, or for those practitioners who are interested in expanding their knowledge base or refining interpersonal skills, selected readings in the field may prove helpful. Individuals who are prepared to meet the challenge of cross-cultural "helping" may better understand the concepts and implications of cultural pluralism and therefore become more effective counselors.

The following list of books and journal articles address the concerns of cross-cultural counseling and the issues related to various ethnic and racial groups. It is by no means complete but it will present valuable information to elementary or middle school counselors.

Books

Asante, M. K., Newmark, E., & Blake, C. A. (Eds.). (1979). *Handbook of intercultural communication*. Beverly Hills, CA: Sage.

This book provides theoretical and conceptual considerations in the field of intercultural communications. Interdisciplinary in approach, the text reviews multicultural issues from several perspectives that are useful for the practitioner. The text also contains training designs, specific case examples, and methods.

Atkinson, D. R., Morten, G., & Sue, D. W. (Eds.). (1983). *Counseling American minorities—A cross-cultural perspective* (2nd ed.). Dubuque, IA: William C. Brown.

These readings are intended to sensitize counselors to the life experiences of culturally distinct populations. The book describes some of the unique needs and experiences of minority individuals. It offers direction for counselors who will assist those who are culturally different. Issues, techniques, and concepts applicable to broad minority groups, as well as subgroups such as handicapped persons, gay individuals, prison populations, and religious groups, are discussed.

Brislin, R. W. (1981). *Cross-cultural encounters—Face to face interaction*. New York: Pergamon Press.

This book defines concepts that are useful in the analysis of all forms of cross-cultural interactions. Individual attitudes, traits, skills, and thought processes are discussed as a basis for understanding reference groups, organizational conflict, and the process of adjustment. Productive cross-cultural encounters are proposed as possible solutions to misunderstandings and conflicts.

Brislin, R. W., Cushner, K., Cherrie, C., & Yong, M. (1986). *Intercultural interactions—A practical guide*. Beverly Hills, CA: Sage.

This is one volume in a series by Sage that is especially useful for practitioners. Interpersonal interactions in cross-cultural settings are examined by a critical incident technique: appropriateness of interpretation, underlying reasons for social-psychological principles, and development of different ways to evaluate responses. A series of case studies and vignettes provide a discussion of alternative actions. The book contains a wealth of practical information.

Henderson, G. (Ed.). (1979). *Understanding and counseling ethnic minorities*. Springfield, IL: Charles C Thomas.

This collection of readings is broken down by ethnic groups (Blacks, American Indians, Chinese Americans, Mexican Americans, Puerto Ricans, and Japanese Americans) that address patterns of family life, language, customs, and aspects of social environments. It is intended for use by school counselors and school psychologists who are concerned with understanding the lives of ethnic minority individuals. This is a classic reference text.

Horowitz, D. L. (1985). *Ethnic groups in conflict*. Berkeley, CA: University of California Press.

This book provides an overview and insight into the importance of ethnic conflict on a global level. It addresses the importance of ethnic affiliation, sources of conflict, party politics, military politics, and interethnic accommodation. It presents the concept of democratic multiethnic politics as a measure of success in interhuman relations and as a means of reducing ethnic conflict.

Ivey, A. E. (1983). *Intentional interviewing and counseling*. Monterey, CA: Brooks/Cole.

Counselors could find this book useful as they develop specific skills and competencies in the interviewing process of a counseling relationship. Readers become aware that different cultural groups have differing patterns of communication. "Microskill" techniques are identified and exercises are suggested. In addition, a form of systematic study of major concepts enables the counselor to increase proficiency in communication across cultural barriers.

Ivey, A. E., & Authier, J. (1978). *Microcounseling: Innovations in interviewing, counseling, psychotherapy and psychoeducation* (2nd ed.). Springfield, IL: Charles C Thomas.

The "microcounseling model" refers to a systematic method of acquiring necessary interviewing skills. A psychoeducational methodology of "helping" in cross-cultural counseling is detailed and calls for improved communication skills when working with individuals of various backgrounds. Microcounseling, as a skill, assists practitioners in helping clients develop constructive personal attitudes and behaviors.

Ivey, A. E., Ivey, M. B., & Simek-Downing, L. (1987). *Counseling and psychotherapy: Integrating skills, theory, and practice* (2nd ed.). Englewood Cliffs, NJ: Prentice-Hall.

This is a foundation text describing counseling theories and the skills necessary for psychotherapy. Relevant authorities reviewed the content on each chapter, one of which is an in-depth chapter on individual and cultural empathy.

Goals, broad constructs, and examples of cultural and group differences are clearly set forth and enable the reader to develop an understanding of techniques that work with one group, yet may be offensive to another.

LeVine, E. S., & Padilla, A. M. (1980). *Crossing cultures in therapy—Pluralistic counseling for the Hispanic*. Monterey, CA: Brooks/Cole.

This book describes counseling techniques that are geared to the cultural, linguistic, and socioeconomic conditions of Hispanics and other minority groups. Case histories and real-life illustrations of principles and suggested modes of intervention are included and make for interesting, beneficial, and concise reading.

McGoldrick, M., Pearce, J. K., & Giordano, J. (Eds.). (1982). *Ethnicity and family therapy*. New York: Guilford Press.

This book examines the manner in which ethnocultural factors affect family relations and suggests how counselors and therapists can assess, communicate, and treat subgroups more effectively by being aware of cultural roots. It discusses a systems approach to over 23 subgroups and provides a wealth of information about cultural profiles as well as specific therapeutic suggestions.

Pasteur, A. B., & Toldson, I. L. (1982). *Roots of soul: The psychology of Black expressiveness*. Garden City, NY: Anchor Press/Doubleday.

This book presents a broad range of Black expressive forms and a discussion on how feelings and emotions affect *folkways*, customs, and personal relationships. It offers a theoretical position with practical provisions for helping Blacks and others attend to interpersonal development and mental health needs.

Pedersen, P. (1988). *A handbook for developing multicultural awareness*. Alexandria, VA: American Association for Counseling and Development.

This book is called "an ideal handbook for teaching cross-cultural counseling." Pedersen provides a practical guide for improving communication skills and cultural awareness. Role-playing techniques and simulation exercises help readers identify and overcome learned stereotypical behavior and responses. Stages of multicultural development are outlined and offer readers the opportunity to develop their own multicultural identity.

Pedersen, P., Draguns, J. G., Lonner, W. J., & Trimble, J. E. (1981). *Counseling across cultures—Revised edition*. Honolulu, HI: University of Hawaii Press.

This valuable text examines the impact of cultural differences on mental health priorities in counseling, specific counselor interventions, and dominant-systems values that lead toward cultural bias. The authors demonstrate the way in which differences in culture, age, sex, life-style, and socioeconomic status can affect communication between counselor and client. This is a well-referenced and highly regarded text in the field of multicultural issues.

Reynolds, D. K. (1980). *The quiet therapies— Japanese pathways to personal growth.* Honolulu, HI: The University of Hawaii Press.

Five Japanese psychotherapies (Marita, Naikan, Seiza, Shadan, and Zen) are presented along with their common themes and techniques. Collectively, through their own methods of introspection, the therapies address the nature of man and offer practical advice and techniques for helping clients cope with problems. Western practitioners will find this empathic, introspective, and operational approach to human experiences to be useful.

Sue, D. W. (1988). *Counseling the culturally different.* New York: John Wiley Publishers.

This is a classic work in the field of cross-cultural counseling. It adds meaning to related issues of counseling all minority groups, identifies differences and similarities among ethnic groups in relation to counseling practices, and addresses our social-political system's impact on cross-cultural counseling delivery services. "Critical Incidents" highlight and illustrate issues and concerns that are likely to arise in typical counseling situations.

Vacc, N. A., & Wittmer, J. P. (Eds.). (1980). *Let me be me—Special populations and the helping professional.* Muncie, IN: Accelerated Development.

A wide array of diverse values and individual differences are identified within each special population (Blacks, Hispanics, Asian Americans, Mexican Americans, various religious groups, elderly citizens, and others). In-depth exploration of life experiences of subgroups provides an awareness of unique characteristics that are useful and meaningful to counselors.

Periodicals

Atkinson, D. R. (1985). A meta-review of research on cross-cultural counseling and psychotherapy. *Journal of Multicultural Counseling and Development, 13*, 138–153.

This article examines cross-cultural research in a manner that provides organizational strategies and objective analysis of research outcomes across ethnic groups, research designs, and research settings. It lists a collective set of major conclusions of the studies and makes recommendations for future studies.

Brandell, J. R. (1988). Treatment of the biracial child: Theoretical and clinical issues. *Journal of Multicultural Counseling and Development, 16*, 176–187.

A significant number of children in the United States are born of interracial couples. Ethnic-racial identity undergoes critical development before the school years. This article is a case study of the identifying problem and course of treatment for a biracial child. A "self-psychological perspective model" illuminates some developmental aspects of biracial self-identity.

Cole, S. M., Thomas, A. R., & Lee, C. C. (1988). School counselor and school psychologist: Partners in minority family outreach. *Journal of Multicultural Counseling and Development, 16*, 110–116.

School counselors and school psychologists can play a vital role in bridging the gap between minority families and the educational system. A comprehensive consultation model is presented that attempts to promote family and community involvement in the educational process of minority youth. Through community awareness, family consultation, and para-professional development, the school counselor can help lessen the tension between schools and ethnic groups.

Gade, E., Hurlburt, G., & Fuqua, D. (1986). Study habits and attitudes of American Indian students: Implications for counselors. *The School Counselor, 34*, 135–139.

A comparison investigation of American-Indian study habits and attitudes to classroom achievement and behaviors is presented. Results show how counselors can increase teacher-counselor feedback, can focus on motivational personal concerns of students, and can promote relevance in the school curriculum to acquisition of life-skills.

Hannigan, T. P. (1988). Culture shock with a happy ending. *Journal of Counseling and Development, 67*, 91.

Hannigan describes adjustment difficulties that arise from living in a foreign country. He states that culture shock is not like the mumps; you can get it again and again. Lessons he learned while living in Europe enrich his abilities to counsel foreign students who come to the United States to seek an education.

Heath, A. E., Neimeyer, G. J., & Pedersen, P. (1988). The future of cross-cultural counseling: A delphi poll. *Journal of Counseling and Development, 67*, 27–30.

A study addresses the future of cross-cultural counseling over the next 10 years. Opinions of groups of recognized experts were solicited to obtain a consensus in the areas of theory and research, training and preparation, and social organization. Many probable changes were indicated and these make for fascinating reading. Top programs, journals, and books in the field are nominated.

Helms, J. C. (1988). Expanding racial identity theory to cover the counseling process. *The Journal of Counseling Psychology, 33*, 82–84.

Helms reviews the Racial Identity Attitude Scale and its use in practice and research. The author critiques previous studies and findings to assess racial identity. The article determines that scale reliability and interpretation problems can be lessened by use of multiple variables that reflect the complexity of racial identity, particularly when studying the counseling process.

Henkin, W. A. (1985). Toward counseling the Japanese in America: A cross-cultural primer. *Journal of Counseling and Development, 63*, 500–503.

Pragmatic observations and insights concerning counseling Japanese-Americans are offered. A brief subcultural history gives background information and distinguishes between the "quiet therapies" of Japan and Western "talk-therapies." Precise suggestions for counselors are presented that may help distinguish between client behaviors that are individualistic and those that are cultural.

Herr, E. L. (1987). Cultural diversity from an international perspective. *Journal of Multicultural Counseling and Development, 15*, 99–109.

The United States is described as a land of immigrants, including the American Indian who has a diverse cultural background. Ethnic traditions and international roots persist over time and have effects that span generations, their behaviors, and interrelationships. One set of therapies will not adequately address the therapeutic needs of all clients. A macroenvironment exists in which all counseling approaches and assumptions must be validated against cultural pluralism.

Makinda, O. (1987). African urbanism: Preparation for multi-ethnic school counselors. *Journal of Multicultural Counseling and Development, 15*, 30–41.

Makinda compares cities in Western Nigeria with cities in Europe and North America by identifying cross-cultural perspectives of the urbanization process. The article describes the importance of home life, physical environment, family structure, parental attitudes, and socioeconomic factors that face counselors who work with students who move to a city from a rural setting and go through adjustment to urbanism.

Parker, W. M. (1988). Becoming an effective multicultural counselor. ***Journal of Counseling and Development, 67*, 93.**

This article relates to the reader the first-year counseling experiences of a young Black man, trained to work with middle-class White clients. Through specific examples, the reader learns that Parker discovers a lack of ability to work with ethnic minority clients. Through study and effort, Parker gains an awareness of his own attitudes, changes negative habits, and develops cross-cultural counseling skills.

Parsonson, K. (1987). Intermarriages—Effects on the ethnic identity of the offspring. ***Journal of Cross-Cultural Psychology, 18*, 363–371.**

This study compares children's ethnic identity of multiple ethnic origin with those children from an endogamous marriage. (The ethnic groups were British, Chinese, Italian, and Ukranian.) The results do not strongly support strong ethnic identity with parents' endogamy. Strength of ethnic identity depended upon the ethnicity in question (varied among groups) and the desire to further practice endogamy.

Ponterotto, J. G. (1987). Counseling Mexican-Americans: A multi-modal approach. ***Journal of Counseling and Development, 65*, 308–312.**

Mexican-Americans are reported to underuse counseling services and have counseling needs that are not currently being met. Ponterotto describes the large intracultural diversity of the population and calls for a model inherently flexible in delivery. Multimodal therapy borrows from traditional techniques and therapies to provide a multifaceted and fully comprehensive counseling process, necessary when working with Mexican Americans.

Rubenstein, J., Feldman, S. S., Rubin, C., & Noveck, I. (1987). A cross-cultural comparison of children's drawings of same and mixed-sex peer interaction. ***Journal of Cross-Cultural Psychology, 18*, 234–250.**

The authors present empirical work in which they attribute children's attitudes and views of peer relations to the ideology of the prevailing culture and child-rearing practices. Culture variations were seen in both themes and the ways in which children alter their relationships when they move from same-sex to mixed-sex groups. The data suggest cultural influences and refine the way sex typing is manifested in childhood.

Sue, S., & Zane, N. (1987). The role of culture and cultural techniques in psychotherapy: A critique and reformulation. ***American Psychologist, 42*, 37–45.**

A critique of specific techniques in counseling and treatment of ethnic minority clients is offered. Cultural knowledge and sensitivity are described as being central in establishing a counseling relationship that builds credibility effectiveness. Therapeutic treatment planning must include process components designed with cultural factors in mind.

Vontress, C. E. (1988). An existential approach to cross-cultural counseling. *Journal of Multicultural Counseling and Development, 16*, 73–83.

This article presents a nontraditional, existential cross-cultural counseling approach. Clients are human, part of an ecological culture, representative of a national and regional culture, and are members of a racioethnic group. Counselors are influenced by cultural identity and must understand how their own cultural identities affect their ability to help culturally different clients.

Conclusion

As any researcher will find, there is a wealth of information and resources in the field of cross-cultural counseling. The bibliography (designed primarily for elementary and middle school counselors) does not pretend to be a definitive or recommended reading list, but rather it presents various authors in the field along with some comments that parallel their stated purpose of content.

The prospects for the field of cross-cultural counseling are extremely good. Heath, Neimeyer, and Pedersen (1988) stated that in the future, knowledge of a client's cultural background will be routinely incorporated into the counselor's delivery.

As the demographics of the United States change, the impact of various racial and ethnic groups will also change. The challenge to "help" in a pluralistic culture is an exciting one. Self-study and review in the field of cross-cultural counseling serve to improve one's counseling skills, help one acquire new knowledge, and also make for very interesting reading.

References

Atkinson, D. R., Morten, G., & Sue, D. W. (Eds.). (1979). *Counseling American minorities: A cross-cultural perspective.* Dubuque, IA: William C. Brown.

Heath, A. E., Neimeyer, G. J., & Pedersen, P. (1988). The future of cross-cultural counseling: A delphi poll. *Journal of Counseling and Development, 67*, 27–30.

Henderson, G. (Ed.). (1979). *Understanding and counseling ethnic minorities.* Springfield, IL: Thomas.

Hollis, J. W., & Wantz, R. A. (1986). *Counselor preparation 1986–1989* (6th ed.). Muncie, IN: Accelerated Development.

Jones, E. E., & Korchin, S. J. (1982). *Minority mental health*. New York: Praeger.
Pedersen, P. (Ed.). (1985). *Handbook of cross-cultural counseling and therapy*. Westport, CT: Greenwood Press.
Sue, D. W. (1981). *Counseling the culturally different*. New York: Wiley.

Chapter 1
Counseling Issues in a Culturally Diverse World

Issues for elementary school counselors to consider about a culturally diverse world:

1. Minority groups have concerns and needs that are unique. Identify some of these concerns and needs and consider how elementary school counselors might address them.
2. Racial problems exist in many of our schools. Identify some components of classroom guidance programs that help to alleviate racial conflict.
3. Elementary school counselors who are not members of a minority group may have problems in meeting the needs of children and parents from minority groups. What can counselors do to gain a better understanding of minority populations?
4. There is often a need to provide counseling services to non-English speaking students. How might elementary school counselors deal with this need?
5. How can elementary school counselors work through professional associations to encourage minority group members to consider counseling as a career?
6. Consider how various counseling theories and techniques might help elementary school counselors work with students from minority populations.
7. Identify some means that counselors can use to advocate for changes that make schools more inviting to minority populations.
8. What are some key resources elementary school counselors can use to keep informed about concerns of minority populations?
9. Identify some strategies elementary school counselors might use in the classroom to promote high self-esteem among children from minority populations.
10. How does cultural diversity enrich the lives of everyone in our schools?

CHAPTER 2

A WORLD OF CHANGING FAMILIES

The so-called traditional family has virtually disappeared in America. Divorce and single parent homes are a fact of life confronting children. Divorce occurs in one of every two marriages and estimates suggest that 80% of the students in some schools come from broken homes. This chapter on divorce and single parent homes helps elementary school counselors understand the effects of changing family structures and suggests ways to promote child growth and development within the context of family change.

Chapter 2 covers a variety of topics related to helping children and parents function effectively within changing family situations. These topics include:

1. Multimodal group counseling for children
2. Group training for single parents
3. Group guidance for latchkey children
4. Counseling interventions with children from single parent families

The articles in Chapter 2 recognize that elementary school counselors must often use broad based approaches for intervening with children who face difficult family circumstances. When children experience divorce, for example, they must often learn new behaviors, examine changing feelings, deal with new sensations and images related to home and family, and cope with challenging new relationships within families. Elementary school counselors need to develop innovative approaches to help children and parents develop in a healthy fashion in spite of the ambiguity created by divorce and single parent families.

The 1990s promise to bring new challenges for elementary school counselors in the area of changing family structures. Counselors will probably want to assume a larger role in preparing children to be responsible parents and family members in later adult life. Most counselors are presently reacting to changing families and helping children to cope. Counselors should assume a more proactive stance by collaborating with teachers in developing and implementing family education programs aimed at preventing some of the difficulties experienced in today's families. Chapter 2 provides a clear challenge for counselors to develop creative approaches in helping family members to work together productively.

A Multimodal Intervention for Group Counseling with Children of Divorce

Margaret Crosbie-Burnett
Laurel L. Newcomer

Increasing numbers of children are bringing divorce-related problems to school. Teachers, administrators, counselors and other support service professionals have begun to respond to this phenomenon in ways that go beyond individual counseling. Because of the large numbers of children who need support and guidance in coping with parental divorce, school counselors often choose a group format in which to address these children's needs. In response to this trend, a variety of models of group counseling for children of divorce can be found in the recent literature. Unfortunately, few of these models included any evaluation measures and even fewer tested the group's effectiveness with an experimental design.

Green's (1978) multimodal model of group intervention for children of divorce, however, has been shown to be successful in changing children's beliefs and attitudes about divorce and in increasing competent behaviors (Anderson, Kinney, & Gerler, 1984). A multimodal approach gives the counselor a framework by which to systematically address the many elements of a child's life that may be affected by parental divorce, as well as the interrelationships between those elements. The elements include health, emotions, self-concept, learning and school performance, interpersonal relationships, and behaviors. Because some children may be experiencing problems in some element of their lives more than other elements, the model lends itself to individualized treatment for each child. Even in a group setting, some individualization is possible. In addition, children who are excelling in an element can serve as role models for children who are having problems in that part of their lives. For a complete explanation of multimodal therapy with children, see Keat (1974, 1979) and Keat, Boswell, and Green (1980); for reviews of multimodal counseling, see Gerler (1981, 1982).

The model presented below is a modification and expansion of Green (1978) with minor contributions from models reported by Hammond (1981) and Wilkinson and Bleck (1977). Green's model is modified in the following ways: (a) The objectives and modes for each session are included, allowing the counselor to identify quickly the areas of concern that the session addresses and the mode used to address them. This gives the counselor more flexibility because the counselor can use the session and activities that are most relevant to the group at that particular time. For example, a group may have greater immediate needs for emotion-related activities at a particular time than for behavioral problem-solving activities. (b) The present model is appropriate for use in nearly all primary grades and middle school. Because the Green model places heavy emphasis on the reading of *The Boys and Girls Book About Divorce* (Gardner, 1970), it is limited to the upper primary grades and middle school because of the reading level required. (c) Divorce-related materials that have been developed since the publication of the Green model are integrated. (d) In addition to the group counseling model, the model presented here is enriched by the inclusion of a classroom component to educate all children about parental divorce and family change. The use of both a classroom component and a small group component is consistent with the developmental, preventive approach to school guidance. The classroom component also provides children with the opportunity to refer themselves to the small group.

Both the classroom and the small-group components of the model are described below. This model has been tested in an experimental study with sixth graders (Crosbie-Burnett & Newcomer, in press); it was found to significantly reduce depression as measured by the Reynolds Depression Inventory (Reynolds, 1987) and significantly improve attitudes and beliefs about parental divorce as measured by the Children's Beliefs about Parental Divorce Scale (Kurdek & Berg, 1987) and some aspects of self-concept as measured by the Self-Perception Profile for Children (Harter, 1985). In addition, counselors have informally reported success in using the model repeatedly with elementary school children of varying ages.

Family Change: A Classroom Guidance Activity

Objectives:

1. To help children of parental divorce by reframing divorce as one form of family change.
2. To suggest various coping strategies for adjusting to change.
3. To provide an opportunity for children to sign up for small group work on divorce-related issues.

Discussion

Types of Families. At least 1 hour should be allowed for the classroom guidance activity. The discussion begins with brainstorming and definitions of the various types of families, including intact/nuclear, single-parent, stepparent, foster, adopted, extended, communal, and any others that the children identify. Students discuss similarities and differences between family types.

Family Change. Counselors explain that all families experience change over time. The counselor and children identify the many situations in which families change developmentally, including births, deaths, separation and divorce, remarriage, and children growing up and leaving home. Counselors may invite children to talk about examples of change in their own families.

Adjustment to Change. Counselors need to explain that when families change, people have to learn how to adjust. Counselors may invite children to talk about how they have adjusted to change in their families or other changes, like changing schools. Then the class discusses the kinds of coping mechanisms that children could try if they are having problems adjusting to change. Common suggestions include the following: (a) *talking* with teachers, parents, friends, counselors, siblings, and other adults; (b) *reading* books about the changes they are experiencing; and (c) *joining* a group with other children with similar experiences.

Introduction To Small Group

Counselors explain that a group for children whose parents have separated or divorced will meet for 8 weeks, once a week, for 1 period, and that the purpose of the group will be to talk about their experiences of living in a divorced family. Then counselors ask for questions about the group. When giving a piece of paper to each child, the counselor directs the students to write their names and indicate "yes" if they would like to join the group and "no" if they do not want to do so. It is important that *all* children return the sign-up sheets so that classmates cannot identify those who express interest in participating in the small group.

Closure

If time allows, the counselor asks the children what they learned from the lesson. Ethically, it is important that the counselor note children who appear distressed by the discussion of family change. If these children do not express interest in the small group, they can be contacted for individual counseling.

Group Counseling Intervention for Children of Separation and Divorce

Selections of Group Members

It is important to individually interview all potential group members, even those who are self-selected. In the interview, the counselor may give each child information about the format, goals, and typical activities of the group. The counselor may also ask the child about his or her interest in the group. At the end of the interview, if the child is still interested and the counselor judges the child to be appropriate for the group, the counselor directs the child to have a parent sign a parental permission slip. Children whose parent(s) has(have) remarried may be included if they appear to have unresolved concerns about the divorce and if the counselor wishes to have a more heterogeneous group.

Overview

Each session is composed of an opening Icebreaker Activity, a central Stimulus Activity, and a Closing Activity, which generally includes some form of homework. The objectives for each session and the mode of behavior to which the activities relate are included at the beginning of each session. The seven modes are organized by the acronym HELPING (Green, 1978). They are the following: H–Health, E–Emotions, L–Learning, P–Personal relationships, I–Interests or Image, N–Need-To-Know, and G–Guidance of Behaviors, Actions, and Consequences.

Session 1: Introduction and Getting to Know You

Objectives:

1. To allow children to become better acquainted.
2. To set rules and goals for the group.

Icebreaker: Name Game. Name tags: Each group member is given a 5" x 7" card and a marking pen. In the center of the card each child writes his or her name. In the upper right corner children write their favorite thing to do. In the upper left corner children write their favorite TV show and star. In the lower left corner children write their three favorite foods. In the lower right corner children write their favorite color. In the center, under the name, each child writes one word that describes him or her.

The children are then paired and spend a few minutes interviewing each other, using the cards as stimuli for questions. The group reassembles and each pair introduces themselves to the group.

Stimulus Activity: Group Goal Setting and Rule Setting. The counselor explains the purposes of the group:

> We are here to privately share all we can about divorce. It is something that many children experience. In fact, everyone in the group has parents that are divorced. Some of the things we'll talk about are what divorce means, how it makes us feel, what we can do about those feelings, ways we can learn from it, what is going on with the people in our lives as we experience divorce, how we see ourselves, what we think or tell ourselves about divorce, and problems that we are having because of divorce. I'd like to talk about what you want out of this group, because it is your group. Let's go around and say what each one of us would like to get out of this group and I'll write down your goals so we can try to cover them all in our 8 weeks together.

The group then mutually decides on goals; each child can contribute personally. Setting group goals encourages commitment and involvement of all the members toward open sharing and growth.

The counselor helps the group identify group rules. The rules might include the following: (a) Confidentiality; (b) Listening to the person speaking; (c) The right to pass up your turn to talk; and (d) No put-downs.

Closing. Counselors explain that in future sessions the leader will give the children something to think about or practice for the next session, and then say, "For next week think about the goals and rules we have set and decide if there's something you would like to add."

Session 2: Divorce and Feelings

Objectives:

1. To help children handle personal relationships, especially within the family.
2. To help children clarify, recognize, and understand feelings and emotions pertaining to divorce.

Modes:

1. Personal relationships.
2. Emotions.

Introduction. The counselor reviews goals and rules and adds any goals or rules that the children generated during the week.

Icebreaker: The House My Family Lives In. The counselor shows the children a drawing of their family that was made prior to the session. The drawing of the family members should be divided into house shapes to illustrate the different homes in which they live. For example, one might draw a mother in one house shape where she lives alone, siblings and their families in separate house shapes, a daughter in a house shape to represent the apartment she lives in with her roommates, and a spouse, self, and other children in another house shape. The counselor describes his or her picture to the group and then asks the children to draw house shapes and family members to show where members of their families live. After the drawings are finished, the counselor lets the children share their drawings and name their family members in each house.

Summing-Up Questions. Is someone still in your family if they live in a different home? Can you love someone who lives in a different house just as much as someone who lives with you? Have you ever thought about living with your other parent?

Stimulus Activity: Creating "Feeling Gauges." The counselor explains to children that people react to divorce with various feelings: sad, angry, scared, or unhappy. Children are encouraged to identify other feelings. The counselor reads relevant sections of *The Boys and Girls Book About Divorce* (Gardner, 1970). Using the pictures as discussion facilitators, the group focuses on what divorce means and the feelings that children can have when parents divorce. Concurrent with that discussion, each child individually completes his or her personal set of five "Feeling Gauges"—figures that resemble thermometers with a circle on top. Thus, children can select the most important feelings they have experienced during the divorce process, write the feeling in the circle, and color in the intensity of the feeling (the higher up the thermometer the color is, the "hotter" the feeling).

Closing. The counselor asks the children to write down any feelings they have about their parents' divorce during the coming week and note the event that caused the feelings. The counselor explains that the children will be invited to share these at the next session.

Session 3: Divorce and the Feelings and Problems It Can Create

Objectives:

1. To continue identifying the feelings surrounding divorce.
2. To begin examining some of the problems it can create.

Modes:

1. Emotions.
2. Need-to-know.

Icebreaker. The counselor finishes the "Feeling Gauges" from the previous week if not completed and asks the children to discuss with the group the feeling with which they most closely identify. The counselor asks them to discuss feelings they experienced during the week and the causes of them.

Stimulus Activity: Movie—"Tender Places." "Tender Places" is a play that was written by a 10-year-old boy whose parents had divorced (Films for Humanity, 1987). It provides an opportunity for the group to see that the problems they may have experienced in their families are not unique. An appropriate alternative is a filmstrip entitled "Understanding Changes in the Family: Not Together Anymore" (Guidance Associates, 1983). After the group views the movie or the filmstrip, the counselor leads a discussion along the following lines.

Closing. Discussion questions could include the following: Why did Eric get so mad when his father offered to buy him a dog if he would come to live with him? Why do you think Eric was so upset when his mother told him she was going to remarry? Do you think it's a good idea for kids to choose which parent to live with? What problems could that create? Why did Eric tell the elderly lady at the end that he didn't want to get a dog? Do you think it's worth the risk to love someone or something even if they sometimes disappoint you?

Session 4: Divorce and What to Do About It

Objective:

To help children learn how to confront and cope with feelings and problems specific to divorce.

Modes:

1. Health.
2. Guidance of actions, behaviors, and consequences.
3. Emotions.

Icebreaker. The counselor reviews briefly the film or filmstrip from the previous week. The counselor also makes a list of feelings and problems regarding divorce using the film or filmstrip as a starting point and expands the list from the children's personal experiences. Brainstorming possible solutions to these problems is also beneficial.

Stimulus Activity: Generating Coping Behaviors:

1. Using problems and feelings generated above in the Icebreaker activity, the counselor has the children complete the following sentence fragment: "When I feel angry, frustrated, unhappy (or any other emotion they wish to name), I can ______________________." The counselor helps the children list ideas that can help them feel better but will not cause problems or hurt anyone or anything. Constructive suggestions

would include listening to music, watching television, reading, walking the dog, running or jogging, playing a favorite sport, taking a warm bath or shower, singing, calling a friend, walking in the park or woods, or playing with friends.
2. Students role play one or two solutions that were brainstormed.
3. The counselor discusses the importance of children regulating their emotions and lives through proper sleep, daily exercise, and nutritional food. The counselor also points out that these may be new responsibilities they must attend to as a consequence of the divorce.

Closing. The counselor directs the children to practice during the week one of the coping behaviors that was discussed or role played in the session. The counselor also suggests that they practice telling themselves and another person how they feel once every day during the coming week.

Session 5: Talking About Divorce

Objectives:

1. To continue exploration of how to cope with feelings associated with divorce.
2. To begin thinking about choices and decisions about actions and behaviors.

Modes:

1. Emotions.
2. Guidance of actions, behaviors, and consequences.

Icebreaker. The counselor discusses the homework: "Who practiced a coping behavior that we talked about last week? What happened when you told someone how you felt? How did you feel when you did that?"

Stimulus Activity: Multimodal Game. The students play the "Family Happenings Game" (Boardman & Boardman, 1983) using the additional cards that pertain specifically to divorce. This is a multimodal game designed to encourage discussion, rehearsal, and role playing of various aspects of children's lives related to divorce. An alternative multimodal game is "The Acting, Feeling, Choosing Game" (Keat, 1978). While playing the game, it is helpful to continue developing the list of divorce-related problems and possible solutions. The counselor provides time to brainstorm, discuss, and role-play expression of feelings and other coping behaviors. The momentum and design of the game help motivate the children to confront some issues that may have been repressed previously. The game fosters attention to emotions, learning about divorce, relations with others, positive images, the need-to-know (rational talk), and guidance of actions, behaviors, and consequences.

Closing. Children are given three blank cards to generate their own entries for the game.

Session 6: More About Divorce

Objectives:

1. To help children develop rational, correct thoughts regarding themselves and divorce.
2. To continue examining possible choices for behavior and actions.

Modes:

1. Personal relations, especially friends.
2. Image.
3. Need-to-know.
4. Guidance of actions and behaviors.

Icebreaker. The counselor has the children draw self-portraits. (The counselors should provide mirrors.) Children write positive, rational statements about themselves on the back of the portraits. Personal examples are helpful. Each child reads two or three of his or her statements to the group. Group members can add to each child's list. The counselor explains how positive images and positive thoughts of oneself can promote feeling good about oneself and letting others know that.

Stimulus Activity: Continuation of Multimodal Game. Students continue playing the multimodal game, but the cards the children developed in the previous week as starters for this session are used because they will generally reveal personally relevant situations and questions. The counselor encourages the children to explore pertinent issues in depth, and to brainstorm and practice problem-solving and coping skills.

Closing. Children continue to add to the list of positive self-statements on the back of their portraits. Each child tells someone else something he or she likes about himself or herself each day of the coming week.

Session 7: Clarifying Attitudes Toward Divorce

Objective:

To help children clarify their attitudes toward divorce and reduce irrational thoughts.

Modes:

1. Learning.
2. Personal relations, especially family and friends.
3. Need-to-know.

Icebreaker. Students discuss new additions to positive statements on the back of self-portraits. Students also discuss reactions to telling someone else qualities they like about themselves.

Stimulus Activity: "Quiz" on Beliefs and Attitudes About Divorce. Children number from 1 to 11 on a piece of paper or the counselor hands out a copy of the "quiz" below. Each sentence is read aloud as the children mark either "A" (agree) or "D" (disagree).

1. _____Once people marry they should never get a divorce.
2. _____Sometimes, when parents divorce, it is the children's fault.
3. _____Children from divorced families can be just as happy as children whose parents are married.
4. _____If children promised their divorced parents that they would be very good, they might be able to get them back together.
5. _____It is better for parents to divorce than to fight everyday.
6. _____A parent who does not live with the child can still love him/her very much.
7. _____All kids whose parents are divorced get into more trouble at school.
8. _____It is better not to tell anyone if your parents are divorced.
9. _____Stepparents are usually mean to children.
10. _____It may be good for the children to live half of their time with their dad and half of the time with their mother.
11. _____When parents divorce, it is a very difficult time for all families.

The counselor corrects any maladaptive beliefs and attitudes. The class discusses statements about which children disagree and statements in which there is much interest.

Closing. The counselor asks children to discuss with their parent(s) at least one item from the "quiz." The counselor also asks children to discuss with one friend one of the changes they have experienced due to their parents' divorce.

Session 8: Integrating the Modes and Group Closure

Objective:

To increase the positive ways in which the children think, act, and feel about their families.

Mode:

All seven modes of the acronym HELPING.

Icebreaker. Children are asked to discuss what it was like to talk about divorce with parents and friends. Each child draws a family shield—a shield that is divided into five sections by drawing a cross in the main area and a horizontal line near the bottom of the shield, making the lower area a fifth section. Children are directed to draw pictures or make statements related to the following topics in each of the five sections of the shield.

1. A positive thing or a good time in your family.
2. An unpleasant time you had with your family.
3. One way to cope with an unpleasant family experience.
4. Reasons why you think your parents got a divorce.
5. Something you would like to see happening to your family in the next year.

The counselor asks volunteers to share their family shields with the group.

Stimulus Activity. Each child is given a large six-pointed star design. Students fill the spaces using pictures, words, or symbols. The center of the star is for the child's image (I). The spaces in the points are for the following: Learning or school (L); Friends (P); Family (P); Feelings he or she has most of the time (E); A positive thought he or she keeps in his or her mind all the time (N); A behavior he or she enjoys doing or has gotten under control (G).

Children are asked to share their stars with the group. Ways of expressing that each child is a unique star are encouraged.

Closing. The group concludes with round robin statements of the following: I learned ________________. I feel ________________. I am ________________. Divorce makes life different by ____________________________. I wish I could ______________________. I think ____________________. A good thing that has happened is _________________. Divorce is _________________. I've changed by ______________________.

Children generate sentence stems if they desire. Ways in which their growth or change is apparent to others are also shared.

Conclusion

The model presented is a two-tiered developmental guidance unit on parental divorce. The classroom unit acquaints all children with divorce as a type of family change; the small group focuses on the needs of children who are coping with parental divorce. The use of a multimodal approach in the small group allows each child to focus on the elements of his or her life that has been most affected by the divorce. This modification of the Green (1978) HELPING multimodal approach to group counseling children of divorce has been tested experimentally and found to have positive effects on depression, attitudes, and beliefs about parental divorce, and aspects of self-concept.

References

Anderson, R. F., Kinney, J., & Gerler, E. R. (1984). The effects of divorce groups on children's classroom behavior and attitudes toward divorce. *Elementary School Guidance & Counseling, 19,* 70–76.

Boardman, R. L., & Boardman, L. (1983). *The family happenings game.* Eau Claire, WI: Kids in Progress, Inc.

Crosbie-Burnett, M., & Newcomer, L. (in press). Group counseling with children of divorce: The effects of a multimodal intervention. *Journal of Divorce.*

Films for Humanity (1987). *Tender places* [Film]. New York: Films for Humanity. 1-800-257-5126.

Gardner, R. A. (1970). *The boys and girls book about divorce.* New York: Bantam.

Gerler, E. R. (1981). The multimodal counseling model: 1973 to the present. *Elementary School Guidance & Counseling, 15,* 285–291.

Gerler, E. R. (1982). Multimodal counseling: Update. *Elementary School Guidance & Counseling, 16,* 261–266.

Green, B. J. (1978). HELPING children of divorce: A multimodal approach. *Elementary School Guidance & Counseling, 13,* 31–45.

Guidance Associates. (1973). *Understanding changes in the family: Not together anymore* [Filmstrip]. Pleasantville, NY: Guidance Associates.

Hammond, J. M. (1981). Loss of the family unit: Counseling groups to help kids. *The Personnel and Guidance Journal, 59,* 392–394.

Harter, L. (1985). *Manual for the self-perception profile for children* (Revision of the Perceived Competence Scale for Children). University of Denver.

Keat, D. B. (1974). *Fundamentals of child counseling.* Boston, MA: Houghton Mifflin.

Keat, D. B. (1978). *The acting, feeling, choosing game: A multimodal game for children.* Harrisburg, PA: Professional Associates.

Keat, D. B. (1979). *Multimodal therapy with children.* New York: Pergamon.

Keat, D. B., Boswell, J., & Green, B. (1980). HELPING children multimodally. *Elementary School Guidance & Counseling, 15,* 172–176.

Kurdek, L., & Berg, G. (in press). *The Children's Beliefs about Parental Divorce Scale: Psychometric characteristics and concurrent validity.* Wright State University and University of Dayton.

Reynolds, W. M. (1987). *Child Depression Scale.* Odessa, FL: Psychological Assessment Resources, Inc.

Wilkinson, G. S., & Bleck, R. T. (1977). Children's divorce groups. *Elementary School Guidance & Counseling, 11,* 205–213.

A Parent Group Training Program for Single Parents

Nancy J. Cunningham
Joe H. Brown

This article outlines a group training program in parenting skills for single parents that emphasizes parent-child communication, child management, and problem-solving skills.

The number of single-parent families is rising rapidly. The largest single factor contributing to the increasing number of single-parent families is the growing rate of divorce (Porter & Chatelain, 1981). The number of children under 18 living in single-parent families doubled from 10% to approximately 20% in the 1970s (U.S. Bureau of the Census, 1980). If this trend continues, approximately 45% of those children born today will spend at least 1 year living in a single-parent home. Although these data are alarming, they do not reveal the emotional turmoil and trauma that face many single parents.

There are a number of serious problems that confront the single-parent family. First, the absence of a spouse often places immediate financial responsibility on the single parent (Wallerstein & Kelly, 1980). Such responsibility can be overwhelming as many single-parent families are headed by women who possess little formal education and who lack the necessary job skills to support their family financially (Cashion, 1982). Second, single parents are often isolated and lack an adequate emotional support system. For a variety of reasons (e.g., unwillingness to help and geographic distance) single parents often are unable to depend on relatives or in-laws to assist with child care. In addition, the pressure of coping with the family requires so much energy that the single parent has no time to build a support system with peers who have similar concerns.

A third problem is that single parents often lack confirmation from another adult in the home. In two-parent families, each parent can support the other's position. A single parent may already be feeling guilty because of the termination of the marriage. The parent may have difficulty when a child does not comply with the parent's rules (Blechman & Manning, 1975). Simple requests, such as household chores, often create conflicts unless the single parent's authority is confirmed by another adult. Without confirmation, the single parent often gives in to the child's position. Absence of confirmation often causes the single parent to have less authority in the family (Weltner, 1982).

The program described herein addresses these problems by providing parent training to single parents through groups. There are several advantages to teaching parenting skills to single parents in a group setting. First, because single parents are often isolated, the group provides support and assistance from other parents for solving problems (Rose, 1974). Second, the group provides positive feedback (e.g., validation) for the parent's role in the family. Third, the group contributes to parent effectiveness by exposing single parents to a variety of models of parenting behaviors available in the group. Finally, the group provides a safe environment where parents can try out new behaviors they have learned.

The Group Training Program

The purposes of the group training are to provide single mothers with a set of skills for working with young children and to provide a supportive environment where mothers can help each other solve problems with their children.

Population

The participants were 45 mothers receiving Aid to Families with Dependent Children (AFDC) who were referred by Family Service Workers, Department of Human Resources, Louisville, Kentucky. All the mothers referred to the program agreed to participate. The parents, 31 Black and 14 White mothers, ranged in age from 23 to 63 and had at least one child in the age range of 3 to 10.

Parent Group Trainers

The trainers were ten female staff members from Family Services Workers from the Department of Human Resources. Two Black and eight White workers participated. Each trainer received 12 hours of instruction in group leader and parent training by two faculty members from the Department of Educational Psychology and Counseling at the University of Louisville. Minimal performance (90%) on criterion tests ensured that each trainee had acquired the necessary skills to lead a parent group.

Training Materials

The training delivered to both the group leaders and the parents is outlined in three training manuals developed for use in the program. *Positive Parenting: Manual for Group Leaders* (Cunningham & Brown, 1979) was used to train the social service staff in group leadership skills. The leaders were given 6 hours of training that focused on the following three skill clusters needed for effective group leadership:

1. *Structuring the Group,* including defining the task and setting expectations;
2. *Responding to Group Members,* including reflecting parent statements, summarizing parent statements, praising parent statements, and praising parents who are helping other parents; and
3. *Encouraging Group Members to Talk,* including prompting desired behavior, responding to undesired parent behavior, redirecting attention to parent statements, and redirecting attention to other parents.

The format for the presentation of each leadership skill included (a) definition of each skill, (b) steps in using the skill, (c) written examples, (d) videotape examples, and (e) written exercises. Review sections, which focused on each skill group and the combination of the three skill groups, included written exercises, videotape exercises, and role-play situations.

Group leaders were also given 6 hours of instruction in the skills they would teach parents. These skills, plus explicit instructions for running the groups, are included in *Positive Parenting: Trainer's Manual* (Brown & Cunningham, 1979a). The parent's manual, *Positive Parenting: Parent's Manual* (Brown & Cunningham, 1979b), is identical to the trainer's manual except for the omission of group leader instructions. The trainer's and parent's manuals include explanations and examples of each skill, written and discrimination exercises, scripts of the videotape examples, and directions for role playing.

In addition, homework forms were provided to encourage practice of the skills before the next group session. Problem sheets in the appendix of the manuals enabled participants to monitor two child problem behaviors daily over the course of training.

The Skill Groups

The parenting skills included in the manuals are clustered into three skill groups.

Skill Group I: Communicating with Your Child

This skill group focused on training parents to both listen to their children and respond in a manner that indicates that they had listened to what the child had communicated.

Skill 1: Encouraging Child Talk. Parents were taught to encourage their children to talk to them about problem areas. Specific training focused on establishing eye contact with the child and using encouraging words.

Skill 2: Responding to the Child. Parents were encouraged to recognize and respond to both the feeling and the content in their children's communication.

Skill Group II: Child Management

This skill group focused on teaching parents what to do in a situation where the child's behavior is a problem for the parent but not for the child.

Skill 3: Stating Directions. Parents were taught (a) when to give directions, (b) how to state directions clearly and positively, (c) how to specify conditions for performance, and (d) how to give praise for following directions.

Skill 4: Rewarding Children's Behavior. Parents were taught (a) how to identify effective reinforcers, (b) when to reinforce, and (c) how to pair reinforcement with praise.

Skill 5: Ignoring Child Misbehavior. Parents were taught to deal with certain problem behaviors through withdrawing reinforcement by either looking the other way or leaving the room.

Skill 6: Expressing Feelings about Child's Misbehavior. Parents were taught to (a) discriminate between the child and the child's misbehavior and (b) express disapproval of the child's misbehavior.

Skill 7: Removing the Child for Misbehavior. Parents were taught the proper procedure for using a time-out strategy when the child engages in harmful behavior or fails to follow parent directions.

Skill Group III: Problem Solving

This skill group focused on teaching parents what to do in a situation where both the parent and child consider something a problem. Parents were taught a logical six-step model for solving problems. It includes (a) identifying the problem, (b) generating alternative solutions, (c) evaluating the solutions, (d) deciding on the best solution, (e) implementing that solution, and (f) evaluating that solution.

Format and Content of Training

Thirty single mothers were assigned to five parent-training groups, with six members in each group. The other 15 single mothers served as a control group. They received regular services from their Family Service Workers but were not involved in the parent training groups. The parent training groups met for 2 hours each week for 7 weeks in area churches. Each group was co-led by two family service workers. At the first meeting, parents signed a contract agreeing to attend all meetings and to complete quizzes and homework assignments. The parents were then asked to identify problem areas they were having with their children. Group leaders assisted parents in translating problems into specific behavioral terms. The problems were recorded on problem sheets at the back of the training manual and were tallied over the course of training.

The last half of the first session and the remaining six sessions focused on specific communication and problem-solving skills, as outlined in the training manual. The format for teaching each skill included (a) introduction of the parent-child communication or child management skill, (b) written discrimination exercise related to the skill, (c) videotape model of the skill by a parent and child, (d) discussion of the videotape, (e) written exercise requiring participants to produce examples of the skill, (f) behavioral rehearsal of the skill, and (g) discussion of the homework assignment related to the skill.

Evaluation Measures

Outcome Measures

Three primary outcome measures were used to assess changes in parent behavior during training. The *Handling Problems Knowledge Test* measured the parents' knowledge of parent-child communication and management skills. This pre-post test of information consisted of 18 multiple-choice items. The parents were required to choose the technique that was most appropriate in a particular parent-child interaction.

The *Attitude Scale* was a pre- and post-assessment of parent attitudes toward their children using 14 items from the Aggression factor of the *Becker Bipolar Adjective Checklist* (Eyeberg & Johnson, 1974). The Aggression factor was selected because of its relationship to child problems most often reported by AFDC mothers (Brown, Cunningham, Birkimer, & Stutts, 1979). The checklist measured the parent's perception of both the child's perceived problem behaviors and general characteristics of the child.

Prior to training, all parents identified one or two specific problem behaviors exhibited by their children. Parents identifying two problem areas ranked them in order of severity, with Problem I being most serious and Problem II less serious. Pre-post ratings on problem behaviors were based on the 3-point *Rating Scale* according to how often the behaviors occurred (0 = never; 2 = often).

Process Measures

Three process measures were used to measure the parents' acquisition and implementation of the skill in the treatment group:

1. Understanding the material in the group was measured by two types of exercises. Discrimination exercises required the parents to recognize examples of the skill being taught in the group. Written exercises required the parents to produce correct examples of the skill being acquired.
2. Demonstration of the skill was measured through role playing.
3. Implementation of the skill was measured through written homework assignments.

Evaluation

The data collected during the course of the sessions indicated that training had a number of positive effects for this population of AFDC mothers. First, on the knowledge measure of parent-child communication and management skills (*Handling Problems Knowledge Test)*, parents who attended more than two of the seven workshop sessions scored higher than both a similar group of AFDC mothers who received no training and those mothers who attended only one or two sessions. These scores indicated that low-income single parents can acquire knowledge of basic child management procedures through a parent group training program. The amount of time spent in group training seemed to be a critical variable in determining knowledge acquisition because parents who attended more sessions demonstrated greater knowledge of appropriate behaviors and skills than parents who attended one or two sessions, even though the latter group also had training manuals.

Second, the parents reported improvement in their children's behavior over the course of training. Of the problem behaviors identified at the first workshop session, 62% were rated as improved by the end of the 7 weeks of training, while 34% were rated as about the same and only 4% were rated as worse. It seems that training helped resolve many of the problems parents were having with their children's behavior in the home. Because parent attitudes toward children showed no change over the course of training, it seems that the change in rating of problem behaviors was due to actual behavior change rather than to parents viewing their children in a more positive manner.

Finally, social service workers reported that no children of parents involved in the training had to be removed from the home during the treatment period. It seems that participation in the group helped the parents cope more effectively with their children in the home setting. The social service staff who led the groups were generally enthusiastic about the program and consequently adapted parts of the program for use in training parents of adolescents.

Several factors that occurred may have contributed to the results of the training. First, there was a significant relationship between the written exercises in which parents were required to produce examples of the skill being taught and the *Handling Problems Knowledge Test* ($r = .79$). Written exercises helped to ensure that parents understood the child management procedures before applying them in role playing and home settings.

Second, the data gathered on the participants seem to indicate that training probably should continue for a minimum of six or seven sessions. Although parents who attended training at least one or two times showed a somewhat higher level of knowledge of parent-child communication and child management skills than parents who received no training, they did not score as well as those parents who attended three or more group sessions.

Third, parent attitudes and perceptions of their children's behaviors often follow change in parents' cognitive behavior. Several studies (O'Dell, 1974; Worland, Carney, & Milich, 1977) have suggested that although knowledge of child management procedures may increase immediately as a result of training, it may take longer for parents' attitudes and perceptions to change accordingly. It may be that 7 weeks was not enough time to change parents' perceptions of their children's behaviors and general characteristics, as measured by the *Rating Scale* and the *Attitude Scale*.

Because child management procedures were introduced sequentially, some procedures (e.g., time-out) were not taught until the fifth or sixth week. The short time interval between training and final evaluation (1-2 weeks) may not have allowed parents enough time to observe the effects of specific child management procedures (e.g., time-out) on their children's behavior (e.g., aggression). Thus, an insufficient amount of time passed to allow parents to develop more positive attitudes toward their children's behaviors and general characteristics. A follow-up assessment might have indicated positive changes in parent attitudes, as well as retention of acquired knowledge of child management procedures. A lack of funds prevented the investigators from conducting follow-up procedures.

Conclusion

The combination of a variety of teaching modes (training manual, written exercises, videotape models, and role playing), coordinated through a group approach to training, seems to be an effective method for training AFDC mothers in basic parenting skills. Feedback from participants indicated that the group provided (a) a means for developing a support system from which friendships developed, (b) concrete suggestions for handling problems with their children, and (c) positive reinforcement for their role as parents. As such, the training helped them manage more effectively in their role as single parents.

References

Blechman, E. A., & Manning, M. D. (1975). A reward-cost analysis of the single parent family. In E. J. Mash, L. A. Hamerlynck, & L. C. Handy (Eds.), *Behavior modification and families I: Theory and research* (pp. 61–90). New York: Brunner/Mazel.

Brown, J. H., Cunningham, G., Birkimer, J., & Stutts, M. (1979, December 15). *Training parents via television.* Paper presented to the Association for Behavior Analysis, San Francisco.

Brown, J. H., & Cunningham, N. J. (1979a). *Positive parenting: Teacher's manual.* Frankfort, KY: Department of Human Resources.

Brown, J. H., & Cunningham, N. J. (1979b). *Positive parenting: Parent's manual.* Frankfort, KY: Department of Human Resources.

Cashion, B. (1982). Female-headed families: Effects on children and clinical implications. *Journal of Marital & Family Therapy, 8,* 77–85.

Cunningham, N. J., & Brown, J. H. (1979). *Positive parenting: Manual for group leaders.* Frankfort, KY: Department of Human Resources.

Eyeberg, S. M., & Johnson, S. M. (1974). Multiple assessment of behavior modification with families: Effects of contingency contracting and order of treated problems. *Journal of Consulting and Clinical Psychology, 42,* 594–606.

O'Dell, S. (1974). Training parents in behavior modification: A review. *Psychological Bulletin, 81,* 418–433.

Porter, B. R., & Chatelain, R. S. (1981). Family life education for single parent families. *Family Relations, 30,* 517–525.

Rose, S. D. (1974). Group training of parents as behavior modifiers. *Social Work, 19,* 156–162.

U.S. Bureau of the Census. (1980). Marital status and living arrangements. *Current Population Reports,* Series P-20, No. 349.

Wallerstein, J. S., & Kelly, J. B. (1980). *Surviving the breakup.* New York: Basic Books.

Weltner, J. (1982). A structural approach to a single parent family. *Family Process, 21,* 203–210.

Worland, J., Carney, R., & Milich, R. (1977, December). *Multiple criteria assessment of group and home operant parent training*. Paper presented at the 11th Annual Convention of the Association for Advancement of Behavior Therapy, Atlanta.

Helping Latchkey Children: A Group Guidance Approach

Michael L. Bundy
Judith Boser

The term *latchkey* refers to children who are left at home alone or in the care of an under-age sibling for a significant portion of the day (Long & Long, 1984). These school-age children between 5 and 13 years old usually spend 2 to 3 hours on most days in self-care arrangements. They prepare themselves for school on mornings when their parents have left for work, or they come home after school to an empty house and wait for their parents to arrive home from work. They are named latchkey children because many carry their house keys on a string or chain around their necks.

The exact number of latchkey children is unavailable. It has been estimated, however, that about 6.5 million American children are currently in this category; by 1990 there may be 18 million (Scofield & Page, 1983).

Several societal and familial trends have led to the increase in unsupervised children. The rise in the number of single-parent families (Bundy & Gumaer, 1984) creates situations in which adequate adult supervision of children becomes difficult. The increase in the number of working mothers (Levitan & Belous, 1981) and the necessity of dual wage earners for many families (Waldman, 1983) create situations in which parents are unable to be with their children when they arrive home from school. The changing residences by many American families (U.S. Bureau of the Census, 1984) contributes to the rise in the number of children who are home alone. As the mobility of families increases, it is less likely that grandparents or other relatives can be available to provide child care assistance.

Given the current trends in family structures and patterns of family lifestyles, it is reasonable to assume that more and more school-age children will be spending time in self-care or in the care of another under-age child on a regular basis. It is appropriate to ask: "What effect does being home alone have on children?"

Impact of Self-Care Arrangements on Children

School counselors and others are aware of the growing number of children left regularly without adult supervision before or after school. Although research on the impact of self-care arrangements on children is limited, children will talk with counselors about their positive and negative feelings regarding being at home alone. Most children in late childhood tend to enjoy the responsibility of being on their own after school rather than being in the charge of a baby sitter (Long & Long, 1984). It is a normal expectation of late childhood for children to seek independence from family and adults and to desire the companionship of peers (Gumaer, 1984).

Researchers are finding negative consequences, however, when children are left without adult supervision. Studies have reported that children who are in self-care arrangements for regular periods of time tend to report high levels of worry and fear (Long & Long, 1984; Strother, 1984; Zill, 1983). From interviews with latchkey children, Long and Long (1984) found that children who routinely care for themselves experienced more fear than did children who were supervised by adults. The fear most often mentioned was that someone might break into their homes while they were alone and hurt them. They also reported being worried or afraid of noises in the dark, fire, losing their house keys, and severe weather. In the National Survey of Children conducted by Temple University in 1976, it was found that children who are routinely left in self-care are more fearful than are those who receive adult supervision (Strother, 1984).

Feelings of loneliness and boredom are often experienced by children who spend regular amounts of time alone at home (Long & Long, 1984). When children go straight home after school and are not allowed to have friends over to play, they develop symptoms of loneliness and boredom. The long, lonely hours spent at home without others produce stress and anxiety in children (Long & Long, 1983).

Another effect of self-care on children whose parents cannot be with them before or after school seems to be that of diminished performance in school work (Robinson, 1983; Strother, 1984). In a review of three studies, Strother (1984) found that children in self-care situations tended to have lower academic achievement than did children whose parents were not employed full time and could spend time with them. Moreover, there is a clear indication that school grades drop when children are given the responsibility for care of younger siblings (Smith, 1984).

Garbarino (1980), however, suggested that children who are regularly left unsupervised in the suburbs fare better than do those in the city. In a study of children from a rural setting, Galambos and Garbarino (1983) compared supervised and unsupervised children using teacher ratings and found no significant differences in their level of fear, school adjustment, classroom orientation, or academic achievement. Because this study was conducted in an environment that was less threatening than the urban settings of others (Long & Long, 1984;

Smith, 1984; Strother, 1984), there seems to be some indication that the neighborhood of latchkey children has an influence on their level of fear and their school performance.

Parent-child communication is often hindered by self-care arrangements. Long and Long (1984) found that some children will persuade their parents to allow them time to stay home alone so they will seem mature and responsible to both peers and parents. When they develop difficulties or begin to worry about situations that arise when home alone, however, they are reluctant to talk with their parents about those problems. Children tend to withhold sharing their worries because they think parents will make other child care arrangements or because they wish to protect their parents from further worries (Long & Long, 1984).

The special demands made on children when they are without adult supervision increase stress for many of them. Elkind (1981) has argued that latchkey children are expected to take on too much responsibility for their age. These youngsters tend to develop a higher rate of depression and personality problems during adolescence or later in life than do their peers. Because latchkey children are being expected to assume more responsibility for the care of their siblings or themselves, there seems to be a strong need to give these children more comprehensive instruction in survival skills (Long & Long, 1983).

Being in Charge: A Curriculum Response

"Being in Charge" is a guidance unit designed to provide intermediate and middle grade children with the skills to cope more effectively with taking care of themselves while home alone. A basic assumption of the program is that each child will periodically experience self-care situations at some point in time; consequently, all children can benefit from exposure to the program. Furthermore, a central theme of the activities addresses the age-appropriate need for children to become independent of parents and to develop confidence by gaining more control of their lives. The program was written to be used in a developmental guidance curriculum. In addition to developing self-care survival skills, each of the six sessions has a homework component that encourages parent involvement and fosters parent-child communication.

Format of Each Session

Each session contains four phases: warmup, review of homework, presentation of the skill, and assignment of homework.

1. The warmup phase is designed to set the frame of reference for the group session by asking students to complete such sentence stems as "When I am alone at home, I feel . . ." and share them with the group.
2. The review of homework stage is designed to encourage children to talk with their parents about the material and issues related to each session.
3. The activity phase helps students develop specific skills for being in charge when parents are away. At this point, the group members participate in carefully designed activities such as role playing, creating mental images, brainstorming, and group discussions.
4. In the final activity of each session, the assigning of homework, each student is asked to take home the material presented in the meeting and discuss it with his or her parents.

Objective and Content for Each Session

Being in Charge was written to be presented in six 45-minute sessions. The following is an outline of the objectives and content for each session of the program.

Session 1: Introduction. Students are told the purpose and given an overview of the program. They also develop a combined list of their existing home rules and current responsibilities when home alone.

Session 2: Setting up a self-care arrangement. A model is presented, showing how children should work with their parents to set up their self-care arrangement (e.g., finding a contact person, establishing routine communication, and determining special home rules and responsibilities).

Session 3: Personal safety when home alone. During this session, students rehearse ways of safely answering the door and telephone when home alone. Group discussion focuses on the reasons for each of the safety tips that are listed on specially developed handouts.

Session 4: Emergency and non-emergency situations. Group discussion focuses on helping children distinguish between emergency and non-emergency situations. Role-playing activities help students practice emergency action procedures.

Session 5: Special problems of being in charge. Group members brainstorm ways to overcome boredom and loneliness when home alone. A group discussion generates tips for coping with worries and fears.

Session 6: Other topics for being in charge. Role-playing activities help students practice ways to talk with their parents about concerns and problems that arise while home alone. Tips are provided to help students learn how to take care of younger children.

During each session special handouts are provided that give suggestions and tips relating to the topic under discussion. For example, one handout outlines how to make an emergency telephone call. The counselor asks students to take each handout home and discuss it with their parents. Because parent involvement and promotion of parent-child communication are goals of the program, this request of students is made under the guise of homework. Thus, the time set aside during each session to review the homework assignment is really an opportunity for the counselor to encourage children to talk with their parents about Being in Charge activities. The program stresses that parent support is vital if children wish to assume new responsibilities and to cope safely with being at home alone. In fact, parents are notified by letter of the classroom meetings that focus on being alone at home and are urged to discuss the program materials with their children each night after the sessions.

Program Evaluation

To determine the effectiveness of the program, we conducted field tests in an urban elementary school with a K–6 student population. The program was conducted by the senior author, who is a certified elementary school counselor.

Participants

Five classes of students, two sixth grades ($n = 50$) and three fifth grades ($n = 65$), were the participants. This included all the students in those two grades. The students were heterogeneously grouped in each grade by the school principal so that each class would have equal numbers of able and less able students. Approximately 22% of the students were from single-parent homes, and 25% of the students reported being home on a regular basis without adult supervision. Socioeconomic level of the population was generally middle to lower class, and the racial composition was approximately 13% Black, 4% Asian, and 83% White.

Design

One class at each grade level was randomly selected to receive the treatment first ($n = 48$), with the remaining classes serving as control classes ($n = 67$). The design called for pretesting all fifth- and sixth-grade students, presenting the program only to the treatment class at each grade level while the control classes continued their regular activities, posttesting all classes (Posttest 1), presenting the program to the control classes, and posttesting the control classes after their exposure to the treatment (Posttest 2). In addition, a retention test was administered approximately 5 months later to all available students who had participated in the program. When the retention test was administered to students the following September, the sixth-grade participants had matriculated to the junior high school, so the retention test was administered by personnel at that school.

Instruments

The test was an 18-item cognitive test on program content. All items were multiple choice with four possible answers. Readability of the written test was assessed by a certified reading teacher to be at the third-grade level. Test items were presented in a different order on the posttest than they were on the pretest. Response options for each question were also rearranged. Test scores were corrected for guessing before statistical analysis was done.

A 13-item parent questionnaire was used in the fall to assess parents' perceptions of the children's behavior when home without adult supervision and the parents' feelings about such situations. Questionnaires were received for 38 of 50 former fifth-grade participants who were still enrolled in the same school in the fall.

Results

Mean scores (corrected) are shown in Figure 1 for all testings. The numbers of students for whom paired scores were available for analysis over the various time periods differ because of absentees and withdrawals from the school. There was a significant difference between gains (corrected for guessing) of treatment and control groups between the pretest and Posttest 1 using a paired t test (t = 12.38, df = 113, $p < .001$). Comparison of scores (again corrected for guessing) for the control students for Posttest 1 and Posttest 2 showed the average increase of 5.21 to be significant (t = 17.48, df = 54, $p < .001$). Thus, the test results showed that participation in the program seemed to be responsible for increasing students' knowledge of self-care practices.

Comparison of the posttreatment and retention scores (corrected for guessing) for all students (treatment and control) for whom paired scores could be obtained showed only a slight decay in scores (–.51) from the posttreatment mean of 16.53 to the retention mean of 16.02 (t = 2.17, df = 69, $p < .017$). This change occurred over a period of approximately 5 months, in which there was no planned reinforcement administered by the counselor.

According to parent perceptions recorded on the parent questionnaires, most of the children kept the door locked (89%), answered the telephone (88%), did not admit to strangers that there was no adult home (85%), and did answer the

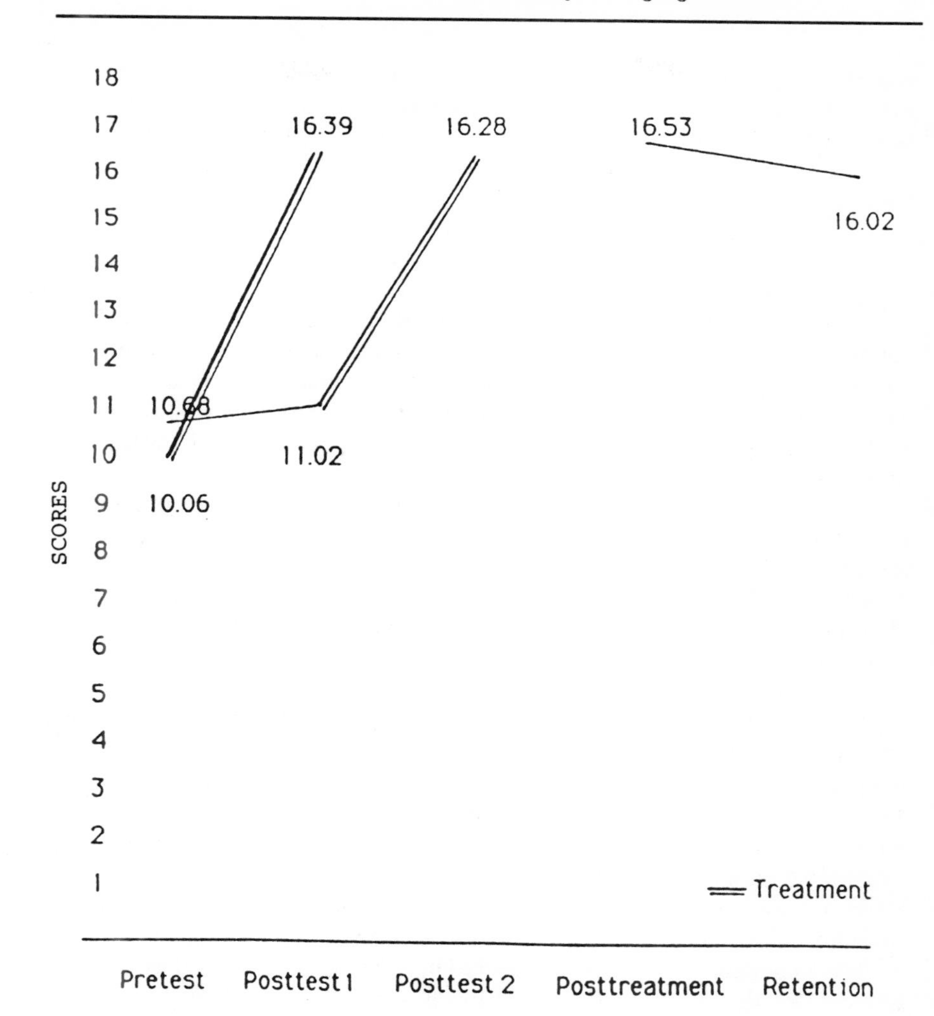

Figure 1

Change in Mean Scores Across Time

door (72%) but kept it closed when doing so (93%) when home without an adult. Most homes (92%) had a list of special telephone numbers by the telephone, and parents thought the children knew in what circumstances to use the various numbers (92%). All except 11% believed that the child felt more confident about staying home without adult supervision since having the program, and all except one parent reported feeling more comfortable personally about the child's ability to take care of himself or herself since completing the program.

Discussion and Conclusion

The program conducted by the school counselor was designed to increase children's knowledge about how to set up a self-care arrangement and what to do when home alone or with siblings when there was no adult present. The children became more knowledgeable about the procedures they should use, and the knowledge stayed with them over the summer. The parents who responded to the survey indicated more confidence in their children's skills in taking care of themselves after completing the program.

Incidental evidence of the program's impact was provided when a teacher told the counselor of an occasion on which a call to a student's home was necessary. The call was answered by a fifth grader who was alone and who had participated in the Being in Charge program. When the teacher asked to speak to the child's mother, the reply was: "I'm sorry, but my mother cannot come to the phone now. May I take a message?" This is the precise statement role played in the program.

Extensive training is not necessary for school counselors to implement this program successfully. School counselors in two different school systems used the program with students in Grades 3-8 after attending only a brief orientation session on the program and using the program materials and resources. Although adaptations were made to fit their respective time schedules and there was no validation that the program was followed, the students in all groups made posttest gains on the written test that were similar to gains in the original research.

It is important that school counselors implement programs such as Being in Charge. During the group sessions of this program, children tended to express strong emotions about times when their parents were away from home and they were in charge. In situations that require processing of affect, the skills and experience of a trained counselor are needed to help children work through their feelings. Furthermore, the school counselor is able to help children develop confidence about being at home alone and to help children recognize when they should seek help from stresses and worries that arise from being unsupervised at home.

As society continues to change the ways in which its children are reared, greater demands will be placed on children. The role of the school counselor becomes increasingly vital in helping schools and parents to become more effective in meeting the changing needs of children. The Being in Charge program is evidence of one such effort.

References

Bundy, M. L., & Gumaer, J. (1984). Guest editorial: Families in transition. *Elementary School Guidance & Counseling, 19*, 4–8.

Elkind, D. (1981). *The hurried child.* Reading, MA: Addison-Wesley.

Galambos, N. L., & Garbarino, J. (1983). Identifying the missing links in the study of latchkey children. *Children Today, 40*, 2–4.

Garbarino, J. (1980). Latchkey children: Getting the short end of the stick. *Vital Issues, 30*(3), 14–16.

Gumaer, J. (1984). *Counseling and therapy for children.* New York: Free Press.

Levitan, S. A., & Belous, R. S. (1981). Working wives and mothers: What happens to family life? *Monthly Labor Review, 104*, 26–30.

Long, T., & Long, L. (1983). *Latchkey children.* Urbana, IL: ERIC Clearinghouse on Elementary and Early Childhood Education. (ERIC Document Reproduction Service No. ED 226 836)

Long, T., & Long, L. (1984). *The handbook for latchkey children and their parents.* New York: Berkley.

Robinson, V. M. (1983, May). 5,000,000 latchkey children. *PTA Today, pp.* 13–15.

Scofield, R., T., & Page, A. C. (1983). Afterschool care and the public schools. *Tennessee Education, 13*(1), 40–47.

Smith, T. E. (1984). School grades and responsibility for younger siblings: An empirical study of the "teaching functions." *American Sociological Review, 49*, 248–260.

Strother, D. B. (1984). Latchkey children: The fastest growing special interest group in the schools. *Phi Delta Kappan, 66*, 290–293.

U.S. Bureau of the Census. (1984). *Current population reports, 20*(393), *Geographical mobility: March 1982 to 1983.* Washington, DC: U.S. Government Printing Office.

Waldman, E. (1983, December). Labor force statistics from a family perspective. *Monthly Labor Review*, pp. 16–19.

Zill, N. (1983). *American children: Happy, healthy, and insecure.* New York: Doubleday-Anchor.

Strategic Interventions with Children of Single-Parent Families

Wade Lewis

Single-parent families have rapidly become a way of American life. During the past two decades, the number of families consisting of at least one child and one biological parent has doubled, and single-parent families are increasing at a rate 2 1/2 times that for families with a husband and wife (McLanahan, Wedemeyer, & Adelberg, 1981; Smith, 1980). Unfortunately, the fields of psychology and counseling have seemingly not kept pace with the emerging prevalence of single-parent families. It is encouraging to note, however, the increased concern with the unique structural, organizational, and developmental aspects of these families, which has correspondingly enlarged the range of effective interventions.

This article focuses on the school-related problems of children of single-parent families. A way of conceptualizing such problems from a family systems perspective is presented, as well as examples of interventions based on strategic family therapy (Haley, 1976; Madanes, 1980).

Social Context of Children's Problems

When a school counselor is requested to intervene because of a child's disruptive classroom behavior, defiant attitude toward teacher authority, physical aggression with peers, or repeated academic failure, there are obviously numerous ways of viewing how the problem developed. One way of conceptualizing a problem is to examine its social context and to assume that the problem has occurred in relation to the behavior and actions of others. From this perspective, all behavior in a particular context is interrelated and each behavior provides both a cue for the next behavior as well as feedback for the preceding behavior. Thus, behavior operates in a circular fashion and social systems such as families consist of repetitive sequences of action (Haley, 1976).

Translating systems theory into a pragmatic framework for understanding school-related problems involves emphasis on one point: When faced with a difficult child, a thorough analysis of the familial system must occur before a means of intervening is determined. As the primary social determinants of a child's behavior, the family's structure, hierarchical organization, and generational boundaries must be assessed. This does not mean that the solution to all school-related problems is to be found in a family-oriented intervention, but this system should certainly be the initial area of investigation with severe or chronic problems and extremely abrupt changes in children's behavior.

Basic Systemic Assumptions

Several systemic concepts must be kept in mind when designing interventions for children of single-parent families. Hierarchy refers to the way a family is organized so that there is an order that describes who is in charge of whom and who has power over whom. For example, it is assumed that a single parent must be effectively in charge of a child, rather than the child possessing power over the parent, for the family to function effectively. Misbehavior, however, often allows a child to control actions of the parent and essentially puts the child in charge of the parent (Haley, 1976).

Boundaries are the family rules that define who participates in what, and how (Minuchin, 1974). Boundaries help a family organize into an effective hierarchy by delineating areas of responsibility, action, decision making, and privacy. Thus, it is assumed that a single-parent family must have a clear generational boundary between parent and child. This boundary allows each party to recognize the needs and tasks of the other. It is also assumed that unclear or diffuse boundaries and repeatedly crossing or intruding established boundaries often result in symptomatic behavior (Haley, 1976; Minuchin, 1974).

Another example of crossing boundaries is the formation of coalitions, alliances established by two people who occupy different positions in the hierarchy and therefore different levels of responsibility and power. Coalitions may result in the "perverse triangle," in which two people of different status join together against a third person (Haley, 1976). This arrangement may often result in behavioral problems. A prevalent example is when a parent and child form a coalition against a teacher, which undermines the teacher's authority. Likewise, a teacher and child may form a coalition against a single parent with similar results.

Systems theory also describes behavior as operating in a circular fashion. Symptoms or behavioral problems involve repetitive sequences of interaction that must be interrupted for the family system to evolve to a higher, symptom-free level of functioning (Hoffman, 1981). This interactional view indicates the importance of understanding what occurs before and after the behavior is presented. Altering the precipitants and consequences of the behavior is an important therapeutic strategy.

Protective Function of Symptoms

There is another systemic concept that is especially important. Madanes (1980) has described how a child's problem may serve a protective or helpful function in a family. This premise is particularly relevant to single-parent families, which may have been abruptly formed because of divorce, death, or abandonment and which are suddenly confronted with personal, economic, social, and developmental hardships. In such cases, a child's problem may induce a parent to maintain self-control and temporarily put personal problems aside so that he or she can focus on helping the child. Parents are helped or protected by the child's problem because "it provides a respite from the parents' own troubles and a reason to overcome their own difficulties" (Madanes, 1980, p. 66).

In a single-parent family, the helpfulness of the child's problem may be very specific: A child may refuse to go to school so the parent does not have to face looking for a job; the parent of a failing student may stay home evenings to help with schoolwork and, thus, not have to deal with developing social activities and forming new relationships; a child's conflicts with the teacher may cause the parent to be angry with the teacher rather than be depressed over a recent divorce. The systemic approach, therefore, examines what the function of a symptom may be and, in particular, looks at how the problem may be helpful to or protective of another person.

Strategic Interventions

From this family systems perspective, there are a number of strategic interventions a school counselor may choose to use with children of single-parent families:

Reframing requests for participation. The parent may be asked during the first interview to help the school solve the child's problem. It is emphasized that the parent is the only true expert regarding the child, and the school needs this special expertise. The school counselor must use every opportunity to emphasize the parent's competence. Blaming the parent in any way for the child's problem will probably result in poorer functioning by the parent, thereby increasing the need for the child to misbehave or fail as a way of further protecting the parent. This simple tactic also clearly places the parent in charge of the child, draws an appropriate generational boundary, and establishes an effective hierarchy.

Describing the nature and extent of parental responsibilities. To ensure consistency and cooperation among the "helpers," the teacher, therapist, and parent should agree on a specific plan designed to solve the presenting problem. Each person's part must be clearly defined, and the limits of responsibility for the parent are particularly important. If a parent is to help the child complete unfinished classwork each evening, a limit must be placed on the length of time the parent will assist the child. If disruptive classroom behavior is to be managed with both a consequence at school and another consequence at home (such as no television), then the exact details of these consequences must be prescribed. It is essential that all parts of the "helper system" function together in a supportive manner to avoid covert coalitions. The parent must also be appropriately put in charge of the child's problem to establish a correct hierarchy. As such, the nature and extent of the parent's involvement must be carefully determined and monitored.

Encouraging age-appropriate activities for the child. The school counselor may suggest that the child is at least partially experiencing problems because of underdeveloped social skills with peers or not enough physical activities for the child's energy or mental outlets for the child's abilities. The counselor may encourage the parent to seek specific age-appropriate extracurricular activities for the child. This intervention also interjects appropriate distance into the parent-child relationship and establishes a functional hierarchy within the family. The child's involvement with peers is also increased while the child's involvement in the parent's life is decreased, which strengthens appropriate generational boundaries.

Encouraging appropriate parent activities. By emphasizing the importance of the parent in solving the child's problem, the school counselor may encourage the parent to pursue social and physical activities, particularly those involving peers, as a way of "maintaining your energy and motivation and recharging your batteries." This approach of taking care of oneself in order to help the child may direct the parent into those pursuits that had previously been avoided. Such involvement should improve the parent's adjustment, increase the support network, decrease the need for protection, and strengthen generational boundaries.

Removing the function of the problem. The counselor may make the function of the problem a consequence for its occurrence. For example, if a child's misbehavior in school keeps the parent overinvolved and distracted from making social contacts, the parent may be directed to go out twice during the weekend instead of once when the child misbehaves. The explanation may be that the parent will require this extra rest and relaxation to have the energy necessary to manage the child's misbehavior. Thus, the repetitive sequence of parent-child interaction has been changed and the helpfulness of the problem removed. Instead of helping the parent to avoid something, the problem now causes it to occur.

Prescribing other nonsymptomatic ways of being helpful. The counselor may state that the child has a need to be helpful to the parent and elicit suggestions as to what other ways help may be provided. It is best, however, not to describe openly the child's problem as an attempt to be helpful. From these suggestions, an age-appropriate means of help is selected and a ritual prescribed whereby both parent and child participate. It may be decided that the child will read a story to the parent every day at 4:00 p.m., after which they will have milk and cookies together. This ritual will bring the parent and child together for an event other than the problem and give the child a means of being helpful without presenting a problem.

Summary

A family systems model provides a clear and useful way of perceiving the school problems presented by children of single-parent families. The techniques briefly outlined in this article have been used alone and in various combinations with both elementary and junior high school students. The use of such systems-oriented interventions may result in rapid change and effective short-term therapy, the goals of any school counselor. A more elaborate and difficult strategy to implement, which is applicable to the interventions presented here, is the pretending technique (Madanes, 1980). Counselors experienced in family therapy are referred to Madanes's work for a thorough description of this technique.

References

Haley, J. (1976). *Problem-solving therapy.* San Francisco: Jossey-Bass.

Hoffman, L. (1981). *Foundations of family therapy.* New York: Basic Books.

Madanes, C. (1980). Protection, paradox, and pretending. *Family Process, 19,* 73–85.

Madanes, C. (1981). *Strategic family therapy.* San Francisco: Jossey-Bass.

McLanahan, S., Wedemeyer, N., & Adelberg, T. (1981). Network structure, social support, and psychological well-being in the single-parent family. *Journal of Marriage and the Family, 43,* 601–612.

Minuchin, S. (1974). *Families and family therapy.* Cambridge, MA: Harvard University Press.

Smith, M. (1980). The social consequences of single parenthood: A longitudinal perspective. *Family Relations, 29,* 75–81.

Chapter 2
Counseling Issues in a World of Changing Families

Issues for elementary school counselors to consider about a world of changing families:

1. You are a new counselor in an elementary school where single parent families are common. What can you do to meet some of the special needs of the children from these families?

2. What topics would you want to include in a divorce group for third and fourth grade students? How would you determine the effectiveness of your group?

3. You are counseling a student who has been consistently disruptive in class. During a counseling session the student begins to cry and tells you that she doesn't know what to do about her parents getting a divorce. What would you do to help this student?

4. How might an elementary school counselor initiate a divorce group for parents? What topics should be included in the divorce group sessions?

5. What is unique about the multimodal approach to divorce groups for children?

6. A teacher informs you that a student from a single parent family has had problems completing class assignments. This student has typically been conscientious, but since his parents' divorce, he has not been getting his work done. What specific interventions would you use to assist the child?

7. What role should elementary school counselors have in family counseling?

8. How can elementary school counselors help latchkey children deal with the lonely hours they spend at home?

9. When parents divorce, some children feel that they have been abandoned. How might elementary school counselors help children who feel abandoned and who lack self-esteem?

CHAPTER 3

A WORLD OF DRUG ABUSE

Research has shown that students often begin to experiment with drugs in elementary school and that early experimentation frequently leads to abuse and addiction in adolescence. Moreover, research has documented the problems of children from families made dysfunctional by alcoholism and drug addiction. It has been estimated that 6.5 million children under 18 years old and 22 million persons over the age of 18 have been reared by problem drinkers. William Bennett, the coordinator for drug policy under President George Bush, has commented that "the most serious threat to the health and well-being of our children is drug use." This chapter on substance abuse (a) helps elementary school counselors understand the scope and implications of substance abuse and (b) presents drug education programs that are designed to prevent drug abuse and to help children overcome the effects of substance abuse in their families.

The focus of Chapter 3 is on substance abuse prevention. The first article, "Perspectives on Substance Abuse Prevention," presents a clear picture of how important it is for children to be able to say "no" to drugs. However, as the authors of the article point out,

> Focusing on the simple mechanics of saying "no" may be of little value when a more basic choice problem such as "If I say no, I may not be liked by this individual or group" is evident. Thus, training in how to generate alternatives (e.g., learning to say "no" in such a way as to minimize alienating protagonists, discovering how to break into social circles having more compatible values, etc.) may be highly relevant.

With this more basic choice problem in mind, other articles in Chapter 3 provide innovative programs for counselors to implement, including, the broad-based approach of Quest's "Skills for Growing Program" and the cognitive development approach of "Dilemma Discussion in Drug Education" and "Moral Reasoning in Early Adolescence: Implications for Drug Abuse Prevention." Elementary school counselors will find exciting new ideas in each of the substance abuse prevention programs discussed in this chapter.

Chapter 3 concludes with the article, "Helping Children of Alcoholic Parents: An Elementary School Program." This article recognizes the serious effects of parents' alcoholism on children's development and presents a compassionate approach to helping these young victims receive help whether or not their parents are willing to accept help. The 1990s will undoubtedly bring new problems in the area of substance abuse, but the decade will also witness advances in drug education.

Perspectives on Substance Abuse Prevention

John J. Horan
Andres Kerns
Christine Olson

Some years ago, one of us opined that the drug educator of the 1960s had a lot in common with Christopher Columbus: both were seeking a newer world, but then again, both started out not knowing where they were going; both ended up not knowing where they had been, and both did it all on government money (Horan, 1974). In this article we provide a terse tour of substance abuse prevention programming over the past 2 decades. Showing where we've been is a helpful backdrop for suggesting where we might go in the future. To illustrate that government money can, indeed, be well spent, we describe an empirically promising approach based on teaching assertiveness and decision-making skills and cite the results of a longitudinal evaluation of the assertive training component. We conclude with a description of our current program in the context of our ongoing evaluation efforts.

Prevention Programming

There is an enormous body of literature written in the name of drug education (see Blum, 1976; Evans, D'Augelli, & Branca, 1976; Goodstadt, 1974; Ostman, 1976; Shain, Riddell, & Kelty, 1977). Very little of it, however, is of use to practicing counselors seeking to discover and employ empirically verified prevention programs. Horan and Harrison's (1981) review, for example, indicated that only 26 published references were to intervention endeavors that included drug-related outcome measures. Moreover, only a third of the studies cited met the main requirement of true experimentation, namely, random assignment to experimental conditions. Also, some projects were apparently conducted in the absence of a coherent theoretical base, and most were not replicable because of the undefined or undefinable nature of the independent variable. Furthermore, data-analysis errors seemed to be the norm rather that the exception. Finally, "prevention" by definition, implies a reduced probability of future substance abuse; yet, only 4 of the 26 projects in the Horan and Harrison (1981) review included any sort of the follow-up evaluation effort.

Schaps, DiBartolo, Moskowitz, and Churgin (1981) were able to locate 75 citable projects (of which 69% were unpublished) and expressed similar dismay about the lack of design quality in the literature. Their exhaustive review categorizes the literature into 10 intervention strategies: information, persuasion, affective-skill, affective-experiential, counseling, tutoring/teaching, peer group, family, program development, and alternatives. Only 10 studies met their minimal criteria for design quality and service delivery intensity, and of these only two showed an impact on drug use. Given that this exhaustive compilation of 75 documents contained 127 evaluated programs, the fact that two should emerge as promising is not surprising and, indeed, might be expected by chance alone.

Information-based programming is the most common prevention modality deployed over the past 2 decades, and thus warrants a closer look. The logic of information-based programming can ultimately be traced to classical decision theory (see Bauman, 1980; Broadhurst, 1976; Bross, 1953; Horan, 1979; and Mausner, 1973); however, such linkage is rarely articulated. Thus, the failure of information-based programming to receive favorable review may well be because of implementation inadequacies rather than to deficiencies in the conceptual basis of the approach.

In any event, according to classical decision theory, our choice between two or more alternatives (e.g., consuming drugs or abstaining from them) depends upon the utilities inherent in each alternative and their probabilities of occurrence. Essentially, we act to maximize subjectively expected utility (SEU); that is, we pick the alternative with the greatest likely payoff.

The purpose of information-based programming thus becomes fairly clear: if we provide our youth with an awareness of the dangerous consequences of drug use (negative utilities) and indicate to them that these consequences are indeed highly probable, the drug avoidance option is virtually assured. No rational human being would select an alternative with a comparable low SEU value.

Unfortunately, drug educators and counselors, however well intentioned, have a long history of distorting the facts about drugs to such an extent that the potential user is apt to find more correct information about drugs in the drug culture than in the classroom. Most accompanying instructional materials (e.g., films, poster, and pamphlets) likewise attempt to miseducate (e.g., see Globetti, 1975; and National Coordinating Council on Drug Education, 1972). Consequently, student skepticism is a highly reactive obstacle to drug education program evaluation.

From an empirical standpoint, Horan and Harrison's (1981) review indicated that compared to no-treatment control groups, information-based drug education curricula can raise drug knowledge levels (as measured by achievement tests keyed to the particular program). Such findings are not particularly noteworthy, given that we might expect parallel outcomes from any curriculum in math or spelling. Information-based programming is not likely to alter attitudes or drug use behavior meaningfully until its implementation corresponds to the decision-theory framework on which it ought to be based (e.g., the information needs to be perceived as accurate and relevant to the consumption decision). Data confirming that possibility remain to be collected.

Quo Vadis?

Where do we go from here? It might be helpful to step back and view this pessimistic data from a slightly different historical perspective. By the early 1970s, our profession had stumbled to a consensus that drug abuse prevention programs should be directed at fostering one or more of the following objectives: (1) increasing knowledge about drugs, (2) promoting healthy attitudes about drugs, and (3) decreasing potential drug abuse behavior in the general population (Horan, Shute, Swisher, & Westcott, 1973; Warner, Swisher, & Horan, 1973).

To be sure, these objectives were found to be fraught with a number of conceptual and methodological difficulties (see Horan, 1974). It was soon noted, for example, that drug users already knew more about drugs than nonusers, so an invidious misunderstanding of correlation and causality led to widespread fears that drug education may be "pushing rather than preventing."

Moreover, there was considerable disagreement on just what constituted a healthy drug attitude; for example, some professionals advocated stiffer penalties for marijuana consumption, while others argued just as passionately for its legalization. Thus, items on Likert scales used to assess attitude changes had serious shortcomings in content validity.

Finally, behavior changes were difficult to register, given that prior to high school only a small percentage of our nation's youth are actually drug-involved. The problem is one of statistical power; that is, the evaluator must use extremely large sample sizes and wait several years after the program has ended (when the seducing effects of history and maturation have taken their toll), before collecting behavioral data suitable for meaningful analysis.

Rather than confront and attempt to resolve these difficulties, by the late 1970s, many drug educators had abandoned the concept of drugs from drug education! They instead pursued popular humanistic goals; fashionable examples of non-drug drug education included Parent Effectiveness Training (Gordon, 1970), the DUSO Kit (Dinkmeyer, 1973), and the Magic Circle technique (Ball, 1974). If evaluated at all, the outcomes of a typical drug education program in that era were likely to be assessed with measures of self-esteem rather than surveys of substance abuse. (We have no quarrel with the pursuit of humanistic goals, however, we do believe that such endeavors ought to be supported with their own resources, rather than with redirected funding for the prevention of substance abuse).

As we advance through the 1980s, it is clear that some lessons have not been learned. The tired miseducation strategies of the 1970s, for example, proliferate the professional marketplace along with a plethora of unpromising affect-oriented programs in fancy packages (As Yogi Berra said, "It's like deja vu, all over again").

The wise shopper, however, might take note of the emerging evidence in support of social skills approaches to prevention (see Botvin, 1983; McAlister, 1983; and Pentz, 1983). Nancy Reagan's popular "Just say 'no'" campaign, for example, owes its uncited theoretical base to the assertion training literature. Saying "no," of course, presumes that one has reasons for, as well as the personal-social competence to do so; unfortunately, however, many individuals do not have those resources. Thus, let's take a closer look at the rationale and demonstrated effectiveness of a more fully articulated approach to assertion training.

Assertion Training as a Prevention Program

Assertion training as a drug abuse prevention strategy owes a portion of its theoretical base to classical decision theory. Recall from our discussion of information-based programs, that we select the alternatives with the highest "subjectively expected utility" (i.e., SEU = utility x probability), or in less technical terms, the greatest perceived payoff.

The probable role of peer approval as a utility (or disapproval as a negative utility) accruing from drug abstinence or consumption is virtually self-evident. In the first place, of all the psychosocial correlates of drug use, most conspicuous are the relationships between an individual's use of drugs and the drug-taking behavior of peers (Swisher, Warner, & Herr, 1972); reported correlations are consistent across all drug categories including smoking (Levitt & Edwards, 1970), drinking (Kandel, Kessler, & Margulies, 1978), and the consuming of illegal substances (Kandel, 1974a, 1974b). Second, the power of peer influence has been *experimentally* demonstrated on alcohol consumption (Dericco & Garlington, 1977) and in the formation of expressed drug attitudes (Shute, 1975; Stone & Shute, 1977). Finally, there is some evidence that drug users lack assertiveness skills (Horan, D'Amico, & Williams, 1975); such a deficit could easily increase one's vulnerability to drug-use peer pressure.

Assertion training is an extremely popular and thoroughly documented vehicle for enabling individuals to do "what they really want" in particular social situations (e.g., Alberti, 1977; Galassi, Galassi, & Litz, 1974; Heimberg, Montgomery, & Madsen, 1977; Holmes & Horan, 1976; Kwiterovich & Horan, 1977; McFall & Marston, 1970). As a drug abuse prevention strategy, assertion training rests on the assumption that many youths, who would otherwise abstain from taking drugs, reluctantly imbibe because they lack the social skills necessary to extricate themselves from social situations in which drug use is imminent. Of course SEUs other than those pertaining to the likelihood of peer approval-disapproval are relevant to drug decisions. For example, the potential user also may estimate (however crudely) the probabilities of euphoric and adverse physiological consequences. Thus, the role of assertion training as a drug abuse prevention strategy is limited to simply shoring up the possibility of free choice. Following such training, youths could still decide to take drugs (on the basis of other SEUs), but in doing so, they would not be capitulating to peer pressure because they would have the competence necessary to finesse themselves away from the drug consumption option without losing face.

To test this theoretical perspective, Horan and Williams (1982) randomly assigned 72 nonassertive junior high students to assertion training (in which one-third of the training stimuli involved drug-use peer pressure), or to placebo discussions focused on similar topics, or to no treatment at all. The experimental assertion training and placebo treatments were delivered in the context of five small-group counseling sessions of 45 minutes duration over a 2-week period. Each treatment group was composed of three same-sex subjects plus the counselor.

The assertion training treatment was based on the intervention model of Galassi, Galassi, and Litz (1974), 10 general assertiveness (non-drug) training stimuli borrowed from McFall and Marston (1970), and five additional training situations involving peer pressure to use drugs. Sessions began with the counselor's instructing about assertiveness and live modeling of an assertive response to a particular training stimulus. Subjects rotated twice in the roles of speaker, listener, and responder for each stimulus. The counselor provided feedback plus additional instruction and modeling when appropriate after each subject's role-played response. Three training stimuli (one involving drugs) were used in each counseling session. Typical examples are as follows:

> *General assertiveness training stimulus:* Picture yourself just getting out of class on any old weekday morning. Hmm. You're a little hungry and some candy or some milk would taste good right about now, so you walk over to the machines and put your money in. You press the button . . . and . . . out it comes. You open it up. Mmm. Whatever it is you just bought, it sure tastes good. It's a good break, right after class. Oh, oh. Here comes your mooching friend again. This person is always borrowing money from you. He's getting closer now, and as he gets

closer your relaxation sort of changes to irritation. Oh, here he comes. Moocher: "Hey, I don't have any money and I'm hungry. How 'bout loaning me 50 cents for a candy bar?"

Drug-specific assertiveness training stimulus: You are out for the day with a group of close friends. While eating some food at a snack shop, you notice a friend you have not seen for a while and you invite him or her over to talk. During the conversation, your friend says: "I just got back from the greatest vacation. I was up in the mountains with some friends of my older brother. We really had a wild time! Hey! You should have been there. I got a chance to try a lot of different drugs that some of the other kids had. I've got some stuff at home. My family isn't home. Come on over and I'll give you some. You all will have the greatest time! Are you coming?"

The results of this study were very promising. At posttest, compared to control subjects, the experimental students showed highly significant gains on behavioral and psychometric measures of assertiveness as well as decreased willingness to use alcohol and marijuana. At 3-year follow-up, these students continued to display higher levels of assertiveness and less actual drug use.

Is That All There Is to It?

The role of assertion training as a drug abuse prevention strategy is limited to that of fostering the competence to say "no" in peer pressure situations focused on drug use. More fully developed social skills programs are currently being designed and evaluated with promising preliminary results (see Botvin, 1983; McAlister, 1983; Pentz, 1983).

Although social skills are critical to adaptive decisions about drugs, other competencies are also relevant. Thus, to maximize benefit in applied settings, we suggest a comprehensive programming approach. At the core of such a program we envision an instructional unit conforming to the implications of classical decision theory. Namely, accurate information regarding the utilities of drug use and abstinence along with their probabilities of occurrence should be readily available (including synopses of dissenting opinions). The misinformation contained in most drug prevention endeavors is educationally and ethically abhorrent.

But classical decision theory is actually inadequate to the task. For example, it assumes that all alternatives are known and that all utilities are rational. Consequently, when developing intervention curricula, drug educators and counselors should pay close attention to the expanding problem-solving and decision-making literatures, which include strategies to help students (a) define their choice problems, (b) enlarge their response repertoires, (c) identify pertinent information, and (d) implement their desired alternative (Horan, 1979; Moskowitz, 1983).

Current Work at Arizona State

A variety of projects in substance abuse prevention are underway at Arizona State University. For example, due to the generous support of the Sally M. Berridge Foundation, we are in the process of revising the assertive training program described above. Although its effectiveness from an empirical standpoint is clear, the stimuli were developed in the 1970s. They need to reflect the language and "zeitgeist" of the current decade.

The problem of exporting effective programs to the practitioner community continues to vex us as researchers, as does the ever present burden of cost benefit analysis. Professional labor-intensive programs or those requiring high-level expertise to implement will rarely escape a dusty bookshelf destiny. Although, the general strategy of assertion training is within the bailiwick of most practicing counselors, when applied to substance abuse prevention, there are fine nuances that may not be in the professional public domain.

Therefore, we are attempting to commit our program to a videotaped delivery format. We also expect to provide potential assertion trainers with detailed implementation instructions. We envision, for example, a filmed display of various peer pressure situations, that can be stopped and discussed prior to viewing similar vignettes that explicitly model effective assertive responses. The leader's guidebook will call for role-played practice situations, wherein students receive detailed feedback about the proficiency of their rehearsed assertive behavior.

A program of this sort would make no assumptions about the level of practitioner expertise. Counselors already highly proficient in assertion training might use our program as a point of departure; others might follow it verbatim.

We will also be embedding the assertion training component into the larger context of teaching effective decision-making skills. For example, a student may already have a high level of assertive competence (i.e., the ability to say "no" to given peer-exerting pressure). Focusing on the simple mechanics of saying "no" may be of little value when a more basic choice problem such as "If I say no, I may not be liked by this individual or group" is evident. Thus, training in how to generate alternatives (e.g., learning to say "no" in such a way as to minimize alienating protagonists, discovering how to break into social circles having more compatible values, etc.) may be highly relevant. Moreover, frontal assaults on irrational cognitions may be apropos as well. In this case, cognitive restructuring a la Ellis (1962) along the lines of "One's worth as a person does not depend on being liked by any individual or clique" may be highly productive.

As might be expected, organizing a comprehensive, yet focused, instructional unit for enhancing relevant decision-making skills is a formidable task. Committing it to an interactive videotaped format to aid in exportability increases the burden exponentially. Nevertheless, we feel confident about the ultimate utility of this approach, and are currently in the process of piloting our intervention materials.

References

Alberti, R. (1977). *Assertiveness: Innovations, applications, issues.* San Luis Obispo, CA: Impact.

Ball, G. (1974). *Human development program. Level V activity guide.* La Mesa, CA: Human Development Training Institute.

Bauman, K. E. (1980). *Predicting adolescent drug use: The utility structure and marijuana.* New York: Praeger.

Blum, R. H. (1976). *Drug education: Results and recommendations.* Lexington, MA: Brooks.

Botvin, G. J. (1983). Prevention of adolescent substance abuse through the development of personal and social competence. In T. J. Glynn, C. G. Leukefeld, & J. P. Ludford (Eds.), *Preventing adolescent drug abuse: Intervention strategies.* (National Institute on Drug Abuse Research Monograph 47, pp. 115–140). Washington, DC: U.S. Government Printing Office.

Broadhurst, A. (1976). Applications of the psychology of decisions. In M. P. Feldman & A. Broadhurst (Eds.), *Theoretical and experimental bases of the behavior therapies.* Chichester: Wiley.

Bross, I. D. J. (1953). *Design for decision: An introduction to statistical decision-making.* New York: Macmillan.

Dericco, D. A., & Garlington, W. K. (1977). The effect of modeling and disclosure of experimenter's intent on drinking rate of college students. *Addictive Behaviors, 2,* 135–139.

Dinkmeyer, D. (1973). *Developing understanding of self and others manual.* Circle Pines, MN: American Guidance Service.

Ellis, A. (1962). *Reason and emotion in psychotherapy.* New York: Lyle Stuart.

Evans, K., D'Augelli, J., & Branca, M. (1976). *Decisions are possible.* University Park: Addictions Prevention Laboratory, Pennsylvania State University.

Galassi, J. P., Galassi, M. D., & Litz, M. C. (1974). Assertion training in groups using video feedback. *Journal of Counseling Psychology, 21*(5), 390–394.

Globetti, G. (1975). An appraisal of drug education programs. In R. J. Gibbins, Y. Israel, H. Kalant, R. E. Popham, W. Schmidt, & R. G. Smart (Eds.), *Research advances in alcohol and drug problems*. New York: Wiley.

Goodstadt, M. S. (Ed.). (1974). *Research on methods and programs of drug education*. Toronto: Alcoholism and Drug Addiction Research Foundation.

Gordon, T. (1970). *PET: Parent effectiveness training*. New York: Wyden.

Heimberg, D. G., Montgomery, D., Madsen, C. H., & Heimberg, J. S. (1977). Assertion training: A review of the literature. *Behavior Therapy, 8*, 953–971.

Holmes, D. P. & Horan, J. J. (1976). Anger induction in assertion training. *Journal of Counseling Psychology, 3*(2), 108–111.

Horan, J. J. (1973). Preventing drug abuse through behavior change technology. *Journal of the Student Personnel Association for Teacher Education (SPATE), 11*, 145–152.

Horan, J. J. (1974). Outcome difficulties in drug education. *Review of Educational Research, 44*, 203–211.

Horan, J. J. (1979). *Counseling for effective decision making. A cognitive behavioral perspective*. North Scituate, MA: Duxbury.

Horan, J. J., D'Amico, M. M., & Williams, J. M. (1975). Assertiveness and patterns of drug use: A pilot study. *Journal of Drug Education, 5*, 217–221.

Horan, J. J., & Harrison, R. P. (1981). Drug abuse by children and adolescents: Perspectives on incidence, etiology, assessment, and prevention programming. In B. B. Lahey & A. E. Kazdin (Eds.), *Advances in clinical child psychology* (Vol. 4). New York: Plenum.

Horan, J. J., Shute, R. E., Swisher, J. D., & Westcott, T. B. (1973). A training model for drug abuse prevention: Content and evaluation. *Journal of Drug Education, 3*, 121–126.

Horan, J. J., Westcott, T. B., Vetovich, C., & Swisher, J. D. (1974). Drug usage: An experimental comparison of three assessment conditions. *Psychological Reports, 35*, 211–215.

Horan, J. J., & Williams, J. M. (1982). Longitudinal study of assertion training as a drug abuse prevention strategy. *American Educational Research Journal, 19*(3), 341–351.

Kandel, D. B. (1974a). Inter- and intra-generational influences on adolescent marijuana use. *Journal of Social Issues, 30*, 107–135.

Kandel, D. B. (1974b). Interpersonal influences on adolescent illegal drug use. In E. Josephson & E. E. Carroll (Eds.), *Drug use: Epidemiological and sociological approaches*. Washington, DC: Hemisphere.

Kandel, D. B., Kessler, R. C., & Margulies, R. Z. (1978). Antecedents of adolescent initiation into stages of drug use: A developmental analysis. In D. B. Kandel (Ed.), *Longitudinal research on drug use: Empirical findings and methodological issues*. Washington, DC: Hemisphere.

Kwiterovich, D. K., & Horan, J. J. (1977). Solomon evaluation of an assertiveness training program for women. *Behavior Therapy, 8*, 501–502.

Levitt, E. E., & Edwards, J. A. (1970). A multivariate study of correlative factors in youthful cigarette smoking. *Developmental Psychology, 2*, 5–11.
Mausner, B. (1973). An ecological view of cigarette smoking. *Journal of Abnormal Psychology, 81*, 115–126.
McAlister, A. L. (1983). Social-psychological approaches. In T. J. Glynn, C. G. Leukefeld, & J. P. Ludford (Eds.), *Preventing adolescent drug abuse: Intervention strategies.* (National Institute on Drug Abuse Research Monograph 47, pp. 36–50). Washington, DC: U.S. Government Printing Office.
McFall, R. M., & Marston, A. R. (1970). An experimental investigation of behavioral rehearsal in assertion training. *Journal of Abnormal Psychology, 76*, 295–303.
Moskowitz, J. M. (1983). Preventing adolescent substance abuse through drug education. In T. J. Glynn, C. G. Leukefeld, & J. P. Ludford (Eds.), *Preventing adolescent drug abuse: Intervention strategies.* (National Institute on Drug Abuse Research Monograph Series 47, pp. 233–249). Washington, DC: U.S. Government Printing Office.
National Coordinating Council on Drug Education. (1972). *Drug abuse films.* Washington, DC: Drug Abuse Council.
Ostman, R. E. (1976). *Communication research and drug education.* Beverly Hills, CA: Sage.
Pentz, M. A. (1983). Prevention of adolescent substance abuse through social skill development. In T. J. Glynn, C. G. Leukefeld, & J. P. Ludford (Eds.), *Preventing adolescent drug abuse: Intervention strategies.* (National Institute on Drug Abuse Research Monograph Series 47, pp. 195–232). Washington, DC: U.S. Government Printing Office.
Schaps, E., DiBartolo, R., Moskowitz, J., & Churgin, S. (1981). A review of 127 drug abuse prevention program evaluations. *Journal of Drug Issues, 1*, 14–44.
Shain, M., Riddell, W., & Kelty, H. L. (1977). *Influence, choice, and drugs.* Lexington, MA: Heath.
Shute, R. (1975). Impact of peer pressure on the verbally expressed drug attitudes of male college students. *American Journal of Drug and Alcohol Abuse, 2*, 231–243.
Stone, C. I., & Shute, R. (1977). Persuader sex differences and peer pressure effects on attitudes toward drug abuse. *American Journal of Drug and Alcohol Abuse, 4*, 55–64.
Swisher, J. D., Warner, R. W., Jr., & Herr, E. L. (1972). Experimental comparison of four approaches to drug abuse prevention among ninth and eleventh graders. *Journal of Counseling Psychology, 19*, 328–332.
Warner, R. W., Swisher, J. D., & Horan J. J. (1973). Drug abuse prevention: A behavioral approach. *National Association of Secondary School Principals Bulletin, 57*, 49–54.

Putting It All Together: Quest's Skills for Growing Program

Hank Resnik

What really works in drug education and prevention? What needs to happen for prevention to be effective? After 2 decades of trial and error, and several generations of funding cycles and drug "crises," some clear answers are beginning to emerge.

Following are several basic premises to consider. All of these are supported by years of research and dozens of books, articles, and reports (Edmonds, 1982; Hawkins, Lishner, Catalano, & Howard, 1986; Johnston, Bachman, & O'Malley, 1985; NIAAA, 1986; Polich, Ellickson, Reuter, & Kahn, 1984; Search Institute, 1984).

1. It is time to put behind us the notion of a "quick fix" to the drug problem. School assemblies, informational pamphlets, and even widely publicized drug awareness and health events are not enough. Although they can be helpful in a more comprehensive prevention effort, there is little evidence that, by themselves and isolated from other prevention activities, they can change young people's behavior.
2. Parent and family involvement is central to effective prevention programming. At one time, it was considered helpful and desirable; increasingly, it is being recognized as a key element.
3. Effective prevention programming takes time. A commitment of as much as 3 to 5 years is not overly ambitious. This does not mean that after 3 to 5 years a prevention program is "over." Rather, by that time, it should have been thoroughly internalized and institutionalized.
4. Good drug education and prevention programs are positive, constructive elements in the life of a school and its community. They lead to a community-wide emphasis on healthy living, positive activities for youth, improved education, and family involvement. A good program does not focus exclusively on the drug and alcohol problem; rather, it promotes a long-lasting, community-wide commitment to the development of human potential, especially the well-being of children and youth.
5. For school-based programs, effective prevention programming is closely associated with better teaching, happier and more successful kids, more involved parents—in a nutshell, better schools.

All of these premises have guided Quest International in the development of its newest program, Skills for Growing, which is targeted at grades K–5. A not-for-profit educational organization, Quest is already well known for two other programs that have a similar focus. Skills for Living is directed at grades 9–12 and has been adopted by more than 900 school districts throughout the United States and in seven other countries. Skills for Adolescence, developed in close cooperation with Lions Clubs International, is the principal drug education and prevention program of Lions Clubs throughout the world. It is now being used in more than 10,000 middle and junior high schools and has been translated into five languages, in addition to English. Skills for Adolescence is a broad spectrum approach to drug abuse prevention addressing such areas as behavior, cognition, and personal relations. (Gerler, 1986) (See author's note) Skills for Growing has already attracted wide-ranging attention and support. It is being disseminated through a collaborative working relationship with Lions Clubs International and the National Association of Elementary School Principals.

The Quest Conceptual Model

Like all of Quest's programs, Skills for Growing is based on a conceptual model for effective prevention programming that integrates theoretical approaches and research from several related disciplines. The programs of Quest International have two main goals:

1. To help young people develop positive social behaviors such as self discipline, responsibility, good judgment, and the ability to get along with others.
2. To help young people develop positive commitments and bonds in four key areas of their lives: family, school, peers, and community.

Represented graphically in Table 1, the conceptual model can be seen as a simple formula: A + B = C + D. If certain (A) external and (B) internal conditions are met, young people will exhibit (C) positive social behaviors and will develop (D) positive commitments. When these two goals are accomplished, young people will be more likely and better prepared to lead productive, healthy, drug-free lives.

External Conditions

The external conditions envisioned in the Quest Model can be divided into two major categories: environment and skill instruction. Quest has identified seven features of the environment that encourage young people's development of positive social behaviors and commitments. The environment must do the following:

Table 1
Quest International Conceptual Model for K-12 Programming

External Conditions	+	Internal Conditions	=	Positive Social Behaviors	+	Commitment
Environment		Self-perception		Self-discipline		Family
Opportunity						
Expectation						
Caring		Motivation		Responsibility		School
Predictability						
Reciprocal interaction						
Safety		Cognition		Good Judgment		Peers
Reinforcement						
Skill				Getting Along with Others		Community
Instruction						
Thinking skills						
Social skills						

1. Provide opportunities for young people to engage in positive social behavior
2. Clearly communicate expectations that young people will behave in positive ways
3. Be warm and caring
4. Be predictable and consistent (but not rigid)
5. Provide reciprocal interaction with adults and peers so that young people learn mutual respect
6. Be emotionally safe
7. Provide appropriate reinforcement and support for positive social behaviors

In Quest's programs, skill instruction focuses primarily on thinking and social skills. Thinking skills include problem solving, critical thinking, decision making, and goal setting. Social skills include building relationships, enhancing communication, and being able to say "No" to potentially harmful influences.

Another important component of Quest's approach is conveying information—about alcohol and other drugs, for example—through short lectures, independent study, and classroom activities that encourage students to learn in interesting and motivating ways. Nevertheless, the model focuses more on purpose than content, especially at the elementary level.

Internal Conditions

Quest's programs are also designed to affect internal conditions—the child's self-perceptions, motivation, and cognitive development. Self-perception is important because people who are successful in school and in life have a strong sense of being capable. They value themselves and believe that they are worthwhile. They have a sense of control (Glenn & Nelson, 1987). Another key internal condition is motivation, the desire or drive to behave in positive, healthy ways. Especially in a program that emphasizes social skills, students need to be interested and see the relevance of a skill or concept in order to learn it. Three areas of cognition have particularly important implications for skill instruction: memory, understanding, and reasoning. All are combined in Quest's programs in an emphasis on continual information gathering and critical thinking.

Positive Social Behaviors

Positive social behaviors are a principal outcome of Quest's programs. These behaviors can be divided into four categories: self-discipline, responsibility, good judgment, and the ability to get along with others.

Self-discipline consists of respecting oneself, persevering to attain one's goals, and postponing gratification, when necessary. Responsibility involves making and keeping commitments, acting with integrity, being direct and honest, and following through on one's values and beliefs. Good judgment includes considering alternatives and consequences. It involves making wise, informed decisions. Getting along with others is associated with a wide range of social interactions, such as helping, sharing, and cooperating.

Positive Commitments

Another main outcome of the Quest approach is positive commitments and bonding in four critical areas of children's lives: the family, the school, the peer group, and the community. The stronger the positive commitments to these systems, and the more systems to which the child is bonded, the less likely it is that negative and problem behavior will develop.

The Components of Skills for Growing

Given the broad scope of the conceptual model, all of Quest's programs are noteworthy for their comprehensiveness. Each provides a complete set of curricular materials and a variety of components. Each requires that participating teachers undergo an intensive training workshop before receiving the program materials. Each views the involvement of the total school-community as vital to success.

Skills for Growing was pilot-tested for the first time in the spring of 1988 in ten schools of the United States and Canada. The number of schools expanded to 41 in the fall of 1988, and full implementation of the program will begin in the fall of 1989. The program revolves around five components:

Classroom Curriculum. The curriculum consists of five units, each focusing on a specific theme (for example, "Building a School Community" and "Choosing to be Drug-Free") and offering a series of six lessons. Throughout, the emphasis is on interaction—between the students and the teachers, and the students and each other. The curriculum also provides extensions that relate each lesson objective to various aspects of the standard elementary curriculum.

Positive School Climate. The program establishes a School Climate Committee, made up of teachers, administrators, support staff, students, parents, and community representatives. The basic goal is to involve everyone in the school in the program's positive approaches and activities. A principal task of the committee is to organize and direct efforts to implement the curriculum themes school wide.

Parents as Partners. Parents are encouraged to take an active role in the program through activities they do at home with their children. These activities are outlined in a series of family newsletters for each unit. Parents are also encouraged to become involved in the School Climate Committee. The program provides a series of meetings and booklets for parents that offer practical tips on child rearing in connection with the program's main themes. The emphasis throughout the parent component is on strengthening the family and creating positive links between home and school.

Community Support. Skills for Growing helps to create a team of school and community volunteers whose mission is to increase community involvement in the school and focus community efforts on the needs of children. This component suggests ways to develop cooperative working relationships among community groups and build effective school-community partnerships.

Training. Every classroom teacher in the program must complete an intensive, 3-day workshop led by Quest trainers. The workshop provides both an overview of the program and hands-on experience with the materials. School staff, parents, and community leaders who will play key roles in the program, are strongly encouraged to participate in the training as a team.

The program provides a wide range of materials, including curriculum guides, booklets for students and parents, audiovisual media, and newsletters. After the first year of program implementation, teachers will be kept in touch and up-to-date through a newsletter called *The Living Curriculum*, which will offer lessons, ideas, and activities to expand the program. Program participants will also be invited to attend regional networking meetings and advanced training workshops sponsored by Quest. In addition, Quest operates a toll-free phone line through which experienced Quest staff members offer practical assistance and answers to questions about the program.

Beyond Drug Education

Skills for Growing was developed by a team of more than 100 educators, psychologists, and curriculum specialists throughout the United States and Canada. It represents a collective lifetime of thinking, experimenting, researching, and innovating in the area of drug abuse prevention and education. One of the main premises of the program is that drug abuse prevention programs must reach far beyond any traditional notion of "drug education" to be effective.

What Skills for Growing is really about is making schools healthier, happier places for children, adults, and the wider school community. Although this is far from being a radically new concept, Skills for Growing provides the tools—the training, the materials, and the organizational support—to make it happen.

Even in the program's early developmental stages, the potential impact was evident. Many teachers and administrators who participated in the pilot project clearly recognized that the program can create important positive changes in elementary schools. Reflecting on the Skills for Growing training, one principal commented, "We are not the same folks today that we were (before training) . . . There is a genuine and gentle warmth, coupled with a sense of caring about who we are and what we do or say to others."

The spirit of cooperation and caring that the program can develop throughout a school is exemplified by one of the pilot school teams that included a bus driver. He became so enthusiastic about the program, the training, and the importance of school-wide cooperation that when he returned to school, he developed a workshop for all the other bus drivers to tell them how they could have a positive impact on children. "I never really thought of it this way before," he told one of the Quest trainers. "A bus driver can set the tone for a child's day. I'm one of the first people the child sees in the morning. I can be an important part of that child's education."

References

Edmonds, R. R. (1982). Programs of school improvement: An overview. *Educational Leadership, 40*, 4–11.

Gerler, E. R. (1986). Skills for adolescence: A new program for young teenagers. *Phi Delta Kappan, 67*, 436–439.

Glenn, S., & Nelson, J. (1987). *Raising children for success.* Fair Oaks, CA: Sunrise Press.

Hawkins, J. D., Lishner, D. M., Catalano, R. F., & Howard, M. O. (1986). Childhood predictors of adolescent substance abuse: Toward an empirically grounded theory. *Journal of Children in Contemporary Society, 18*, 11–48.

Johnston, L., Bachman, J., & O'Malley, P. (1985). *Use of licit and illicit drugs by America's high school students: 1975–1984.* Washington, DC: U.S. Government Printing Office.

National Institute on Alcohol Abuse and Alcoholism. (1986). *Literature review on alcohol and youth.* Rockville, MD: National Institute on Alcohol Abuse and Alcoholism.

Polich, J. M., Ellickson, P. L., Reuter, & Kahan, J. P. (1984). *Strategies for controlling adolescent drug use.* Santa Monica, CA: Rand Corporation.

Search Institute. (1984). *Young adolescents and their parents: A national portrait.* Minneapolis: Search Institute.

Author's Note: Information about Quest programs may be obtained by writing Quest International, 537 Jones Rd., Box 566, Granville, Ohio 43023–0566.

Dilemma Discussion in Drug Education

Edwin R. Gerler, Jr.

Dilemma Discussion in Drug Education

The current state of drug education is ambiguous at best. Many of the programs offered to counselors for implementation in elementary and middle schools have not been tested empirically and do not have adequate theoretical underpinnings (Horan & Harrison, 1981). Theory-based prevention programs that have been tested or that are currently being tested offer hope that drug education will improve dramatically over the next few years. Horan and Williams's (1982) assertiveness training program, for example, designed to help adolescents resist peer pressure, shows the value of drug education that is grounded in theory and adequately tested. Similarly, the "Skills for Adolescence" curriculum developed by the Quest National Center in Columbus, Ohio, which takes a broader theoretical approach than the Horan and Williams program, seems to be a solid drug education program that is undergoing thorough testing.

It is apparent, however, that even promising approaches to drug abuse prevention do not focus sufficiently on the way young adolescents think when confronted with opportunities to use drugs. The need to correct this deficiency in drug prevention efforts is particularly apparent from recent research (Mohr, Sprinthall, & Gerler, 1987), which showed that middle school students reason at lower levels of maturity when confronted with drug related dilemmas than when faced with other kinds of dilemmas. This finding suggests that drug prevention programming needs to take into consideration theoretical perspectives such as Loevinger's (1977) on ego development, Kohlberg's (1979) on moral development, and Selman's (1981) on interpersonal reasoning.

What follows is a description of a 10-session program, based largely on cognitive-developmental theory that is aimed at helping middle school students progress in their reasoning about using drugs. The program challenges students' current reasoning about using drugs, provides role-taking experiences that allows students to consider the perspectives of peers, and provides students with opportunities to reflect on thoughts and feelings about drug-related issues.

The Dilemma Discussion Program

Participants take part in 10 one-hour, small group sessions that are ideally conducted over a 10-week period. Following each session, students write their thoughts and feelings in personal journals. Students may discuss their journal entries during any session but are not required to do so.

Phase 1: Getting Acquainted, Group Guidelines, and Drug Information

This phase involves three group sessions incorporating such elements as get-acquainted activities, presentation of guidelines for behavior in group sessions, discussions about the possible side effects of substance abuse, and consideration of social situations in which drug use might be encountered.

Session 1. The group leader involves members in an exercise that asks members to pair off, separate from the group for about 5 minutes, and get acquainted with each other. When members return to the group, they briefly introduce each other to the entire group. Following introductions, the leader discusses the purpose and nature of the dilemma discussion groups, namely, to challenge students' thinking and to prepare students to confront difficult decision-making situations. The leader also identifies guidelines for the group:

1. The group will begin and end on time.
2. Group members should attend every session.
3. Members should keep group discussions of personal matters confidential.
4. Participants should be active in discussions.
5. Members should listen carefully to each other.
6. Members should be considerate in responding to each other.
7. Members should maintain a journal that contains personal reactions to each session.
8. Participants will have opportunities to discuss their journal entries at the beginning of each session.

Session 2. This session provides members with the opportunity to talk about why they want to participate in a dilemma discussion group related to drug use and abuse. Members usually share what they know about drugs, how much peer pressure plays in drug use among students, and how media encourages use of alcohol and other drugs. Discussion of the latter topic usually involves lively conversations about alcohol advertisements associated with television sporting events and about particularly compelling magazine advertisements of alcoholic beverages. Students may also wish to discuss warnings on cigarette advertisements. The leader may challenge students to come up with appropriate warnings for containers of alcoholic beverages.

Session 3. This session begins with students reflecting on their journal entries and, particularly, on discussion in Session 2, about peer and media pressure to use drugs. Next, the leader offers opportunities for members to discuss not only what they know about drugs, but also how they feel about the use of various types of drugs, including over-the-counter drugs for medical purposes, prescription drugs for medical purposes, legal drugs such as alcohol for recreational purposes, and illegal drugs for recreational purposes. Finally, the leader presents students with the following information about consequences of abusing drugs and encourages students to discuss their feelings about the short- and long-term consequences of drug use:

Alcohol — The effects of alcohol include decreased heart rate, blood pressure, and respiration, as well as impaired coordination, slurred speech, and fatigue. Long-term use of alcohol results in psychological and physical dependence, liver damage, stomach difficulties, and vitamin depletion. Alcohol abuse also results in traffic injuries, and death, as well as Fetal Alcohol Syndrome.

Nicotine — This drug results in increased blood pressure and heart rate, as well as reduced appetite and sensitivity to pain. Long-term effects include cancer and heart disease.

Cannabis — Abuse of marijuana results in red or glassy eyes, increased appetite, impaired coordination, forgetfulness, reduced attention span, animated behavior, and fatigue. Long-term effects include damage to the respiratory system and possible heart damage.

Stimulants — These substances cause loss of appetite, hyperactivity, and paranoia. High doses of certain substances, particularly amphetamines, result in delirium, panic, aggression, hallucinations, psychoses, weight loss, and heart abnormalities.

Inhalants — Use of these substances causes slurred speech, impaired coordination, drowsiness, runny nose, and appetite loss. High doses result in respiratory depression, unconsciousness, and, in some cases, death. Chronic use has adverse physical effects on liver, kidneys, and bone marrow.

Cocaine — This drug causes decreased appetite, weight loss, dilated pupils, periods of tirelessness followed by extreme fatigue, irritated nostrils, anxiety, irritability, and paranoia. Chronic use causes serious health problems, including heart attack, brain hemorrhage, liver and lung damage, seizures, and respiratory arrest.

Psychedelics — These substances alter the senses and often cause panic, nausea, and elevated blood pressure. Large doses of certain psychedelics result in death from brain hemorrhage, heart and lung failure, or repeated convulsions.

Depressants These drugs cause impaired coordination, slurred speech, fatigue, and decreased respiration, pulse, and blood pressure. When used with alcohol, depressants may be fatal.

Narcotics Narcotics cause decreased respiration, blood pressure, and pulse rate, as well as fatigue, constricted pupils, watery eyes, and itching. They may also result in nausea and vomiting. Coma, shock, respiratory arrest, and death may result from high doses. When these drugs are injected with unsterile needles, AIDS may be an outcome.

Designer Drugs The effects of designer drugs are greater than the imitated drug. Designer narcotics may cause drooling, paralysis, tremors, and brain damage. Other designer drugs may create impaired vision, chills, sweating, and faintness.

Phase 2: Beginning Dilemmas

This phase involves three sessions, wherein students discuss and roleplay drug-related situations described by the group leader. These dilemmas stimulate the students to think about social pressures to use drugs. The leader's role during these sessions consists of listening actively, encouraging and supporting roleplay, and asking questions to promote higher levels of reasoning about drug use.

Session 4. This session begins with students reflecting on their journal entries and on previous discussions about consequences of substance abuse and about social pressure to use drugs. Next, the group leader presents students with their first drug-related dilemma for discussion.

> Just before the beginning of the new year, Tony's parents moved into the community and enrolled him in school. He had lived in the same house since birth. Moving was certainly not his idea.
>
> Now, here he was at a new middle school, 400 miles from where he was born and where he wanted to be. Three weeks had passed, and he still didn't know anyone. His new school was an unfriendly place. Kids passed him in the hall as if he didn't exist. Lately, he didn't even feel like getting out of bed in the morning to come to school.
>
> Today, a guy, named Joe, from his English class walked down the hall beside him to the cafeteria and asked him if they could eat together. Things might be looking up for Tony.
>
> Lunch was great. Tony enjoyed telling Joe about his old school, and Joe seemed really interested, asking a lot of questions in between bites of pizza. Tony looked forward to having a new friend.

> There was just one hitch. As they walked out of the cafeteria, Joe casually said, "I've noticed you haven't looked too happy about being here, Tony, and I've got something in my pocket that'll fix you right up, make your troubles go away." Joe patted his pants pocket and smiled knowingly.
>
> Tony, feeling embarrassed and uncertain, said nothing.
>
> "No rush, Tony, they'll keep," Joe said. "See you later," and he turned to go down the hall to his locker as the bell rang.
>
> Tony walked on, wondering if Joe wanted him for a friend or what. Tony wanted a friend, but he wasn't sure if he wanted to get involved in drugs. What should Tony do? (Wilkinson, 1988, p. 8)

The leader asks participants to reflect on Tony's situation. During the discussion of the dilemma, the leader challenges students' thinking with questions such as the following:

1. What is Tony's dilemma?
2. What factors enter into Tony's decision? What kinds of statements might Tony be making to himself about his predicament?
3. What alternatives does Tony have? Consider all the choices he has. Which one(s) is he most likely to choose?
4. How do students make friends? Do all new students have problems similar to Tony's? Why or why not?
5. What makes a good friend? Would Joe make a good friend? Why or why not? Would Tony make a good friend? Why or why not?
6. What responsibilities do students already enrolled in school have toward new students?
7. We don't know anything about Tony's race, nationality, or religion. Would these make any difference in Tony's attempts to find new friends? (Wilkinson, 1988, pp. 8–9)

Session 5. Students begin this session by reflecting on journal entries about their first dilemma discussion. Typical student comments include those listed below:

1. I would never be friends with Joe. He's just looking to take advantage of a new kid.
2. Tony is probably a geek. Joe *will* fix him all right.
3. Tony needs to talk with his parents so that Joe will not ruin his life.
4. I would turn Joe in, if he couldn't find out who did it.
5. Joe just wants to help Tony fit in.

Following discussion about journal entries and a review of the dilemma from Session 4, the leader presents another dilemma:

> Carrie is walking on air! She has her first, real, live boyfriend. Craig is not just any boyfriend either. He is a grade ahead of her in middle school. She has liked Craig for several months and now he has begun to like her. Craig has asked Carrie to go with him. Everyone at school knows and admires Craig, and now, everyone knows Carrie. She wants to do everything she can to hang on to him.
>
> On Saturday evening Craig invites Carrie to go out with him. She goes with him to see his friends, but she is surprised that it actually turns out that most of his friends are smoking pot. Craig takes his turn and then offers his cigarette to Carrie. Carrie refuses to take part. On the way home, Craig tells Carrie that she really needs to grow up, to make some decisions for herself, and to have some good times in life. He says that she needs to stop ruining fun for everybody else. Craig says that if she is to continue going with him and his friends, she will have to enjoy an occasional smoke.
>
> Carrie is faced with the realization that if she says, "No," she will lose Craig forever, but if she says, "Maybe the next time," she can keep him for the present and avoid embarrassment with her friends. She also thinks that if she can put him off a few weeks, maybe he will like her enough that he will change his mind.
>
> How should Carrie reply to Craig's demands? (Paisley, 1987, p. 113)

After listening to this dilemma, students roleplay the situation, offering several ways for Carrie to reply to Craig's demands. Students also roleplay various alternative responses from Craig and offer subsequent suggestions for Carrie. During and following roleplay, the leader poses questions challenging students to think more maturely about Carrie's situation.

Session 6. Participants begin this session reflecting on their journal entries and on Carrie's dilemma considered in the previous session. Many students find Carrie's dilemma "close to home" and, thus difficult to discuss. The following are sample journal entries in reaction to Carrie: (Students volunteer to share and discuss their journal entries.)

> I feel sorry for girls like Carrie. Boys are always trying to get girls to do things that are bad for them. Drugs and sex are all boys think about. If girls give in to pot, the next thing is sex, and maybe with all of the boy's friends. Girls should stick with their own age group and not go with older boys. I am tired of thinking about poor Carrie. I think she will give in. I wouldn't even for the greatest boy. (eighth-grade girl)

> Craig has all the luck—good looks, a great body, all kinds of friends, and a nice girl friend. I wish I [were] in his shoes. I would like to have a girl friend especially. I wouldn't force her to smoke pot either. (eighth-grade boy)

> Carrie is too nice to be real. She needs to loosen up and have some real fun. Craig knows how to live. I don't really mean any of this. (eighth-grade boy)
>
> Carrie is too sweet. Her experience with Craig will make her a lot smarter about the way the world is. (eighth-grade girl)

Following participants' voluntary reflections on journal entries, the leader asks students to begin thinking about how to write their own drug-related dilemmas before the next group session. Students express their feelings about the dilemmas already presented and discussed in the group. They also discuss the main components of the dilemmas previously discussed. These components (Galbraith & Jones, 1976) include the following: (a) focus on a genuine problem, (b) action centering about a main character, (c) the presence of choice that has no apparent correct answer, and (d) a question posed about what the main character in the dilemma should do. The leader asks students to prepare a brief dilemma for discussion in the next group session.

Phase 3: Personal Dilemma

This phase includes three sessions in which students write their own drug-related dilemmas and discuss the dilemmas in the group. The leader's role is again to encourage discussion and roleplay and to ask questions that challenge students to reason at higher levels about using drugs.

Session 7. This session begins with only brief reflections on journal entries from the previous session. Next, the students discuss how it felt to write dilemmas on their own. Students who did not write dilemmas, for whatever reason, also participate in this discussion and talk about feelings that led them not to complete the assignment. Some comments during the discussion include the following:

1. Dilemmas are easy to write if they don't come from your own real life.
2. I hate to write these things. This is beginning to be like a class.
3. I don't have any dilemmas in my life and nothing to write about.
4. I just made up something. I don't think anybody will want to talk about it.
5. I have lots of hard choices but none about drugs. I will never use drugs.
6. I like talking about our own dilemmas. They are more realistic than the other dilemmas.

Following this discussion, some students volunteer to read their dilemmas and each is discussed briefly. The leader then forms the participants into small groups of three or four to write dilemmas during the session. The leader circulates among the groups, encouraging participants to stay on task and to complete dilemmas for discussion at the next session.

Session 8. Students briefly discuss their journal entries. The leader asks for a volunteer to read one of the dilemmas created in the previous session. The following is an example from an eighth-grade group:

> Chris is an up-and-coming young basketball player. He shows a lot of academic promise as well. However, Chris has a problem. No matter what he does, he just can't seem to wake up in the morning. He's tried many different things, such as using two alarm clocks, having his parents turn on the overhead light in the bedroom, even just having his parents come in and try to shake him out of bed, but nothing works.
>
> One day, Chris overheard some of his friends talking. It appeared that they were having the same types of problems, but they had found a solution. They were taking amphetamines. Chris asked them about it and they said that it really helped. They said that after using it, they had no trouble waking up in the morning, and it made them more alert in class. Chris began to wonder, "Is this the only way?"
>
> Chris knew that drugs were bad for you, and he had never planned to use them. He also knew that amphetamines would solve his problem, and that they might be the only way to remedy the situation. What would you do if you were in Chris' shoes?

The leader and group members together raise and discuss questions about the dilemma faced by Chris. These questions include the following:

1. What is Chris' dilemma?
2. What might be causing Chris to sleep too much? How will amphetamines affect his problem? Why did Chris think of using amphetamines?
3. What other alternatives does Chris have? Consider all possible choices he has. Which might he choose?
4. Do all kids have trouble waking up? Why or why not?
5. What makes a kid want to keep sleeping in the morning? What makes a kid want to wake up?
6. What responsibilities does Chris have that should make him get up on time?
7. What would you do to help Chris if you were his friend?
8. Where would you go for help if you were Chris?
9. Will Chris try amphetamines to solve his problem? Why or why not?

The leader asks students to write a dilemma for discussion at the next group session. The leader urges everyone to try to complete the assignment this time.

Session 9. Students reflect briefly on their journal entries, particularly thinking about the dilemma of Chris discussed in Session 8. Students then share and discuss the dilemmas they were assigned to write. At this point in the group process, many of the dilemmas are quite personal and sometimes difficult for students to discuss. The following is an example of a personal dilemma written by an eighth grader.

> Greg's father is an alcoholic, but Greg does not know it. He's seen his father come home drunk a few times and be late for work the next day. Greg's mom always calls his boss when this happens, however, and things turn out all right. To Greg, there is no real problem.
>
> Some of Greg's friends invited him to a party. Everyone seemed to be enjoying him or herself. Then one of Greg's friends walked up to him and offered him a beer. Greg started to say "yes," but he stopped and thought for a moment.
>
> Greg knows he is too young to drink, but he sees his father drink all the time. However, Greg also knows that alcohol is a drug. If you were in Greg's place, what would you do?

As student dilemmas are read and discussed, the group leader and group members ask challenging questions to stimulate thinking about each of the difficult situations presented.

Phase 4: Closing the Group

This phase consists of one meeting that brings closure to the group. During this time, students reflect on how their thinking about drug dilemmas has progressed. The leader's role is to paraphrase and summarize the students' views on their progress.

Session 10. At the beginning of this session, the leader asks the students to read through each of their journal entries from the nine previous sessions. This provides students with the opportunity to observe progress they have made during the group. Students discuss feelings about their progress or lack of it. The leader invites students who have made progress to describe the program for all in the group to hear. The leader then encourages participants who see no movement in their own thinking to discuss their feelings and to consider how their thinking might change in the future.

Does the Dilemma Discussion Approach Work?

Preliminary research (Paisley, Gerler, & Sprinthall, 1988) in drug education involving dilemma discussion has indicated that the approach is effective in helping young adolescents increase their level of reasoning when confronted with drug dilemmas. When compared with control students, students in drug dilemma discussion groups showed significant increases in principled reasoning about drug-related situations. These increases, of course, do not guarantee that participating students will avoid drugs, but the increases suggest that these students will be better prepared than other adolescents to think maturely about whether or not to use drugs. The ultimate success of such discussion groups in promoting advanced levels of reasoning in students lies in Hunt's (1971) notion about the need for a manageable mis-match between students' present levels of development and educational interventions.

In conclusion, middle school counselors who are planning programs in drug prevention should consider using dilemma discussions. Also, counselors who already coordinate drug education programs should think about including dilemma discussions is existing drug curriculum. Counselors should be aware that the dilemma discussion approach, because it helps students practice language arts skills, is appropriate for use in regular academic courses such as social studies and English classes. In short, counselor and teacher collaboration is a good possibility in drug education efforts that include dilemma discussions. This innovative approach offers the hope that drug education will be perceived as more than an elective or ancillary part of curricula in middle schools.

References

Galbraith, R. E., & Jones, T. M. (1976). *Moral reasoning: A teaching handbook for adapting Kohlberg to the classroom*. Anoka, MS: Greenhaven Press Inc.

Gerler, E. R. (1986). Skills for adolescence: A new program for young teenagers. *Phi Delta Kappan, 67*, 436–439.

Horan, J. J., & Harrison, R. P. (1981). Drug abuse by children and adolescents: Perspectives on incidence, etiology, assessment, and prevention programming. In B. B. Lahey & A. E. Kazdin (Eds.), *Advances in clinical child psychology* (Vol. 4). New York: Plenum.

Horan, J. J., & Williams, J. M. (1982). Longitudinal study of assertion training as a drug abuse prevention strategy. *American Educational Research Journal, 19*, 341–351.

Hunt, D. (1971). *Matching models in education*. Toronto: Ontario Institute for Studies in Education.

Kohlberg, L. (1979). *Measuring moral judgment*. Worcester, MA: Clark University Press.

Loevinger, J. (1977). *Ego development*. San Francisco: Jossey-Bass.

Mohr, P. H., Sprinthall, N. A., Gerler, E. R. (1987). Moral reasoning in early adolescence: Implications for drug prevention. *School Counselor, 35*, 120–127.

Paisley, R. (1987). *A cognitive developmental dilemma based model for substance abuse prevention.* Unpublished doctoral dissertation, North Carolina State University, Raleigh.

Paisley, R., Gerler, E. R., & Sprinthall, N. A. (1988). *The dilemma in drug abuse prevention.* Manuscript submitted for publication.

Selman, R. (1980). *The growth of interpersonal understanding.* New York: Academic Press.

Wilkinson, C. (1980). *Dilemma discussion in the classroom.* Unpublished manuscript, North Carolina State University, Department of Counselor Education, Raleigh.

Moral Reasoning in Early Adolescence: Implications for Drug Abuse Prevention

Phyllis H. Mohr
Norman A. Sprinthall
Edwin R. Gerler, Jr.

School counselors are concerned about preventing substance abuse among adolescents. This concern is especially justified in light of the national school survey conducted at the University of Michigan's Institute for Social Research (McEneaney & Fishbein, 1983), which showed that, of the nation's high school seniors, (a) 66% reported using illicit drugs at some time in their lives, (b) 43% reported using an illicit drug other than marijuana, (c) 7% reported using marijuana daily, and (d) 31% preported using marijuana before entering high school.

Peer pressure is perhaps the most frequently mentioned reason for the high rate of drug abuse among adolescents. In a research report from the National Institute on Drug Abuse, Carter (1983) concluded:

> In the peer group, attitudes, values, parental behavior, the school, and society are discussed and judged. As participants in these groups, teenagers are influenced by their desire to conform to group expectations. Teenagers most strongly influence each other regarding dress and appearance, choice of leisure-time activities, language, and use of alcohol and drugs. (p. 25)

School counselors have tried various means to help adolescents withstand the peer pressure that often contributes to drug abuse. Counselors in many sections of the United States, for example, are helping teachers to implement the "Skills for Adolescence" curriculum, a new approach to drug abuse prevention developed by the Quest National Center in Columbus, Ohio. This curriculum is an attempt to help adolescents deal effectively with peer pressure and to consider positive alternatives to drug use. Early findings about its effectiveness have been positive (Gerler, 1986).

Some other promising findings about how to reduce the effects of peer pressure among adolescents have come from a study by Horan and Williams (1982), which indicated that junior high school students, when trained to behave more assertively, were significantly less inclined toward drug abuse than were nonassertive youngsters. The researchers concluded that students who are able to act assertively probably "have the competence necessary to finesse themselves away from the drug consumption option without losing face" (p. 342).

If counselors are to be more effective in preventing adolescent drug abuse, however, they need more and better information about how adolescents decide for or against the use of drugs. To supplement the findings of previous studies there is a need for basic research with adolescents—particularly with young adolescents—to determine the thinking processes they use when confronted with the dilemma of whether or not to abuse drugs. It is apparently true that social behavior skills play an important role in adolescents' abilities to resist the peer pressure that contributes to drug abuse; yet, it seems equally plausible that adolescents' reasoning also contributes.

Advances in theory and research about cognitive-developmental functioning, particularly in the area of moral reasoning (Kohlberg, 1979), make investigation of adolescent judgments about drug use especially intriguing. Because previous research (Hedin, 1979) has indicated that educational programs need to be based on the participants' level of reasoning about the issues at hand, both practicing school counselors and researchers might find it useful to know whether adolescents' reasoning about drug use is at the same level as their reasoning about other social dilemmas. Counselors and researchers might also benefit from knowing whether there is a difference between the sexes in their reasoning about the dilemma of drug use. Limited previous research (Gilligan, Kohlberg, Lerner, & Belenky, 1979) has found few, if any sex differences in moral reasoning levels. Nevertheless, if sex differences occur in reasoning about drug use, prevention programs need to be designed accordingly.

The purpose of this study, therefore, was to examine the following questions about adolescent thinking as it relates to judgments about abusing drugs:

1. When confronted with social dilemmas that are "close to home" (e.g., whether or not to use drugs at a weekend party), do young adolescents use the same level of moral reasoning as when dealing with abstract dilemmas that are somewhat removed from daily living?
2. Do male and female adolescents reason at similar levels in resolving drug-related dilemmas?

Understanding how adolescents reason as they make difficult choices about drug use might provide considerable help in building successful prevention programs.

Method

Participants

Students from two eighth-grade classes—a health education class and a physical education class—were selected from a public middle school to participate in this study. There were 54 participants, 33 boys and 21 girls. They came from a variety of cultural and socioeconomic backgrounds.

Instrument

The measure of students' reasoning used in this study was a modified version of Rest's (1979) Defining Issues Test (DIT). The modified DIT consisted of four dilemmas, two taken directly from the DIT and two drug-related dilemmas modeled after the Rest dilemmas. The two dilemmas taken from the DIT are titled the "escaped prisoner" and the "newspaper" dilemmas. Appendix A is a sample of a drug related dilemma.

Procedures for scoring the modified DIT were the same as those outlined by Rest for scoring the DIT. Responses to the modified DIT yielded scores that were converted to indicate the percentage of student reasoning at Level 1 (preconventional), Level 2 (conventional), or Level 3 (postconventional, principled). Sprinthall and Collins (1984) have noted that (a) preconventional moral reasoning is based in "external, quasi-physical happenings, in bad acts, or in quasi-physical needs rather than in persons and standards," (b) conventional reasoning is based in "performing good or right roles, in maintaining the conventional order, and in meeting others' expectations," and (c) postconventional reasoning is based in "principles that can be applied universally" (p. 179). The modified DIT also yielded scores, which were converted to indicate the percentage of student reasoning devoted to "meaningless" items listed on the instrument. (These items help to determine if a student is reasoning about items or simply responding to their pretentiousness.)

Although there are no reliability and validity data available on the modified DIT used in this study, the DIT itself has been studied thoroughly and has been shown to have high levels of concurrent validity (correlations ranging from .20 to .50 on variables such as achievement, aptitude, and intelligence quotient), construct validity (correlations ranging from .40 to .70 on variables such as cognitive ability and comprehension of moral values), and criterion-group validity (Davidson & Robbins, 1978). Studies of the DIT's reliability have resulted in test-retest correlations in the .80 range (Rest, 1979).

Results

Students responded at all three levels of reasoning measured by the modified DIT. On the four dilemmas combined, the mean percentage of responses at Level 1 = 18.51 (SD = 10.07), at Level 2 = 56.97 (SD = 12.07), and at Level 3 =

20.23 (*SD* = 11.23). As shown in Table 1, there were significant differences between the responses to the DIT dilemmas and the responses to the drug-related dilemmas. (A paired *t* test was used to analyze the differences in group means because the scores from the two DIT dilemmas and the two drug dilemmas were paired for each individual. Therefore, the information for each pair of scores was not independent. Glass and Hopkins [1984] noted, "When each observation in group 1 can be linked to or paired with an observation in group 2, the two sets of observations are dependent or correlated" [p. 240].)

Table 1
A Comparison of 54 Eighth Graders' Moral Reasoning Scores on Two DIT Dilemma and Two Drug-Related Dilemmas

	DIT Dilemmas		Drug Dilemmas		*T*-test results	
Score levels	Group *M*	*SD*	Group *M*	*SD*	Paired *t*	*p*
Level 1	9.54	8.14	28.70	19.11	-6.82	<.0001*
Level 2	61.11	16.18	52.32	20.94	2.37	<.0250*
Level 3	26.02	15.97	13.80	13.94	4.14	<.0010*
Meaningless items	3.33	6.73	3.37	5.88	-0.03	>.4000

Note. DIT = Defining Issues Test.
*Statistically significant

The greatest differences in mean percentage of responses to the two types of dilemmas were at Levels 1 and 3. At Level 1 (preconventional) the difference in means was 19.16 percentage points ($t = 6.82, p < .0005$) with the drug dilemmas having the higher percentage. At Level 3 (postconventional) the difference in means was 12.22 percentage points ($t = 4.14, p < .0005$) with the two DIT dilemmas having the higher percentage. At Level 2 (conventional) the difference in means was 8.79 percentage points ($t = 2.37, p < .025$) with the two DIT dilemmas again having the higher percentage. There were no significant differences in percentage of responses to meaningless items.

Table 2 shows the comparisons between the girls' scores and the boys' scores on the DIT and the drug-related dilemmas. Girls and boys did not differ significantly in their responses at any level of the two DIT dilemmas. Girls and boys differed significantly, however, in their responses at Levels 1 and 2 on the drug-related dilemmas. The boys' percentage of responses at Level 1 on the drug dilemmas was 33.33 whereas the girls' percentage was 21.43 (t = 2.32,

$p < .025$). At Level 2 on the drug dilemmas, the percentage of female responses was higher, equaling 60.71; the percentage of male responses was 46.97 (t = 2.46, $p < .01$).

Table 2
A Comparison of Moral Reasoning Scores for 21 Eighth-Grade Girls and 33 Boys on Two DIT Dilemmas and Two Drug-Related Dilemmas

Score levels	*M* for girls	*M* for boys	Unpaired *t*	*p*
Level 1				
DIT	7.62	10.79	-1.39	<.10
Drug	21.43	33.33	-2.32	<.03*
Level 2				
DIT	61.19	61.06	0.03	>.40
Drug	60.71	46.97	2.46	<.01*
Level 3				
DIT	28.57	24.39	0.94	<.38
Drug	15.00	14.24	0.19	>.40
Meaningless items				
DIT	2.62	3.79	-0.62	<.38
Drug	2.86	3.70	-0.51	<.38

Note. DIT = Defining Issues Test.
*Statistically significant

Discussion and Implications

This study resulted in two important findings: (a) middle school students seem to reason at higher stages of moral development on abstract social dilemmas than on drug-related dilemmas, and (b) adolescent girls seem to reason at higher stages of moral development on drug-related dilemmas than do adolescent boys. These findings have implications, first, for counselors' work in planning and implementing drug education programs and, second, for extending theory and research on moral reasoning. Both counselors and researchers should note, however, that this study consisted of only a small sample of eighth graders and that the outcomes should be viewed from the perspective of this important limitation.

Implications for School Counselors

Although this was not an intervention study, it has important implications for counselors' efforts in preventing drug abuse. There have been few effective educational methods in drug abuse prevention. Among the exceptions is Horan and Williams's (1982) assertion-training program, which succeeded in preventing drug abuse among junior high students. This program, when viewed in light of the cognitive-developmental findings of our study, may be regarded as having promoted growth in students' reasoning about drug use and as having helped students to be more autonomous, more individuated in their thinking, and therefore less apt to be victimized by the short-term attractiveness of the "forbidden fruit." These results suggest that it may be necessary for school counselors to provide developmental goals for drug programs, particularly goals that are tailored to promote growth in students' levels of reasoning.

One approach counselors can use to promote growth in students' levels of reasoning about drugs is through regular discussions of drug-related dilemmas with groups of students (see Appendix A for an example of a dilemma). The process of such discussion groups consists of these phases:

Phase 1: This phase consists of a few group sessions (2 to 3) incorporating such elements as get-acquainted activities, presentation of guidelines for behavior in group meetings, discussions about the nature and possible causes of drug abuse, and general discussions about dilemmas regarding drug use that adolescents may encounter. The counselor's role in these sessions is to provide information and to encourage active listening among all group participants.

Phase 2: This phase is made up of a few sessions (2 to 3) in which participants discuss and role play situations involving drug-related dilemmas described by the counselor. These dilemmas stimulate adolescent thinking about social pressures to use drugs. The counselors' role in these sessions is to listen actively, to encourage lively interaction and role play among the participants, and to ask open-ended questions that begin to promote higher levels of reasoning about drug use.

Phase 3: This phase consists of a few sessions (2 to 3) in which participants write their own drug-related dilemmas and discuss the dilemmas in the group. The role of the counselor in these sessions is again to encourage both discussion and role play and to ask open-ended questions that promote higher levels of reasoning about drug use. During this phase counselors also try to reinforce participants' motivation to ask questions that stimulate growth in reasoning.

Phase 4: This phase consists of final sessions (1 to 2) that bring closure to the group. Here the participants reflect on how their thinking about drug dilemmas has progressed. The role of the counselor in this phase is to paraphrase and summarize the participants' views on their progress. (We are currently studying this entire counseling process. Further information and an outline of group sessions may be obtained by writing the third author.)

This kind of counselor-led developmental group seems to have promise for drug abuse prevention. There may be a problem, however, of differing effects of such a developmental program on students (and in the case of this study, male students) who may be reasoning at significantly lower levels than many other members of the group. Hedin (1979) was the first to show that developmental programs may need to be differentiated more clearly according to the present level of the participants' thinking. A meta-analysis of earlier work (Sprinthall, 1981) showed that not all high school or college students, for instance, benefit equally from a general developmental intervention such as peer counseling. Hedin also found that some students (those at more "modest" levels of development) needed substantially more structured learning experiences than do those who are at average or above average stage levels for their age. Thies-Sprinthall (1984) found the same need for structure for adults, namely, in-service teachers. These studies suggest the need to follow Hunt's (1971) notion of a manageable mismatch between students' present levels of development and educational interventions. Too great a discrepancy may invite a developmental version of "ships passing in the night."

Implications for Theory and Research

In addition to having implications for the work of school counselors, this study also has implications for theory and research in moral development. Rest (1979) suggested that one of the major difficulties with early research in moral development was the lack of a complex model to specify the relationship between cognitive structure and content. He noted that the so-called "simple state model," denoting global, unified, qualitative, invariant, and contextual independent elements, was not adequate to encompass theory. Rest's suggestions, of course, were theoretical. Gilligan et al. (1979) proved his point empirically. They found systematic variation in levels of moral reasoning by content. When contemplating sexual dilemmas as opposed to standard dilemmas, the reasoning levels of both boys and girls in the sample fell. In other words, the study demonstrated an interaction between content (standard versus more personal) and the structure of cognition.

Our study demonstrates one outcome similar to that of the Gilligan et al. (1979) study and one that is different. The similarity is that our study showed an interaction between content and structure: The group scores declined overall between the standard and the drug-related dilemmas. This finding is also similar to that of another study (Joyner, 1984), which demonstrated systematic variation by content between standard dilemmas and personal dilemmas at the college level (i.e., the more personal the dilemmas the lower the scores). Yet, in another study, Tucker and Locke (1986) also found a systematic difference in the level of reasoning, based on how personal the dilemma was, by altering the ethnic identification of the protagonists in dilemmas. It seems possible, therefore, to conclude with some measure of cross validation that content and structure interact and that Rest is correct in calling for a more complex model of developmental growth in moral reasoning.

The second outcome of this study, a finding that differs from that of Gilligan et al. (1979), is the sex interaction. In that study, no sex differences were found. Both boys and girls exhibited a similar decline in reasoning. In our study, on the other hand, sex differences appeared. The boys' level of reasoning declined further than did the girls' level as the content of dilemmas changed from standard to drug related. The boys seemed more adversely affected by the change in content and were much more apt to choose preconventional reasons than were the girls. The boys and girls in the eighth grade may not be starting at the same cognitive level. Whether this is unique to early adolescence, of course, cannot be confirmed without at least some cross-sectional replication, perhaps using students in Grades 8, 11, and college. In any event, further research is needed regarding the content, structure, and sex interaction to elaborate on the basic understanding of stage variation and to determine possible causal explanations.

Conclusion

Advances in understanding cognitive development have important implications for school counselors' work in drug education and for the work of theorists and researchers who are studying moral reasoning. Our findings suggest that adolescents may reason at lower levels about drug use than they do about other issues and thus may be unable to make responsible decisions in drug-related matters. Prevention programs, therefore, should probably focus on drug issues rather than on peripheral, abstract matters of judgment. Our findings also indicate sex differences in reasoning that counselors need to consider in designing drug prevention programs and that researchers need to explore further. As counselors learn more about this important area from additional research, they should be able to design programs for drug abuse prevention that will be more effective than the educational programs currently available.

References

Carter, D. (1983, October 24). Why do kids use drugs and alcohol, and how do we help them stop? *PTA Today*, pp. 15–18.

Davidson, M. L., & Robbins, S. (1978). The reliability and validity of objective indices of moral development. *Applied Psychological Measurement, 2*, 391–403.

Gerler, E. R. (1986). Skills for adolescence: A new program for young teenagers. *Phi Delta Kappan, 67*, 436–439.

Gilligan, C., Kohlberg, L., Lerner, J., & Belenky, M. (1979). *Moral reasoning about sexual dilemmas*. Washington, DC: U.S. Commission on Obscenity and Pornography.

Glass, G. V., & Hopkins, K. D. (1984). *Statistical methods in education and psychology*. Englewood Cliffs, NJ: Prentice-Hall.

Hedin, D. (1979). *Teenage health education: An action learning program to promote development*. Unpublished doctoral dissertation, University of Minnesota, Minneapolis.

Horan, J. J., & Williams, J. M. (1982). Longitudinal study of assertion training as a drug abuse prevention strategy. *American Educational Research Journal, 19*, 341–351.

Hunt, D. (1971). *Matching models in education*. Toronto: Ontario Institute for the Study of Education.

Joyner, G. (1984). *Moral reasoning and discipline choices: Differences among students, faculty, and administration in a liberal arts college*. Unpublished doctoral dissertation, North Carolina State University, Raleigh.

Kohlberg, L. (1979). *Measuring moral judgment*. Worcester, MA: Clark University Press.

McEneaney, K., & Fishbein, P. (1983, February 8). Drug abuse among young adolescents. *PTA Today*, pp. 75–79.

Rest, J. (1979). *Manual for the Defining Issues Test*. Minneapolis: University of Minnesota.

Sprinthall, N. A. (1981). A new model for research in the service of guidance and counseling. *Personnel and Guidance Journal, 59*, 487–493.

Sprinthall, N. A., & Collins, W. A. (1984). *Adolescent psychology: A developmental view*. Reading, MA: Addison-Wesley.

Thies-Sprinthall, L. (1984). Promoting the developmental growth of supervising teachers: Theory, research, programs, and implications. *Journal of Teacher Education, 35*, 53–60.

Tucker, D. O., & Locke, D. C. (1986). The manipulation of race in moral dilemmas: Implications for moral education and human relations. *Educational and Psychological Research, 6*, 99–109.

Appendix A

A Sample Drug-Related Dilemma Used to Measure Students' Levels of Reasoning

It's Friday night. Don and his friend, Bart, are at their school's football game. They have been friends for many years, are very close, and go to all the football games together. Last week, Bart was elected president of a school club that Don has been trying to get into for the past year. Don now has a good chance of getting into the club with his friend as president. At halftime, some members of the club come up to Don and ask him and Bart to join them behind the stands for a "little partying." Don says, "Sure—great," because this is a chance to get to know these folks better and, perhaps, be asked to join their club. As they leave the stadium to go behind the stands, they pass a policeman. There are always two policemen on duty at the football games in case there is any trouble. When the group finds a quiet spot, everyone sits down and a couple of the kids pull out beers from their coat pockets. One guy rolls a joint and passes it and a beer to Bart, who takes a toke and chases it with beer. Bart then passes the joint to Don. In the past, Don has tried pot and kind of liked it, but he has tried to stay away from it because he does not want to get into any trouble.

Don's parents have made an agreement with him that they will pay all the cost of putting him through college if his grades are pretty good and he does not get into any serious trouble. Don has already picked the college he would like to attend. If he gets caught getting high, he will have broken the agreement with his parents. However, to refuse the joint from his best friend, Bart, in front of this group will hurt Don's chances of getting into the club. Bart asks, "What's wrong, Don? Come on! Relax! We're all friends here." If he does not take the joint and smoke it, his friendship with Bart will be seriously hurt. The club members will ignore Don and not include him in their group anymore.

What should Don do? (circle one): (a) should smoke the joint, (b) can't decide, (c) should not smoke the joint.

The selection of responses includes the following 12 options. (The student is asked to rate the importance of each on a 5-point scale—*great, much, some, little, no*):

1. Whether the policeman catches them
2. Whether Don breaks the agreement he willingly made with his parents
3. Whether Don's father will physically punish him
4. Whether Don recognizes the need for societal values that protect mental and physical health
5. Whether or not Don wants Bart's approval and acceptance
6. The overall factors of Don's mental images and concepts

7. Whether Don loses his new stereo tape deck, which his parents have just given him
8. Don's desire to have a good time
9. Whether the city's laws and the school's rules are going to be upheld
10. Whether or not Don is elected to the club
11. Whether Don likes to watch television
12. Whether it is Don's duty to obey the law to maintain order in the community, even though he would like to smoke marijuana

Helping Children of Alcoholic Parents: An Elementary School Program

Ruth B. Davis
Patricia D. Johnston
Lena DiCicco
Alan Orenstein

Most alcohol education programs are directed toward junior and senior high school students—adolescents beginning to drink regularly. Younger children, however, also have problems with alcohol. To illustrate, the following are some issues raised by second to sixth graders who kept journals for their alcohol education groups:

- Do you think when kids have a drink at the park that it is okay?
- Why do people drink and get mad?
- Why does my father drink?
- My mother drinks nearly all the time. My father put her in the hospital, but after she came out, she still drinks beer and comes home drunk. Can you tell me what to do?
- Sometimes I think: Am I going to drink when I grow up?
- When my father drinks, he says bad things to me. Then after, he's nice. Why does he do that to me and not to my sister? Is that because I care about him more, or does he dislike me more?
- I am an alcoholic. I drink beer. But I hate to drink. (age 7)
- I have felt I wanted to tell someone something, but I'm always afraid.
- When my father gets drunk, why do I feel responsible for him, and why do I think it's my fault?

These children were part of an experimental program in Somerville, Massachusetts, a predominantly Irish and Italian working-class community of 80,000, adjacent to Boston. School surveys show that the proportion of teenagers who drink heavily (at least once a week and large amounts per occasion) is about 50% higher than comparable national estimates, both for boys and girls. The community's response to these indicators of alcohol abuse must begin by addressing the concerns of its youngest citizens.

Alcohol education conducted by classroom teachers in the early primary grades is an important first step. Teachers can provide information, address fears, and make the entire topic of alcohol use less stigmatizing, so that children will be more open to discussion and advice in later years when they start to drink and hide their behavior from adults. In addition, teachers in Somerville find that when alcohol is discussed in the classroom, some children display such marked changes in behavior that it is clear that something is wrong. It was these reactions that led us to develop more therapeutically oriented alcohol education groups in elementary schools, which may help children cope with the emotional distress of living with family alcoholism and prevent them from using alcohol abusively in their teenage years or as adults.

Program Structure

The groups meet during school hours for 45-minute periods over 10 weeks. They have 8–12 participants with an age span of not more than 3 years. The sessions are co-led by a staff member at the school, often a guidance counselor, and a psychologist/educator experienced in providing treatment services to children of alcoholics. The meetings include games, movies, puppet shows, coloring books and storybooks, arts and crafts, and other activities adapted from *Decisions About Drinking* (CASPAR, 1978), the alcohol education curriculum used at all grade levels in Somerville.

The program recruits participants in a number of ways. Letters describing the program and seeking parental consent are sent to the families of children receiving special education services. Group leaders visit regular education classrooms, where they talk about the program and distribute permission forms to any child wishing to attend. Teachers, counselors, and parents make referrals, and children encourage their friends to join. Over 4 years, there have been 42 groups at four elementary schools, reaching about 480 children in grades 2 to 6. There currently is a waiting list of students who cannot be served because of limited resources.

About half of the children in the groups come from families in which a parent is alcoholic, although only a small number are in treatment. Of the participants in grades 4–6, 105 responded to a questionnaire at their first group meeting. This sample will be referred to throughout this article. Of this sample, 51% said "yes" to the statement: "Sometimes I think about how much my mother or father drinks." Because this is an unlikely response if the drinking were not disruptive, it can serve as a rough indicator of which children come from alcoholic homes.

In a community with many alcohol problems, when we allow children to volunteer for treatment, encourage parent referrals, and purposely select children with academic and behavior problems, we virtually ensure that many group members will be children of alcoholics, despite the fact that the groups are open to all. Also, because a wide range of children are attracted by the adult attention as well as by the topic, the groups are not stigmatizing for either the children who attend or, more importantly, their parents, whose permission is required and who might not want their child singled out because of the family's problems.

What Is Taught About Alcohol

Working with younger children highlights the goals of alcohol education. With adolescents, there is a tendency for teachers to emphasize the dangers of alcohol use to prevent misuse, although these scare tactics are rarely effective. The children in our groups are already afraid of alcohol. For example, at their first group meeting, 85% of our group members agree drinking alcohol is "bad"; 90% recognize that "nice people act not nice" when they drink too much; 80% report that most teenagers drink too much; 59% of the children of alcoholics and 42% of other group members believe that most adults drink too much; 36% feel that "people who drink always drink too much"; and under 5% say that drinking helps solve problems but 92% say that people who drink "cause problems for others."

It is not surprising that children of alcoholics hold negative attitudes toward alcohol. More surprising is that the other children in the groups are almost as negative. These feelings seem to reflect the ambivalence of adults. Americans drink "wet" but think "dry" and feel guilty about drinking, so even parents who drink moderately often feel they should teach their children that alcohol is evil. In addition, in a community with considerable alcohol abuse, parents are likely to explain to children that "bad" events—from fights to highway accidents to juvenile delinquency—are due to drinking. In other words, children are socialized to be afraid of alcohol, although this does not stop them from later alcohol abuse. Schools that simply reinforce this socialization are equally ineffective.

An alternative approach is to emphasize an individual's capacity to control alcohol. For example, because of their observations at home, many children equate drinking with drunkenness. They have trouble recognizing as drinking any intake of alcohol that does not have drunkenness as its goal, and they are unaware of the pleasurable feelings and increased sociability many people associate with controlled, moderate social drinking. When we teach these children that alcohol can be a normal and healthy part of family occasions and celebrations, we are showing them that drinking need not be disruptive and that people have a capacity to make decisions about how they drink. We do not want to reinforce the view that alcohol is a scary substance with overwhelming, uncontrollable, and evil effects.

A child who fears alcohol has something to "prove" when he or she enters a drinking situation. A child who has been taught either directly or indirectly by his or her parents that alcohol is an uncontrollable substance may fulfill the prophesy. Rather than scaring children away from misuse by emphasizing abstinence, the groups recognize that most children will eventually drink and try to provide social support for models of moderate drinking behavior. The goal is to make alcohol less emotionally charged—to remove some of the fears and apprehensions that may prevent children from acting responsibly when they enter drinking situations.

What Is Taught About Alcoholism

In addition to learning about alcohol, many of the children in our groups need to learn about alcoholism. Group activities are designed to reinforce a set of messages that are believed to be so basic that they should be communicated by any helping professional who is interacting with the child of an alcoholic.

First, *you are not alone*. Children of alcoholics need to learn that many other young people also live with alcoholism and that their guilt, shame, confusion, and anger at both their alcoholic parent and sober parent (who may ignore the child to attend to the alcoholic) are normal responses, not indications that something is "wrong" with them. Groups in which children can compare experiences are a powerful instrument for making this point.

Second, *your parents' drinking is not your fault*. Children often feel responsible for their parents' behavior. In part, this is because one or both parents may use normal childhood transgressions as an excuse or justification for drinking. In part, the inconsistent pattern of rewards and punishments in an alcoholic home make it difficult for children to know how to act, producing a pervasive sense that they must be doing *something* wrong. Among the group members, one of the most striking findings concerns the following item: "When children do something bad, it makes their parents drink." Although only 13% of other children agree to this statement, 39% of the children of alcoholics agree, suggesting that many understand their parents' drinking in a way that is damaging to their own self-images.

Third, *alcoholism is a disease*. Although adult opinions range from people who view alcoholism as an illness to those who view it as a mechanism for coping with emotional problems, children have a need to know that their alcoholic parent is not a bad person and that drinking is not a sign that their parent does not love them. Treating alcoholism as a disease explains the compulsive quality of their parent's drinking without blaming the parent or the child. It also interprets particular behaviors—for example, the personality changes that alcoholics undergo when drinking lead to an unpredictability that upsets children; the physical phenomenon of blacking-out leads to broken promises; and withdrawal symptoms are often interpreted by children as a terminal illness, unless they are provided with some basic information.

Fourth, *alcoholics can and do recover*. Children who see a mother or father passing out or being sick the next morning or falling down the stairs are terrified about their parent's safety and need some hope that things can be better. In addition, for children living with alcoholism, their own unhappiness is rarely a sufficient reason to seek help. They go out looking for a way to help their alcoholic, and only then come to recognize their own needs. These youngsters need to believe that recovery is possible, although they must also come to understand that neither their parent's drinking nor their parent's recovery is their responsibility, is under their control, or depends on their behavior.

Finally, *you are a person of worth who needs and deserves help for yourself.* Children must be taught that it is not "selfish" to look after their own needs, that they are as deserving of a good time as their friends, and that they have a right to protect themselves and their siblings in threatening situations. Many children of alcoholics will need continuing support. Hopefully, early contact with helping agents who directly confront rather than ignore the central importance of parental drinking will encourage more children to seek help when they need it.

A Prevention Issue

There is accumulating evidence that during childhood, the offspring of alcoholics exhibit a wide range of problems, including erratic school attendance and poor performance, psychosomatic symptoms, depression, and low measured self-esteem (Deutsch, 1982). When these symptoms, however, lead children to care-givers such as school, mental health, and probation personnel, as they often do, the focus of the intervention is rarely on the child's guilt, shame, and feelings of responsibility for the alcoholic's drinking. The child may deny there are drinking problems at home or may not understand the connection between these drinking problems and his or her feelings.

The counselor may feel that asking about drinking is too great an intrusion into the family or may feel powerless to do anything about the parent's drinking. Therefore, the counselor focuses on the child's current disruptive behavior without addressing the causes of this behavior, since these are seen as irremediable or requiring intervention with the entire family, which is often beyond the counselor's role. The groups attempt to help the child acknowledge and cope with how he or she feels about parental drinking. The group experience has shown that children can learn to feel better about themselves and attend to their own needs, whether or not their parent stops drinking.

There is also convincing evidence that as adults, the offspring of alcoholic parents are more likely (some say twice as likely) to become alcoholic, which raises the issue of what to advise about drinking (Woodside,1982). Some prevention specialists recommend that children of alcoholics be encouraged not to drink at all (O'Gorman, 1981). This runs the risk of increasing fear and apprehension about alcohol among the great majority who eventually will drink, which may increase their susceptibility to drinking problems.

In part, this issue depends on the weight assigned to different causal factors, on which there is little agreement among experts. If genetic inheritance could be shown to be the major factor in the transmission of alcoholism, this might make abstinence the best advice, since even moderate drinking behavior would lead to a high probability of alcoholism. If the key factors in the development of alcoholism, however, are social and cultural and reflect the models of drinking behavior and coping with unhappiness that children learn in their homes, then inculcating new models of moderate drinking behavior and providing information about the warning signs of alcoholism seem to be more crucial tasks.

For older children of alcoholic parents, it is certainly appropriate to suggest that responsible drinking behavior for them should involve greater caution than for others. For the younger children in the groups, who are already afraid of alcohol, it is emphasized that most people can drink moderately and responsibly, that alcohol abuse among teenagers is mostly volitional, and that the illness of alcoholism develops among a relatively small number of (mostly) middle-aged adults, usually after several years of insufficiently controlled drinking. In other words, while we acknowledge that their parents may be unable to control alcohol because they have developed the disease of alcoholism, we simultaneously emphasize the child's potential to control his or her own drinking as teenagers and as adults.

Program Results

Questionnaires given at the first and last group meetings illustrate the kinds of changes we hope to encourage. First, the facts taught about alcohol are retained. For example, although only 37% on the pretest knew that the amount of alcohol in a can of beer, a glass of wine, and a shot of whiskey are the same, 86% understood this equivalency by the posttest, while the percentage for those who believe that coffee can make someone less drunk dropped from 66% to 39%.

Second, alcohol comes to be perceived as more controllable. For example, the percentage for those who say that people who drink always drink too much dropped from 36% to 19%, while those who feel that drinking alcohol is bad dropped by 15%. Some of the ambivalence that children feel about their own alcohol use is also reduced. One item reads: "Is it okay for a child to have a drink at a family celebration, like a wedding or holiday?" Although 61% said "yes" at the program's start, 89% agreed by the end, with greater changes for children of alcoholic parents who enter more fearful about their own current and future alcohol use. Perhaps because it contradicts an observed reality for children living in families with alcoholism, there were only small changes in the number of those who reported that most adults and most teenagers drink too much.

Finally, there are changes in how children understand alcoholism. Recognition of alcoholism as an illness increased from 73% to 93%. Among children of alcoholics, the percentage for those who say that bad children make their parents drink declined from 39% to 24%. The willingness to admit that children sometimes think that parental drinking is their fault increased from 59% to 81%, with a larger increase among children of alcoholic parents.

Of course, these paper-and-pencil tests hardly begin to describe the growth evident in the groups, at least for some children. For example, a fourth-grade boy from a very disrupted alcoholic family heard us read *Pepper* aloud—a story about a dog who comes to understand that his master has not stopped loving him, although he sometimes forgets to feed him or let him out for walks. This happens because he is alcoholic and sick. When we asked the child to write in his journal about what made Pepper feel better, he wrote: "Knowing what the matter was."

A fourth-grade girl said she was tired because she stayed up every night until her father fell asleep, to keep him from drinking. After a long discussion as to whether this was her responsibility, the next week she said that she was not tired because it was her father's job to keep himself sober, not hers. Later that spring, her teacher stated that she did not know what had happened in the group, but the child was like a new person—more carefree and more able to interact with classmates. This girl has recently registered for her third elementary school group.

After the seventh meeting, during which the group saw a film about alcoholism's effect on families, a fifth-grade girl wrote in her journal that her father is alcoholic, that there is fighting and drinking at home, and that she has never told this to anyone in the world before. She asked us to promise that we would not tell anyone else. Her little sister, who had been in a previous group, had never mentioned her father's drinking, although we had suspected something was wrong because she was so withdrawn when alcoholism was mentioned. Two months later, the fifth grader excitedly approached one of the group leaders in the hallway to say that her father was in detoxification for the first time and was now going to get better. We shared in her happiness but reminded her that recovery was often a bumpy process, as had been discussed in the group. This was a message she seemed to understand and represents a type of support that could only have taken place because of her group participation. Now, a year later, both she and her sister have enrolled again in a group.

Finally, some teachers have increased their referrals to the groups because they say that children who have attended groups act out less frequently in class. This is being investigated more systematically.

Whatever its immediate impact, a 10-week group is likely to have limited effects. Traditionally, of course, it was felt that children of alcoholic parents could be helped only by "curing" their parent, and if services were provided for children at all, it was as part of the parent's recovery process (Woodside, 1982). Today, more programs are being designed in which the child is the primary client. These programs recognize that children need help, whether or not their parents are willing to accept help. The elementary school groups described in this article are viewed as part of the community's total response to alcoholism.

In Somerville, alcohol education is required in grades 7, 8, and 10 and encouraged at other grades. One-fourth of the teaching staff of 600 has undergone a 20-hour workshop to equip them to teach a five-to-ten-period alcohol education unit. For children in grades 7–12, there is an after-school alcohol education program in which groups are run by trained high-school-aged peer leaders. The mental health center runs groups for children of alcoholic parents who are enrolled in alcohol groups in addition to whatever other therapy they receive. We hope to establish a student assistant program in the high school, and Alateen groups remain an important community resource.

In other words, a network of services is emerging, structured somewhat differently at each age level, but all reiterating the same messages about alcohol use and alcoholism. As these "pieces" are put into place, children who receive support at one age level will be able to connect with similar services later and will know that help is available when they need it.

References

CASPAR. (1978). *Decisions about drinking.* Somerville, MA: CASPAR Alcohol Education Program.

Deutsch, C. (1982). *Broken bottles, broken dreams: Understanding and helping children of alcoholics.* New York: Columbia University, Teachers College Press.

O'Gorman, P. (1981). Prevention issues involving children of alcoholics. In *Services for children of alcoholics* (Research Monograph 4, DHHS Publication No. ADM 81–1007). Washington, DC: Government Printing Office.

Woodside, M. (1982). *Children of alcoholics.* Albany, NY: New York State Division of Alcoholism and Alcohol Abuse.

Chapter 3
Counseling Issues in a World of Drug Abuse

Issues for elementary school counselors to consider about a world of drug abuse:

1. Why have substance abuse prevention programs often failed?
2. Your school principal has asked you to coordinate the drug prevention program in your school. Describe the steps you would need to follow in developing the program. What resources would you use? How would you enlist the support of teachers, parents, students, and school administrators for your program?
3. What might be harmful about drug education that simply provides students with drug information?
4. You want to develop a support group for children of alcoholic parents. How would you identify the students? What are some of the major concerns you need to address in the group?
5. Write a drug abuse dilemma which children might face at school. How might you use this dilemma to improve children's decision-making about using drugs?
6. Several parents inform you of their concern about the prevalence of drugs in their neighborhood. What can you do to assist these parents?
7. How might elementary school counselors incorporate discussions of values into a drug education program?
8. During a group counseling session a student says that he drinks at home with his parents. How would you handle this situation in the group?
9. How can an elementary school counselor incorporate advertisements for alcoholic beverages into a drug prevention curriculum?
10. What steps should an elementary school counselor take upon learning that parents are using illegal drugs at home in the presence of a child?

CHAPTER 4

A WORLD OF CHILD ABUSE AND NEGLECT

Child abuse and neglect are rampant in our society. This chapter on abuse includes the article "A Profile of the Physical Abusers of Children" in which the authors conclude:

> The physical abuse of children is acknowledged as a serious problem in our society, one not clearly understood by school counselors. Educators recognize that children are our most valuable resource as a nation. When children are physically abused, emotional and psychological scars are created that may last a lifetime.

In spite of maltreatment, however, healthy development may occur, provided children are surrounded by strong environmental resources and positive interpersonal interactions. This chapter suggests ways that elementary school counselors can build a positive school environment for youngsters who suffer from abuse and neglect.

Chapter 4 presents a variety of articles to aid elementary school counselors in the area of child abuse prevention and treatment. The topics include:

1. Parent support groups to prevent physical abuse of children
2. Ways to identify potential child abusers
3. Problems and possibilities with preventive sexual abuse programs
4. Myths and realities of counseling child sexual abuse victims

The articles in Chapter 4 recognize that elementary school counselors cannot work alone in preventing and treating child abuse. Counselors, of course, need to develop close working relationships with social services and other community agencies that frequently advocate for victims of abuse and neglect. Counselors also need to work closely with teachers to help them thoroughly understand signs of abuse and to acquaint them with correct referral procedures. Counselors and teachers need to collaborate to insure that abused and neglected children experience a warm and caring environment at school. The elementary school classroom, in fact, may be the most stable setting neglected and abused children experience and may provide the empathy and positive regard needed to help children cope with their ordeal. Chapter 4 helps elementary school counselors become increasingly sensitive to the victims of abuse and to the need for effective counseling programs in this troublesome area.

Parent Support Groups to Prevent Child Abuse

C. Jerry Downing

New federal and state statutes requiring and aiding the reporting of abuse of children have contributed to an awareness of the problem (Griggs & Gale, 1977). The pressures of modern living have quite likely contributed to an increase in abusive parental behavior. The definition of child abuse has become more stringent and specific in recent years. There seems to be universal agreement among professional helpers that a child abuse problem exists in the United States today (Moore & McKee, 1979).

A new-found awareness of the extent of child abuse seems to be growing in the United States. Because child abuse is most often concealed, available statistics are uncertain; and it is difficult to determine if such behavior is actually increasing (Clarizio, Craig, & Mehrens, 1977). It is clear that a large number of children are victims of abuse. It is also evident that the professional helpers of children are almost desperate in their search for successful intervention techniques (Walters & Grusec, 1977). This article provides a description of the organization and training of a parent support group whose purpose is to help prevent child abuse in homes.

The parent support group was the brainchild of a nurse practitioner and pediatrician team, and was organized with the cooperation of school counselors, university personnel, church members, and the medical community. In their practice, the members of the medical team encountered many mothers under obvious stress. Many were mothers for the first time with little or no training in child rearing. Often these women were far from their own mothers or other support persons who could provide assistance. Other mothers presented evidence of stress related to their finances, unhappiness in their marriages, difficulties as a single parent, and personal physical concerns. The medical team became increasingly aware that although the children being seen in their office might not be abused as yet, the mothers were often very close to that point. These professionals believed many of these women would be aided by the support of a friend. This view was supported by some of the counseling literature (Slager-Jorne, 1978; Westcott, 1980). The nurse practitioner began to search for caring people who could act as friends of these women.

With the aid of a local clergyman, the nurse practitioner discovered a small group of women concerned about child abuse and willing to help. After some cursory organizational meetings, a parent support group was developed. The initial concept involved the introduction (by a medical team colleague) of a member from the support group to possibly abusive mothers. The support group members expected to limit their activities to being a friend on call. The early response was generally positive from the mothers; however, there was soon a near panic call from the support group: "We need some training."

Requesting training assistance, the support group contacted a local university faculty member who developed a training and supervision team containing a counselor educator, two school counselors, and the nurse practitioner. Together with the parent support group, they developed a training and supervision model.

Training Program

Format

The parent support group agreed on a series of weekly evening meetings, augmented with two all-day Saturday training sessions. The local school district provided a meeting place affording comfort and privacy.

Purpose

The training team believed it was critical that the parent support group establish clearly the purpose of the group and its support activities. Three aspects of this phase of training seem important. First, the determination of purpose needed to surface from the support group. Second, all members of the group needed to be in agreement as to the purpose. Finally, the specifics of the purpose needed to be defined in terms of member behavior.

Two evening meetings were spent in a problem-solving process to clarify the group's purpose. This process resulted in a purpose of establishing supportive friendships with the assigned mothers. Such friendship efforts would include the following: social contacts, listening actively to concerns, sharing general child care tips—experiences, and referral encouragement when concerns developed.

During the purpose-determination process, it became apparent to the training team that some attitudinal matters needed to be resolved. Some of the support group members viewed child abusers as highly disturbed people in need of intensive psychotherapy. Other members saw abusive mothers as persons in need of their pity. As a result, the first part of the training was devoted to assisting the parent support group members in becoming aware of their own attitudes toward child abusers.

Attitudes

The first step in this training phase involved the member exposure to some of the professional literature related to child abuse. The support group devoured the available literature related to child abuse, child rearing, and relationship development. Bibliotherapy in counseling has proven helpful in assisting abused children understand their ideas and feelings about themselves (Watson, 1980). In this situation, the literature seemed to be of assistance to helpers as well.

A structured group activity (Pfeiffer & Jones, 1975) was used to identify strongly held attitudes regarding child abusers. The results of this exercise indicated a variety of attitudes held by the support group members. These were summarized as follows:

- Child abusers are just people like us.
- Child abusers have specific problems or needs.
- Child abusers should be objects of our sympathy.
- Child abusers are repulsive animals.

This identification of attitudes exercise led to some active discussion of causes of child abuse. The training team members were able to contribute information and experiences from their professional backgrounds. Of greater importance was the fact that the support group members shared a surprising understanding of the antecedents of abuse. All members of the support group had children of their own. All had experienced examples of severe stress related to their children. The lengthy discussion led to considerable insight into the nature of child abuse.

The support group developed a series of guidelines as a result of this discussion:

1. We will try to remember that the people we seek to help are just people like us.
2. Our task is not to solve the helpees' problems.
3. Everyone has some strength—look for it.
4. People approaching child abuse do not need our pity—they need a friend!

As the guidelines developed, group members readily identified some skill needs. The remainder of this phase of training was devoted to these minds.

Specific Skills

Listening skills were identified as a critical to a support group member. The training team used the "pattern for helping" model as presented by Gazda

(1973). Role plays, audio- and videotapes, and demonstrations were used in teaching listening skills. By far the most effective material for this group was the genuine child-rearing concerns that support group members shared with one another as they practiced their listening skills. The women seemed to have an unending supply of concerns and shared them openly.

The major stumbling block in this phase of the training had to do with problem solving. The support group members genuinely wanted to help and as a result were intent on finding solutions to the problems presented by the potentially abusive mothers. Again, the work with actual child-rearing concerns of the helpers aided with this hurdle. The support group soon realized that *they* did not need or want someone else's answer to their own problems. They wanted an opportunity to *process* the concern. As a result, they were better able to *help* the mothers seek answers of their own.

Referral sources and appropriate procedures for making referrals were other major training points. All support group members received a directory of helping service personnel in the community. The group became familiar with the directory and the services available to people in need.

For this group, the desired course of referral was through the nurse practitioner and physicians. It was assumed, however, that situations would arise in which this referral chain could not be used. The suggested technique involved a process of listening carefully to stated needs of the helpee and reflecting those needs. When the helpee clearly identified a need beyond his or her capacity for resolution, the helper learned to guide him or her in a search through the directory.

The final phase of the training involved a discussion of handling confidential information. The support group was identified as a professional colleague group for purposes of staffing. Procedures for protection of the identity of mothers to be helped were discussed and agreed upon. Because so much personal data had been shared by the group members, they could readily see the value of confidentiality.

Supervision

The key to this plan for a parent support group involved ongoing supervision. Because the nurse practitioner would make the initial introduction of helper to helpee, she was seen as the logical supervisor. Support group members checked in with the nurse practitioner on a weekly basis when working with a helpee. These contacts were usually telephone calls to brief the nurse on the status of the helping relationship.

When more detailed discussion was needed, the helper arranged to have a bag lunch meeting with the nurse practitioner in the nurse's office. This procedure was developed as least disruptive to the office schedule, was the most readily available time, and allowed for professional confidentiality.

In addition, the parent support group asked to have a monthly supervision group meeting. These were held in members' homes on evenings when other family members would not be present. The nurse practitioner was the responsible supervisor, but usually included one or more of the school counselors in the groups.

Several benefits resulted from these sessions. First, they served a support function for the helpers. Second, they provided an excellent model for sharing case (identity protected) experience. Finally, they provided an opportunity for ongoing training activities for the support group members.

Case Example

The following case summary is presented as an example of the work being done by support group members. The parent in this example is fictitious; the concerns of the parent are taken from actual cases. This example is typical of the type of assistance the support group provides for potentially abusive parents.

Mrs. Jones sought services from the medical team shortly after the birth of her first child. Because of an upper respiratory infection, she brought her 3–week old infant to see one of the pediatricians. It became apparent that Mrs. Jones was experiencing a great deal of stress in her efforts to care for the child. The illness had increased the tension between mother and child, if for no other reason than sleep deprivation.

The nurse practitioner met with Mrs. Jones to assist her with some home care procedures. In this interview, some details of the Jones's family system were shared. The couple had moved to this community just three months before the birth of their baby. Mrs. Jones had made very few friends in the area. Mr. Jones's career caused him to be away from home an average of two nights per week. He had told his wife that he was not into babies and he expected her to take care of the infant.

To add to Mrs. Jones's problems, both sets of grandparents lived approximately 400 miles away. After the infant had been home for one week, the maternal grandmother returned to her home and Mrs. Jones was on her own.

In the opinion of the nurse practitioner, Mrs. Jones was at risk of becoming an abusive mother. The frustration levels being experienced by the mother were becoming intolerable. The mothers' physical health was questionable, and her energy level was dangerously low.

At this point, the nurse introduced Mrs. Jones to Judy, a parent support group member. For several weeks, Judy visited with Mrs. Jones on a regular basis, at least two to three times weekly. Judy was also available for telephone conversations when needed. During this time these women became good friends. By exhibiting good listening skills, Judy was able to help Mrs. Jones vent some of her frustration, anger, and resentment. From her own experience as a mother, Judy helped Mrs. Jones acquire some effective child care procedures. Judy was also verbally active, noting the positive growth of the baby. This resulted in some reinforcement for the mother's efforts.

After approximately three months, Judy introduced Mrs. Jones to a group of women with a common interest activity. Mrs. Jones was also provided assistance in locating baby-sitting help.

Judy continued to be available for friendly visits and for telephone conversations with Mrs. Jones. Their contact, however, has gradually been reduced as Mrs. Jones has found other friends more nearly her own age.

Summary

With the cooperation of a nurse practitioner, physicians, school counselors, and interested community members, a parent support group for potentially abusive parents was established to aid in preventing child abuse. A training program was offered and continuing supervision provided. Indicators from helpers and helpees suggest this to be an effective, preventive strategy to deal with the plaguing problem of child abuse.

References

Clarizio, H. F., Craig, R. C., & Mehrens, W. A. (1977). *Contemporary issues in educational psychology*. Boston: Allyn & Bacon.

Gazda, G. A. (1973). *Human relations development*. Boston: Allyn & Bacon.

Griggs, S. A., & Gale, P. (1977). The abused child: Focus for counselors. *Elementary School Guidance and Counseling*, *2*, 187–196.

Moore, H. B., & McKee, J. E. (1976). Child abuse and neglect: The contemporary counselor in conflict. *School Counselor*, *26*, 293–298.

Pfeiffer, J. W., & Jones, J. E. (1975). *A handbook of structural experiences for human relations training: Vol. V.* La Jolla, CA: University Associates.

Slager-Jorne, P. (1978). Counseling sexually abused children. *Personnel and Guidance Journal*, *57*, 103–105.

Walters, G. C., & Grusec, J. E. (1977). *Punishment*. San Francisco: Freeman & Co.

Watson, J. J. (1980). Bibliotherapy for abused children. *School Counselor*, *27*, 204–209.

Westcott, N. A. (1980). Sexually abused children: A special clientele for school counselors. *School Counselor*, *27*, 198–203.

A Profile of the Physical Abusers of Children

Pat Alford
Don Martin
Maggie Martin

The physical abuse of children is acknowledged as a serious problem in our society, one not clearly understood by school counselors. Educators recognize that children are our most valuable resource as a nation. When children are physically abused, emotional and psychological scars are created that may last a lifetime (Wilson, Thomas, & Schuette, 1983). It takes a conscious effort seasoned with insight and proper treatment for an abused child to grow up to be an effective parent. Thus, if violence occurs in the home, it is likely to have a major impact on the subsequent behavior of a child.

Statistics regarding child abuse are alarming. In 1978, approximately 200,000 cases of suspected child abuse and neglect were reported in America (Kempe & Kempe, 1979). The Department of Health, Education, and Welfare estimated that a more realistic figure would exceed 1 million cases per year (Camblin & Prout, 1983; Newberger, 1982). More recent estimates range from 60,000 to 4 million cases of child abuse per year (Williams & Money, 1980). The difficulty in determining the actual number of abuse cases lies in the fact that the majority of cases remain unreported. It is believed that reported cases represent only the tip of the problem (Ebeling & Hill, 1975). Professionals, such as school and medical personnel, social workers, and law enforcement officers, are reluctant to report suspected abuse. Many professionals tend to report cases as accidental; they rely on someone else who encounters the family at a later date to be more responsible than they have been. Other officials simply ignore the evidence, hoping the problem will cure itself (Helfer & Kempe, 1976).

Unfortunately many known cases proceed unchecked until the tragedy is too blatant to ignore (Ebeling & Hill, 1975). In 1981, 2,000 children were reported to have died as a direct result of parental abuse or neglect (Newberger, 1982). Buchanan and Oliver (1977) stated their belief that violence-induced handicaps should be recognized as a major cause of mental malfunctioning. It has been estimated that 25% to 30% of abused children who survive have neurological damage directly related to the abuse (Williams & Money, 1980). Buchanan and Oliver (1977) suggested that at least one-fourth of harshly attacked children become intellectually impaired, rendering them subnormal as a consequence of the battering they received.

Demographic Characteristics

Although researchers have attempted to ascertain a specific profile of the child abuser, few would argue that any one trait is inherent in this population (Bowers, 1978/1979; Kertzman, 1978/1980; Milner & Ayoub, 1980; Rosen, 1979). It seems, rather, that there are a number of stimuli frequently active within an abusive parent. The precise combinations of these factors seem to vary, and the level to which any one element contributes to the abusive pattern is inconsistent and peculiar to each situation (Helfer & Kempe, 1976).

In understanding the principal components that constitute and define the characteristics of child abusers, however, the following are especially important: (a) the majority are married adults who are living together at the time of the abuse; (b) the parents tend to marry young; (c) marital conflict is common to them; (d) a high proportion of abused children were conceived before their parents' marriage; (e) abusive parents were probably mistreated by their parents; (f) the parents are often isolated; (g) the average age of an abusive mother is 26; (h) the average age of an abusive father is 30; (i) studies yield conflicting results concerning which parent is more likely to be the active abuser; (j) the most serious injuries are inflicted by the mother; (k) the majority of abuse occurs in homes of low socioeconomic status; (l) regardless of the family's social standing, abusive families frequently experience financial distress; (m) the use of alcohol or drugs by the parents is often an agent involved in an abusive episode; and (n) the most common instrument of abuse is a hairbrush (Blumberg, 1980; Justice & Justice, 1976; Kaiser, 1977).

Violence Breeds Violence

An important trait associated with child abusers is that they were themselves victims of negative childhood experiences (McKee & Robertson, 1975). Researchers indicate that these experiences can be psychologically detrimental to the child (Rosen, 1979; Kaiser, 1977).

Child abusers may have strong, conscious desires to be good parents, but often find themselves reliving their own childhood while performing the cruel role of the parent (Kempe, Silverman, Steele, Droegemueller, & Silver, 1962). This may seem paradoxical. It could be speculated that they would rather sympathize with the abused child and henceforth vow never to put their own children through the same anguish.

The ability of formerly abused children to abuse their own children may be partly explained by the processes occurring within the abused children during the assaults. When pain is inflicted on children by their parents and when the terrifying punishment is accompanied by an angry voice and facial expression, the children learn to fear the parent and attempt to avoid repetition of the incident that triggered the violent outburst. These children are faced with an overwhelming dilemma. They must look for care and support from the same person who victimized them.

It is hypothesized (Helfer & Kempe, 1976) that helpless children who are unable to adequately protect themselves from their oppressors identify with their attackers. By mentally assuming the role of aggressor rather than victim, they condone and incorporate the values of the victimizer into their own personality (Helfer & Kempe, 1976; Martin & Rodeheffer, 1976). The child assumes the values of an inconsistent, hostile adult. When the victims internalize their harasser's value system, they see themselves as the guilty parties who provoked the justifiable punishment. As parents, the victims conceive of their own children as naughty and deserving of severe forms of discipline (Ebeling & Hill, 1975). Indeed, investigators tend to believe that the type of care that parents received in their childhood is the most consistent predictor of how those parents will treat their children and whether the abuse will be generational in nature (Belskey, 1980).

Unrealistic Expectations of Appropriate Behavior

In many cases, abusive parents tried desperately as children to fulfill the impossible regimen imposed by their parents. Likewise, these parents tended to set unreasonable standards for their child's behavior, expecting the child to perform tasks inconsistent with normal development. For instance, a parent might tell a 6-year-old to wash and iron the family's laundry or command children to conduct themselves in ways inappropriate to their physical capabilities, such as requiring a 5-year-old to sit perfectly still watching television for 6 hours. Frequently, abusive parents are simply ignorant of what constitutes appropriate behavior in relation to normal development (Helfer & Kempe, 1976; McKee & Robertson, 1975). They do not look on children as developing human beings but instead as persons with fully integrated personalities, capable of understanding parental wishes and carrying them out.

Role-Reversal Phenomenon

Numerous clinicians have suggested that abusive parents yearn for children whom they fantasize will love and care for them, making up for all the emotional needs they were deprived of in their own childhood (Ebeling & Hill,

1975; Gaines, Sandgrund, Green, & Power, 1978). If children never grow beyond this symbiotic relationship or if they are always expected to fulfill the parasitic needs of others and never have their own needs for dependency gratified, they will incessantly seek out someone to respond to their needs. All too often, the one looked on as a "savior" by abusive parents is a child.

Abusive parents may view their child as a "transference object," a substitute for parental nurturance (Spinetta & Rigler, 1972). What could be more natural than for such parents to look to their own child for the same need fulfillment they were expected to provide their parents (Blumberg, 1980). With the birth of a child, this destructive role reversal is accomplished and the cycle continues.

Another genre of role reversal occurs when parents perceive themselves as victims and the child as villain. The parents imagine that the child is big and powerful and that they are weak and helpless. The abusive parent views the child as a culprit who provokes the incident by soiling diapers, spilling food, or willfully frustrating the parent. The parents rationalize their abuse and believe that if only the children would behave, they would not be forced to take the extreme measure of physical assault (Ebeling & Hill, 1975).

Perfectionism and Feelings of Inadequacy

Abusive parents will not tolerate anything less than precise compliance from their children. As children, these parents were expected to be perfect in a milieu that had changing definitions of what perfection meant. They were required to anticipate parental needs and whims, making sure the parent's desires were satisfied (Rosen, 1979). Abused children are supposed to conform entirely to the parent's wishes in a world infected with violent outbursts and unknown rules about everything (Cameronchild, 1978). Even an accident such as breaking an object may be misunderstood and met with blows (Belskey, 1980). Because the caretakers often expect the impossible from their children, no one can ever measure up to what is demanded of them. These youngsters are criticized, rejected, and made to feel like worthless failures (Rosen, 1979). They develop low self-esteem and display inadequate and insecure feelings (Ebeling & Hill, 1975; Kinard, 1978/1980).

Parental models are also very insecure. In 29% of the child abuse cases investigated for a recent study, one or both parents had attempted suicide (Roberts & Hawton, 1980). Abusive parents make more repeated suicide attempts within 1 year after they attempt suicide than do others of the same age who attempt suicide.

To compensate for their poor self-concepts, child abusers hope to have a child of their own who will be so perfect and supportive that they will feel better about themselves. The children are incapable of achieving the unrealistic prerequisites they inherit from birth, so the dejected parents take out the inevitable disappointments and anger on the children. To raise their self-esteem, the parents are driven to blame someone else for personal inadequacies. This "someone" is often their own child, who is blamed constantly for not being perfect. The child becomes the established scapegoat in the family (Helfer & Kempe, 1976).

Child abusers are prone to expect perfection from themselves as well as their children. Frequently, the parent demands rigid standards of neatness and order (Derdeyn, 1977). Because of the parents' penchant for faultlessness and their haunting feelings of personal inadequacy, even a child's crying can be misinterpreted as an accusation of poor parenting skills.

Negative Concept of the Child

Abusive parents may see their child as a demanding, scheming, willful ingrate. Sometimes the seed for this negative concept is planted even before birth. The mother may be upset about an unplanned pregnancy or she may be carrying a child that is the product of a rape or an adulterous liaison (Guyer, 1979).

After the birth, the child may be despised because of illegitimacy or may be "type cast" if he or she resembles someone repulsive to one of the parents (Kempe & Kempe, 1978). Children may be born with a congenital disease or a mental or physical handicap, features that arouse intolerable anxiety in the parents, who promptly alienate themselves emotionally from the child. A financial crisis may begin life for the child in a negative fashion (Cameronchild, 1978).

Shortly after birth, the child may be presumed to be the source of marital conflict, especially when one spouse believes the child is depriving this person of the other's attention (Kempe & Kempe, 1978). As children grow older, parents may ascertain that they have behavioral problems or are intentionally splitting the parents and for these things they must pay dearly, regardless of how erroneous the parents' assumptions may be (Charles, 1979/1980; Kempe & Kempe, 1978).

Sanctioning of Corporal Punishment

The Department of Health, Education, and Welfare in 1975 reported that abusive parents have a righteous belief in the intrinsic value of harsh physical punishments as an avenue to prevent the spoiling of children (Williams &

Money, 1980). Many abusers actually conclude that children deserve a beating for their misdeeds (Ebeling & Hill, 1975). It is as if the parent takes the social sanction of corporal punishment as a license to abuse (Blumberg, 1980). Frequently, abusive parents experience an unreasonable fear of overindulging their children. Any action acknowledged as a glimmer of sinfulness in the child represents a trend toward corruption and must be dealt with swiftly and often physically (Kempe & Kempe, 1978).

Abusive parents often implement severe physical punishments under the guise of discipline. Discipline, however, is designed to teach a child a moral lesson or an important principle; abuse, on the other hand, is a means of releasing aggressive tension (Ebeling & Hill, 1975).

The issue of power and control is a vital ingredient in an abusive system (Ebeling & Hill, 1975). Defiance will not be tolerated (Belskey, 1980). The parents are willing to go to almost any length to ensure absolute obedience from their children. Furthermore, they convince themselves that it is their duty to physically reprimand their children, even if it entails almost killing the child (Belskey, 1980). To them, physical punishment seems to be an appropriate and valuable medium for solving conflicts (Blumberg, 1980).

In addition, a particular occasion of explosive aggression is often the culmination of a long period of tension (Williams & Money, 1980). Justice and Justice (1976) argued that life crisis is the chief stressor in abuse cases. Others have suggested that internal conflict, unhappiness, and a strong dislike of self create such an inward battleground than any small incident is liable to ignite the internal dynamite (Belskey, 1980). Still others have intimated that financial difficulties, illness, marital discord, unemployment, and a lack of immediate support by social service agencies are responsible for provoking abuse (Ebeling & Hill, 1975; Williams & Money, 1980).

Whatever the particular stressors may be, the actual circumstances of uncontrolled physical violence are often symbolic of displaced aggression. The parent is unable to confront a person or situation and thus liberates his or her rage by hitting a child.

Implications for School Counselors

Understanding the psychological components of the child abuser and the effects on the child can be very helpful for the school counselor. Although counselors do not interact with parents as much as they do with children, it is important to look for clues in parents if child abuse is suspected or to follow up on parental statements or actions that may indicate abuse. Possibly more important is being aware of the subtle behaviors that "borderline" children may exhibit, including consistent, self-defeating statements, withdrawal, the obsessive need for affection, or behaviors that may not be obvious unless one takes time to investigate.

Because school personnel report only 15% of all abuse referrals on a national level (Camblin & Prout, 1983), we hope that counselors fail to notice abuse because of a lack of knowledge rather than a deliberate avoidance of the problem. In support of this hypothesis, Camblin & Prout (1983) indicated that states that reported a high number of abuse cases had a more comprehensive child abuse informational program in their schools than did other less responsive states.

The counseling literature has included discussions regarding the concern of mental health officials that school personnel are only reporting obvious cases of abuse and are not making a conscientious effort in the area (Broadhurst, 1978; Camblin & Prout, 1983). Conversely, in our workshops and discussions with school personnel, we have found that many school counselors feel inadequate regarding their knowledge of child abuse and also do not believe that human service agencies are responsive to their needs or to those of the child when abuse is reported. If human service agencies and school personnel were more cooperative in both their efforts and their training programs, perhaps some of these problems could be eliminated.

We have found that in addition to reporting suspected child abuse and referring cases to the appropriate sources, school counselors can be very helpful in the prevention and treatment of abuse within the school setting. Some examples of preventive measures that we have seen as effective include:

1. Development of programs for students can span a broad spectrum—from informal discussions in the classroom to group counseling sessions with abused children.
2. Educational programs about child abuse can be helpful to students. If counselors openly share their concerns in this area, students and faculty members may feel more comfortable about sharing any difficulties they are experiencing. Sometimes knowing a person is interested enables a child to share difficult problems. Recent media and video materials can be helpful in this area.
3. Providing inservice programs to teachers and administrators can help individuals become more cognizant in this area. Because child abuse can be "psychologically" painful for the teacher, counselors can help teachers better cope with this dilemma. Special programs developed for parents can also be valuable. Community support can be vital to successfully working with abused children. In our local school district, for example, the theater department of the university developed a play centered on child abuse and incest. It has been well received and provides information in a nonthreatening manner. In addition, the

authors have helped both mental health and school counselors to develop an assertiveness training and awareness program. Children are taught how to be assertive rather than aggressive and what they can do or who they can talk to about problems if they are being abused.
4. School counselors need to constantly upgrade their skills if they are to be effective in an educational system. Courses in marriage and family processes, parenting, and child development are but a few that can be of critical value to counselors seeking to understand abusive families.

This article is not designed to explore in detail the various therapeutic approaches used with abusive families. Some school counselors, however, have been successful in working with this type of situation by using a family therapy or systems approach. The counselor's role in this situation is to teach the parents and children new ways of relating and re-educating the parents to assume a more normal parental role. In most cases, however, the physically abusive family system needs structured and intensive psychotherapy, and referral to a more appropriately trained professional is the recommended course of action.

References

Belskey, J. (1980). Child maltreatment, an ecological integration. *American Psychologist, 35*, 320–335.
Blumberg, M. L. (1980). The abusing mother—Criminal, psychopath, or victim of circumstances. *American Journal of Psychotherapy, 34*, 351–361.
Bowers, J. E. (1978). Stress and physical and verbal aggression in families and the incidence of acute physical illness in preschool children (Doctoral dissertation, Columbia University Teachers College, 1979). *Dissertation Abstracts International, 39*, 2224B.
Broadhurst, D. (1978, January–February). What schools are doing about child abuse and neglect. *Children Today*, pp. 22–36.
Buchanan, A., & Oliver, J. E. (1977). Abuse and neglect as a cause of mental retardation. *British Journal of Psychiatry, 131*, 458–467.
Camblin, L., & Prout, H. (1983). School counselors and the reporting of child abuse: A survey of state laws and practices. *School Counselor, 30*, 358–367.
Cameronchild, J. (1978). An autobiography of violence. *Child Abuse and Neglect: The International Journal, 2*, 139–149.
Charles, G. (1979). Parental expectations and attitudes about child bearing in high-risk vs. low-risk abuse families (Doctoral dissertation, University of Southern California, 1980). *Dissertation Abstracts International, 39*, 3537B.
Derdeyn, A. P. (1977). A case for permanent foster placement of dependent, neglected, and abused children. *American Journal of Orthopsychiatry, 47*, 604–614.

Ebeling, N. B., & Hill, D. A. (1975). *Child abuse: Intervention and treatment.* Acton, MA: Publishing Sciences Group.

Gaines, R., Sandgrund, A., Green, A. H. , & Power, E. (1978). Psychological factors in child maltreatment: A multivariate study of abusing, neglecting, and normal mothers. *Journal of Abnormal Psychology, 97*, 531–540.

Gil, D. G. (1977). Child abuse: Levels of manifestation, causal dimensions, and primary prevention. *Victimology: An International Journal, 2*, 186–194.

Guyer, M. J. (1979). The consciously rejected child: Legal and social issues. *Psychiatry, 42*, 338–350.

Helfer, R. E., & Kempe, H. C. (1976). *Child abuse and neglect.* Cambridge, MA: Ballinger.

Justice, B., & Justice, R. (1976). *The abusing family.* New York: Human Sciences Press.

Kaiser, G. (1977). Child abuse in West Germany. *Victimology: An International Journal, 2*, 294–306.

Kempe, R. S., & Kempe, C. H. (1978). *Child abuse.* Cambridge, MA: Harvard University Press.

Kempe, R. S., & Kempe, C. H. (1979). *Child abuse.* London: Fontana Open Books.

Kempe, C. H., Silverman, F. N., Steele, B. F., Droegemueller, W., & Silver, H. K. (1962). The battered child syndrome. *Journal of the American Medical Association, 181*, 17–24.

Kertzman, D. (1978). Dependency, frustration, tolerance, and impulse control in child-abusers (Doctoral dissertation, State University of New York at Buffalo, 1980). *Dissertation Abstracts International, 34*, 1484B.

Kinard, E. M. (1978). Emotional development in physically abused children: A study of self-concept and aggression (Doctoral dissertation, Brandeis University, 1980). *Dissertation Abstracts International, 39*, 2965B.

Lewis, K. (1977). Child abuse: Causes, effect, and prevention. *Victimology: An International Journal, 2*, 337–342.

Martin, H. P., & Rodeheffer, M. A. (1976). The psychological impact of abuse on children. *Journal of Pediatric Psychology, 1*, 12–15.

McKee, M., & Robertson, I. (1975). *Social problems.* New York: Random House.

Milner, J. S., & Ayoub, C. (1980). Evaluation of "at risk" parents using the child abuse potential inventory. *Journal of Psychology, 36*, 875–884.

Newberger, E. H. (1982). *Child abuse and neglect: Toward a firmer foundation for practice and policy.* Washington, DC: Department of Health, Education, and Welfare, Subcommittee on Child Development and Human Development.

Roberts, J., & Hawton, K. (1980). Child abuse and attempted suicide. *British Journal of Psychiatry, 137*, 312–319.

Rosen, B. (1979). Interpersonal values among child-abusive women. *Psychological Reports, 45*, 819–822.

Spinetta, J. J., & Rigler, D. (1972). The child-abusing parent: A psychological review. *Psychological Bulletin, 77*, 296–304.

Williams, G. J., & Money, J. (1980). *Traumatic abuse and neglect of children at home*. Baltimore: Johns Hopkins University Press.

Wilson, J., Thomas, D., & Schuette, L. (1983). Survey of counselors on identifying and reporting causes of child abuse. *School Counselor, 30*, 299–305.

A Preventative Approach to Child Sexual Abuse

Ann Vernon
Jill Hay

Although school counselors are becoming more aware of the need to help protect children from sexual assault, their role has focused primarily on identification, reporting, or crisis intervention (Anderson & Griffin, 1981; Colao & Hosansky, 1983). Although the significance of these roles must not be discounted, Colao and Hosansky (1983), Fontana (1982), and Hitchcock and Young (1986) advocated a preventative approach to sexual abuse, stressing the importance of equipping children to deal more effectively with issues of this nature that they may be forced to confront.

According to Hay and Struck (1986), the goals of a preventative sexual abuse curriculum include sensitizing children to issues involving touch, feelings about sexual assault, assault by strangers as well as persons known to the child, and strategies for protecting oneself and coping with the situation. Harms and James (1982) cited the need for preventative sexual abuse programs that address self-protective aspects as well as broader issues related to assault. Hitchcock and Young (1986) noted that "elementary school counselors are in a unique position to develop and provide such prevention programs" (pp. 201–202).

In this article we describe a sexual abuse prevention program that we developed and implemented. The program, designed for children in Grades 1 through 6 and implemented the first year in Grades 2, 4, and 6, included lessons on six different components of sexual abuse.

Implementation Process

This program was specifically developed for a small rural district in Iowa, Belle Plaine Community School. The need for such a program was felt by the second author, an elementary counselor who asked to counsel several children who had been sexually assaulted. In working with these children she was concerned about how to help them work through this traumatic experience and believed that if they had been aware of different kinds of touch, how to say no, or their right to protect their bodies, they might not have been sexually abused.

In following up on this concern, the elementary counselor discovered that if any prevention was occurring in the school, it was more of a "stranger-danger" approach and not perceived to be highly effective. She requested a meeting with the principal and teachers to discuss further the perceived problem and possible interventions. The counselor presented information on child sexual abuse as a significant problem (Fontana, 1982); the physical, emotional, and behavioral indicators of abuse (Landau, 1983; Williams, 1981); myths about the offender always being a stranger (Williams, 1981); and the psychological harm to victims (James & Nasjleti, 1983). Because several children in the district had been assaulted, the information seemed relevant, and faculty and administration agreed that some type of prevention program should be implemented. The counselor was advised to pursue various possibilities.

The elementary counselor reviewed several existing programs offered by community agencies. None of these programs were adopted for use because of one or more of the following disadvantages: (a) cost was prohibitive, (b) the focus was too narrow and failed to address broader issues such as self-acceptance and feelings, and (c) most consisted of a one-time-only presentation with little discussion or follow-up.

Additionally, the counselor was concerned about an outside resource person who had no rapport with the children coming into the school to discuss sexual abuse issues. She believed that she could present the program more effectively and decided to develop her own program, which could complement the existing affective education program as well as address sexual abuse specifically.

Before implementation, a letter was sent to all parents discussing the rationale for a sexual abuse prevention program and describing the specific components, lessons, and reinforcement ideas for home use. Because of the rapport the counselor had established with the children as well as parents and the positive support of the elementary school counseling program, no concerns were raised by the parents.

Program Components

To develop the program, the first author contacted the second author at the university. Together we reviewed the sexual abuse literature and analyzed the myriad of associated topics and implications for children. Upon completion of this task, we determined that the areas commonly identified as essential components included awareness of body parts and touch, decision-making (coping) strategies, assertive communication skills, and people who can offer help. In addition, we believed there was a need to include something on awareness and expression of feelings associated with sexual abuse and issues of acceptance of self and others (i.e., offender).

Self-Acceptance

Although this topic seems to be lacking in preventative sexual assault programs, we believed that the issue of accepting oneself as worthwhile after the assault needed to be addressed. Because of the guilt and self-blame resulting from assault, it seemed important to emphasize that the child is still a worthwhile person despite the abuse. As Colao and Hosansky (1983) pointed out, children who feel good about themselves find it easier to stand up for themselves; thus an emphasis on general self-esteem topics in a sexual abuse program is likewise relevant. In addition, some emphasis on the worth of the offender is important; the perpetrator is usually a confused person with problems. This understanding may help children deal with their own confused or negative feelings toward the offender in a more realistic way, especially if the offender is a significant other.

Feelings

In abusive situations, children are likely to experience fear, sadness, anger, guilt, shame, confusion, or helplessness and powerlessness (Kraizer, 1985). Because of these overwhelming feelings, abuse victims and children in general need to develop feeling vocabularies, learn that negative feelings are okay and natural, learn how to express feelings appropriately, and understand that feelings change over time. Perhaps prevention programs that focus on these aspects will better equip children should they encounter a sexual abuse situation.

Body Parts and Touch

Often children are forced to give or receive hugs when they might not feel comfortable because of who does the touching or where the person touches. If children can distinguish between what feels comfortable and uncomfortable, can label body parts and differentiate private from public parts, and can adequately discriminate between appropriate and inappropriate sexual behavior, this may help them learn when to say no to inappropriate or uncomfortable touch (Kraizer, 1985).

Decision Making

Obviously children need to be able to make decisions in order to protect themselves. Decisions involving personal safety, trust, reporting, and coping are critical issues. Helping children weigh alternatives and consequences is an important skill that could help a child avoid or prevent a sexually abusive situation (Crane & Lenett, 1985).

Assertion

"No" is perhaps the most important word a child can say if confronted with a person who is trying to get them to do something uncomfortable. Children have been taught to respect authority, to cooperate, and not to talk back to adults (Crane & Lenett, 1985). Therefore, it is extremely important to help them understand their rights as related to the privacy of their bodies and to touch. Additionally, children need to be taught appropriate times and ways to say no (Crane & Lenett, 1985).

Helpers

An essential component of a preventative program is that of educating children about who to tell and where to go for help (Kraizer, 1985). When a child has resources at hand, anxiety is often reduced, In addition, children need to know that if one adult does not listen, they should keep telling until someone listens and takes action. Although information of this nature is not presented to alarm children, they do need to be aware that there are potentially dangerous situations and that knowing who can help is a way of being prepared.

The topics outlined in each component were developed into three activity clusters for children in Grades 1 and 2, 3 and 4, and 5 and 6. Activities were introduced the first year in Grades 2, 4, and 6; additional activities will be written so that next year each grade level will have a separate set of activities for each component. An example of one activity for each component follows.

Activity Summary

Self-Acceptance

"*Mistakes*" *(Grade 4)*. This activity begins with a general discussion on mistakes. The leader and children share examples of mistakes that they have made, emphasizing the fact that making mistakes does not mean one is a bad person. Following this discussion, a short story that we developed is read. The story focuses on how a child receives a confusing touch from her stepfather and then is upset with herself because by not telling anyone, she was not able to prevent this from happening to her younger sister. Follow-up questions reinforce the concept of being vulnerable and confused and doing the best that one can at the time.

Feelings

"*Express It*" *(Grade 6)*. Hypothetical situations are read, and students are asked to describe how they would feel if that happened to them and how they might express the feeling. Discussion focuses on how feelings are or are not expressed and how people may react differently to the same experience.

Examples of situations presented to the children are:

1. Someone stands behind you in line and tries to touch you on a private place on your body.
2. An older brother or sister keeps walking into your bedroom without knocking while you are dressing.

Body Parts and Touch

"It's Me" (Grade 4). To introduce the private parts of the body, children are given an outline of a child's body. Each child fills in their outline including eyes, ears, hair, and nose. They should put their person in a swimsuit appropriate for their sex. Discussion should focus on private body parts, parts of the body that people do not see or touch, and parts of the body that are not private that are okay for others to touch if the child gives permission.

Assertion

"I Can Do It" (Grade 2). Students are divided into small groups and roleplay the following situation as their favorite television, comic book, or movie hero: "You are playing in the park when someone you do not know very well asks you to go for a ride. You are trying to decide what to do when your hero appears and helps you out of the situation." Discussion focuses on how their heroes handled the situation. The leader presents the idea that in real life a super hero will not appear and the child will have to handle the situation. Discussion can then compare how the heroes might handle the situation with how the students would cope.

Decision Making

"What Do You Do?" (Grade 2). This activity is introduced by discussing the fact that there are usually several choices a person has when confronted with any situation and that it is important to think about which choice is the best one. The leader reads specific situations to the children and asks them to discuss the best choice with a partner. The children then share their responses and reasons for their decisions.

Sample situation and choices: "It's getting dark and you are in a hurry to get home. You are supposed to be home by 8:00 and it is 7:55. If you are late you'll be grounded. What do you do?"

1. You take a shortcut through an unlighted alley. By doing this you will get home on time.

2. You walk home on a lighted street. By doing this you will be late.
3. You ask for a ride home from someone you've seen before in town who is driving by. By doing this you will get home on time.

Helpers

"Who Helps?" (Grade 4). As a class, the children list all of the people who may at some time have a chance to touch them (i.e., counselor, teacher, minister, parent, friend). The children then think of one person who has touched them in the past week and to recall how they felt about that touch. The leader discusses with students who they could go to for help if the touch they received felt uncomfortable. Discussion includes the consequences of asking for help and appropriate actions to take if the person does not listen or believe the story.

Reaction

Children seemed to be very responsive to the program and were comfortable discussing the topic of abuse. Although no formal evaluation was conducted, teachers noted that children seemed to welcome the chance to discuss appropriate reactions and safety precautions and seemed willing to identify and discuss different types of touch, ways to ask for help, and assertive ways to say no.

In addition, to the students, the staff was accepting of the material and lessons. During the lesson presentations the teachers became more aware of the topic and were able to reinforce various aspects about touch in the classroom and on the playground.

Parental response was also positive. The parents were comfortable with the content of the program, and some requested that the topic be covered every year in every grade. Another benefit of the program was that two parents shared with the second author information about their children's sexual victimization and asked that she work with their children.

Conclusion

The activities in this article illustrate an approach that informs children about various aspects of child sexual abuse. Elements of sexual abuse within a preventive program encourage children to be more alert to potentially dangerous situations and the possible outcomes of those situations. As children learn to identify the issues and discover that there are ways to deal with this problem, they become less vulnerable and better able to help themselves physically and psychologically. As professionals dedicated to the promotion of healthy youth, the counselors' role in the prevention abuse programs is very significant.

References

Anderson, L. S., & Griffin, C. L. (1981). The neglected and abused child: New roles and responsibilities for the school. *Elementary School Guidance & Counseling 16,* 24–30.

Colao, F., & Hosansky, T. (1983). *Your children should know.* New York: Bobbs-Merrill.

Crane, B., & Lenett, R. (1985). *It's o.k. to say no.* New York: Tom Doherty Associates.

Fontana, V. J. (1982). Sexual child abuse. In J. Bulkley, J. Ensminger, V. J. Fontana, & R. Summit (Eds.), *Dealing with sexual child abuse* (pp. 1–2). Chicago: National Committee for Prevention of Child Abuse.

Harms, R., & James, D. (1982). *Talking about touching: A personal safety curriculum.* Seattle, WA: Judicial Advocates.

Hay, J., & Struck, C. (1986). *Take charge of your body.* Waterloo, IA: Family and Children's Council of Black Hawk County.

Hitchcock, R. A., & Young, D. (1986). Prevention of sexual assault: A curriculum for elementary school counselors. *Elementary School Guidance & Counseling, 20,* 201–207.

James, B., & Nasjleti, M. (1983). *Treating sexually abused children and their families.* Palo Alto, CA: Consulting Psychologists Press.

Kraizer, S. K. (1985). *The safe child book.* New York: Dell.

Landau, L. J. M. (1983). *Touch that hurts: Talking with children about sexual abuse.* Portland, OR: Author.

Williams, B. G. (1981). Myths and sexual child abuse: Identification and elimination. *The School Counselor, 29,* 103–110.

Counseling Child Sexual Abuse Victims: Myths and Realities

Lynn W. England
Charles L. Thompson

The goal of the authors is to (a) create an awareness among counselors about the nature and prevalence of child sexual abuse, (b) examine myths and realities about the topic, and (c) present recommendations for interviewing suspected victims of child sexual abuse.

Reports of child sexual abuse continue to rise, and, in all probability, many more cases go unreported (Conte, 1986). Counselors often feel unprepared, however, to work effectively with sexually abused children; the existence of various myths and misinformation further compound the problem. Perhaps significantly, a computer search we recently conducted using various child sex abuse headings revealed that most citations were found in social work and medical journals. Few were in counseling journals. Therefore, the purpose of this article is threefold: (a) to enhance counselors' awareness about the nature and prevalence of child sexual abuse, (b) to examine myths and realities about the topic, and (c) to present some recommendations for interviewing suspected victims of child sexual abuse.

One of us (Lynn England) has worked as a child abuse coordinator for the army and now works in a similar position in a state department of mental health. The other (Charles Thompson) is a counselor educator specializing in counseling children. Our total caseload experience with clients involved in child sexual abuse includes over 120 children, 70 adult female victims, and 40 male offenders.

We have identified, through our work with numerous counselors, teachers, parents, and children, six sexual abuse myths. Each is discussed below.

Myths and Realities

Myth Number 1

Incest rarely occurs, but when it does it is found primarily in poorly educated families of low socioeconomic status.
In 1984 there were 100,000 reports of child sexual abuse; however, this figure may be a gross underestimate of actual abuse. Depending on the particular

study, between 15% and 38% of women have been sexually abused as children; the number of male victims, also high, is often cited at 10% (Conte, 1986). It is generally accepted that 1 of every 4 girls and 1 of every 7 to 10 boys will have some kind of sexual encounter with an adult before reaching age 18 (Seattle Institute for Child Advocacy, 1985). Peters, Wyatt, and Finkelhor (Finkelhor, 1986) conducted an in-depth study of the prevalence of child sexual abuse in North America. They found considerable variation in the prevalence rates based on existing studies. The ranges were 6% to 62% for girls and 3% to 31% for boys. Further support for this wide range of figures can be found in Wyatt and Peters (1986), Wyatt (1985), and Finkelhor and Hotaling (1984). Is is suspected, however, that actual rates of child sexual abuse are much higher.

Professionals have been aware of child sexual abuse for some time. Brown (1979), for example, stated: "The literature during the 1950's and 1960's shows the sexual misuse of children was a noticeable clinical entity in psychiatric clinics before it became an issue under child protective laws" (p. 435). It must be remembered that the above estimates are based on reports and that the actual number of incidences is probably much higher. Child sex offenders know no social class or educational boundaries, and it seems that differences in the ethnic compositions of samples do not affect prevalence rates (Finkelhor, 1986).

Myth Number 2

Child molesters are attracted sexually to their victims.

Many prominent writers in the field believe that sexual assault of children (and other persons) is an act of power rather than sex. Groth (1979) described it as the sexual expression of power and anger. Sgroi (1982) pointed out that even though *pedophilia* is defined in textbooks as a sexual variation, individuals who are sexual offenders against children do not seem to be motivated primarily by sexual desires. Instead, they tend to engage in sexual behaviors with children in the service of nonsexual needs, especially the need to feel powerful and in control.

I (Lynn England) have found similar trends in my treatment of sex offenders. Often, I discover that my adult male clients have been experiencing emotional valleys in their lives. Literally nothing was going well for them in their work, interpersonal relations, and feelings of self-worth. They turned to controlling a child to once again feel powerful. As with adult rape, sex was used as a controlling tool. These offenders have been described as regressed pedophiles (Mayer, 1985). An exception to the above rule and infinitely more rare is the fixated pedophile, a male molester whose emotional and psychological development was arrested at an early age, often at the age when he was molested (Mayer, 1985). This is the stranger that we constantly remind our children to avoid. The fixated pedophile *is* sexually attracted to children (usually of the same sex) and is not motivated by power needs (Burgess, Groth, Holstrom, & Sgroi, 1978). As are other forms of sexual deviance (American Psychiatric Association, 1987), pedophilia is addictive (Burgess et al., 1978; Carnes, 1983).

Myth Number 3

Most child molesters are strangers (unknown) to their victims.
Perhaps this is the most difficult reality to accept. Unfortunately, most sex offenders are related to their victims. According to a Committee for Children report (Seattle Institute for Child Advocacy, 1984), in 80% to 90% of the cases the offender is someone the child loves and trusts. In nearly one-half of the cases in which the child knows the offender, this trusted adult is a father or stepfather. The known offender exploits the child's innocence, dependence, and eventual fear. Between 20% and 30% of the offenders are in the child's immediate family (brothers, uncles, grandfathers, and cousins) (Finkelhor, 1979; Pierce & Pierce, 1985; Sgroi, 1982), leaving an estimated 10% to 20% known but not related to the child (e.g., baby-sitters, youth leaders).

It can be assumed, therefore, that so-called "stranger" child molesters are quite rare. Rather, they are people we know, those we see at the grocery check-out lane or in the next church pew. The vast majority of all offenders are men. According to most estimates, men constitute well over 90% of the sex offender population (Finkelhor, 1979, 1984; Mayer, 1985).

Myth Number 4

Child sexual abuse is a modern phenomenon, probably resulting from the sexual revolution.
Children have been sexually victimized by adults for centuries. In fact, Finkelhor (1979) found that it was quite common for adults to be sexual with children in the 16th, 17th, and 18th centuries in Europe.

Perhaps counselors can learn a valuable lesson from one interpretation of Freud's experience with his sexually abused patients. Freud accurately recognized the descriptions of his female patients as sexually abusive episodes perpetrated by fathers and brothers, but he could not accept the reality of the shockingly large number of reports that he heard. Ridicule and scorn from his colleagues in Vienna apparently influenced Freud to sublimate his patients' realities into his well-known Oedipus complex theory. Probably, it was much easier to believe that children unconsciously wanted or desired their opposite-sexed parent than to believe that they were actually in sexual contact with them. Freud was one of the first victim blamers and set a precedent for not believing patients' reports of childhood sexual experiences (Finkelhor, 1979).

Child pornography also flourished during the Victorian Era. One of the more famous child pornographers was Charles Lutwidge Dodgson (1832-1898), a clergyman (deacon) at Oxford University's Christ Church College. Dodgson kept exacting descriptions of his photographs in his diary. His first entry was dated May 21, 1867, where he referred to photographing a nude, 6-year-old girl. Dodgson abandoned his hobby in 1880, apparently to avoid scandal. After his death, portions of his diary were deleted by his nephew to avoid further notoriety. Dodgson's artistic talents were not limited to photography, however. He was also a fiction writer and authored many books. One of his favorite characters was a young, innocent girl named Alice who was taken on some very unusual journeys, to say the least. Dodgson's pen name was Lewis Carroll (Tyler & Stone, 1985).

Because of the "sexual revolution," we now have pornographic material readily available in magazines and videocassettes. Childhood prostitution is rampant. Of the estimated 600,000 children involved in child prostitution in the United States, 50% are male. Of the pornographic material (called kiddie porn), 7% involves the graphic, pictorial display of adults engaged in sexual activity with children or children with children. Many of the children photographed were and currently are victims of pedophiles who had lured them into this activity (Mayer, 1985).

Pedophiles have devised sophisticated organizations and networks to further their cause. The credo of the Rene Guyon Society is, "Sex before eight or else it's too late." The Childhood Sexuality Circle (CSC) exchanges child pornography, and its members send each other detailed descriptions of their victims and activities. The North American Man/Boy Lovers Association (NAMBLA) has proposed that "adult society has neither a moral nor legal right to limit a child's selection of sexual partners." The British Pedophile Information Exchange (PIE) advocates the lowering of the age of consent for sex to age 4 (Mayer, 1985).

Myth Number 5

The sexual abuse of a child is usually a single, violent incident.

Again, it may be easier to believe those incidents where adults under the influence of alcohol or other drugs commit a violent act similar to adult rape. Reality is quite different. There are more sexual adult-child contacts involving fondling, oral sex, masturbating, and exposing than incidents involving penile-vaginal or anal intercourse. The entire continuum of sexual activity is defined as abusive if it involves adults with children (Finkelhor, 1979; Sgroi, 1982). The classic dynamics of incest described below are seen in case after case.

According to Sgroi (1982), incest follows some common dynamics or phases. Beginning with the engagement phase, it moves through sexual interaction, secrecy, disclosure, and the repression or recantation phases.

During the engagement phase, the child is gradually taught (conditioned) to accept sexual acts. This teaching is done in a loving fashion for the most part. Human beings are not born with a working knowledge of sex. Some offenders often go so far as to instruct children about what to say and what noises to make.

The sexual interaction phase includes a variety of sexual acts, progressing from exposure to vaginal or anal intercourse. Soon the offender will realize the consequences of being discovered and begins threats, bribes, or coercion to keep the child quiet. This secrecy phase keeps him safe and allows the abuse to continue so that he can still feel powerful and in control.

If child victims tell, the abuse is likely to stop, but they may recant when pressure is applied. In reality, however, most children do not tell, and the abuse continues until they are physically able to leave home.

Myth Number 6

Children frequently make up stories about engaging in sexual activities with adults.

There is a general consensus in the literature that children simply do not lie about being abused. Herman and Hirschman (1980), in a review of the literature, found that over 99% of children were truthful in their reports. Great psychological harm is done when a professional does not believe a child (Finkelhor, 1979, 1984; Mayer, 1985; Sgroi, 1982).

Those of us who work with children would probably be very suspicious of a child who confessed to breaking school rules. We assume that children tell stories (lie) to stay out of trouble, not to get into it. Yet, as a rule, we want not to believe when we hear of the sexual abuse of a child.

During the secrecy phase, many threats are made to children to keep them quiet. Violence, disbelief, the breakup of the family, public ridicule of the child, and jail for the offender are some of the more common threats made to the child: If they tell, it will be their fault if their father, stepfather, uncle, or brother goes to jail. Such threats tend to foster enormous amounts of guilt for the child to bear. Many children recant after they realize that most of the threats made to them are actually coming true. Counselors must be aware of these dynamics and anticipate them.

It is not surprising, then, to realize that most sexually abused children grow into adulthood and carry the secret with them their entire lives (Finkelhor, 1979). According to Giarretto (1978), there is a strong tendency for the existence of sexual abuse histories in adult women receiving psychiatric treatment.

For example, he found that of 160 women in treatment for sexual dysfunction, 90% had been sexually abused as children and 23% had been involved in incest with their fathers or stepfathers.

As a result of her personal experiences as a therapist, Mayer (1985) believes that the following effects of not disclosing sexual abuse are far reaching. Victims tend to be indiscriminate or promiscuous in their choice of partners. Also, they are more likely to marry an abuser. Forgotten or repressed episodes of childhood incest may manifest themselves in destructive or self-destructive behavior in adulthood. Tragically, over 70% of female drug addicts and prostitutes were sexually abused as children, and men molested in childhood have a high probability of becoming molesters themselves.

The validation of child sexual abuse is a complicated process and is best left to child protective workers. All states now legally require a good faith report of suspected child sexual abuse. The counselor who possesses a good understanding of sexual abuse dynamics should feel confident in reporting suspected sexual abuse cases.

Counseling Sexually Abused Children

Counselors have the opportunity to become primary advocates for sexually abused children (Erickson, McEvoy, & Colucci, 1984). In many cases, the counselor may emerge as the only trusted adult in the abused child's world. When disclosure occurs, counselors may find themselves in a very unfamiliar position as they try to cope with bizarre and unfathomable descriptions of adult sexual behaviors toward children. A child's story of emotional and personal involvement in incest or molestation often fosters denial as an adult reaction (Finkelhor, 1979; Groth, 1979).

Should counselors find themselves involved in counseling sexually abused children, care should be given to both the setting and interview methods chosen. As in any counseling interview, special consideration needs to be given to building trust and rapport with the child. Based on their personal experience, Thompson and Rudolph (1983) believe that abused children are not easy clients. These children have learned not to trust themselves and other people because they have been hurt by the inconsistent behavior of the adults in their lives. In working with sexually abused children, the relationship of trust between counselor and client becomes even more critical.

In regard to the interview setting, children respond better to playroom and informal settings than to office-type atmospheres. Cheerful colors, thick carpets, beanbag chairs, floor pillows, anatomically correct dolls, puppets, doll houses, art materials, and other assorted, age-appropriate toys can assist the counselor in building the trust and cooperation needed for effective communication. Also, the playroom is less threatening and should help children feel safe and in control. Counselors have a better opportunity to observe children in their own environment in the playroom setting. Play is the natural medium for communication and self-expression for children. It may even help, before beginning the interview, to say to preschool children, "Let's go to the playroom (or my room) where I keep my toys." Of course, older children and adolescents would not respond well to a playroom designed for younger children. It is necessary, however, to maintain an informal atmosphere that communicates to the victim the message, "You are not in trouble." Just the reverse is true for the offender, who needs the more formal office setting to get the message, "I'm in trouble and I need help."

Questions that can be answered with a yes or no often are answered "no." For example, in response to a question such as "Would you like to go to my office and play with some toys?" the preschooler may wish to remain with Mom and say no. Because it is necessary to conduct the interview in private, toys may help younger children separate from their mothers for the duration of the interview.

After entering the playroom setting, sit next to the child rather than behind a desk or table. Speaking in a language that he or she understands, you might begin by explaining what you want to do in the interview (e.g., "I would like to have you tell me about your family" or "I would like to have you tell me about other people you know"). The puppets, dolls, and doll house can be helpful to children in describing their family, their acquaintances, and their typical day. Counselors often must help younger (toddlers) select toys appropriate for their stage of development. Again, in speaking in a language understandable to children, we have found it helpful to know how children refer to their genitals. Use of these genital nicknames makes children feel more comfortable in talking about their bodies.

Care must be taken to teach sexually abused children that what happened to them was not their fault and that they are not wrong for telling what happened. During a recent interview with a 6-year-old girl who had difficulty keeping her hands off other children during weekly group guidance meetings, the counselor was able to identify sexual abuse by the girl's 14-year-old brother when she was able to help the girl feel less guilty about what had occurred. During the interview it became apparent that the girl was replicating at school a "game" she played with her older brother. When the counselor asked her if her brother touched "down there," she said no. When the counselor rephrased the question and asked "Does he do it some of the time?" she replied yes. Following the "some of the time" style of questioning, the counselor was able to get a clear picture of the nature of the sexual abuse and referred the case to the Department of Human Services.

Ask children to clarify words, phrases, nicknames, pronouns, and other verbal and nonverbal expressions that you do not understand. Use proper names rather than pronouns that could confuse the child. Be sure to limit your interview comments and questions to one thought at a time with preschool children. Although you may need to reinforce each interaction that children make, allow them to tell their own story about what happened without leading them into telling what they think you want to hear. Leading or closed questions should be avoided. For example, asking "Did your daddy touch your private parts?" is grossly leading and therefore unacceptable. Children will tend to give the answer they believe you want. Rather, a question such as "Can you tell me about a time something happened to you that made you feel funny or uncomfortable?" allows the child to answer without being led. It is best to avoid "why" questions because such questions have been overused in situations where parents and teachers have tried to trap children into confessions about misbehavior. Thus, "why" questions tend to put children on the defensive.

The interview also can be damaged if the counselor displays shock and disapproval of the child, the parents, or the content of the story. The counselor can be most effective by maintaining a neutral but empathic position of a listener, summarizer, and clarifier. Three things need to be done as you close the interview. First, without overinforming, tell children how the information given will be used. Second, explain what will happen next. Third, thank them for helping you with such a problem. For in-depth discussion, readers are referred to Sgroi's (1982) excellent suggestions on interviewing.

Unfortunately, false reports do occur. Recently, a falsely accused psychologist (whose career had been ruined) received national attention on a television news program. In this case, the accusation had come from an ex-wife rather than a child. Extra caution should be used when handling adult disclosures (Grayson, 1986; Pierce & Pierce, 1985). The motives for these reports may be squabbles with neighbors, custody battles, dislike for a teacher, and so forth. Of course, all adult disclosures are not invalid. It is a sad reality that along with a raised public awareness of sexual abuse comes the notion of using it as a weapon.

Summary

We have reviewed the current literature on child sexual abuse as a way of defining some myths and realities about the topic. In general, we found support for the following conclusions: (a) child sexual abuse is more common than many people believe, (b) sexual attraction is not the primary motive for most child sexual abuse, (c) most child molesters are known to their victims, (d) child sexual abuse is not a reflection of the sexual revolution, (e) child sexual abuse is most often part of a behavior pattern between the adult and child rather than a single, violent incident, and (f) children tend to be truthful about their self-reports of sexual abuse.

References

American Psychiatric Association. (1987). *Diagnostic and statistical manual of mental disorders* (3rd ed.). Washington, DC: Author.

Brown, S. (1979). Clinical illustrations of the sexual misuse of girls. *Child Welfare, 58*, 435–442.

Burgess, A., Groth, N., Holstrom, L., & Sgroi, S. (1978). *Sexual assault of children and adolescents.* Lexington, MA: Lexington Books.

Carnes, P. (1983). *Out of the shadows: Understanding sexual addiction.* Minneapolis: CompCare Publications.

Conte, J. (1986). *A look at child sexual abuse.* Chicago: National Committee for Prevention of Child Abuse.

Erickson, E., McEvoy, A., & Colucci, N. (1984). *Child abuse and neglect: A guidebook for educators and community leaders.* Holmes Beach, FL: Learning Publications.

Finkelhor, D. (1979). *Sexually victimized children.* New York: Free Press.

Finkelhor, D. (1984). *Child sexual abuse: New theory and research.* New York: Free Press.

Finkelhor, D. (1986). *A sourcebook on child sexual abuse.* Beverly Hills, CA: Sage Publications.

Finkelhor, D., & Hotaling, G. (1984). Sexual abuse in the national incidence study of child abuse and neglect. *Child Abuse and Neglect, 8*, 22–32.

Giarretto, H. (1978). The humanistic treatment of father-daughter incest. *Journal of Humanistic Psychology, 18*, 59–76.

Grayson, J. (1986). Child sexual abuse complaints: Determining the truth. *Virginia Child Protection Newsletter, 20*, 1–4.

Groth, A. (1979). *Men who rape.* New York: Plenum.

Herman, J., & Hirschman, L. (1980). *Father-daughter incest.* Cambridge, MA: Harvard University Press.

Mayer, A. (1985). *Sexual abuse: Causes, consequences and treatment of incestuous and pedophilic acts.* Holmes Beach, FL: Learning Publications.

Pierce, L. & Pierce, R. (1985). Analysis of sexual abuse hotline reports. *Child Abuse and Neglect, 9*, 37–45.

Seattle Institute for Child Advocacy, Committee for Children. (1985). *Talking about touching: A personal safety curriculum.* Seattle: Author.

Sgroi, S. (1982). *Handbook of clinical intervention in child sexual abuse.* Lexington, MA: Lexington Books.

Thompson, C., & Rudolph, L. (1988). *Counseling children.* Monterey, CA: Brooks/Cole.

Tyler, R., & Stone, L. (1985). Child pornography: Perpetuating the sexual victimization of children. *Child Abuse and Neglect, 9*, 313–318.
Wyatt, G. (1985). The sexual abuse of Afro-American and White American women in childhood. *Child Abuse and Neglect, 9*, 507–519.
Wyatt, G., & Peters, S. (1986). Issues in the definition of child sexual abuse in prevalence research. *Child Abuse and Neglect, 10*, 231–240.

Chapter 4

Counseling Issues in a World of Child Abuse and Neglect

Issues for elementary school counselors to consider about a world of child abuse and neglect:

1. How can elementary school counselors serve as advocates for victims of child abuse and neglect?
2. What are some of the main community resources that counselors can use to help child abuse victims?
3. Play therapy is a means that may help children to express their feelings about sexual abuse. Consider how an elementary school counselor might use play therapy to counsel a sexual abuse victim. How might puppets be used in these play therapy sessions?
4. What steps should counselors follow in planning a parent support group to prevent child abuse?
5. What is the most important legal information counselors need to have about reporting child abuse?
6. How can you identify children that may be experiencing abuse at home? What steps must you follow to help these children?
7. Every state has passed legislation dealing with child abuse. Obtain a copy of the law in your state. Consider how well your school system is following the law.
8. What are some of the main characteristics of adults who physically abuse children?
9. Some people believe that corporal punishment is little more than physical abuse. How do you feel about corporal punishment? What are some of the key issues involved?

CHAPTER 5

A WORLD OF EXCEPTIONAL CHILDREN

The noted personality theorist, Harry Stack Sullivan, once noted, "In most general terms, we are all much more simply human than otherwise." There are many children in our schools, however, who are labelled exceptional and find it difficult to accept that they are "simply human." These children need to feel accepted and to use their exceptional characteristics in extraordinary ways. Children who are not so-labelled need to learn ways of benefitting from those who are exceptional. The parents and teachers of exceptional children also need to find ways to understand and assist these youngsters. This chapter helps elementary school counselors build a supportive learning environment for exceptional children.

Chapter 5 begins with Elizabeth Conroy's discussion of a counseling group for parents of gifted children. As Conroy states, parents of gifted youngsters have unique needs resulting from misunderstandings created by "myths, stereotypes, and the small number of gifted children in the population." Charles Humes follows with an excellent case example of counseling with parents of handicapped children. Humes notes that "counseling for parents does exist in the schools, but not to the depth or extent necessary for special education cases." Next, Judy Berry presents a counselor-led training program designed to help teachers work more effectively with parents of handicapped children. Berry observes that the teacher "is in a position to develop an active, ongoing relationship with parents but may lack the training to provide effective counseling support."

Carolyn Bauer concludes the chapter with her provocative article on using books to help children become increasingly sensitive to the needs of handicapped students. She points out that "children's books can play a positive role in breaking attitudinal barriers for the handicapped." The article is filled with practical suggestions about which books are the most helpful in such areas as visual handicaps, speech handicaps, learning disabilities, auditory impairments, intellectual handicaps, and orthopedic impairments.

The 1990s will bring new challenges for elementary school counselors in working with exceptional children. Counselors can best meet these challenges by collaborating with parents and teachers to make the school environment increasingly sensitive to the needs and aspirations of exceptional children.

Primary Prevention for Gifted Students: A Parent Education Group

Elizabeth H. Conroy

During the late 1970s and early 1980s, there has been renewed concern about meeting the needs of gifted children in the educational system. Several authors (Culross, 1982; Dettman & Colangelo, 1980; North Carolina Association for the Gifted and Talented [NCAGT] Task Force, 1986) have discussed the role of the school counselor in this effort. Among the most recent research is a 4-year study by Cox (1986). These results demonstrated that counseling services are essential in successful educational programs for gifted students.

School counselors can have many different functions in helping gifted students. Some of these functions, such as program selection and career and college advisement, are more necessary in the secondary school setting than at other levels. Counseling with students in response to social, emotional, and academic problems is important at all levels. At the elementary school level, counselors need to exercise their function of consultation with administrators, teachers, and parents. Culross (1982) urged counselors to become involved in preventing problems by encouraging the healthy growth and development of gifted children. Elementary counselors can help provide the psychologically safe environment recommended in Cox's (1986) report by consulting with those people who design programs and those who live and work with gifted children every day.

In her summary of research, Herbert (1982) established the importance of identifying a child's talents and abilities early so that these traits can flourish. Van Tassel-Baska (1985) stated that one of the current national trends in gifted education is the increase in programs at the elementary school level. This trend provides an opportunity for elementary school counselors to be instrumental in clarifying the needs of gifted students and promoting the development of appropriate educational strategies. Glennon (1985) suggested that counselors assess the advantages and disadvantages of the three major current approaches to meeting the educational needs of gifted children: (a) enrichment, (b) special grouping, and (c) acceleration. Counselors need this kind of information to consult effectively with administrators, teachers, and parents in designing or evaluating educational approaches or activities.

Parent Consultation

Communication with parents is an essential function of an elementary school counselor. Traditionally, counselors have joined with teachers in meeting with parents individually when a concern has arisen about a student's progress in school. In recent years, counselors have been urged to spend more of their time in preventive efforts (Dinkmeyer & Dinkmeyer, 1984). Because parents are the major influence on the mental health of their children, changing parents' attitudes or behavior can have a significant impact on the development of children.

Some research has demonstrated that parent education is an effective way to help parents develop healthy attitudes toward their children and useful techniques for raising them (Bundy & Poppen, 1986; Dembo, Sweitzer, & Lauritzen, 1985). Parent education approaches have been shown to affect family environment (Campbell & Sutton, 1983), parent-child communication (Bredehoft & Hey, 1985), child-rearing behavior, student motivation, academic achievement (Bundy & Poppen, 1986), and child learning (Bergan, Neumann, & Karp, 1983). Some of the most commonly used parent education programs include *Parent Effectiveness Training* (Gordon, 1970), *Systematic Training for Effective Parenting* (Dinkmeyer & McKay, 1976), *Parents Are Teachers* (Becker, 1976), and *Self-Esteem: A Family Affair* (Clarke, 1978). School counselors have used these and other approaches in parent education groups.

Needs of Parents of Gifted Children

Parents of gifted children have many needs that are similar to those of all parents and some needs that are unique. The unique needs are based on the exceptionality of their children. Because of myths, stereotypes, and the small number of gifted children in the population, gifted children are frequently misunderstood. Parents may react with mixed emotions to the awareness of their child's special abilities. Parents may be uncomfortable knowing their child is "different" and may be confused about their role in the process of educating their child. They may not share their concerns or seek help because they do not want to sound "elitist."

Dettman and Colangelo (1980) recommended that school counselors and parents of gifted children use a partnership approach in which the "parents and counselor make joint decisions on the best direction to meet the educational needs of the gifted child" (p. 160). One way to begin a partnership and give parents information to make well-informed decisions is to offer them a parent education group. An appropriate time to offer such a group is when the school system first identifies their children as gifted. At this point, parents may have a need to understand the meaning of the term and ways to cope with their feelings. If they have been aware of their child's exceptional abilities, the school's data may be the first confirmation of these abilities. If the parents have not realized how exceptional their child is, they may have numerous questions about how to raise such a child.

A group approach is a very effective way to meet these needs. Parents can be provided with information regarding the results of research in gifted education and can be made aware of available literature and resources. For the counselor, such information can be shared more efficiently in a group. Another advantage of the group approach is the interaction among parents. When they discover that other parents have similar needs, a supporting network develops. Additionally, their perspective will be broadened by being exposed to issues relevant to other parents. To accomplish these goals, a group that offers both information and participation is most useful. The school counselor, as leader of the group, can establish a relationship with parents that will be beneficial throughout the child's school career.

The Parent Education Group

With these considerations in mind, I developed a three-session parent workshop. The purpose of the group was twofold: (a) to help parents develop a better understanding of their children and (b) to increase their comfort in raising their gifted children. The workshop was offered at two different times for 1 hour on 3 consecutive Saturdays. It was held during an enrichment program for gifted children sponsored by the Durham, North Carolina, chapter of Parents for the Advancement of Gifted Education (PAGE), a statewide organization affiliated with NCAGT. Although attendance varied somewhat, 23 parents participated in each group.

Session 1: Definition and Identification

The purpose of the first session is to help parents understand the meaning of the label *gifted*. Parents are asked to introduce themselves and tell the names, ages, and enrichment classes of their gifted children.The leader begins by presenting several current definitions of giftedness. First, the group leader introduces the traditional definition and identification in use since the 1920s, which equated giftedness with high intelligence quotients. Subsequently, the leader explains that identification systems used since 1980 involve the use of multiple measures (e.g., achievement test scores, classroom performance, checklists completed by teachers and parents, student products, intelligence test scores). Renzulli's

(1978) three-ring conception of giftedness is then introduced. Renzulli suggested that individuals who are considered gifted have a combination of task commitment, creativity, and above-average intelligence. This definition enlarges the percentage of gifted students. After presenting these definitions of giftedness, the leader discusses the local school definition and identification standards.

The last part of the session is a presentation of characteristics that have been used to describe the gifted. The parents are given copies of descriptive characteristics by different authors, such as Juntune (1985) and Clark (1983). The leader asks the parents to look carefully at Clark's list of characteristics, needs, and concomitant problems. This leads to the topic of the next session, a discussion of needs and problems of gifted children. Additionally, the information provided in this session helps the parents identify their children's gifts without depending completely on evaluations based on test scores, which, in turn, will help them note and foster strengths in the children that may not be addressed by school programs. In the final 10 minutes of the session the leader invites comments and questions from the parents.

Session 2: Needs and Problems

This session is designed to cover cognitive and social-emotional needs of gifted children, some approaches used to meet these needs, and problems often faced by gifted children. After reviewing the main points from the previous session, the leader explains one approach to understanding cognitive needs. An outline of Bloom's taxonomy (1956) is reviewed, and the leader presents the recommendation by many educators of the gifted that gifted students should spend less time with activities requiring the lower levels of thinking (i.e., knowledge, comprehension) and more time on application, analysis, synthesis, and evaluation. Teaching that meets the cognitive needs of the gifted can be accomplished in various ways: (a) through administrative arrangements, such as enrichment within the regular classroom, ability grouping, or acceleration by individual students to higher grades for all or part of the day, or (b) through curriculum modifications that can be used in any setting. Curriculum modifications include such approaches as (a) acceleration in subject matter, (b) enrichment of topics covered in the regular curriculum, (c) opportunities for students to pursue their interests in constructive ways, and (d) opportunities for students to use their learning to solve real-world problems (Aubrecht, 1986).

Many of the social-emotional needs of the gifted children are similar to those of all children, and gifted children may have problems getting their needs met. In this session, the leader presents the following issues for discussion: (a) positive self-concept, (b) family and adult relationships, (c) peer relationships,

(d) communication skills, (e) discipline, and (f) freedom from stress or depression. Gifted children frequently have different attitudes, sensitivities, and interests than do other children their age. These discrepancies can cause difficulties with relationships and self-satisfaction. The challenging nature of helping gifted children develop social skills and emotional health is discussed with the parents using information from Webb, Meckstroth, and Tolan (1982).

During the last 30 minutes of the session, parents are invited to discuss questions, concerns, or problems of their own children. When I led this session, parents discussed issues such as their children's (a) unwillingness to try new things because of a fear of failure, (b) extremely high expectations of themselves, (c) lack of motivation in school, (d) difficulties with peers, (e) being bored in school, (f) not wanting to leave the regular classroom to go to a gifted resource room, and (g) sibling relationships. Parents are encouraged to respond to others and share experiences and ideas with each other.

At the end of Session 2, parents are given an assignment for the following week: to write a brief paragraph describing a problem with which their child is confronted and how it is resolved. Copies of suggestions for rearing gifted children are distributed. These suggestions are taken from various sources, including Ginsberg and Harrison (1977), Hall and Skinner (1980), Jackson (1985), and Sebring (1986). In addition, parents are invited to check out folders containing more information and explanation of additional topics such as acceleration, activities at home, creativity, discipline, sibling relationships, stress and perfectionism, and underachievement.

Session 3: Resources

The purpose of the final session is to discuss successful approaches to educating and rearing gifted children and to inform participants of ways to obtain additional information. This session begins with the leader asking parents to share positive experiences in resolving problems faced by their children. Examples sometimes shared by parents are (a) developing an individualized program in a public school, (b) encouraging a gifted child to try new things, and (c) deciding to accelerate to a higher grade.

After 30 minutes of discussion, the leader summarizes the discussion and lists various resources on the chalkboard. These resources include (a) books; (b) magazines; (c) national, state, and local organizations; (d) local school personnel; (e) local consultants on gifted education; and (f) community resources available for enrichment activities. Finally, an evaluation questionnaire and copies of resources are distributed. The resources include (a) an article by Sawyer (1984), (b) an application for the National Association for Gifted Children, (c) an application for NCAGT, (d) a cover page of *Gifted Child*

Monthly, (e) an application for the *1987 Educational Opportunity Guide,* published by Duke University's Talent Identification Program (Sawyer & Rigsby, 1987), and (f) a bibliography for parents.

Evaluation and Implications

I designed this workshop to help parents better understand their gifted children and to assist them in feeling more comfortable in their role as parents. I expected that this feeling of comfort would result from the following experiences: (a) a better understanding of the label *gifted,* (b) an awareness that gifted children have special needs and problems, (c) a recognition that some needs and problems of their children may be related to their giftedness, (d) a realization that most suggestions for rearing gifted children include familiar ideas, and (e) the knowledge of available resources for help and further information. Parents' awareness of resources such as school staff, other parents, organizations, and literature, should help them continue to be able to meet the needs and resolve the problems of their children as they grow and develop.

After participation in this group, most parents demonstrated understanding of the need for gifted children to (a) develop higher level thinking skills, (b) pursue their own interests, and (c) learn self-discipline. Parents also increased their personal comfort level by discussing the needs and problems of their gifted children. One parent expressed her relief in recognizing that some of her daughter's problems were common to other gifted children. After each of the three sessions, parents stayed to discuss personal situations in more depth with the leader. Many parents indicated a desire for more sessions and an interest in getting to know other participants better. Teachers and administrators noted comments made by participating parents that indicated a growth in understanding.

After a workshop of this nature, a variety of options for follow-up are possible. Counselors can (a) consult with parents, individually or in group meetings, about common issues faced by gifted students; (b) join resource or classroom teachers in annual reviews or occasional meetings; (c) publish or contribute to a parent newsletter with hints, reminders, and updates on material presented in the workshop; and (d) offer counseling groups in which parents explore concerns and problems more deeply. Counselors should become involved with teachers and parents of gifted children to plan appropriate services for these students throughout their school careers.

Educators of gifted children have concluded that parent education and guidance are necessary components of education for gifted children (Dettman & Colangelo, 1980). Offering a parent education group is one effective way for counselors to begin a partnership with parents. Because parents are ultimately responsible for the education and mental health of their children, they need information to make good decisions. Schools need cooperation and information from parents to plan an effective educational program for their gifted students. Elementary counselors can be instrumental in beginning a positive relationship between home and school while implementing parent consultation strategies as a means of primary prevention for gifted children.

References

Aubrecht, L. (1986). *Teaching the gifted individual class.* Raleigh: North Carolina State University.

Becker, W. (1976). *Parents are teachers.* Champaign, IL: Research Press.

Bergan, J., Neumann, A., & Karp, C. (1983). Effects of parent training on parent instruction and child learning of intellectual skills. *Journal of School Psychology, 21*, 31–37.

Bloom, B. (1956). *Taxonomy of educational objectives: Handbook 1. Cognitive domain.* New York: McKay.

Bredehoft, D., & Hey, R. (1985). An evaluation study of self-esteem: A family affair. *Family Relations, 34*, 411–417.

Bundy, M., & Poppen, W. (1986). School counselors' effectiveness as consultants: A research review. *Elementary School Guidance & Counseling, 20*, 215–222.

Campbell, N., & Sutton, J. (1983). Impact of parent education groups on family environment. *Journal for Specialists in Group Work, 8*, 127–132.

Clark, B. (1983). *Growing up gifted.* Columbus, OH: Merrill.

Clarke, J. (1978). *Self-esteem: A family affair leader guide.* Minneapolis: Winston Press.

Cox, J. (1986). *Educating able learners: Programs and promising practices.* Austin: University of Texas Press.

Culross, R. (1982). Developing the whole child: A developmental approach to guidance with the gifted. *Roeper Review, 5*, 24–26.

Dembo, M., Sweitzer, M., & Lauritzen, P. (1985). An evaluation of group parent education: Behavioral, PET, and Alderian programs. *Review of Educational Research, 55*, 155–200.

Dettman, D., & Colangelo, N. (1980). A functional model for counseling parents of gifted students. *Gifted Child Quarterly, 24*, 158–161.

Dinkmeyer, D., & Dinkmeyer, D., Jr. (1984). School counselors as consultants in primary prevention programs. *Personnel and Guidance Journal, 62*, 464–466.

Dinkmeyer, D., & McKay, G. (1976). *Systematic training for effective parenting.* Circle Pines, MN: American Guidance Services.

Ginsberg, G., & Harrison, C. (1977). *How to help your gifted child.* New York: Monarch Press.

Glennon, A. (1985, May). Old issue renewed. *ASCA Counselor*, 4–5.

Gordon, T. (1970). *PET, Parent Effectiveness Training: The tested new way to raise responsible children*. New York: New American Library.
Hall, E., & Skinner, N. (1980). *Somewhere to turn: Strategies for parents of the gifted*. New York: Columbia University, Teachers College Press.
Herbert, D. (1982). *Counseling gifted students* (ERIC/CAPS Fact Sheet). Ann Arbor, MI: Counseling and Personnel Services Clearinghouse.
Jackson, C. (1985, May/June). Communication with your gifted child. *G/C/T* [Gifted/Creative/Talented], p. 7.
Juntune, J. (1985). *Is your child gifted? Parent information*. Circle Pines, MN: National Association for Gifted Children.
North Carolina Association for Gifted and Talented Task Force. (1986). *What is an appropriate education for a gifted student?* Raleigh, NC: Author.
Renzulli, J. (1978). What makes giftedness? Re-examining a definition. *Phi Delta Kappan, 60*, 180–184.
Sawyer, R. (1984, June). Advice for parents: Open doors, show love, relax. *Psychology Today*, p. 36.
Sawyer, R., & Rigsby, C. (1987). *1987 educational opportunity guide*. Durham, NC: Duke University.
Sebring, D. (1986). *Problems of the gifted*. Paper presented at NCAGT annual conference, Raleigh, NC.
Van Tassel-Baska, J. (1985). *Current trends in gifted education*. Paper presented at NCAGT annual conference, Charlotte, NC.
Webb, J., Meckstroth, E., & Tolan, S. (1982). *Guiding the gifted child*. Columbus: Ohio Psychology Publishing.

Parent Counseling in Special Education: Case Description of a Novel Approach

Charles W. Humes

Counseling for the parents of handicapped children is required by the Education for All Handicapped Children Act of 1975 (P.L. 94-142), but is poorly implemented in most school districts (Humes, 1978; McDowell, 1976). Formal services are not materializing for a number of reasons such as lack of money or time, not enough trained school staff, and the work schedules of parents (McDowell, 1976). As a result, attempts by school districts to implement this counseling have fallen short of the requirements (Humes & Munsey, 1984). Gargiulo (1985) stated that barriers have been erected between parents and professionals and this has exacerbated the situation. Although school counselors often do counsel parents, such counseling is not conducted to the extent required by the Education for All Handicapped Children Act. In addition, other pupil services and special education staff have not met the need.

Parents in a number of locations have reacted to the perceived lack of service by developing the parent-as-partners concept. For example, the following programs exist: the Center to Assist Parents—Professionals (CAP-P) in Des Moines, Iowa; the Parent Facilitator Program in San Diego, California; and the Parent Advocacy Coalition for Educational Rights (PACER) in Minneapolis, Minnesota. These organizations were formed by parent groups to work cooperatively with school personnel and to bring about understanding of and participation in special education programs for their children. Until then the history of parent-professional partnerships in special education had not been productive (Gallagher, Beckman, & Cross, 1983). This movement to improve parent-professional partnerships was probably influenced by the peers-as-helpers idea that exists in other settings and populations.

Some of these parent groups plan formal group meetings and produce information on the special needs of children. Others emphasize the understanding of federal and state laws regarding the rights of parents and their handicapped children. Most of the programs train parent facilitators who work with other parents to listen to concerns, help formulate annual goals, attend team meetings as advisers, and help in determining a child's placement. In addition, the parent facilitators help parents to accept a child's handicap and to set realistic goals for the child in terms of physical, mental, and emotional development. Thus, the emphasis is on offering a continuum of parental training and counseling.

One goal of these parent facilitation programs is to gain cooperation and support from pupil services staff, particularly school counselors, psychologists, and social workers. The most successful efforts use pupil services staff as part of the instructional cadre. This is a desirable strategy because it offers professional assistance to the parent facilitators and enables school staff to express points of view, define parameters, and provide cautions. Such professional participation also seems to defuse the notion that the intent is only child advocacy and adversarial action.

In this article I described the conceptualization and evolution of a parent facilitation program in one school district. This program evolved spontaneously and not as a result of direct knowledge of other similar efforts. It was a grass roots idea spearheaded by a few activist parents who sensed that relationships were not good between dissatisfied parents and the pupil services-special education community. The program description is not presented as a model or paradigm for success. It delineates how such a project was started, implemented, and evaluated and also describes how counselors can participate. The project's title—Parent Assisters—was selected with great care to convey to both parents and professionals alike that it was facilitative in intent.

Parent Assisters

Parent Assisters is a cooperative, school-based support program for parents of handicapped children at all grade levels in a small, suburban school district. The school district includes 15 schools with a total of approximately 9,000 pupils. The school population is heterogeneous in socioeconomic makeup, and there are few minority students. The school district has good local financial support for public education.

The Parent Assisters program consists of a group of trained parent volunteers who are available to help parents on a one-to-one basis to understand the Individualized Education Program (IEP) process and to exercise appropriately rights and responsibilities toward their children. The need for such a group of volunteers was first recognized by the parents. In fact, most progress in the school's special education program has been made in response to parental pressure in some form (Hummel & Humes, 1984). As parents began wrestling with the mandates of the Education for All Handicapped Children Act of 1975 in their efforts to help each other, they circulated a mass of subjective information based on their own experiences. Furthermore, there was a tendency for some parents to promote biased points of view on the mistaken assumption that what is an appropriate educational program for one child is equally good for another. Too often, an adversarial relationship developed between parents and staff members. Clearly, more structure and cooperation were needed.

This parent assistance program, in cooperation with the public school system, was proposed under the leadership of a local community organization concerned with excellence in all aspects of public education. A philosophy and policy statement was developed, and a plan for the program was designed and presented to the superintendent of schools. The proposal was reviewed and approved; then the director of pupil services was asked to assist in its implementation. The superintendent of schools volunteered to provide the financial resources necessary.

Initiation of Project

The first step was to ask for outside help. A well-known and respected special education specialist from the state department of education was enlisted as a consultant. She was known to both school staff and parents, and her participation was welcomed.

The second step was to appoint a steering committee with representatives from the school's administration, pupil services, and special education departments, as well as from the students' parents. The purpose was to develop a structure and formulate a viable program. The group's intentions were announced to all staff members, and comments were solicited.

The steering committee met six times over a period of 5 months primarily to define the role and limitations of a parent assister. Predictably, there were many concerns. Some professional staff members feared the group would attempt to do what was really the staff's responsibility or might give advice that would interfere with what the staff was trying to accomplish. It was difficult to persuade many staff members that a parent assister might actually improve essential communications. These meetings were invaluable and were used to revise the wording of statements, clarify meanings, and build a degree of trust between parents and staff members. A structure was developed that reflected (a) general agreement on principles, (b) a job description with known responsibilities and limitations, and (c) accountability to both the superintendent of schools and the community organization.

Selection of Parent Assisters

The selection of volunteers to become parent assisters was the primary concern and required procedural safeguards. Each volunteer was recruited and screened by the community organization and then interviewed by pupil services staff. There was final agreement on the potential of all the recruits selected. Anyone who could not accept the basic philosophy of cooperation or make the essential time commitments was eliminated.

Training

The training program was a 4-day workshop designed by the state consultant and presented by pupil services staff from the schools, representatives from the state department of education, and staff from community agencies. The format was as follows: 1st day—overview of handicapping conditions and background on federal and state regulations; 2nd day—school procedures and continuum of services available; 3rd and 4th days—role playing with emphasis on listening and communication skills using an adaptation of a relationship model (Egan, 1975).

Throughout the training it was emphasized that the assisters were not to be advocates. The role of the presenters was not to tell parents what to do but rather to help them to understand their options. The training was continuous and was followed by monthly meetings to upgrade the skills and knowledge of new or upgraded school services. One or two pupil services staff members, usually counselors, always met with the group to discuss events and problems of the month. These pupil services staff members performed a vital liaison function, which became an integral part of training the parents.

Placement of Assisters

The request for a parent assister was always made by a parent in need. This request was usually a telephone call to the volunteer coordinator, who made all the assignments. There were several important guidelines the coordinator followed in deciding which assister was to help a particular parent. These included not assigning anyone to help a good friend or to become involved with school personnel who were dealing with that parent's own child. The assisters' competencies, as reported by parents and staff, were reviewed periodically, and those who consistently fared poorly were given limited assignments or none. The absence of an assignment was explained only if the assister expressed concern.

Evaluation

During the 1st year of operation, 30 parents received one-to-one help, including assister attendance at team meetings. Another 12 parents called for answers to specific questions but did not require further assistance. Although there were no easy solutions and some serious confrontations, communication seemed to improve as a result of assister participation. Program evaluation was accomplished through a survey questionnaire developed jointly by the director of pupil services and coordinator of volunteers, then distributed to all participants. Most parents indicated that they acquired a better understanding of their children's problems and understood what the school staff hoped to accomplish through the IEP. They also believed that they articulated their own ideas more effectively and participated more in the decision-making process.

Some parents were not satisfied with the decisions of the placement team or the program offered. The parents who had unresolved differences with the school system sometimes proceeded through due process to mediation and even to hearings. If this was the case, the Parent Assisters were still available. Whatever the outcome, this group of volunteers made a contribution toward mutual understanding, on an individual basis, between parents and the school system.

Implications for Counselors

School counselors can play a key role in the initiation and development of a parent facilitation program. They have the skills and assets needed to work with parents. In the pupil services framework they are the most neutral and least threatening of the pupil services. They have no direct ties to the special education community and can approach parents with a nonjudgmental stance. In addition, counselors have training in group dynamics or counseling that will be useful in implementing such a program. They play a key part in the follow-up and maintenance phase of this project.

The starting point in such a program is the needs assessment. Counselors are the staff persons most often associated with general needs assessment in their prime function of serving the developmental needs of all pupils. A specific needs assessment to determine the requirements of special education pupils and their parents is a logical extension of this function. After an assessment is conducted, the counselor must enlist the cooperation and involvement of a parent organization. In the absence of a special education-oriented group, there is always the Parent Teachers Association (PTA). Such a program can be initiated at either the school or district level. If it begins at the school level and is successful, it will undoubtedly expand to other schools.

The counselor should grasp this opportunity to serve special education students and their parents. Counselors have long been overlooked or played insignificant parts in the special education of handicapped pupils. This is an area in which they can make a contribution that is clearly within their role description.

Conclusion

The Parent Assisters program described here has made an impact on the school system and continues to do so. According to information obtained from an annual survey questionnaire, the program has received good reviews over the past 5 years from counselors and other pupil services staff in the school district.

Counselors and other pupil services specialists reported that although some of the parent volunteers were previously parent activists who could find nothing right with the school district's method of processing handicapped pupils, these attitudes were frequently modified as a result of participation in the program. Dealing with the problems of other pupils had an apparent salubrious effect and helped to place the parents' own concerns in perspective. Many of the assisters ceased to be activists. A tangential effect was better parent and staff preparation for team meetings and a more objective adherence to pupil data and case documentation.

This novel program has significance for all counselors but perhaps especially for those working in the elementary and middle schools where counselors have more frequent contacts with parents and a higher incidence of special education placements. The conceptual approach can be incorporated into a comprehensive guidance program and can be an effective vehicle to meet the requirement for parent counseling of handicapped pupils.

Counseling for parents does exist in the schools, but not to the depth or extent necessary for special education cases. Special educators have neither the time nor training to conduct such counseling; thus, the responsibility reverts to counselors and other pupil services specialists. This is why a Parent Assisters program can be a valuable resource for school counselors. After the need for more parent counseling has been established, the counselor can take a leadership role in the form of parent training, its implementation, and subsequent evaluation. Finally, this novel approach has the considerable potential to be a first-rate public relations tool for both counselors and guidance programs.

References

Education for All Handicapped Children Act of 1975, § 100–121, 45 U.S.C. § 1401 (1977).

Egan, G. (1975). *The skilled helper.* Monterey, CA: Brooks/Cole.

Gallagher, J., Beckman, P., & Cross, A. (1983). Families of handicapped children: Sources of stress and its amelioration. *Exceptional Children, 50,* 10–19.

Gargiulo, R. M. (1985). *Working with parents of exceptional children.* Boston: Houghton Mifflin.

Humes, C. W. (1978). School counselors and PL 94-142. *School Counselor, 51,* 210–215.

Humes, C. W., & Munsey, B. W. (1984). Parent counseling of the handicapped: A contemporary status report. *Journal of the International Association of Pupil Personnel Workers, 28,* 25–31.

Hummel, D. L., & Humes, C. W. (1984). *Pupil services: Development, coordination, administration.* New York: Macmillan.
McDowell, R. L. (1976). Parent counseling: The state of the art. *Journal of Learning Disabilities, 9,* 614–619.

A Program for Training Teachers as Counselors of Parents of Children with Disabilities

Judy O. Berry

Public Law 94-142, The Education for All Handicapped Children Act, brought the team approach to public schools. The process is now firmly in place, but numerous refinements are still needed so that the public school interdisciplinary team will provide maximum benefit to students receiving special education services and to their families. The school counselor is a team member who has the training necessary to provide emotional support for families of children with disabilities, but he or she often has very little time to fulfill this role. The teacher, on the other hand, is in a position to develop an active, ongoing relationship with parents but may lack the training to provide effective counseling support. A study by Westling, Koorland, and Rose (1981) demonstrated that superior special education teachers establish more intense relationships with parents, and yet teachers and other professionals report feeling inadequate and somewhat threatened (McWilliams, 1976) as well as anxious (Price & Marsh, 1985) about performing a counseling role with parents.

It is well documented that parents of children with disabilities want and need an empathic approach from the professionals who work with their children (Sonnerschein, 1981; Turnbull & Turnbull, 1985). Buscaglia (1983) spoke of "the desperate need disabled persons and their families have for good, sound, reality-based guidance, and the tremendous resultant despair and loss of human potential when it is not forthcoming" (p. 5). So the problem becomes one of merging the counselor's training with the teacher's ongoing relationship with parents. Training programs to meet this need have, for the most part, focused on the Individualized Education Program (IEP) conference (Bailey, 1984; Kameen & McIntosh, 1979). Although extremely important, this conference is only the first step in providing support and establishing a positive relationship with parents of children with disabilities.

The purpose of this article is to present the basic components of an in-service training program that can be used by counselors to train teachers to work more effectively with parents through integration of counseling theory and special education practice. This program was developed through counseling consultation, both brief and intense, that I have provided during the past 7 years. For 3 years, I provided consultation to a program at the University of Tulsa serving preschool age children with disabilities and their families. Four special education teachers each year served young children, both in a school setting and through home visits. I developed a four-session training program for the teachers, and follow-up support was available as needed throughout the school year. Since that time I have provided 12 in-service training programs, based on consumer needs assessments, to special education teachers, regular classroom teachers with mainstreamed students, and speech-language pathologists. I provided these programs for school systems in the Tulsa, Oklahoma, area. The time available for these sessions ranged from 3 to 6 hours, so adaptations were made to accommodate time restraints and needs of the training audience, which ranged from 25 to 50 participants. Each of the following four topical areas should be covered in the in-service training. Preferably, they should be presented in four separate sessions.

Session 1

In the first session, teachers are introduced to the concept of the grief response following loss (Kubler-Ross, 1969). They are told that parents of children with disabilities are likely to experience feelings of guilt, anger, and depression; that they may deny that their child has problems; and that they may bargain or "shop" for diagnostic results that predict a more favorable outcome for their child. An important focus of this session is to point out that parents (especially parents of children with more severe disabilities) have two crucial tasks to handle. One task is adjusting to the loss of the normal child that they expected to rear, and the other is coping with the many challenges of daily living with a disabled child. In discussing the grieving process, it is important to note that the emotional responses of parents will vary relative to the child's age and time of diagnosis. Parents with older children who have known of the diagnosis for a longer time will have worked through much of their grief and will have a greater need for coping strategies. An article by Berry and Zimmerman (1983) is used as a framework for this session, and the teachers are given specific suggestions on how to be supportive of grieving and how to facilitate coping.

Session 2

In the second session family systems theory, or the view of the family as an interactional system (Minuchin, 1974), is applied to families with a disabled member. Turnbull and Turnbull (1986) have done significant work in applying "the family systems approach in the context of exceptionality across the life-cycle" (p. iv). Their work is helpful in providing discussion topics for this session and is a useful resource for future reference. The counselor conducting this session can draw a contrast between families with and without a disabled member. The presence of a disabled child will affect family resources, family interactions, and the ways in which families can function. It is also important for teachers to consider the influence of family structure, particularly the presence of siblings and the impact of the disabled child on the siblings. The involvement or noninvolvement of extended family members, especially grandparents, is important as well. Alfred Adler's work (Bischof, 1964) concerning birth order and inferiority-superiority can also be useful in presenting this session. Of special help is the issue of *Individual Psychology* (Huber, 1983) in which Adlerian psychology is linked to children with special needs.

It has been my experience that an in-depth discussion of family dynamics helps increase the teacher's sensitivity to the stresses faced on a daily basis by the families of their students. As the teachers become more aware of family systems and family strengths and weaknesses, they are in a better position to provide positive support for families as well as to link families with community programs such as respite care, foster grandparents, sibling support groups, and financial resources.

Session 3

The focus of the third session is parental self-esteem. Teachers need to know that the parents of the children in their class have suffered rejection and humiliation by a society that is not comfortable with the differences their children display. This rejection, combined with the difficult task of meeting the special needs of their children, can undermine their confidence in their ability to be effective parents. In the book *Parents Speak Out: Then and Now* (Turnbull & Turnbull, 1985), parents of handicapped children write candidly of this "battering" of their self-esteem in which, unfortunately, professionals sometimes have a role. Examples from this book are helpful in demonstrating the difficulties these parents face.

Teachers are in a unique position to nurture parental self-esteem, and the third training session presents some strategies for facilitating this endeavor. The importance of being congruent, of being an empathic listener, and, especially, of providing unconditional positive regard are stressed (Rogers, 1961). Being generous with praise of the child and of the child's abilities and accomplishments, as well as of parental involvement in school activities and home programs, is a simple but highly effective way to improve parental self-esteem. Leo Buscaglia's (1983) work is also helpful for this session because of his view that "parents are people first" (p. 77).

Session 4

In the final session teachers are given specific "how to" information for facilitating ongoing communication with the parents of their students. Strategies discussed include assessing needs, planning effective conferences, and enhancing parent involvement in team conferences. Less formal communication is also stressed, including telephone conferences, notes to parents, newsletters, and parent involvement in the classroom. The work of Kroth (1975) and Kroth and Simpson (1977) is helpful in this session.

The principal message of this session is that teachers must view each parent as an individual and must know that individual differences will have a major impact on the level and amount of parent involvement. Grieving reactions, family dynamics, and self-esteem all affect parent involvement, both for parents as a group and for any individual parent over time. Therefore, the understanding that parents gain in the first three sessions is crucial to the successful implementation of the activities presented in the fourth session.

Conclusion

The problem with a program of this type remains one of balancing major needs and limited resources. The intense training that was provided in the preschool setting was very successful but was time consuming and expensive. Evaluation results following the brief sessions have also been gratifying. Long-term evaluation has been limited, but clearly the results are better if the educator receives follow-up support from a counselor in addition to the basic sessions. The recommended reading material has been praised highly and has provided a sound, if impersonal, backup for the educators. This program can be a useful and satisfying way for counselors to provide training for teachers, and it can be adapted to the personnel needs and time constraints of a variety of settings.

References

Bailey, D. B. (1984). A triaxial model of the interdisciplinary team and group process. *Exceptional Children, 51*, 17–25.

Berry, J. O., & Zimmerman, W. W. (1983). The stage model revisited. *Rehabilitation Literature, 44*, 275–277, 320.

Bischof, L. (1964). *Interpreting personality theories*. New York: Harper & Row.

Buscaglia, L. (1983). *The disabled and their parents: A counseling challenge.* Thorofare, NJ: Slack, Inc.

Huber, C. (Ed.). (1983). Adlerian psychology and special needs children (special issue). *Individual Psychology, 39*(4).

Kameen, M. C., & McIntosh, D. K. (1979). The counselor and the individualized educational program. *Personnel and Guidance Journal, 58*, 238–244.

Kroth, R. L. (1975). *Communicating with parents of exceptional children.* Denver: Love.

Kroth, R. L., & Simpson, R. L. (1977). *Parent conferences as a teaching strategy.* Denver: Love.

Kubler-Ross, E. (1969). *On death and dying.* New York: Macmillan.

McWilliams, B. (1976). Various aspects of parent counseling. In E. J. Webster (Ed.), *Professional approaches with parents of handicapped children.* Springfield, IL: Charles C Thomas.

Minuchin, S. (1974). *Families and family therapy.* Cambridge, MA: Harvard University Press.

Price, B. J., & Marsh, G. E. (1985). Practical suggestions for planning and conducting parent conferences. *Teaching Exceptional Children, 17*, 274–278.

Rogers, C. (1961). *On becoming a person.* Boston: Houghton Mifflin.

Sonnerschein, P. (1981). Parents and professionals: An uneasy relationship. *Teaching Exceptional Children, 14*, 62–65.

Turnbull, A. P., & Turnbull, H. R. (1986). *Families, professionals and exceptionality: A special partnership.* Columbus, OH: Charles E. Merrill.

Turnbull, H. R., & Turnbull, A. P. (1985). *Parents speak out: Then and now.* Columbus, OH: Charles E. Merrill.

Westling, D. L., Koorland, M. A., & Rose, T. L. (1981). Characteristics of superior and average special education teachers. *Exceptional Children, 47*, 357–363.

Books Can Break Attitudinal Barriers Toward the Handicapped

Carolyn J. Bauer

Mainstreaming is the practice of providing educational programs for handicapped students in environments that maximize contact with nonhandicapped peers. This practice reflects changes in attitudes about educating the handicapped that have resulted in federal mandates and court decisions. Both require that handicapped students have access to educational and social opportunities that are afforded to their nonhandicapped peers.

Although a major reason for mainstreaming handicapped children into regular classrooms is to increase their contact with nonhandicapped children and decrease their isolation, studies of mainstreaming have found problems with the social integration of handicapped children (Semmel, Gottlieb, & Robinson, 1979). As a group, handicapped children are not chosen as friends as often as other children in the class. Even though they are physically in the mainstream, they often continue to be socially isolated. Helen Keller asserted that the heaviest burdens of disability arise from personal interaction and not from the impairment itself (Baskin & Harris, 1977). Although counselors can exert little control over the reality of the disability, they can help change other children's attitudes and foster a more beneficial social climate.

These studies and comments suggest that our society is contaminated with negative perceptions regarding the handicapped. What can be done to break the barrier and foster nonhandicapped children's positive attitudes toward handicapped persons? Increased contact with handicapped individuals can help, but teachers and parents should not overlook another important tool for breaking the barrier—the honest, objective depictions of handicapped individuals in literature. Books that children read or have read to them provide continuous stimuli through their formative years, and latent and overt messages in stories of exceptional individuals accumulate to form subsequent perceptions.

Research on how children are influenced or changed by books is a recent phenomenon. Although most studies agree that literature is potentially important in the child's value development, the extent of that learning and its permanence have yet to be determined (Waples, Berelson, & Bradshaw, 1958). The results of a study done by Berg-Cross and Berg-Cross (1978) indicated that the expressed attitudes and values of 4-to-6-year-old children can be significantly changed by reading to them a picture storybook that espouses different attitudes.

The research by Monson and Shurtleff (1979) indicated that the use of nonprint media can influence children's attitudes toward people with physical handicaps, particularly when cooperating teachers provide good models and encourage positive attitudes. The research of Gottlieb (1980) found that in the regular classroom, the attitudes of students toward retarded children could be improved by using group discussion. These studies lead to the question: What books can be used to influence children's attitudes toward the handicapped?

A search was made through bibliographies and library collections for books that could develop positive attitudes toward the handicapped. Because attitudes are formed early, the titles were limited to those for use at the elementary level, particularly for the primary grades. Emphasis was put on quality literature that accurately reflects the reality of impairment and avoids false impressions. Because of the abundance of books published about handicaps or handicapped persons, the titles included are necessarily selective. Books dealing with the more prevalent handicaps of mainstreamed young children are listed in eight categories: visual handicaps, speech handicaps, emotionally disturbed, learning disabled, auditory handicaps, intellectual impairments, orthopedically handicapped, and general. The books are appropriate for use from preschool through level three.

Visual Handicaps

Stories about glasses predominate in the books relating to visual handicaps, while one title deals with blindness. The foggy, fuzzy, preglasses state of the heroine is detected in a medical examination during kindergarten in *Katie's Magic Glasses* (Goodsell, 1965). The situation is corrected, and information is given on how visual problems cause social misperceptions. *Jennifer Jean, the Cross-Eyed Queen* (Naylor, 1967) is a picture book portraying a feisty, determined heroine and her discomfort resulting from the rehabilitation process. *Spectacles* (Raskin, 1969) is an amusing and entertaining picture book; Iris adamantly resists getting glasses until a clever optician wins her over by suggesting that the right frames will make her look like a movie star. Mike and Sally are teased because they are the only children who wear glasses in *The Cowboy Surprise* (Wise, 1961), but the situation is remedied when Wild Bill, a bespectacled cowboy, comes to school and explains why some people need glasses. Apprehension about blindness is replaced by a desire for friendship as two young brothers become acquainted with a blind man who plays a harmonica and lives in the same apartment building in *Apt. 3* (Keats, 1971).

Speech Handicaps

A void exists for quality primary-level books dealing with the speech handicapped. The topic is considered in *A Certain Small Shepherd* (Caudill, 1965), but it cannot be evaluated on a literary basis since it is a religious parable.

Emotionally Disturbed

No books dealing with the emotionally disturbed were found for young readers.

Learning Disabled

The frustrations of youngsters who have learning problems are presented in two books for young children. The image of sibling affection, the exploration of frustration, and the accuracy of information presented are strengths of *He's My Brother* (Lasker, 1974). Jamie's disability creates difficulties in school and on the playground. *Leo, the Late Bloomer* (Kraus, 1971) is a fanciful story about a baby tiger who cannot do anything right; he cannot read, write, nor draw; he is a sloppy eater and never talks. His mother assures his father that Leo is a late bloomer, and in his own good time, he blooms!

Auditory Impairment

There are few trade books for the primary level on auditory impairment. The two fiction titles are about girls, and the nonfiction title has a matter-of-fact approach. *Lisa and Her Soundless World* (Levine, 1974) tells how 8-year-old Lisa's handicap was discovered and how hearing aids, lipreading, and sign language were used in treating her disability. The book provides good background on hearing and speaking processes and promotes empathy and understanding. A show-and-tell story in which Angela tells how her hearing deficiency was detected and corrected with a hearing aid is told in *A Button in Her Ear* (Litchfield, 1976). Encouraging evidence of increasing social acceptance of auditory impairment is found in the factual book, *A Show of Hands: Say It in Sign Language* (Sullivan & Bourke, 1980). In cartoon-type drawings and narrative text, it demonstrates the manual alphabet and more than 150 signs, while dealing in a matter-of-fact way with problems of what it is like to be deaf in a hearing world.

Intellectual Impairment

The importance of love and understanding from a supportive family is presented in the book for young readers about intellectual impairment. Even though *One Little Girl* (Fassler, 1969) suffers from a lack of focus as to its appropriate audience, it does emphasize the importance of positive attitudes toward a slow learner. Laurie has intellectual and visual impairments, and her parents and teachers see her improved response after they stop thinking and saying that she is slow and begin emphasizing her abilities.

Orthopedic Impairment

The books for young readers about orthopedic impairments focus on individual characters, and the tone is one of encouragement, hope, and normalcy as the youngsters, despite their handicaps, lead full lives. The problems of daily living associated with cerebral palsy are presented in *Howie Helps Himself* (Fassler, 1975). A real value of the book lies in its honest, accurate, and direct presentation of the problems of a severely physically handicapped child. *Rachel* (Fanshawe, 1975) depicts a young child who enjoys life fully and ignores whenever possible the inconvenience of using a wheelchair. An Alaskan Indian folk tale that treats disability as a mark of favor is found in *At the Mouth of the Luckiest River* (Grieses, 1969). Tatlek, who has a weak, pronated foot, is encouraged by his grandfather's assertion that a good spirit is looking after him. Tatlek deals with his "difference" in a natural, pragmatic fashion.

General

One title is especially noteworthy because it encourages children to imagine themselves in various situations faced by the disabled. *What if You Couldn't . . . ? A Book About Special Needs* (Kamien, 1979) is an informational book about many disabilities that asks the reader to imagine that he or she is a person with a disability and then introduces experiments that help to understand how it feels to have that disability. Hearing and visual impairment, other physical handicaps, emotional disturbances, and learning disabilities are among the conditions included. The direct and matter-of-fact text is an excellent resource book to help dispel ignorance about both the causes and consequences of specific handicaps.

One distinctive feature of books about the handicapped for elementary school children is that they are in general written about children, and the majority are about an individual child. Also, most books deal with only one handicap rather than multiple handicaps. Almost all the recent books focus on the handicapped character's positive outlook on life and the great gains he or she has made despite a disability.

Implications for Guidance Counselors

Good books about the handicapped are important for two reasons. They provide handicapped children with images and situations with which they can identify, and they help nonhandicapped children achieve an intelligent understanding of the handicapped. In addition, books of this type deal with many sound values, among them courage, understanding, and fair play, which are important to communicate to all children.

Several methods of using books to affect attitudes are available to counselors. Oral reading, group discussion, exposure to aids and appliances of the handicapped, guest speakers, tapes, filmstrips, and films are among the techniques available. Regardless of the method, it is particularly important that the adults provide good models and encourage positive attitudes.

Counselors should emphasize the importance of helping each child fit in and helping others to understand and accept handicapped students. The most crippling handicap is in the mind, not in the body, and that handicap is the attitudinal barrier. Children's books can play a positive role in breaking attitudinal barriers for the handicapped.

References

Baskin, B. H., & Harris, K. H. (1977). *Notes from a different drummer: A guide to juvenile fiction portraying the handicapped.* New York: Bowker.

Berg-Cross, L., & Berg-Cross, G. (1978). Listening to stories may change children's social attitudes. *The Reading Teacher, 31*, 659–663.

Caudill, R. (1965). *A certain small shepherd.* New York: Holt, Rinehart and Winston.

Fanshawe, E. (1975). *Rachel.* Scarsdale, NY: Bradbury.

Fassler, J. (1969). *One little girl.* New York: Human Sciences Press.

Fassler, J. (1975). *Howie helps himself.* Chicago: Whitman.

Goodsell, J. (1965). *Katie's magic glasses.* Boston: Houghton Mifflin.

Gottlieb, J. (1980). Improving attitudes toward retarded children by using group discussion. *Exceptional Children, 47*, 106–111.

Grieses, A. A. (1969). *At the mouth of the luckiest river.* New York: Crowell.

Kamien, J. (1979). *What if you couldn't . . . ? A book about special needs.* New York: Scribner's.

Keats, E. J. (1971). *Apt. 3.* New York: Macmillan.

Kraus, R. (1971). *Leo, the late bloomer.* New York: Windmill.
Lasker, J. (1974). *He's my brother.* Chicago: Whitman.
Levine, E. S. (1974). *Lisa and her soundless world.* New York: Human Sciences Press.
Litchfield, A. (1976). *A button in her ear.* Chicago: Whitman.
Monson, D., & Shurtleff, C. (1979). Altering attitudes toward the physically handicapped through print and nonprint media. *Language Arts, 56,* 153–170.
Naylor, P. (1967). *Jennifer Jean, the cross-eyed queen.* Minneapolis: Lerner.
Raskin, E. (1969). *Spectacles.* New York: Atheneum.
Semmel, M. I., Gottlieb, J., & Robinson, N. M. (1979). Mainstreaming: Perspectives on educating handicapped children in public schools. In D. C. Berliner (Ed.), *Review of research in education* (Vol. 7, pp. 223–279). Washington, DC: American Educational Research Association.
Sullivan, M. B., & Bourke, L. (1980). *A show of hands: Say it in sign language.* Reading, MA: Addison-Wesley.
Waples, D., Berelson, B., & Bradshaw, F. (1958). What reading does to people. *Research in the three R's.* New York: Harper & Row.
Wise, W. (1961). *The cowboy surprise.* New York: Putnam.

Chapter 5
Counseling Issues in a World of Exceptional Children

Issues for elementary school counselors to consider about a world of exceptional children:

1. How can elementary school counselors and special education teachers collaborate to help parents deal with the needs of exceptional children?
2. Consider some advantages of support groups for parents of exceptional children.
3. What are some of the special problems faced by gifted children?
4. Consider your graduate work in counselor education. What did you learn that has helped you deal with the special needs of exceptional children? What additional training do you need in this area?
5. How can exceptional children improve the learning environment in regular classrooms?
6. Identify several problems that families with gifted children may have. How can elementary school counselors provide support for these families?
7. What are some of the key issues involved in developing support groups for parents of exceptional children? What should be the major goals of these support groups?
8. How can elementary school counselors use books to help educate parents and students about the needs of exceptional children?
9. Discuss what is wrong with the following statement: "Elementary school counselors do not need additional work and should avoid significant roles in the education and support of exceptional children."
10. Discuss the following statement: "All children are exceptional."

CHAPTER 6

A TECHNOLOGICAL WORLD

Technological advances have changed education, work, and leisure in our society. Although most people experience the benefits of these advances, most also know the anxiety and frustration that accompany rapid technological change as well as the alienation generated by impersonal aspects of technology. Elementary school counselors need to help children develop emotionally and socially in the context of rapid technological change. Counselors often need to deal first with their own concerns about technology before helping children understand the benefits and limitations of technology. This chapter helps elementary school counselors to explore their own feelings about technology and to learn how technology may be used as a counseling tool.

The chapter begins with an article by Garry Walz who observes:

> The computer is an invention of unparalleled significance. In the last decade several innovations have been heralded as having the power to change how we live. Probably none, however, has the potential of the computer to affect our lives in general and education in particular.

The chapter includes articles which examine the need for elementary school counselors to acquire competencies with computers, to overcome anxieties about using the technology, and to integrate computer technology into counseling programs. These articles raise theoretical issues, practical issues, and ethical issues about the counselor's use of computers.

Although Chapter 6 is mainly limited to issues related to computer technology, several of the articles suggest that technology includes a wide range of useful tools for counselors especially in the area of video recording. The elementary school counseling literature in the next decade needs to explore imaginative uses of video technology to improve elementary school counseling

The central issue of this chapter is not whether technology is here to stay or if technology will affect the services elementary school counselors provide. Instead the issue is whether counselors will take charge of technology to improve their services and to make schools more humanistic institutions. The articles included in Chapter 6 argue that technology can make education and counseling more human.

As Nelson and Krockover note in the concluding article of this chapter, computers have the humanizing advantage of being blind to "sex, race, ethnic group, and socioeconomic status, showing virtually limitless patience to individuals from any group who happen to take longer than others to develop particular skills."

Role of the Counselor with Computers

Garry R. Walz

The computer has the potential to affect significantly the role of the counselor. Changing counselor roles are examined in light of recent computer innovations.

The computer is an invention of unparalleled significance. In the last decade several innovations have been heralded as having the power to change how we live. Probably none, however, has the potential of the computer to affect our lives in general and education in particular.

Certainly part of the reason for the tremendous impact of the computer on education is the time of its arrival. Education is currently under attack from dissatisfied constituencies who are demanding that students acquire a great deal more from their schooling. Postsecondary education, after a decade of emphasis on equity, is now being called upon to place greater emphasis on excellence and achievement. New strategies for educating both adolescents and adults are extending learning beyond school and college walls to a variety of self-managed educational experiences. These cries for greater excellence in education and improved student performance are occurring at a time when the costs of education are rising rapidly. The demand and the need for a quantum leap in improving education is so great that if the computer did not exist, something akin to it in potential, power, and impact would have been invented.

The computer is having a strong influence on school districts across the country, on state educational plans, and on policy pronouncements for both public and postsecondary education. The clamor for the computerization of education is becoming a din. Yet even before computers have become established in the educational enterprise, some people are decrying both their potential and the way they are being used. Are computers merely "electronic page-turners," or do they have the capacity to affect significantly how students and adults learn? Will school systems, training institutions, and organizations be able to use them to change and enhance the learning process? These questions are paramount. The difficulty in answering them is compounded by the fact that the real development and contribution of computers is only now emerging. The "computational powers equivalent to that of present-day super computers . . . will be available in a micro-process system for under $100 by 1990" (*Computers in Education*, 1983). Clearly, any discussion about the role of the counselor with computers needs to focus not on present activities or past experience but on possible and probable developments for computers and their impact and influence on counseling and human services in the near future.

Characteristics of Computers and Technology

There is an understandable tendency today to deal in simplistic generalizations about the computer's super powers and how it will revolutionize all that it touches, with little discussion of the concepts basic to the constructive use of computers. A discussion of computers that focuses on hardware alone overlooks the fundamental power of the computer. This is especially true in counseling, where the applications of the computer are still miniscule compared with the needs and opportunities.

Four characteristics of computers and technology will have significant effect on their adoption and use. First discussed by Walz (1970) in a *Personnel and Guidance Journal* special issue on technology and guidance, these characteristics have proven to be important in considering possible roles for computers in counseling and human services: (a) generation of both positive and negative outcomes; (b) increased visibility of conflict between choices and values; (c) the duality of depersonalization and individualization; and (d) influence of the social setting.

Generation of Both Positive and Negative Outcomes

Computers will create new opportunities to counsel differently and better and to perform counseling functions that have not been feasible in the past. But while the computer makes possible the achievement of new goals, some loss in the achievement of older goals may occur (e.g., greater opportunity to examine pertinent information may result in less one-to-one counselor interaction). The same technology and process will bring about both the gain and the loss.

Thus, the positive attributes of using computers must be weighed against the negative. In this process it is likely that different people will apply different criteria as to what is desirable or undesirable. Counselors with a strong interpersonal relationship orientation may have a different view than those with a guidance curriculum or a learning orientation. The fact is that even a very sophisticated technological innovation such as the computer has negative aspects. This explains why computers engender so much fear and resistance on the part of some counselors and in some educational settings.

Increased Visibility of Conflicts Between Choices and Values

Using computers in counseling forces program developers to delineate clearly their values and goals. In this process people may recognize greater conflicts than were apparent when goals or means were not sharply defined. In traditional counseling settings individual counselors have operated independently, and conflicts, if they existed, could be ignored or allowed to exist without much attention or fuss. The introduction of computers into a counseling program dramatizes the need to make hard decisions about values and outcomes. Although some may bemoan the conflict associated with computers and technologies and long for the days when counselors could "do their own thing" without the necessity for such choices, the very discussion necessary for the appropriate use of computers can sharpen the programmatic focus to a degree that strengthens the entire guidance program.

The Duality of Depersonalization and Individualization

In the year of Orwell's *1984* we are all sensitized to technology's potential to become the master rather than the servant. The very thought of such mechanistic processes entering the highest realm of humanistic interactions (i.e., counseling and education) convinces many that the survival of the individual as an existential being is possible only by opposing the adoption and use of computers.

The fact that 1984 is upon us and that few of the doomsday outcomes horrifyingly described by Orwell have occurred speaks to the ability of human beings to mediate and control the use of technology to serve their best interests. Furthermore, there is increasing evidence that in our complex world only technology can preserve and make possible the freedom and rights of humankind that we cherish so dearly. The storage and memory capacity of the computer provides the means to respond to people as individuals. When large numbers are involved, only the grossest identification and response is possible by any means other than the computer. Many who have experienced computer-assisted counseling feel that it was an extremely "personal" experience because the interaction with the computer was so focused on them.

The Influence of the Social Setting

The social setting for the computer has a strong influence on whether or not, to what extent, and in what ways the benefits of the computer will be realized. It is undesirable, even dangerous, to either discuss the usefulness of a computer without reference to the setting in which it is to be used or generalize about the usefulness of computers from one setting to another. An adult counseling center committed to providing accurate information about career opportunities and choices is likely to use a computer very differently than a secondary school guidance program concerned with helping adolescents deal with important life plans and decisions. The computer, as a component in a highly variable social setting, is ungeneralizable because it both shapes and is shaped by the particular program in which it is used, the school or agency where it is located, or the larger community. However primitive our knowledge about computer-assisted counseling, our knowledge about how to adopt and implement computer-assisted counseling in different counseling and human services programs is even more primitive. Generalizations across different levels and settings are of little real value.

New and Emerging Counselor Roles in Using Computers

Systematic Exploration and Use of Computers

No role for counselors in using computers is easily generalizable or clear-cut. The level, the setting, and the particular program culture will determine how the computer can be used most effectively and what outcomes will accrue. Therefore, an essential first step for counselors in defining their role will be practical experience with a variety of strategies and procedures. There is no substitute for counselor familiarity and comfort with computers. The difficulties of acquiring such experience probably have been greatly overstated. Short courses offered by computer vendors or a variety of educational institutions can provide a relatively quick, basic understanding and skill level.

Counselors can begin immediately to explore possible computer applications and use in two areas. The first, computer-managed counseling (CMC), assists counselors with the clerical and administrative tasks associated with their work, tasks that frequently inhibit their ability to undertake meaningful counselor interactions (Bleuer & Walz, 1983). Practical applications of computer-managed counseling include the following: client-student recordkeeping, counseling activity logs, student and client attendance records for both individuals and groups, scheduling of individuals and groups, records of grades for easy production of transcripts, resource files for the counselor's personal use, and general word processing (e.g., report writing and personalized letters). In these areas the computer can alleviate some of the tedium and monotony of present counseling duties and allow time for more meaningful counselor-client interactions. Many existing software programs enable counselors to perform all of these tasks without great skill or expense.

A second area of exploration for counselors is computer-assisted counseling (CAC), which is to counseling what computer-assisted instruction (CAI) is to teaching. This is an interactive counseling technique in which the computer is used to present information, elicit and monitor responses, and select and present additional information in accordance with individual client needs (Bleuer & Walz, 1983). CAC offers three significant contributions to the counseling process: objectivity, availability, and the capacity to store and retrieve a great deal of information. Objectivity is an important aspect of any educational decision and planning relationship, and the computer is certainly objective. Availability, or the opportunity for ready access to information, is also a decided contribution of CAC. After initial instruction, clients can often use the computer with sufficient reward that additional direct interaction with a counselor is unnecessary; in other cases, clients are better prepared to have meaningful discussions with the counselor about their decisions and plans. Perhaps the greatest contribution of present-day CAC is the computer's capacity to store and retrieve many kinds of information. This ability is evident in computer software that provides career and educational information, skill-building in such areas as problem solving and decision making, interest and ability assessment through computerized testing modules, and test practice and preparation such as for the SAT.

Exploring and trying out CMC and CAC will help counselors discover ways to reduce the time they devote to repetitive, monotonous tasks that the computer can perform better. Providing clients with some of the same meaningful experiences and learnings by computer that are possible in one-to-one counseling may also lead to improved quality for one-to-one counseling interactions.

An Active Stance for Quality Assurance

Many are inclined to judge the quality of a computer program by the complexity and the quantity of the hardware. Simply stated, some people believe that the more computers are used, the more advanced and sophisticated the program. In fact, program effectiveness is more a function of quality and appropriateness of the software than of expense or quantity of computers. The available software for counseling and guidance can be used on relatively few computers. Therefore, the first consideration in selecting a computer is to make sure that it is compatible with software that meets the needs and interests of a particular clientele. It is just as important to make sure that the chosen software is of high quality. A vital counselor role, then, is a quality assurance review of all software to be used. This is particularly important for two reasons. First, unlike print media, software programs cannot be reviewed quickly or casually. The assumptions and values inherent in the construction of each program are not readily apparent and require careful analysis. Second, unlike many guidance procedures, computer software frequently will be used by students or adults without further reference to the counselor. Such independent access makes the need for careful scrutiny all the more important. This is a responsibility that counselors cannot delegate and must carry out if computers are going to make a truly viable contribution to counseling.

Evaluation of the Use of Computers

The effects of computers in counseling processes are only beginning to be known. Although there is an emerging consensus among researchers about the positive benefits of computer-assisted counseling, the actual contribution of computers to counseling must be determined separately in each program.

Perhaps the greatest deterrent to systematic and ongoing evaluation of counseling and human services innovations has been uncertainty about how to do it. Consequently, many initially attractive innovations have been abandoned because their value could not be sufficiently substantiated to justify the added effort or expense. Computers, however, can compile the data needed to evaluate the quality of their services.

Counselors must be committed to gathering specific data about what computers do or do not do to achieve significant outcomes. One approach, *SHAPE—Self Help Approach to Program Evaluation* (Collet, Walz, & Collet, 1983), presents a readily usable method for program self-evaluation and suggests a variety of sources for judging the value of using computers in counseling processes. This program provides a systematic approach to evaluation that does not require external consultants or complex statistical procedures. The inevitable pendulum swing will bring about questioning of the use and worth of technology in education and counseling. If counselors fail to evaluate their programs, it is likely that others will do it for them, and most likely from a nonobjective and possibly hostile perspective.

Computers as an Indiscriminate Discriminator: A Commitment to Equity

Client response to computers is varied and not universally positive. Based on previous experiences, clients may approach computers with either trepidation or pleasure. Women and minority group members may show less interest or desire to use computers than do White males. Clients with linear cognitive styles may find the computer less appealing than do those with inferential thinking and learning styles. Previous experience with computer games can also influence people's response to computers.

Special efforts to minimize anxieties and to clarify false assumptions about computers could be necessary if many clients are to benefit from using them. Most users do enjoy the computerized components of a counseling experience, finding reinforcement and reward. It is a major responsibility of counselors to attend to initial attitudinal and experiential differences and to ensure that they do not keep certain individuals or groups from profiting from the counseling process.

A Systematic Adoption and Implementation Process

Ask a group of counselors how they first introduced computers into their program and you will receive as many descriptions as there are counselors. Patterns range from imposition from higher administrative authority to a strong counselor initiative to broaden the resources available within the guidance program. Evident in many of the adoption procedures used, however, is the lack of an orderly and systematic process. More often than not, decisions about installation and implementation are based on availability of funds or administrators' desires to computerize the program. The resultant patchwork quilt of usage is not conducive to realizing the full potential of computers in counseling.

A seven-step model for developing and implementing a high-tech counseling program has been described by Bleuer and Walz (1983). This model emphasizes the need for customizing the computer to the particular goals and needs of a given human services program and provides a step-by-step process for counselors to follow. The steps in the model are: (a) analyze the program for potential computer applications; (b) investigate available computer resources; (c) select computer uses that will meet program needs; (d) match software to program needs; (e) match hardware to software; (f) invest in personware; and (g) implement and evaluate. Basic to this model is purposeful and planful adoption rather than an impulsive, thoughtless approach that rushes to the end state (the purchase and installation of computers) before the necessary groundwork has taken place.

The counselor should encourage excited interest in the adoption process, but should also make sure that the necessary thinking and planning occur before decisions are made or actions are taken that might later hinder or negatively affect the program. The computer has the potential for providing great individuation and flexibility within the counseling program. Unwise decisions, however, may lock the counseling staff into either behaviors or resources that actually negate their ability to respond flexibly and that could result in a more rigid program than if they had not attempted to use computers and technology at all. This is a time when counselors must stand firm and insist on careful planning and judicious implementation.

Exploration into New Uses of the Computer

Computers can help counselors accomplish old tasks in new ways or undertake new functions not previously thought of because the necessary methodology was lacking. Unfortunately, the tendency exists to try to mold this new innovation, the computer, to existing modes of thinking and behaving. Thus, in some cases computers are used primarily as efficient storage banks that offer an advantage over traditional methods of filing and retrieving information. Admittedly, this is a useful role. But counselors need to explore exciting new uses for computers in counseling.

Listed below are a few of the avenues by which counselors may use computers to enhance the scope of counseling and the quality of counseling outcomes (*Computers in Education*, 1983):

Tutoring. The computer can be an excellent tutor in different aspects of career and life decision making and problem solving. It is patient and can readily adapt to a variety of individual differences and needs.

Diagnosis. Computers can help to diagnose individual students' knowledge and cognitive style. Counselors can use this information to plan more appropriate learning strategies that build on the strengths and weaknesses of a given student.

Game technologies. Computer games can provide motivation and interest for extensive practice in the problem-solving abilities associated with making major life plans and decisions. They also can serve a diagnostic function, helping to determine where individuals need additional help and practice in planning and decision making. It is possible to develop games that resemble exploratory learning environments, enabling the user to simulate deciding and behaving in actual life situations.

Networks. Through the use of telecommunications or special computer programs, it is possible to create communities or networks of participants regardless of physical location. Students interested in exploring a particular career, for example, could develop a support network using computer telecommunications. They could then interact with students in other classes or in other schools without any need for physical meetings or travel. Resources developed during the day could be shared with parents in the evening, providing an opportunity for parent-child interactions currently missing in many families.

The above are just a few of the many possibilities for using computers in counseling. Counselors must provide a creative impetus for the use of computers. They must be unwilling to accept their being able to perform old tasks better as the major or sole contribution that computers can make to counseling.

Counselor Role Priorities

The computer has the potential to affect significantly the role of the counselor. But it is only a potential. The addition of computers to a human services program does not guarantee that the program will be either more efficient or more effective. Rather, it is the clear identification of outcomes and the means selected for reaching those outcomes that will determine whether or not a computer will enhance the counselor role. Several considerations are paramount in redefining the counselor's role vis-à-vis the computer.

1. In light of the enormous potential of the computer, we must look to the creative redesign of counseling. There is a real danger that we will automate the status quo—settling for doing what we do with a little more pizzazz and in a labor-saving mode, but with little significant change in how we define our role or interact with clients. Physical scientists have used computer programs as a way of testing the soundness of their theories. We need to use computers to assess the soundness of our counseling strategies and to determine how we may better achieve our goals, using the computer.

2. We must define our developmental efforts as a joint enterprise. Perhaps one of the most exciting aspects of using the computer in counseling is the opportunity it provides for individuals to work together as a team—clients, counselors, parents, and community members—to design programs that best meet individual and joint needs. In most of the areas in which counselors work, significant others play a vital role in the movement from idea to action. Making those significant others an integral part of the learning environment is fascinating and potentially beneficial. Joint planning concerning the ways computers can be used to reach a variety of counseling objectives is likely to whet the interest of these various groups regarding computer use and help to ensure that objectives are met.

3. Many aspects of the use of computers in counseling create uncertainty. Is there a synergism that will encourage students to become involved in other learning experiences, computer or otherwise? Will the increased use of computers by students disturb parents? Will extensive use of computers enhance the counselor role and encourage new, higher-level personal interactions, or will counselors become mere functionaries in an automated system? What effects will computers have on the motivation of students and adults? Will they be encouraged to seek other learning experiences and more computer interaction, or will they be less inclined to seek out new learning challenges? We need to address questions such as these as we consider broad-term effects of computers on clients. Vital to the new counselor role is a willingness to observe, identify, and assess behaviors associated with computers, on the part of both those who use them and those who provide them. This must become an important subject of discussion and analysis as we move toward a computer-enhanced counselor role.

4. Emerging research in cognitive science tells us that dialogue is a particularly meaningful way for students to learn, especially when it is followed

by regular practice. This suggests a learning model not unlike typical counseling interactions and may mean that subject-oriented educational programs will be moving closer to the style of the counselor. This is an exciting opportunity for counselors to influence educational processes, leading toward discovery learning and individual planning and decision making. The computer may be the instrument for breaking down the massive walls of isolation erected by counselors over the years, prohibiting or limiting their interaction with other educators and the community. The computer can be the means for achieving coalescence. Counselors may be in a position to expand their influence in areas far wider than the traditional counseling realm.

Counseling today is still relatively untouched by technology. Although tape and video recorders and programmed instruction are a regular part of most counselor preparation programs, they are hardly ever used in day-to-day counseling. The computer, however, offers a new vision for counselors—the opportunity not only to do better what they now do but to redefine what counseling is and how it is delivered. The ultimate effectiveness of tomorrow's counselors will depend somewhat on advances in the development of hardware and relevant software, but most of all on personware—the attitudes and feelings of counselors about the adoption of a powerful new tool. It will require their giving up some of what they have done well in order to take on new means and goals. The most important new role for counselors in the use of computers may well be a sense of creative risk-taking that encourages, stimulates, and models for clients a change in viewpoint regarding the counseling experience and how to use it.

References

Bleuer, J. C., & Walz, G. R. (1983). *Counselors and computers.* Ann Arbor: ERIC/CAPS, The University of Michigan.

Collet, J. C., Walz, G. R., & Collet, L. S. (1983). *SHAPE: Self-help approach to program evaluation.* Ann Arbor: ERIC/CAPS, The University of Michigan.

Computers in education: Realizing the potential. (1983). Chairmen's Report of a Research Conference, Pittsburgh, Pennsylvania, November 20–24, 1982. Washington, DC: Superintendent of Documents, U.S. Government Printing Office.

Walz, G. R. (1970). Technology in guidance: A conceptual overview. *Personnel and Guidance Journal, 49*, 175–182.

High Touch and High Technology: The Marriage that Must Succeed

JoAnn Harris-Bowlsbey

Counselors should view the computer and its associated technology as partners in helping students and clients achieve their counseling goals. The extent to which this collaborative effort is feasible or considered desirable, however, is related to the theoretical perspective the counselor adopts. Affective theoretical positions, in which high touch is seen as a powerful remediating force, will view the computer as a much less welcome partner than will cognitive theoretical perspectives, in which systematic processes and learning goals can be defined. For the future survival of the profession, it is essential that the appropriate merger of high touch and high technology be accomplished and that counselors be trained to implement the synthesis.

The computer, introduced into the counseling field in the 1960s, is just now reaching a period of high adoption, owing to the advent of microcomputer technology, the existence of several well-tested products from which to select, and the extensive marketing effort of both commercial and not-for-profit organizations in the field. It is particularly relevant, then, that in the 80s the counseling and guidance profession come to grips with an appropriate merger of high technology and high touch to assist clients/students in accomplishing the goals and objectives defined for the counseling or guidance relationship.

Before embarking on such a significant task, it is appropriate to define the terms *high technology* and *high touch* (Naisbitt, 1982). High technology is defined as any mode of delivery of counseling or guidance services in which a computer or an interactive videodisk is central to the accomplishment of client/student objectives. High touch is defined as any mode of delivery of counseling or guidance services in which human, empathic interpersonal skills are central to the accomplishment of client/student objectives.

The purpose of this article is to assist counselor educators, supervisors, and practicing counselors to determine conditions under which high technology alone, high touch alone, or the purposeful combination of the two may be the preferred mode of treatment. To begin this process, at least three assumptions seem apparent. First, high technology will never replace high touch in the human resource development field. Although robots may make automobiles better and faster, my assumption is that human beings will never be better counseled or guided by robots, computers, or interactive videodisks. A second assumption is that high technology and high touch should be viewed not as opponents, but as potential partners. This article will suggest under what conditions and in what ways they may become powerful partners. Third, presumably the profession's thinking about the merger of high technology and high touch is new and tentative; therefore the counselors whom we educate and supervise will need preservice and in-service training to think in ways suggested in this article.

Counseling and guidance practice need to flow from a theoretical base, and each of the major schools of counseling theory has its attendant tools, techniques, and modes of service delivery designed to facilitate the client's accomplishment of goals deemed worthy and appropriate. My contention is that the degree of involvement of high technology in assisting individuals to reach those goals is, or should be, related to the theoretical perspective the counselor or helper adopts.

The following pages elaborate on this statement in detail. Each major theoretical perspective will be examined in regard to its hypotheses about the self, the environment, and the interaction of the two.

Theoretical Perspectives of Counseling: Affective Approaches

Rogers

The work of Carl Rogers (1951, 1961) has made a major impact on counseling theory and practice. Like other theorists, Rogers deals with the self, the environment, and the interaction of the two. The self is a learned attribute consisting of individuals' pictures of themselves. The aware organism is constantly experiencing in a perceptual field. The part of the field that the individual accepts or experiences as separate from the remainder becomes the *self.* The individual by nature strives toward integration and actualization of potential. For this reason, the self of the healthy individual becomes increasingly differentiated over time into an organized, fluid, consistent conceptual pattern of perceptions together with values attached to these concepts. Ideally, as the individual actualizes, the concept of self becomes increasingly harmonious and increasingly consistent with experience. Growth consists of the continuing acceptance and integration of experience as a part of the self-structure.

The environment, says Rogers, is that part of the perceptual field other than the self. In other words, *reality* for a given individual consists totally of that individual's unique perceptual field. The part of the field that is claimed as self is excluded from the environment, although the two are in continuing, dynamic relationship to each other.

The interaction between self and environment has at least two important aspects. First, the environment is the source of the individual's need fulfillment; the growing individual reaches out into the environment to find those things that are needed for self-actualization. Second, the environment is the place in which experience occurs. Optimally, experience is integrated into the self so that the two are coterminous or nearly so. Experience, therefore, may at times be a part of the environment (that is, not yet integrated into the self), and at other times be a part of the self (that is, accepted and integrated into the self-picture).

The primary goal of counseling is to create an environment in which an individual can release the natural tendency to self-actualize. Such a growth environment must allow the client to examine experience without judgment, to accept it, to integrate it into the self, and to reach out into the environment to seek ever new experience to fulfill needs and enhance the differentiation of the self. The counselor's role is to create this environment. Its characteristics are warmth, understanding, acceptance, supportiveness, empathy, and encouragement. The primary technique is skillful reflection, which enables and encourages the client to look at experience, environment, and self with increasing perception and awareness.

The hallmark of the Rogerian theory and approach is high touch. In fact, high touch is the absolutely necessary condition for any forward movement in understanding and developing the self, the environment, and the interaction of the two. The Rogerian approach is a very personal, subjective one. The world of educational and vocational options doesn't even exist unless it becomes a part of the individual's live perceptual field, and until it does, it would be impossible to deal with. The growing individual will reach for such options only when a need is felt for them, and when the self is ready to integrate them into experience and awareness.

High technology is anathema in this theoretical perspective. The human counselor, and well-sharpened perceptive and reflective skills are absolutely critical to reaching valid counseling goals. The only imaginable place for a computer in this framework is as a method of explaining selected parts of the environment (e.g., occupations or colleges) when an individual feels a need to reach out of self to access unknown elements of the environment. Even in such an event, the counselor would be a critical entity in assisting the individual to integrate the new-found information from the environment as a part of the self and the self-experience.

Gestalt

Akin to Rogers's approach, in that emphasis is placed on the affective, is Perls's Gestalt therapy. The Gestalt view emphasizes the position that human beings are more than the sum of their parts and that individuals must be perceived and must behave as wholes. Since humans are viewed as wholes, the organism cannot be separate from the environment. The self is contained within an *ego boundary,* the recognized division between the individual and the environment. Humans are constantly plagued with a Freudian-type controversy between *topdog* and *underdog*, Perls's terms for the Freudian *superego* and *id.*

The environment is a place from which to select activities, experiences, and people to fulfill needs. The aware individual senses needs and seeks a means whereby to meet them. This awareness catalyzes the absorption of elements from the environment into the individual in order to make the organism more nearly whole and more stable as a psychological system. The interaction between the individual and the environment, then, is a dynamic, fluid one. The ideal is a kind of homeostasis in which the individual's needs are amply met and the individual has "owned" all of the experiences and attitudes that are a part of a very aware "now."

As in the Rogerian approach, the mode of counseling is a direct one-to-one human intervention approach. Techniques include dream analysis, role playing, and active confrontation. Counseling goals are the raising of awareness, the acceptance of responsibility for one's own behavior, and independence.

Also as in the Rogerian approach, this theoretical perspective does not lend itself to the application of high technology. This one is a high touch, totally human delivery mode, applied one-to-one and in groups. Emphasis is given to development and maturation of the self, with the assumption that life's decisions and choices can be adequately handled once such responsible maturity is achieved.

Two predominant theories that emphasize the affective approach to counseling have been reviewed. From these perspectives the spotlight is on the individual and the development of the self. All of life's choices are viewed as extensions of the self into the environment. It is assumed that the individual will be aware only of those choices that are a part of the perceived phenomenological field. Furthermore, it is assumed that wise choices will be made from among the known alternatives if the individual has sufficient integration and awareness. In short, attention needs to be given only to the self in order to ensure successful interaction with the environment.

Theoretical Perspectives of Counseling: Cognitive Approaches

Trait and Factor

The trait-and-factor approach has its roots in the work and theory of Williamson (1939, 1972). In this approach humans are viewed as rational beings composed of a variety of measurable personality factors. If individuals adequately understand their capabilities, including both strengths and limitations, they can use these capabilities in a planned way to lead purposeful lives and to maximize the potential they have. It is assumed that with adequate cognitive understanding of self, the individual will be able and motivated to take purposeful action.

The environment is viewed as a place in which jobs and educational opportunities have differing requirements. Given the individuals' potential to have clear self-pictures of their capacities and for the requirements of jobs and educational programs to be measured, it is possible to match the one with the other. To the extent that accurate matches can be made, both the individual and the environment can function productively and harmoniously.

To implement this counseling theory, it is necessary to have accurate assessment tools to measure the characteristics of both the individual and the environment. Obviously, in order to create meaningful matches between the two, it is necessary to measure the same aspects of both in the same terms so that linkages can be made.

Given the availability of assessment tools, then, the role of the counselor consists of several aspects. First, the counselor needs to use the assessment tools to accurately analyze the individual to gain and to transmit an accurate understanding of self-variables to the client/student. Second, the counselor must synthesize data about the client in order to understand the client's strengths and weaknesses. Diagnosis of problem areas or strengths that need cultivation follows. Prognosis provides predictive data about probabilities of success in alternative occupational or educational pursuits. Counseling is a period of making plans and taking action steps to bring about adjustment or the next steps of action. This period might typically be followed by a more formal one of follow-up evaluation.

The trait-and-factor approach lends itself beautifully to high technology and can minimize high touch, which has never been a significant variable in the mix. There are several reasons why this approach lends itself to high technology. First, it is a cognitive, logical step-by-step sequence with clearly identifiable branches and outcomes. These characteristics make it totally amenable to flow-charting, systemization, and therefore to computerization. Second, the assessment instruments inherent in the approach can be administered, scored, interpreted, and compared to a variety of norm groups by computer with more precision, more objectivity, and faster feedback than by humans. Third, it is a relatively short-term definable process, although it may need to be repeated at intervals, and therefore may be presented by computer and associated devices in a finite number of cost-feasible sessions. Finally, the variety of possible alternative interpretations, questions, and relationships can be identified so that the resulting computer program can allow an amazing degree of personalization through multiple branching opportunities.

Rational-Emotive

The rational-emotive point of view focuses on the individual's belief system. Albert Ellis (1967), the theorist behind this position, has defined 11 irrational ideas, one or more of which every human being believes. To believe an irrational idea, such as "Every adult human being should be loved or approved by virtually every significant other person in his community," will cause negative emotions. There is a direct relationship between belief and emotion. Changing the belief set will change the emotional set. The important focus, therefore, is to identify which of the 11 irrational ideas a client accepts and to actively and persuasively convince the client that these beliefs are in error. Once a belief, that is, a self-statement, can be corrected, the emotions associated with it can be changed. The self, therefore, is a complex structure of beliefs learned from parents and the larger society. The environment is the stage on which these beliefs are set. The interaction between the two and the quality of the emotional response of the client/student can be substantially altered by the modification of beliefs.

The counselor in this model is a very forceful teacher. Once the number and magnitude of the irrational beliefs are assessed, the counselor sets out to attack the client's beliefs forcefully and directly in an attempt to correct them. Little or no attention is given to feeling states; it is assumed that they will correct themselves as beliefs are changed and tested in the environment.

Although this position has always cast the human counselor in the role of an intervention agent, the approach is not high touch. Little value is awarded to warmth, genuineness, rapport, or any of the other counselor characteristics so valued by other approaches. The counselor needs to be an attacker, a nagger, an arguer, and a confronter. Computers can do that! Although it has not been done to my knowledge, it would seem possible to create an on-line, detailed, branching analysis of the degree of a client's commitment to each of the 11 irrational ideas. The material could be laid out in much the same way adaptive testing items are. If the client responds in a way that indicates that a given irrational idea does not exist for him or her, the computer soon abandons it and goes on to the next idea. Alternatively, if some responses indicate a degree of adoption of a given irrational idea, this idea might be pursued in great depth and ferreted out so that it could be forcefully attacked. The "attack" might be enhanced with the audiovisual power of a videodisk as well. This kind of program could comprehensively assess the degree of belief each client holds in each of the irrational ideas. Strong prescriptive treatment could be supplied for each of several levels of belief in each idea.

Behavioral Counseling

Behavioral counseling explains behavior in relation to the stimulus-response learning theory (S-O-R). Desired behavior can be learned, and learning takes place through positive reinforcement for acceptable behavior or approximations of it. Undesirable behavior can be unlearned through negative reinforcement or lack of reinforcement, thus extinguishing the behavior. The self, then, is a set of learned behaviors and responses; the more appropriate and the broader the repertoire of these behaviors, the more developed or refined is the self. The environment is a very important focal point of this counseling persuasion because it is the source of the learning. The environment can either perpetuate or extinguish desired or undesired behaviors. Its value may even be more important than that of the self. Surely reality, learning, and adjustment reflect the quality of the interaction between the environment and the individual.

In this theoretical perspective, the counselor serves two primary roles: manipulating the environment to set up necessary learning conditions to achieve desired ends, and assisting the individual to understand the interaction that is taking place. Of these two roles, the first is by far the most important. The tools of this approach, then, are those involved in setting up learning conditions to teach desired behaviors. The counselor must be a creative engineer of experience for the client and must become expert at modifying the person-environment interaction when there is a variation from the desired end goals worked out in consultation with the client.

As we have noted with other cognitive approaches, behavioral counseling is a defined system. It therefore lends itself to a fair degree of computerization. The computer could be used to generate prescriptions for clients by simulation methods like those used for computer diagnosis of patients or trips into space. Given that the computer program had a "knowledge" of reinforcement theory, client goals and specific behavioral problems could be entered into the computer, and the computer could provide the counselor and the client suggested plans for environment change or manipulation. If a first try at this approach did not completely achieve the desired end goals, the computer could prescribe "corrections" to the original plan based upon input of data about the success of the plan.

Besides being used as a drafter of plans for the counselor, the computer could also serve as a direct teacher for the client. It could provide direct didactic material about learning. It could ask the client to enter specific problems and desired end goals, and it could set up computer and videodisk-provided positive and negative reinforcers in simulated situations.

Application of Theories to Career Counseling

Any one of the counseling theories reviewed could be used to assist a client/student in making educational or vocational decisions, often called career counseling or guidance. Historically, the trait-and-factor approach has been heavily applied to decisions in the career arena. Even counselors who typically use the approaches described earlier in "personal" counseling often make a transition to an eclectic, trait-and-factor, or Parsonian approach when helping a client make educational and vocational choices. The Parsonian approach (Parsons, 1909) is a logical three-step one: (a) clients should become aware of their interests and abilities as these relate to work; (b) clients should become aware of the many alternatives available in the environment, that is, available occupations, paths of education, and schools; and (c) clients should be helped to put these two domains of information together to identify feasible personal options. Counselors have used the work of John Holland (1973) so well and so enthusiastically because it "measures" the person and the environment in the same three-letter terms, thus making the relationship between the two easy to understand. The computer has already been used extremely effectively to help implement the trait-and-factor and Parsonian models.

The Presenting Problem

Extensive review has been provided of the most common theories of counseling. Some inferences have been drawn in regard to the degree of fit between these theories and the use of the computer as a tool. Another dimension that needs to be considered in the mix is the nature of the presenting problem that the client/student brings to the counseling situation. Considerable research data (Garis, 1982) indicate that the computer is a very effective tool when career choice is the primary if not exclusive presenting problem. In the Garis study, findings indicate that with this population the best treatment is a combination of counselor and computer; the second best, the computer alone; and the third best, the counselor alone. All three of these experimental groups made significant gains in aspects of vocational maturity and specification of career plans over the control group, which had no treatment. The body of research on the effects of one-to-one and group counseling with personal-social presenting problems would lead us to believe that the priority order of effective treatments would be quite different and would place the counselor in first place as the most effective mode of treatment.

Summary

There seem to be two relevant dimensions on which to assess the potential effectiveness of the computer as a tool in counseling and guidance. The first is the theoretical base of the counseling approach. The greater the extent of the cognitive emphasis of the approach, the greater the potential for effective computer intervention. More specifically, the computer lends itself well to approaches that have the following characteristics:

1. The counseling process can be described as a systematic step-by-step process;
2. The interpersonal skills of the counselor are not the primary ingredient of the counseling process; and
3. The improvement of the client/student depends on the acquisition of skills, knowledge, or information.

The second dimension is the nature of the presenting problem. The greater the confinement of the presenting problem as a career choice problem, one that is related specifically to educational and vocational choice, the greater the potential for the computer alone or in combination with the counselor to be an effective mode of intervention. The expectation would be, therefore, for the computer's effectiveness to be significant in the following priority order:

1. With "pure" career guidance concerns, with counselor support, combined with a cognitively based theoretical perspective;
2. With pure career guidance concerns, without counselor support, combined with a cognitively based theoretical perspective;
3. With counseling concerns other than career guidance, with counselor support, with a cognitively based theoretical perspective;
4. With counseling concerns other than career guidance, without counselor support, with a cognitively based theoretical perspective;
5. With counseling concerns related to career guidance, with counselor support, with an affectively based theoretical perspective;
6. With counseling concerns related to career guidance, without counselor support, with an affectively based theoretical perspective;
7. With counseling concerns unrelated to career guidance, with counselor support, with an affectively based theoretical perspective;
8. With counseling concerns unrelated to career guidance, without counselor support, with an affectively based theoretical perspective.

This priority order is currently based on judgment, rationality, and a limited amount of research data. This is a fertile area for extensive future research.

Implications for the Education and Supervision of Counselors

This article began with the premise that the merger of high touch and high technology must be a marriage that succeeds. Few, if any, marriages succeed without planning, hard work, and learning. The same will be true of the high touch/high technology marriage. If it does not succeed, counselors must have preservice and in-service training specifically designed to provide the following:

1. A general base of computer literacy, especially in regard to microcomputer technology;
2. Good cognitive knowledge of the various theoretical perspectives for both career and personal-social counseling and of their preferred techniques;
3. Understanding of the strengths and weaknesses of computer delivery of services;
4. Understanding the systematic approaches of the delivery of guidance, especially of career guidance, and of the role of the computer in these approaches;
5. An understanding of the combinations of modes that can be used for delivery of services and under what conditions single and combination modes of delivery are most effective.

To address these concerns, counselor education programs need to modify and add to curriculum. They need to provide counselors with already-existing knowledge about and experience with computer software as well as with skills to develop the systems of the future. Counselor supervisors need to give attention to the in-service training of their staffs and to the acquisition of computer-based systems to provide significant assistance in the areas of counseling and guidance, in which the computer's effectiveness has already been proven. The technology of the computer is with us to stay, and that of the interactive videodisk is on its way. If we cannot integrate these technologies into our work effectively, we will find ourselves as out of date as did the cloistered scribe after the introduction of the Gutenberg printing press. If we can integrate these technologies, the result of the new union will be greatly improved and expanded services to our clients.

References

Ellis, A. (1967). *Reason and emotion in psychotherapy.* New York: Lyle Stuart.

Garis, J. W. (1982). *The integration of the DISCOVER computer-based guidance system in a college counseling center—its effects upon career planning* (Doctoral dissertation, Pennsylvania State University).

Holland, J. L. (1973). *Making vocational choices.* Englewood Cliffs, NJ: Prentice-Hall.
Naisbitt, J. (1982). *Megatrends: Ten new directions transforming our lives.* New York: Warner Books.
Parsons, F. (1909). *Choosing a vocation.* Boston: Houghton-Mifflin.
Perls, F. S. (1971). *Gestalt therapy verbatim.* New York: Bantam Books.
Rogers, C. (1951). *Client-centered therapy.* Boston: Houghton Mifflin.
Rogers, C. (1961). *On becoming a person.* Boston: Houghton Mifflin.
Williamson, E. G. (1939). *How to counsel students.* New York: McGraw-Hill.
Williamson, E. G. (1972). Vocational counseling: Trait-factor theory. In B. Stefflre & W. H. Grant (Eds.), *Theories of counseling.* New York: McGraw-Hill.

Counselor Computer Competencies

Don Dinkmeyer, Jr.
Jon Carlson

The first automobiles were often viewed as dangerous, noisy machines. Villages forced drivers to send men with red flags ahead of the automobiles, warning pedestrians and horses of the oncoming vehicles.

Men with red flags are not being sent ahead of the computers entering our schools. Microcomputers, however, are replacing many traditional methods in education. Counselors who understand the purpose and potential of computers will be able to use the machines to increase their effectiveness; thus they need to acquire a specific set of computer competencies.

A quarter million microcomputers (small, portable computers that are sometimes called "personal computers" because of their use in homes and schools) will be in our schools this fall. Computer manufacturers want to donate machines to each of the 83,000 schools in the nation. Revenues for computer-assisted instruction reached $2 billion in 1981 and are expected to exceed $13 billion in less than 5 years (*Computers: Focus on the Classroom*, 1982). The microcomputer is quickly becoming as common as blackboards or notebooks. It is not a passing fad.

If you doubt the ability of microcomputers to assist the educational process, consider these situations:

- A counselor is asked by the principal to make student assignments for next year, taking into consideration parent requests, teacher requests, and a fair balance of the best and worst students in each grade.
- A teacher sends a second-grade student to the counselor because the student does not learn at the same pace as the majority of the class. Discouraged and disruptive, the student is labeled a "behavior problem" that the counselor is expected to solve for the teacher.
- A counselor's position is threatened because the school board does not know what the counselor really does. Is there any hard evidence as to the number of student contacts, parent and teacher conferences, and outcomes?

All of these challenges can benefit from computer assistance. The first and third problems can be solved with the help of the record-keeping abilities of computers. The second-grade child may be helped by the self-pacing, tireless, and reinforcing abilities of the microcomputer in computer-assisted instruction (CAI).

Computer Competencies

We suggest four specific competencies that counselors need to acquire:

1. An elementary knowledge of microcomputer components and some of the vocabulary surrounding computers.
2. An awareness of the current uses of microcomputers by students, teachers, and counselors.
3. The ability to identify and act upon inherent ethical issues concerning the present and future uses of computers in the schools.
4. A willingness to see and act upon potential opportunities for the use of microcomputers.

What is a Computer?

The computer is simply a machine that does some tasks incredibly well and incredibly fast. It has absolutely no ability to do these things unless a person has written a program that will instruct the machine for this task. Once this program (software) is created, the applications are almost limitless.

The microcomputer's basic parts can be simply described:

- A keyboard, similar to a typewriter keyboard, allows you to "enter data" (give instructions to the machine). Computer keyboards have more keys than regular typewriters. The additional keys are often used to move the cursor (a flashing line or square that indicates your position) on the screen or to give frequently used commands to the machine. For example, instead of typing "print this document," by pressing one of these additional keys you can achieve the same result with a single keystroke.
- A viewing screen (sometimes called a video display terminal [VDT]) allows you to see your work. Because you are often working with words and numbers, a regular television set does not work well as a VDT. The words and numbers look broken up and are hard to read.
- The processor is the place where the actual computing takes place; it is the "brain" of the machine.
- Disk drives are used to read and store data. Most software programs and the information you create with them are stored on 5 1/4-in. (13.3-cm) magnetic diskettes. The drives act like tape recorders: They can "play" information into the machine as well as "record" information you have entered with the keyboard or the processor has created. The small diskettes can hold large amounts of information. More than a quarter million bytes (keystrokes) can fit on a single diskette.

- A printer creates a permanent copy of the information. Dot-matrix printers, which may be familiar to you from such computer printouts as test scores, billings, or form letters, achieve high speeds of 100 or more letters per second by forming letters with groups of dots. For example, using six dots in the specific pattern that forms the letter *i* is faster for a printer than finding an *i* key.

A Brief History

Computers have been part of our society for a quarter century. Compact, portable, and less expensive machines have been developed during the past decade. Although 100 companies manufacture microcomputers, the type of machine that is becoming accepted in the schools seems to be one of about a dozen brands. Fierce competition for our business is already producing widely accepted hardware and software as well as obsolete machines and programs.

Microcomputer advances are an outgrowth of the U.S. space program. We could not send heavy and underpowered calculating and data storage machines into outer space. The first manifestations of miniaturization were the pocket calculators and digital watches now commonplace in the schools. First-generation computers the size of a classroom have been replaced by microcomputers that can fit in the palm of a child's hand.

Computers are affecting the quality of our life. Microcomputers and microprocessors (the calculating component of a computer) are found in automobiles, microwave ovens, automatic bank tellers, and supermarket check-out lines. Many tasks can be performed more quickly and efficiently with the assistance of computers.

A computer has two major advantages. It can store large quantities of information (data), never forgetting a single item (unless the power fails!). It can work on this data in milliseconds—faster than the blink of an eye. The advantages of volume and speed are now being used in our schools in several areas:

Administration. Grades, records, and achievement tests have been stored, scored, and printed by computers for years. The machines that perform these tasks are often quite large and located in a central office. Recent advances now place these capabilities in the counselor's office. Case loads, student records, scheduling, and assessment can now be stored and accessed on a microcomputer. The advantages over past methods are speed, clarity, accessibility, and cost effectiveness.

Computer-assisted instruction (CAI). Students now work at their own pace in advanced, regular, or tutoring applications of educational software. The computer can store a seemingly endless number of drills, reinforcement, and lessons. The first uses of CAI were in mathematics, and several years ago over 95% of educational software was devoted to mathematical applications. As the Alert—Update department of this issue indicates, software is now reaching areas such as language and vocabulary development, foreign languages, social studies, and career development.

Counselor assistance. Because classrooms are a larger market, development of software for counselors has been much slower. Currently, however, a number of programs allow counselors to record accurately their time, analyze their interactions and time expenditures, and provide information that can increase their knowledge of the students and teachers they serve. Counselors can also use readily available programs to serve their needs for student records, word processing (once called "writing"), and an increasing variety of tasks.

Can Computers Counsel?

In a word, no, not yet. Programs that have demonstrated the computer's ability to listen reflectively (actually drawing on a large set of options programmed into the machine) are not yet sophisticated enough to replace the counselor. It is improbable that computers of any size or capacity will ever replace the counselor. Machines do not have the ability to make decisions, share feelings, or make judgments as effectively as the counselor or therapist.

But computers can help counselors (a) by freeing time otherwise spent in administrative tasks; (b) by performing initial assessment and data search functions, such as intelligence test reports, career search information, and identification of specific trends or groups within the school population; (c) by providing otherwise discouraged children with a positive learning experience with a computer; (d) by providing an inexhaustible resource for gifted students; and (e) by providing teachers with an effective teaching assistant in the classroom.

If a computer cannot counsel, it can increase the time available for counseling. It can provide accurate information for counseling and decision-making tasks. The microcomputer is, at the very least, a time saver and an organizational tool.

Practical Issues

We must be able to speak some of the language of computers. As the glossary in this issue indicates, a specialized vocabulary has been developed to communicate the unique aspects of these machines. Just as special education, reading, or other areas develop terms to convey meanings, computer users have created a vocabulary. You do not need to be fluent in "computerese," but your understanding of computers and their applications can be greatly enhanced, for example, if you know the difference between hardware and software. *Hardware* is the machine, *software* the programs that give instructions to the machine.

We must also know what computers can and cannot do for our students, teachers, and ourselves. To the uninformed, *computer* is a nebulous term that conjures images of all-seeing, all-knowing machines that would justly threaten us if these images were indeed fact. From our life experience, computers are the culprits when we are unable to correct a billing mistake with our local department store. We have personal evidence that these machines cause aggravation.

Fortunately, computers are only as good as the people behind them. There is absolutely no judgment capability in a computer. It only follows orders given by humans. Just as the refrigerator door does not have the good sense to shut itself when left open, neither does the computer have the ability to think. It can only work with what it is given. Human ability allows these machines to perform these tasks.

Computers cannot do anything we do not want them to do, and they cannot do anything we are unable to tell them to do. We must overcome our prejudices against the machines, remembering that people are responsible for any unpleasant experiences.

The effectiveness of microcomputers for counselors has been limited by a lack of useful software. We cannot expect each counselor to become a programmer (you do not have to become a mechanic to drive an automobile), but we can anticipate that software will be developed that meets our needs. We must have the ability to identify useful software from the large number of programs being sold.

Ethical Issues

Are we now using computers ethically? Technology has created a situation in which abuses are easy to start but difficult to stop. Awareness of potential abuses of the information stored in computers is a necessary computer competency for counselors. Sampson and Pyle (1983) identify three areas of potential abuse:

1. Is confidentiality of student records maintained? It is now possible for a large amount of information about each of our students to be stored for indefinite periods of time. The number of absences in the second grading period of the first grade can be retrieved 20 years later when a person is being assessed for medical school candidacy. Is this information relevant? At what point do portions of a student's record stop following them? The mass storage abilities now being used must have specific end points. When a child graduates or

transfers out of your school, what is saved and what is passed on to other institutions?

2. Is computer-assisted testing and assessment being used properly? The technology now exists, for example, to mix subjective counselor and teacher observations of a child with test scores, previous observations, parental status, and other variables into a "score." Will this information be used to place children in advanced, normal, or remedial classrooms? Computer technicians have used the term *GIGO*—garbage in, garbage out—to describe inappropriate use of information generated by computers. When testing and assessment is assisted by computers, the results cannot be taken for granted. Results are no better than the assumptions we hold about the data. Erroneous conclusions are worse than no conclusions, even when a computer is involved. The myth of infallibility of computer-generated results must always be challenged.

3. The need for counselor intervention, even when a computer can assist a process, can be overlooked. For example, upper grade students are now using career data bases that provide them with quantities of information no single counselor can provide. But is the total process of successful and meaningful career selection based only on the information or assessment a computer can provide?

We must be aware of computer anxiety too. Although this phenomenon apparently exists more often in adults than in students, we cannot simply tell students to "see the computer; it knows more about this than I do." Successful interaction with a computer requires skills. Everyone falls off the bike when first learning to ride. The ability to use a computer has a similar learning curve. Skinned knees heal more easily than bruised egos. If students and teachers are expected to use these machines, they must be given proper training and encouragement.

We suggest that counselors should be able to answer the following questions concerning computer use in their school:

1. What student information is being stored in computer data bases? What is the expiration date for the storage of this information?
2. Who has access to this information? How do these people use the information?
3. If computers are being used to score test results and provide other evaluations of students, what procedures ensure that the results are accurate and appropriate?
4. When portions of our work with students are turned over to computer-assisted procedures, how do we ensure that human interaction still takes place?

5. What training is being provided for students, teachers, counselors, and administrators interested in computer skills?

The ethical issues concerning computers are not theoretical. Abuses can and do occur. It is our responsibility to ensure that rights are not violated through ignorance.

The Counselor as Computer Consultant

The widespread demand for computers is now forcing educators to become knowledgeable in this field. It is a field that becomes outdated within months, not years, with a confusing array of choices. The counselor can become a valuable resource for administrators, teachers, and students.

Does the counselor really have a choice? If we choose not to use or know about computers, are we in fact incompetent? Hays relates an encounter with a concerned school counselor:

> Recently, an elementary school counselor in an eastern state asked me how the micro can help her in her work with children. We talked about what she does and we came to the conclusion that a micro would not be of assistance to her. Micros are not for all people. One must be careful not to get swept up in a new wave of innovation. It is important to ponder first what you want the micro to do that can help you improve what you are now doing. (Hays, 1983, p. 7)

Even when counselors conclude that the computer does not serve a useful purpose in their settings, they must still become aware of its impact on the administrators, teachers, and students in their schools. It has been estimated that within 5 years at least one microcomputer will be in every school in the nation (*Computers: Focus on the Classroom*, 1982).

Our experiences in researching this field for the special issue and this article have shown us that people can become "haves" (those with some knowledge of microcomputers) with a little effort. By default you may become a "have not" who is unsure of your computer potential or of the available resources for credible and useful information. Some common issues that seem to concern educators include:

How do I get a microcomputer into my school? Competition for your business is fierce. Studies show that the machine you use successfully the first time is the brand you tend to stick with. What better place to make the first impression than the schools?

Manufacturers are constantly offering educational discounts and grants to fund educator purchases of their equipment. Proposed federal and state legislation would allow special tax credits to companies that donate their hardware to schools. This is a controversial proposal, because it allows these companies to get their foot in the door for more lucrative software sales and maintenance contracts. The status of this legislation is always changing and should be monitored by all counselors who anticipate purchases of microcomputer equipment.

Who will teach me? Many districts are now assigning a teacher or support staff member as a "computer specialist." Responsibilities include staff training and support.

We advise that counselors and teachers be given uncomplicated, brief, and practical hands-on exposure to the microcomputer. This allows the potential user to see the usefulness of the equipment.

The value of a microcomputer can be demonstrated within 15 minutes. Training will take from 5 to 50 hours, depending upon the quality of the instruction and the specific hardware and software. Access to "experts" after an initial training period is crucial. Most important, the experts must be able to speak the language of educators.

How much money will it cost? A rudimentary computer costs less than $100, but a realistic figure for a functional system is about $3,000. This is an investment in an office clerk, teacher's aide, and consultant that draws no further salary after the initial purchase.

What is the best equipment for our needs? This is an unanswerable question. It depends upon the needs and goals of the school. A counselor with 200 students will need far less memory in the machine than one responsible for 500. Compatability with district-wide machines and software must be considered. An inexpensive initial purchase may become three items more expensive if unrecognized limitations must be corrected.

The selection rule of thumb is twofold: See what others in similar circumstances are using, and make sure the software you need is now available for the desired hardware. This evaluation and selection process can take 6 months.

Summary

The computer is only as good as the information it is given. We were involved 10 years ago in a pioneering effort to reduce transportation costs to and from a school. After many weeks of entering addresses and coding information, we eagerly awaited the computer's assessment of the best bus routes. Time would be saved for children and parents. Teachers would have less bus duty.

The results were astonishing. The computer had indeed drawn highly efficient schedules and routes but had not accounted for the lack of bridges over some canals within the district. We could either outfit all buses with pontoons or reprogram the computer!

This anecdote demonstrates the need for human input into the computer process. A computer must be told what to do. Unlike the computer "HAL" in the classic movie *2001: A Space Odyssey*, microcomputers in the schools are not intent upon destroying us or our students. The first step in computer competency is knowing what the machine will do better than we can now do with other equipment and human effort.

Counselors are in a unique position in the schools: they have the potential to serve as consultants and proactive users. Counselors can serve their students and teachers more effectively by using microcomputers to create more accurate and useful records of their work and by being aware of the inevitable and ongoing impact of microcomputers on the educational process.

A final word: No computer will ever replace a counselor able to use one.

References

Computers: Focus on the classrooms. (1982, November 23). *New York Times*.

Hays, D. (1983). Do we dare? *ASCA Counselor, 20*, 7–8.

Sampson, J. P., & Pyle, K. R. (1983). Ethical issues involved with the use of computer-assisted counseling, testing, and guidance systems. *Personnel and Guidance Journal, 61*, 283–287.

Getting Comfortable with Computers

Richard C. Nelson
Gerald H. Krockover

> *Change must be accepted . . . when it can no longer be resisted. (Victoria Regina, 1895)*

After a 20-minute introduction, the 45 of us scattered to three learning centers. I watched a secondary school counselor for several minutes as she followed a pattern of simple instructions on an assertiveness program. She was strongly reinforced after completing her responses. The basic message was: "You're exceptionally, appropriately assertive." It occurred to me that she might have responded in the same way to the questions asked of her if she were downright aggressive. Although she was subsequently presented with information differentiating non-assertiveness, assertiveness, and aggressiveness, I wondered if many aggressive people would choose to continue after being given such strong strokes.

I took the chair at the same terminal and ran through a stress management program. By now those around me were feeling playful, so I fed the computer a mixed bag of responses—some demonstrating high stress, others imperturbability. The graph that followed not only reflected inconsistency but was almost incomprehensible. Once again some good information followed. I left that station impressed that, as a novice, I could cope with the computer and even see a software weakness or two.

I moved on to the second learning center, observing that there was plenty of time left in the session but that only a few people remained in the meeting room. I chose a Sesame Street program that was partly designed to help young children become accustomed to the computer, and I greatly enjoyed mixing and matching heads, bodies, and legs of Sesame Street characters. Next I contended with an interesting animals program. As I thought of animals, the computer posed a few questions, asking, for example, "Are you thinking of an elephant?" If I said I was not, it would ask me how my choice, giraffe, differed from an elephant. The program then incorporated my new information, and I was asked to present finer and finer discriminations or be outguessed by the computer. I could imagine youngsters scurrying to encyclopedias to specify some fine difference between a lynx and a cougar while the computer waited patiently.

I moved on to the third station. Now there was only one other member of the audience. At this station I received a brief orientation to a record-keeping program. A counselor could punch a few buttons daily and see displayed on the screen or obtain a printout of the total and average number of minutes spent that month with individual children whose basic concern was friendships. Successes and failures, things to do, fourth-grade children who had volunteered for counseling but had not yet been seen—anything remotely quantifiable—could be recorded for ready recall, modified as changes occurred, and totaled so that reports could be prepared easily.

Now I was alone with the presenters. Had the others ingested the information more quickly than I? Possibly. More likely they had wanted to learn about computers without being willing to be observed, to err, and to allow the computer to demonstrate its infinite patience.

Since then I have been thinking: Counselors need the awareness such a program offers. Are we about to see a new generation gap, separating those who are comfortable with computers from those who are not? Can counselors afford to distance themselves from the children they serve as those children become more comfortable with computers?

—Richard C. Nelson

Why Should Counselors Gain Comfort with Computers?

Until the advent of microcomputers, computers were not "user-friendly"; only a few experts could understand the languages involved. It might have been appropriate then for counselors to avoid computer contact. Now, however, we have entered the age of microcomputers. Disks and tapes have been programmed to reduce complexity so that even preschool children can use computers, and more and more useful software is being developed. Counselors cannot afford to be left behind.

A parallel suggests itself. In the early 1900s drivers of those new-fangled gadgets called horseless carriages had to understand magnetos and sparks, they dealt with balky and dangerous hand cranks, and they needed to be well informed on many aspects of automobile maintenance. Those adventurers were akin to latter-day computer experts. It took a long time for millions of drivers to be automobile-comfortable. Key-operated starters, service stations in abundance, and simpler and safer automobiles have made us a nation of drivers, most of whom have little idea of what goes on under the hood. The parallel breaks down, however, when we consider the time element: The change from unfathomable difficulties to computer friendliness has occurred in just a few years. It is here—today. Those who "cannot fathom" computers will soon feel as out of synchronization with their world as those who cannot drive.

Why should counselors gain comfort with computers? Why, indeed. So that they can live in their own world: today—and tomorrow. And so that they can understand and help children.

Is the computer world a dehumanizing place? Do children become numbers lost in a sea of other numbers? Are children losing their eyesight and becoming muscular imbeciles because they spend so much time at work or play before television and computer displays? Probably to a small degree these things are occurring. If and when they are, then we need counselors who understand uses of the computer that might be harmful and thus are better equipped to put up suitable "road signs" and contribute suggestions to engineers, not merely damn those "new-fangled gadgets."

Can the computer world be a humanizing place? Yes, it can. Children are being helped, patiently and thoroughly, to learn to complete tasks that might otherwise seem odious because they are reinforced for small gains and tolerated through a thousand errors that shape suitable responses. Computers have a humanizing advantage: They are blind to sex, race, ethnic group, and socio-economic status, showing virtually limitless patience to individuals from any group who happen to take longer than others to develop particular skills. Children are learning to complete some tasks more quickly, with the result that they have additional time available for large and small muscle activity. Computers are being programmed to record measurable gains children make in such diverse directions as school subjects and physical skills, with the result that fewer of them give up on themselves.

It was estimated in 1982 that one out of every four public schools had at least one microcomputer (50% of secondary schools and 14% of elementary schools) and that 74% of these schools were using microcomputers (Marks, 1982). Furthermore, it was predicted in 1982 that within the next 4 years 10% of homes in the United States would have computers or terminals with access to distant data bases, and that by the year 2000 these terminals would be common-place in our homes (Long, 1982).

Clearly, computers are here to stay. Counselors who understand uses of the computer will be able to assist software producers to prepare materials that at best are humane and at least shorten tedious processes and leave time for those matters that only human contact and concern can develop. Like automobiles, computers are conveniences for getting somewhere. They may be misused and overused. But, like automobiles, their use is inevitable, and they can be turned to great advantage by those who allow themselves to become comfortable with their use.

Is Computer Literacy Essential?

As a result of the explosion of computer usage in all segments of society, the Information Society has indicated that the job skills needed for the 1990s and beyond include: evaluation and analysis, critical thinking, problem solving, organization and reference, synthesis, application to new areas, creativity, decision making with incomplete information, and communication skills in many modes (Hodgkinson, 1982). These skills may be developed in children and adults as they become "computer literate." Computer literacy may be defined as knowledge of the nontechnical and slightly technical aspects of the capabilities and limitations of computers and of the social, vocational, and educational implications of computers (Moursund, 1975). Johnson, Anderson, Hansen, and Klassen (1980) divided computer literacy into cognitive and affective components. The cognitive components include being able to:

1. Identify the major components of a computer (the hardware)
2. Identify the basic operation of a computer system
3. Distinguish between hardware and software
4. Access a computer
5. Follow simple directions in programming a computer
6. Recognize that a computer needs instructions to operate
7. Recognize that a computer gets instructions from a program written in a programming language
8. Recognize that a computer is capable of storing a program and data
9. Select an appropriate characteristic for organizing data for a particular task
10. Recognize specific applications of computers in all aspects of our society
11. Determine how computers can assist in the decision-making process
12. Recognize the impact that computers have upon our lives

The affective components of computer literacy include:

1. Becoming comfortable with computer experience
2. Gaining confidence in the ability to use and control computers
3. Valuing efficient information processing provided that it does not neglect accuracy, the protection of individual rights, and social needs
4. Valuing the computerization of routine tasks so long as it frees people to engage in other activities and is not done as an end in itself
5. Valuing increased communication and availability of information made possible through computer use provided that it does not violate personal rights to privacy and accuracy of personal data
6. Valuing economic benefits of computerization for the society

7. Enjoying and desiring work or play with computers, especially computer-assisted learning.
8. Describing past experiences with computers with positive affective words such as *fun*, *exciting*, and *challenging*
9. Spending some free time using a computer when given an opportunity

What Uses Might Counselors Make of Computers?

There are six areas of computer usage that are valuable for elementary school counselors. They include: (a) learning from computers via drill, practice, and tutorials; (b) learning with computers via simulations, games, and data collection or interpretation; (c) learning about computers via computer literacy and programming languages; (d) learning about thinking with computers using educational computer languages such as LOGO and PILOT; (e) learning about management with computers via text editing, test generation, data base management, and school management programs; and (f) using the computer as a reinforcer. Counselors should be especially interested in the use of microcomputers for data base management and accountability, text editing, developing specific skills, and as a reinforcer.

Any record-keeping task the counselor does or might do can probably be made easier with the use of a computer. Data base management allows the counselor to construct a data file for each student in the school, district, or community. The data file might include, for example, the student's name, address, telephone number, name(s) of parent(s), emergency telephone number(s), schedule, teachers, standardized test information, grades, and the specific focus of any counseling contact. Hays (1983) suggested that the counselor could keep confidential records very secure by using a password to gain entry to data on a floppy disk. The disk itself could be kept in the possession of the counselor, and considerable data could be stored in a space the size of a 45 rpm record. Once the data base has been established, it can be used to sort, retrieve, and update a student's record. Mailing labels, notes to children, and letters to parents could be filed and retrieved by using defined categories.

Although the initial stages would take some time, accountability would be greatly enhanced if counselors could report the number of children, teachers, and parents contacted and the number of minutes spent on any specified subject. Has group counseling reduced absenteeism for selected children on group meeting dates or other dates? Ask the computer. Has the classroom study skills project affected any specific aspects of achievement? Ask the computer. By using the same program and similarly recorded data, counselors across a school district, county, state, or the nation could pool information and determine whether a specific approach has had a favorable impact on children with low self-concepts or who are low in sociometric standing in their group.

Clearly any of these record-keeping procedures can be conducted without the use of computers; with the new technology, however, the process is made so much easier that the likelihood of improved accountability should increase dramatically as counselors become more comfortable in using computers.

Text editing programs (word processing) allow the counselor to handle large volumes of correspondence more easily. Standard letters can be created for communication to students, parents, and teachers. Corrections or changes in the correspondence can be made without correction fluid, ditto masters, or erasing carbons. A word processing program permits deletion of anything from one character to a paragraph. Phrases, paragraphs, and pages can be relocated within a letter or inserted in another document. Furthermore, the text may be saved on a disk or tape for later use, and it may be printed with many options. These programs allow counselors to improve their communication with all of the constituencies they serve, a significant public relations gain in a time that is critical for the profession.

The current technology provides counselors with a wide range of materials that may be used to inform and educate children in a variety of specific directions, and a software explosion is underway that is resulting in continuous expansion of those materials in many guidance-related directions. There are programs designed for children that teach touch-typing skills, thus developing a usable skill that is applicable in computer literacy and beyond. Repetitious learning processes (e.g., learning the multiplication tables) are readily developed as game-type learning experiences programmed to increase in complexity or demand for speed. Although some of these processes are not guidance functions, it seems inevitable that counselors will on occasion act as individual facilitators of learning, either directly or through a variety of aide and peer tutoring procedures.

Increasingly, self-growth programs, similar to the stress management and assertiveness programs cited in the introductory paragraphs, are appearing on the market as aids in enhancing personal or interpersonal skills for children. In many cases interpersonal skills might be enhanced and reading and related skills developed simultaneously by having two or more children work together at a microcomputer, discussing and choosing responses cooperatively. Applications of computers in informing and educating children seem to be limited only by the imaginations of software producers and individuals who can adapt software to their own uses.

In addition to these uses of computers by counselors for record keeping and accountability and by children for obtaining information and developing skills, it is apparent that the computer offers great potential as a reinforcer for children.

Free time at the computer can be used as a reward for gains or effort. Children can insert a disk or tape of their choosing, play a learning game with or without a partner, and compose music or watch color graphics merge and flow in an endless sequence of kaleidoscopic patterns. Any device or process that is as compelling for most children as the microcomputer can serve as a significant reinforcer. More and more the play aspects of the computer are merging into the work aspects of learning. Children are being helped to learn through intriguing processes that they find highly rewarding. Perhaps the most significant gain that we can expect from the use of computers is that learning will increasingly be seen by children as a rewarding experience in and of itself.

How Should You Get Started?

The best way to begin your computer friendly approach to becoming a computer-literate counselor is to obtain access to one of the microcomputers in your school. Find out the brand and model of the computer. Locate the nearest computer dealer that sells this brand of computer, and purchase a copy of the corresponding self-paced, programmed guide to that computer (your school may already have a copy). This book and the computer manual should be all that you need to begin to become a friendly computer user. You should be able to turn the computer on and off, use tape or disk software, and use some of the basic computer commands such as RUN, SAVE, LIST, and PRINT.

If you are interested in learning programming, these books will also introduce you to the basics. It is not necessary, however, to be able to program a computer to use one. There are computer programming resources readily available in your school and community—maybe a teacher, fourth grader, principal, parent, or computer user club. There is someone who will be happy to help you join the club of computer users. Microcomputer journals can also be very helpful in providing tips for the selection and use of microcomputer hardware and software. Journals such as *Creative Computing, The Computing Teacher, 80 Microcomputing*, and *Incider* serve as excellent resources for those who are learning to use computers.

It seems advisable for counselors who wish to make use of computers to learn something about two computer languages, BASIC and LOGO. Of the two, LOGO is simpler because it is more graphic, and it may therefore provide an easier starting point for the novice. LOGO can be used to draw pictures on the computer's video display by entering instructions at the computer keyboard. A shape on the screen (called a "turtle") responds to the instructions entered by moving around and leaving a trail of color on the screen. LOGO allows children to learn by exploring and involves them in thinking logically about directions, distances, and angles. LOGO gives children vast opportunities to be creative, and there is even a special feature, called "Doodle Mode," for children who cannot read yet. Much has been written about the educational theory behind LOGO-type programs (e.g., Pappert, 1980).

If you are in a position to be able to influence the selection of a microcomputer for purchase by your school, it is important to consider what uses other counselors in your school district are making of hardware and software and to select the same brand of microcomputer if this is feasible. This will allow for the full exchange of software and data management for the preparation of district-wide comparative reports and statistical analyses. Check with other school districts in your region before a decision is made regarding the computerization of elements of your counseling program.

Conclusion

Before the 1980s it took years for textbooks and schools to reflect current events. The schools of the future will need to install more computer terminals and other electronic equipment for using such items as tapes and videodisks to keep pace with the changes and improvements in education and guidance. The electronic microchip is not likely to cause a decline in the teaching and guidance profession, but the status of teachers and guidance counselors and what they do is likely to be quite different as they work at developing our planet's greatest resource: our learners. With the help of the tools for improving learning that the microchip provides, the skills of professionals such as elementary school counselors should help guarantee that the world retains the capacity to move toward a decent, civilized future (Shane, 1982).

Dateline 2001

The telephone rings and the counselor, Mr. Richards, answers via his interactive computer terminal. It is a third grader asking to be scheduled for his fourth-grade mathematics program and his sixth-grade social studies program. Mr. Richards enters the access code into the computer, and Jerry receives a listing of the times and programs available for mathematics and social studies at his levels. At the same time another student, Barbara, is receiving career information regarding the training required for technicians who will work at the moon colony for the next 10 years. Mr. Richards also initiates the administration of several different standardized tests to individual students throughout the district and helps Martha, a fourth grader, get started on a choices program. Upon completion of these early morning chores, as his 9:00 group of fifth graders files in for another session of getting along together, he recalls the "good old days" of 1983 when he had to process everything and prepare complicated reports by hand, work around rather inflexible student schedules and put in extra hours to catch up on his paperwork so he could spend the time he thought was necessary with the children. "Thank goodness we don't have to return to those 'good old days,'" he says to himself. "I might have decided to become an engineer instead of a counselor! Now I have time to counsel!"

References

Hays, D. (1983). Do we dare? *ASCA Counselor, 20*, 8-9.

Hodgkinson, H. L. (1982). What's still right with education. *Phi Delta Kappan, 64*, 233.

Johnson, D. C., Anderson, R. E., Hansen, T. P., & Klassen, D. L. (1980). Computer literacy—What is it? *Mathematics Teacher, 73*, 91–96.

Long, S. M. (1982). The dawning of the computer age. *Phi Delta Kappan, 63*, 312.

Marks, G. H. (1982). Editorial. *Journal of Computers in Mathematics and Science Teaching, 2*, 2–3.

Moursund, D. (1975). What is computer literacy? *Oregon Council for Computer Education, 2*, 2.

Pappert, S. (1980). *Mindstorms: Children, computers, and powerful ideas*. New York: Basic Books.

Shane, H. G. (1982). The silicon age and education. *Phi Delta Kappan, 63*, 307.

Chapter 6
Counseling Issues in a Technological World

Issues for elementary school counselors to consider about a technological world:

1. Discuss the following statement: "Secondary school counselors have far more uses for computers than do elementary school counselors."
2. What should counselor education programs include to prepare elementary school counselors in using computers?
3. What can elementary school counselors do to reduce their anxieties about using computers?
4. What technological advances (other than computers) will play the greatest role in elementary school counseling by the year 2000?
5. What can children teach counselors about the use of technology?
6. How might elementary school counselors make use of computer graphics in classroom guidance?
7. Discuss the pros and cons of the following statement: "Computers have depersonalized education."
8. How can elementary school counselors use video technology to improve their work with children?
9. How might elementary school counselors use computer technology to improve their counseling with individual children?
10. Develop an inservice training program that is intended to reduce teachers' anxieties about using computers in the classroom? How do you feel about elementary school counselors involving themselves in this kind of inservice training?

CHAPTER 7

A CHANGING WORLD OF WORK

As we approach the close of the 20th century, the world in which we live and work continues to change and become more complex. Vast and far-reaching changes are occurring in the nature and structure of the social and economic systems in which people live, and the industrial and occupational structures where they work. Individuals' values and beliefs about themselves and their society are changing as are the ways they look at and understand their own growth and development. This includes their career development as well. More people are looking for meaning in their lives, particularly as they think about the work they do, their situation as a family member and as an individual, their involvement in their community, their role in education and training, and their involvement in leisure activities.

This observation by Norm Gysbers begins Chapter 7 and suggests that elementary school counselors face major challenges as they work with parents and teachers to introduce children to an ever changing world of work. Ken Hoyt reinforces this idea in his stimulating article, "The Impact of Technology on Occupational Change: Implications for Career Guidance." The emphasis on career education, however, seems to have diminished from its peak in the 1970s when Sid Marland and the United States Office of Education demanded high visibility for career education programs in schools. This decline in career education at the elementary school level is unfortunate because economic, political, and social changes have brought women and minorities into the work force in large numbers and have altered how children must be prepared to enter the world of work.

This chapter discusses theoretical and practical issues related to career development and offers suggestions to help elementary school counselors promote students' career exploration. In addition to the issues covered by Gysbers and Hoyt, Chapter 7 presents ideas for practice on such topics as:

1. Using books to enhance career awareness
2. Examining sex-role stereotyping through career exploration
3. Using role models to expand occupational aspirations

Each of the articles in this chapter challenges elementary school counselors to examine creative ways of preparing children for the world of work in the 21st century.

Major Trends in Career Development Theory and Practice

Norman C. Gysbers

As we approach the close of the 20th century, the world in which we live and work continues to change and become more complex. Vast and far reaching changes are occurring in the nature and structure of the social and economic systems in which people live, and the industrial and occupational structures where they work. Individuals' values and beliefs about themselves and their society are changing as are the ways they look at and understand their own growth and development. This includes their career development as well. More people are looking for meaning in their lives, particularly as they think about the work they do, their situation as a family member and as an individual, their involvement in their community, their role in education and training, and their involvement in leisure activities.

*Designing Careers: Counseling to Enhance Education, Work, and Leisure** is, in part, a chronology of these changes as they affect the career development of individuals, but it is much more than a chronology of people, places, and events in the evolution of career development theory and practice. *Designing Careers* helps us to understand these changes and hence career development theory and practice, in the context of the times in which we live and work from sociological, psychological, and economic perspectives. *Designing Careers* is a source of ideas, techniques, and resources to help us work more effectively with individuals and their career development needs, concerns, and plans. Finally, *Designing Careers* is a book that is grounded in the present but looks into the future and what is likely to be in store for career development practitioners and their clientele.

To accomplish these tasks, *Designing Careers* is composed of an introduction and 23 chapters organized into four major parts: (a) The World of Work Today: Personal, Social, and Economic Perspectives; (b) The Knowledge Base of Career Development; (c) Facilitating Career Development: Practices and Programs; and (d) Responding to Emerging Views of Education, Work, and Leisure.

---

*This article is adapted from the book *Designing Careers: Counseling to Enhance Education, Work, and Leisure* published by Jossey-Bass in 1984 for the National Vocational Guidance Association.

It is not the intent of this article to summarize what is in the book. It is, instead, the intent of this article to bring into sharp focus four predominant trends that may have substantial impact on the future of career development theory and practice from among the many trends identified by the chapter authors in this book. What are these predominant trends? They are as follows:

1. The meanings given to career and career development continue to evolve from simply new words for vocation (occupation) and vocational development (occupation development) to words that describe the human career in terms of life roles, life settings, and life events that develop over the life span. Super in Chapter 1, Jepsen in Chapter 5, McDaniels in Chapter 21, and Miller-Tiedeman and Tiedeman in Chapter 22 described and commented on this evolution of meanings.
2. Substantial changes have taken place and will continue to occur in the economic, occupational, industrial, and social environments and structures in which the human career develops and interacts, and in which career guidance and counseling takes place. Goldstein (Chapter 2), Herr (Chapter 3), Borow (Chapter 6), Dawis (Chapter 10), and Striner (Chapter 19) provided indepth analyses of these changes from a variety of perspectives.
3. The number, diversity, and quality of career developmental programs, tools, and techniques continue to increase almost in geometric progression. Crites (Chapter 9), Kinnier and Krumboltz (Chapter 11), Walz and Benjamin (Chapter 12), Harris-Bowlsbey (Chapter 13), and Miller (Chapter 16) discussed these developments in detail.
4. The populations served by career development programming, and the settings in which career development programs and services take place, have increased greatly and will continue to do so. Lotto in Chapter 4, Stumpf in Chapter 7, Hansen in Chapter 8, Miles in Chapter 14, Thomas and Berven in Chapter 15, Miller in Chapter 16, Johnson and Figler in Chapter 17, Knowdell in Chapter 18, and Sinick in Chapter 20 documented and described this major trend in the field.

To carry out the intent of this article, the first section traces and summarizes each of these four trends. The last section of the article brings these trends together and looks briefly at the future of career development.

Evolving Meanings of Career and Career Development

Modern theories of career development began appearing in literature during the 1950s. At that time the occupational choice focus of the first 40 years of career development began to give way to a broader, more comprehensive view of individuals and their occupational development over the life span. Occupational choice was beginning to be seen as a developmental process. It was during this time that the term *vocational development* became popular as a way of describing the broadening view of occupational choice.

By the 1960s, knowledge about occupational choice as a developmental process had increased dramatically. At the same time, the terms *career* and *career development* became popular. Today, many people prefer them to the terms vocation and vocational development. This expanded view of career and career development was more useful than the earlier view of career development as occupational choice because it broke the time barrier that previously restricted the vision of career development to only a cross-sectional view of an individual's life. As Super and Bohn (1970, p. 15) pointed out, "It is well . . . to keep clear the distinction between occupation (what one does) and career (the course pursued over a period of time)." It was also more useful because it made it possible for career development to become the basis for organizing and interpreting the impact that the role of work has on individuals over their lifetimes.

In the 1970s, the definitions of career and career development used by some writers became broader and more encompassing. Jones, Hamilton, Ganschow, Helliwell, and Wolff (1972) defined career as encompassing a variety of possible patterns of personal choice related to an individual's total lifestyle, including occupation, education, personal and social behaviors, learning how to learn, social responsibility, and leisure time activities.

Gysbers and Moore (1975; 1981) proposed the concept of life career development in an effort to expand and extend career development from an occupational perspective to a life perspective in which occupation (and work) has place and meaning. They defined life career development as self-development over the life span through the integration of the roles, settings, and events of a person's life. The word *life* in the definition means that the focus is on the total person—the human career. The word *career* identifies and relates the roles in which individuals are involved (worker, learner, family, citizen); the settings where individuals find themselves (home, school, community, workplace); and the events that occur over their lifetimes (entry job, marriage, divorce, retirement). Finally, the word *development* is used to indicate that the individuals are always in the process of becoming. When used in sequence, the words *life career development* bring these separate meanings together, but at the same time a greater meaning emerges. Life career development describes unique people with their own lifestyles.

Similarly, Super (1975; 1981) proposed a definition of career that involved the interaction of various life roles over the life span. He called it the life career rainbow. "Super emphasizes that people, as they mature, normally play a variety of roles in many different theatres. . . . For Super, the term *career* refers to the combination and sequence of all the roles you may play during your lifetime and the pattern in which they fit together at any point in time" (Harris-Bowlsbey, Spivack, & Lisansky, 1982, p. 17–18).

Recently, the National Vocational Guidance Association (NVGA) updated its definition of career development to reflect these changes. Although the concept of life roles is not explicit, it is implicit in the new definition. The 1982 NVGA definition is as follows: Career development is "the total constellation of psychological, sociological, educational, physical, economic, and chance factors that combine to shape the career of any given individual over the life span" (Sears, 1982, p. 139).

Wolfe and Kolb (1980, p. 1–2) summed up the life view of career development when they defined career development as involving one's whole life.

> Career development involves one's whole life, not just occupation. As such, it concerns the whole person, needs and wants, capacities and potentials, excitements and anxieties, insights and blindspots, warts and all. More than that, it concerns him or her in the ever-changing contexts of his or her life. The environmental pressures and constraints, the bonds that tie him or her to significant others, responsibilities to children and aging parents, the total structure of one's circumstances are also factors that must be understood and reckoned with. In these terms, career development and personal development converge. Self and circumstances—evolving, changing, unfolding in mutual interaction—constitute the focus and the drama of career development.

Changing Environments and Structures

The nature, shape, and substance of career development and the practices of career guidance and counseling are not separate and independent from the economic, occupational, industrial, and social environments and structures in which they take place. Our understanding of career development and how we practice is closely related to what happens in these environments and the changes that have occurred and will occur in the future. Not only are the changes within environments important, but so are the interactive effects that occur across environments as a result of change.

What are some of these changes? Since 1900, our country has undergone substantial changes in its economic, occupational, industrial, and social environments and structures. Occupational and industrial specialization have increased dramatically and apparently will continue to do so in the future.

Social structures and social values have changed and will continue to change, by becoming more complex and diverse. New and emerging social and political groups are challenging established groups by demanding equality. People are on the move from rural to urban areas and back again, and from one region of the country to another, in search of psychological, social, and economic security.

Today, changes such as these and others that have been well documented by previous chapter authors, continue at a rapid pace. Here are just a few specifics to sum up what has been stated previously:

1. We have moved from a goods producing economic base to a service-information economy. This does not mean that goods producing industries are unimportant and that people will no longer find employment in them. What it does mean, however, is that more and more workers will be employed in service-information industries. Two years ago the number one occupation in the United States, which had long been Laborer, became Clerk. The number of workers in agriculture fell to a low of 3.5 percent. Information or knowledge occupations, including all persons who process and disseminate information increased from 17 percent in 1950 to 60 percent today. (National Association of Manufacturers, 1982).
2. We are continuing to experience rapid acceleration in the use of high technology and automation in the work place due to the continued introduction of new and more highly sophisticated automated techniques, machinery, and computers of all types and sizes.
3. We live in a world economy closely linked by fiscal policies, energy resources, multinational corporations, competition for raw materials, and the sales of goods and services.
4. We continue to experience population shifts that find people moving from the north and northeast to the south and southeast.
5. We continue to see changing demographic patterns in our labor force. "After more than two decades of growth, the United States population in the 16–24 age range peaked at 36 million in 1980. The Department of Labor predicts a 10 percent decrease in this age group by 1985 and another 7% drop, to 30 million, by 1990. As the number of younger workers declines, there will be a demographic 'bulge' in the prime-age (24–44) work force from 39 million in 1975 to an estimated 60.5 million in 1990. Many experts also believe there will be a shift away from early retirement" (National Association of Manufacturers, 1982, p. 2).

What about tomorrow? What will likely happen in the future? Experts who study change tell us that the pace of change in the future will be even more rapid. Governor Pierre S. du Pont IV, who chaired a recent ad hoc National

Committee on Displaced Workers, concluded that "it is entirely possible that the changes recorded in the past 80 years, will be matched and surpassed by the changes in the final 20 years of this century" (Ehrbar, 1983, p. 107).

One note of caution is needed, however, as projections are made about what the future will look like. In the same issue of *Fortune* magazine in which the article by Ehrbar appeared, the following statement also appeared: "The far-off will not be that far-out." Although changes will occur, and with increasing rapidity, the familiar lines of our economic, occupational, industrial, and social environments and structures, as we know them today, in all probability, will still be visible.

Increasing Numbers, Diversity, and Quality of Programs, Tools, and Techniques

A number of decennial volume chapter authors documented the rapid expansion in and the almost bewildering diversity of career development programs, tools, and techniques available today to help individuals with their career development. These same authors project that this expansion will continue into the foreseeable future. Also, as previous chapters make clear, these programs, tools, and techniques are better organized, are more frequently theory-based, and are used more systematically than ever before. It also projected that these emphases will continue into the future.

Let us look more specifically at what is involved in this major trend. The theory and research base of counseling psychology has been expanded and extended substantially during the past 20 years but particularly during the past 10 years. The growth in the theory and research base for career psychology has been equally dramatic during this same time period. One result has been an interesting convergence of ideas in counseling and career psychology concerning human growth and development, and the interventions to facilitate it. This convergence of ideas has stimulated a new array of career guidance and counseling programs, tools, and techniques. These new programs, tools, and techniques are emerging from this convergence through the application of marriage and family counseling concepts to career counseling (Zingaro, 1983) and cognitive-behavioral psychology (Keller, Biggs, & Gysbers, 1982). We also are seeing it in the application of contemporary thinking about personal styles (Pinkney, 1983), learning styles (Wolfe & Kolb, 1980), and hemispheric functioning to career guidance and counseling.

A recent publication by the National Vocational Guidance Association also documents this trend from another perspective. The publication is titled "A Counselor's Guide to Vocational Guidance Instruments" edited by Kapes and

Mastie (1982). In it are reviews of career guidance and counseling instruments. A number of them have been around for a long time. Some have been developed more recently, and they represent new directions for the field. There are new instruments in the traditional category of interest inventories but the new directions for the field are in the category of work values, career development and maturity, and card sorts.

There also are encouraging signs that career and labor market information, important tools in career guidance and counseling, are continuing to improve. Not only have the nature and content of career and labor markets been improving, but so have the relationships between the producers and users of career and labor market information (Drier & Pfister, 1980). A major step was taken in 1976 to facilitate this trend through the establishment of the National Occupational Information Coordinating Committee (NOICC) and the corresponding State Occupational Information Coordinating Committees (SOICCs) by the Vocational Education Amendments of 1976. Their charge was to improve communication and coordination between federal and state agencies that produce career and labor market information and those agencies and individuals that use it. NOICC and the SOICCs also are charged to develop and implement an occupational information system to meet the common occupational information needs of vocational education and employment and training programs at the national, state, and local levels. Finally, NOICC and SOICCs are mandated to give special attention to the labor market information needs of youth, including such activities as encouraging and assisting in the development of local job outlook data and counseling programs for youth who are in correctional institutions and those who are out of high school.

Recently, NOICC joined forces with other government agencies, including the Department of Labor and the Department of Defense, to upgrade the career and labor market information knowledge of counselors. The effort is called the Improve Career Decision Making project. It is designed to assist counselors in training as well as those on-the-job to become knowledgeable about career and labor market information concepts and sources and become skillful in their use.

In addition, there are encouraging signs that delivery systems for career and labor market information using state-of-the-art technology are being put into place with increasing frequency across the country. In 1979, NOICC assumed responsibility for assisting states to develop and implement career information delivery systems. Commercial vendors, publishers, and others also have become very active in making such systems available for use in a wide array of settings with an equally wide array of people.

Finally, it is clear that career guidance and counseling programs, tools, and techniques are more frequently theory-based. Matthews (1975) pointed out several years ago that there were some missing links between materials and people; and that one of the missing links was the lack of an organizing philosophy. "In essence," she stated, "we are now confronted with random materials in search of a philosophy" (Matthews, 1975, p. 652). According to a number of authors of decennial volume chapters, this point has been recognized; now, theorists, researchers, and practitioners are devoting more time and energy organizing and using career guidance and counseling programs, tools, and techniques in comprehensive, systematic ways that are theory-based.

Expanding Populations and Settings

At the turn of the century, career guidance and counseling (then called vocational guidance) was designed to help young people in the transition from school to work; to make occupational choices in line with their understandings about themselves and the work world through a process called true reasoning (Parsons, 1909). Today, young people are still the recipients of career guidance and counseling and will be in the future. Additional populations to be served by career guidance and counseling have been added over the years and have included such groups as individuals with handicapping conditions, college students, the disadvantaged, and unemployed individuals. As the world in which we live and work continues to become more complex, the needs of people in these populations for career guidance and counseling will increase, not decrease.

As new concepts about career and career development began to appear and evolve, it became obvious that people of all ages and circumstances had career development needs and concerns, and that they and society could and would benefit from comprehensive career development programs and services. Two such concepts, in particular, had an impact. First was the shift from a point-in-time focus to a life span focus for career development. And second, was the personalization of the concept of career (the human career) relating it to life roles, settings, and events. By introducing these two concepts, the door opened for career guidance and counseling personnel to provide programs to a wide range of people of all ages in many different kinds of settings.

These newer concepts of career and career development emerged as a result of and in response to the continuing changes that are taking place in our social, industrial, economic, and occupational environments and structures. Because of these changes, adults and adult career development became a focal point for an increasing number of career development theorists and practitioners in the 1970s (Campbell & Cellini, 1981). This focus continued into the 1980s and, in all probability, will continue to do so into the future. As a result, institutions and agencies, who serve adults traditionally, have added career development components. And, new agencies and organizations were established to provide adults with career development programs and services where none had existed.

Career development programs and services in business and industry also became a focal point in the 1970s and 1980s. This trend, too, will continue and probably be intensified in the foreseeable future. More businesses and industries as well as many other organizations are realizing the benefits of career development programs and services for their employees. And, if employees benefit, then the organizations benefit also.

The Future

The four predominant trends discussed in this chapter—the evolving meanings of career and career development; the changing environments and structures in which people live and work; the increasing numbers, diversity, and quality of career development programs, tools, and techniques; and the greater number and variety of people and settings being served—are not separate and discreet. They are closely linked and related. This brief look at the future examines the collective impact these trends may have on the theory and practice of career development.

The behavior of individuals is, in part, determined by their thought processes. The language people use represents their underlying conceptual schemes, and, in turn, their conceptual schemata determines their behavior (Gerber, 1983). As definitions of career and career development have evolved, and become broader and more encompassing, particularly during the past 10 years, there has been a corresponding broadening and expansion of programs and services to people of all ages and circumstances. What was once thought of as mainly for young people, is now for everybody. What was once thought of as a program in schools, is now taking place in a whole new array of settings including public and private agencies, institutions, and business and industry.

Although it is clear that a broad definition of career and career development opens up more possibilities and opportunities for programs and services for individuals and groups than a narrow definition, it is equally clear that other variables are involved. The changing economic, occupational, industrial, and social environments and structures in which people live and work have created conditions and needs not previously present. Individuals must now give more attention to their career development. In addition, a more complete understanding of human growth and development from counseling and career psychology, and the corresponding improvement of intervention strategies and resources, have helped in the expansion and extension of career development programs and services for more people in more settings than ever before.

As these trends converge they have begun to shape a new focus for career development programs and services for the future. What will be the focus of career development programs and services in the future? Will future programs and services be remedial, emphasize crises, and deal with immediate concerns and issues in peoples's lives? Will they be developmental and emphasize growth experiences and long range planning activities? Or, will they do both? The sense of the trends discussed in this chapter and in the literature in general clearly indicate that career development programs and services of the future will respond to the developmental, long-term career needs of people as well as to their more immediate career crises needs.

Traditionally, career development programs and services focused on immediate problems and concerns of people. Personal crises, lack of information, a specific occupational choice, and ineffective relationships with spouse, children, fellow employees or supervisors are examples of the immediate problems and concerns to which counselors are asked to respond. This focus for career development programs and services will continue and new and more effective ways of helping people with their problems and concerns will continue to emerge. To help people meet the challenges they may face in the future, however, this focus for programs and services is not sufficient. What is needed is a developmental focus.

The developmental focus for career development programs and services is not new. It has been part of professional literature for a number of years. Gordon (1974), for example, pointed out that traditional practices tended to overemphasize selection and placement instead of nurturing interests and aptitudes. Tennyson (1970, p. 262) made the same point when he stated that "guidance personnel have been inclined to capitalize upon aptitudes already developed rather than cultivating new talents" in their clientele. What is new now is the sense of urgency about the importance of helping people toward the goal of becoming competent, achieving individuals and of helping people focus on their competencies (skills) rather than only on their deficits as they are involved in their career development over the life span.

What began at the turn of the century under the term vocational guidance, with a selection and placement focus, and then shifted in the 1920s and 1930s to a focus on personal adjustment, has now assumed a developmental focus. Selection, placement, and adjustment remain but are encompassed in the concept of career development over the life span. Societal conditions, interacting with our more complete knowledge of human growth and development in career terms, as well as with the broader array of tools and techniques, have brought us to the realization that career development is a life span phenomenon and that all individuals can benefit from career development programs and services, whatever their ages or circumstances.

References

Campbell, R. E., and Cellini, J. V. (1981). A diagnostic taxonomy of adult career problems. *Journal of Vocational Behavior, 19*, 175–190.

Drier, H. N., and Pfister, L. A. (Eds.). (1980). *Career and labor market information: Key to improved individual decision making*. Columbus, OH: National Center for Research in Vocational Education.

Ehrbar, A. F. (1983). Grasping the new unemployment. *Fortune, 107*(10), pp. 107–112.

Gerber, A., Jr. (1983). Finding the car in career. *Journal of Career Education, 9*, 181–183.

Gordon, E. W. (1974). Vocational guidance: Disadvantaged and minority populations. In E. L. Herr (Ed.). *Vocational Guidance and Human Development*. Boston: Houghton Mifflin.

Gysbers, N. C., and Moore, E. J. (1975). Beyond career development—Life career development. *Personnel and Guidance Journal, 53*, 647–652.

Gysbers, N. C., and Moore, E. J. (1981). *Improving guidance programs*. Englewood Cliffs, NJ: Prentice-Hall.

Harris-Bowlsbey, J., Spivack, J. D., and Lisansky, R. S. (1982). *Take hold of your future*. Iowa City, IA: The American College Testing Program.

Jones, G. B., Hamilton, J. A., Ganschow, L. H., Helliwell, C. B., and Wolff, J. M. (1972). *Planning, developing and field testing career guidance programs: A manual and report*. Palo Alto, CA: American Institutes for Research.

Kapes, J. T., and Mastie, M. M. (Eds.). (1982). *A counselor's guide to vocational guidance instruments*. Washington, DC: National Vocational Guidance Association.

Keller, K. E., Biggs, D. A., and Gysbers, N. C. (1982). Career counseling from a cognitive perspective. *Personnel and Guidance Journal, 60*, 367–371.

Matthews, E. (1975). Comment. *Personnel and Guidance Journal, 53*, 652.

National Association of Manufacturers. (1982). *Perspective on national issues: America's human resources—Keys to productivity*. Washington, DC: Author.

Parsons, F. (1909). *Choosing a vocation*. Boston: Houghton Mifflin.

Pinkney, J. W. (1983). The Myers-Briggs type indicator as an alternative in career counseling. *Personnel and Guidance Journal, 62*, 173–177.

Sears, S. (1982). A definition of career guidance terms: A National Vocational Guidance Association perspective. *Vocational Guidance Quarterly, 31*, 137–143.

Super, D. E. (1981). The relative importance of work. *Bulletin—International Association of Educational and Vocational Guidance, 37*, 26–36.

Super, D. E. (1975). Vocational guidance: Emergent decision making in a changing society. *Bulletin—International Association of Educational and Vocational Guidance, 29*, 16–23.

Super, D. E., and Bohn, M. J., Jr. (1970). *Occupational Psychology*. Belmont, CA: Wadsworth.

Tennyson, W. (1970). Comment. *Vocational Guidance Quarterly, 18*, 261–263.
Wolfe, D. M., and Kolb, D. A. (1980). Career development, personal growth, and experimental learning. In J. Springer (Ed.), *Issues in career and human resource development*. Madison, WI: American Society for Training and Development.
Zingaro, J. C. (1983). A family systems approach for the career counselor. *Personnel and Guidance Journal, 62*, 24–27.

The Impact of Technology on Occupational Change: Implications for Career Guidance

Kenneth B. Hoyt

The impact of technology on occupational change will probably vary greatly from nation to nation in the next decade. The need for an exchange of views between nations is obviously great. As a beginning effort, I have prepared a short summary of the situation in the United States. This summary includes some basic facts on a number of aspects of the problem. For each set of facts, implications for career guidance are considered. In my opinion, the best source of data relative to expected occupational changes during the next decade in the United States is the *Occupational Outlook Handbook,* published biannually by the U.S. government (U.S. Department of Labor, 1986). The 1986-87 edition indicates, among other things, that the civilian work force is expected to grow from 114 million in 1984 to 129 million by 1995, a 14% increase. Furthermore, women will account for more than three-fifths of the labor force growth during this period. These two statistics alone are helpful in understanding both (a) how some so-called "declining industries" will actually have more workers in 1995 than they did in 1982, and (b) how the two-worker family is changing America's occupational structure.

When all occupations are divided into either the *service-producing or goods-producing* category, about 70% of current occupations are in the service-producing category. About 75% are expected to be so classified by 1995. Service-producing industries are projected to account for about 9 out of 10 new jobs between 1984 and 1995. It is only in this sense that America can now be said to be a "service type" occupational society. That is, although service industries are the fastest growing part of service-producing industries, they will, even by 1995, represent only about 31.2 million jobs—a fraction of the total of 129 million jobs. (The *Occupational Outlook Handbook* classifies *service industries* as one of seven service-producing industries. *Butler,* for example, is one occupation within the service industries. *Education* is a kind of service-producing industry, but it is not included within the service industry set of occupations.)

To clarify further, data in the *Handbook* make clear that it is absolutely false to contend that America has moved from an agricultural to an industrial to a post-industrial occupational society. Goods-producing industries are still alive and well in America. As a matter of fact, they are expected to increase 22% between 1982 and 1995 (from 27.1 million to 33.0 million). Today's popular myths about the disappearance of factory jobs because of the "high tech" revolution seem to stem primarily from the fact that Americans have lost about 500,000 jobs in the smokestack industries associated with automobile and steel production (Rosenthal, 1985). Job abolishment is no myth for displaced workers in these industries, but it would be mythical to apply that example to goods-producing industries in general.

Given facts such as these, it seems safe to say that in terms of work, America has moved from being primarily an agricultural society to being primarily an industrial society to being primarily a service, information-oriented, and high technology society (Morris, 1975; Naisbitt, 1982). No one seems sure what one should call the emerging society or exactly how far America is into it (Cook, 1983; Reich, 1983). What is certain is that neither the agricultural society nor the industrial society has disappeared. True, the proportion of the work force engaged in agriculture in America has dropped from about 40% in 1910 to 3% in 1980 (Rumberger & Leven, 1984). It is true that, in a relative sense, service-producing industries are growing at a more rapid rate than are goods-producing industries, but manufacturing jobs are expected to grow by about 1.3 million jobs between 1984 and 1995—a 7% increase.

Further insights into America's probable occupational future can be found in statistics on entrepreneurship (U.S. Small Business Administration, 1984). Small businesses today furnish two-thirds of all new jobs being created in the United States. Women-owned businesses are growing at an all-time high rate: In 1983, 2.8 million sole proprietorships were owned by women (4 times the number of women-owned businesses in 1977). In the 1980–1985 period, entrepreneurs created almost 3 million new corporations. By 1990, nearly one-quarter of the U.S. population—60 million people—will be between 30 and 45 years old, the prime ages for launching new businesses.

Statistics such as these hold multiple implications for professionals in the career guidance movement. Certainly, they make clear the inadvisability of adding one's voice to those urging today's youth to assume, when making career decisions, that the industrial age has disappeared. Similarly, they should help both counselors and those they counsel recognize that, contrary to some popular myths, most of tomorrow's jobs will not be in service occupations. The "certainty of uncertainty" being predicted by many for today's youth is not as inevitable as some have claimed. Finally, it is very clear that career guidance professionals are going to have to pay much more attention to the topic of entrepreneurial careers than most do today. A steady and continuing increase in the number and variety of small businesses in the United States seems certain.

Expected Rate of Occupational Change

Serious arguments exist regarding the expected rate at which America's occupational structure will change over the next 10 years. Some experts have seemed to concentrate on emphasizing how relatively little change can be expected (Kirkland, 1985; Rumberger, 1984). They have pointed out, for example, that most of the 19 million new jobs expected to be generated during the 1980-1990 period will be in very traditional kinds of occupations (e.g., sales clerks, janitors, waiters and waitresses, truck drivers). Jobs in high-tech industries will represent only a small proportion of these 19 million new jobs. Those occupations requiring the greatest numbers of new workers will not be characterized by high technology (Samuelson, 1983). Furthermore, most jobs in the so-called "high-tech" industries will be in "low-tech," not high-tech, occupations (Rumberger & Leven, 1984). High-tech occupations are, at best, no more than 6.2% of America's current work force and, even with expected rapid growth, cannot be much higher than that by 1995 (Rosenthal, 1985).

Those on the other side of this argument seem to delight in identifying what they predict will be new occupations that today's youth should be seriously considering (Bridges, 1983; Borchard, 1984; Feingold, 1983). Illustrative of such new occupations are (a) aquaculturist, (b) artificial intelligence technician, (c) energy auditor, (d) genetic biochemist, (e) information broker, and (f) space mechanic. There seems little doubt that new occupations such as these—and many more—will be part of America's occupational society by the time this year's kindergarten pupils finish high school.

Career guidance professionals must consider all these data and both sides of this argument as they prepare to help persons choose careers. Personal values of clients will undoubtedly be major factors in career choices. For example, those valuing a high probability of finding any job may choose those occupations expected to employ the greatest numbers of persons in the next decade. Those who value being in on the "ground floor" of occupations just now beginning to grow rapidly may choose occupations that today have relatively few job openings.

There seems little doubt that those who are arguing that tomorrow's occupational society will very much resemble today's are more nearly right than those arguing the case for completely new occupations. Another U.S. Department of Labor publication, *Occupational Projections and Training Data* (U.S. Bureau of Labor Statistics, 1986, pp. 12–13), contains the following data with respect to occupational growth between 1984 and 1995:

Largest Job Growth Occupations	**Fastest Growing Occupations**
Cashiers	Paralegal personnel
Registered nurses	Computer programmers
Janitors and cleaners, including maids and housekeepers	Computer systems analysts, electronic data processing (EDP)
Waiters and waitresses	Medical assistants
Wholesale trade sales workers	Data processing equipment repair
Nursing aids and orderlies	Electrical and electronics engineers
Salespersons, retail	Computer operators
Accountants and auditors	Travel agents

Clearly, although several of the fastest growing occupations are high-tech in nature, no high-tech type occupations are included in the list of the 10 occupations expected to employ the most new workers between now and 1995. With an expected 120 million or more employed workers, even an increase in a high-tech occupation, of, say, 500,000 employees would not change the overall statistics very much. Career guidance professionals need to be cognizant of the remarkable degree of stability to be expected in America's occupational structure over the next 10 years. If this perspective is kept clearly in mind, then relative growth or decline in a given occupation can be interpreted to clients in a much more realistic fashion.

Effects on Availability of Jobs

There is no clear consensus in the United States with respect to the effect high technology will have on availability of jobs. Both optimists and pessimists can be found among manpower experts. Predictions range all the way from those who predict that jobs will be plentiful (Main, 1982) to those who claim that, unless drastic countermeasures are taken, unemployment in the United States could exceed 25% of the labor force by 1995 (Schwartz & Neikirk, 1984). The official position of the U.S. government, as expressed in the 1986–87 edition of the *Occupational Outlook Handbook* is:

> The overall impact of technology will be to increase the amount of goods and services each worker can produce. Output of goods and services is expected to increase rapidly, however, so that employment should continue to increase in most industries and occupations. (p. 16)

Part of this argument centers around the probable impact of robots on the availability of jobs in the future. The robots are coming; that is certain. It seems that one robot displaces approximately 1.7 workers in an assembly plant and 2.7 workers in a manufacturing plant (Main, 1982). The fact that, to date, robots seem to have replaced more U.S. workers in the automobile and steel industries than in the clothing and apparel industries seems to have more to do with the relatively high wages of automobile and steel workers than with susceptibility of each industry to robotics. There seems to be general agreement that, if robots can deliver the same skills as humans at the same or lower hourly cost, it is preferable to use robots. After all, as Clapp said, "Robots don't unionize, get pregnant, call in sick, or drop Twinkies in the machinery" (Clapp, 1983).

One apparently conservative argument is that although technology destroys some jobs, it creates others. For example, it has been predicted that robots will eliminate 100,000 to 200,000 jobs by 1990 while creating 32,000 to 64,000 new ones (Hunt & Hunt, 1983).

The capability of robots to displace workers is unmistakable and is growing rapidly as expertise in artificial intelligence develops. But robots cannot really care about persons with whom they work in a human way, and some experts believe that this, in itself, will be enough to ensure that "the office of the future will keep a human face" (Kirkland, 1985, p. 43). Furthermore, robots have not yet become cheap enough to be good investments for most small businesses, and that is where a majority of new jobs will be found in the coming decade (U.S. Small Business Administration, 1984).

Questions of probable availability of jobs in the future extend beyond simply the impact of high technology on job availability. For example, the problem in the United States is further complicated by the great increase in the various subpopulations seeking to enter the labor force. The growing numbers of women, structurally displaced middle-aged workers, minority persons, illegal immigrants, and senior citizens seeking jobs have greatly compounded the prediction problem over what it was when the prime source of new workers was expected to be people recently leaving school. As noted above, the U.S. Department of Labor can and does make 10-year predictions of numbers of persons likely to be employed. It does not, however, make similar predictions regarding numbers likely to be unemployed. Thus, data-based predictions of how many will be unsuccessful in seeking employment are not available.

Even if assumptions of very rapid technological diffusion are accepted, it has been predicted that the maximum number of jobs to be eliminated by the year 2000 is 20 million—or 11% of all the jobs that would exist in the absence of further technological diffusion (Rumberger & Leven, 1984). Several implications for professionals in career guidance are obvious. They can be briefly summarized as follows:

1. No matter how many persons lose jobs because of technology, the human need of all human beings to work will remain. If, for some

persons, that need cannot be met through paid employment, then counselors must provide help in meeting it through unpaid work done as part of productive use of leisure time.

2. Workers whose jobs are displaced by robots are very likely to find it necessary to enter occupations with lower pay scales than those in the jobs they formerly held. This will create serious career guidance problems for both individuals and families.
3. The continuing growth in both service-producing industries (where a personal touch is an important ingredient in success) and small businesses (that cannot afford robots) has great implications for the ways that career guidance professionals deal with clients. The importance of human interactions in career decision making is almost sure to increase.
4. High technology will have some impact by destroying some current jobs while creating others. Its greatest impact seems likely to be on the number of times a given person is forced to change occupations during his or her career.
5. The ability of any nation to compete successfully in the world marketplace is a function of producing higher quality products at lower costs. To whatever extent that goal can be better met by robots than by people, robots can be expected to dominate. The reverse is equally true. The challenge to career guidance professionals clearly includes encouraging clients to produce high quality efforts at a wage that enables the employer to make a reasonable profit.

Effects on Education Required for Jobs

American experts strongly disagree about the likely impact that high technology will have on the amount and kinds of education required to fill tomorrow's jobs. Some emphasize the expected increases in worker dissatisfaction resulting from a combination of a much better educated work force and the "deskilling" of many occupations made possible by high technology (Leven, 1983). The general principle involved in this dissatisfaction is that as machines become more sophisticated through applications of high technology, the knowledge required to operate such machines declines (Rumberger & Leven, 1984). Others seem very optimistic regarding the positive potential of high technology for relieving the drudgery of routine tasks, for freeing individuals to be more creative in their thinking, and for multiplying options available to workers with respect to both where they work and when they work (Aspen Institute for Humanistic Studies, 1982).

Most writers on this subject, however, seem to make dual kinds of predictions; that is, they predict that occupations will become more challenging and exciting for those in highly skilled occupations while simultaneously becoming even less meaningful than today's jobs in occupations at the lower end of the occupational wage scale (Edgerton, 1983; Main, 1982; Schwartz & Neikirk, 1984).

The basic argument is clearly seen in the following contrasting statements:

> Future job growth will favor service and clerical jobs that require little or no post secondary schooling and that pay below average wages. (Rumberger & Leven, 1984)

> We are moving from a work force in which 38% have the . . . skills associated heretofore with the college-bound to a labor market in which nearly half the new hires will be expected to be so qualified. (Honig, 1985)

Obviously, both views cannot be right. Returning to the *Occupational Outlook Handbook* (1986-87 edition) as a prime source of data, the following quotes are germane:

> Between 1970-1984, employment of college graduates grew 127% . . . the proportion in professional technical/managerial occupations declined . . . because . . . [they] . . . did not expand rapidly enough. As a result, 1 of 5 college graduates (1970-1984) took jobs not usually requiring a college degree. This oversupply of college graduates is likely to continue through the mid 1990s. (p. 14)

> Through the mid-1990s, most jobs will become available as the result of replacement needs. . . . Occupations with the most replacement openings generally are large, with low . . . training requirements. (p. 21)

Another set of implications for career guidance professionals seem apparent here. These implications include:

1. Career guidance professionals should not be surprised to discover that most of tomorrow's jobs are expected to require no more than a high school education. After all, that is true for today's jobs, and as pointed out above, profound change in the total occupational society will not occur very rapidly.
2. It is not necessarily inappropriate for career guidance professionals to continue helping their clients attend 4-year college and university settings. After all, the *Handbook* provides clear evidence demonstrating that (a) the chances of having no job at all decline as one's educational level increases, and (b) college programs that last 4 years or longer provide qualifying training to more workers than do all other types of schooling combined (U.S. Bureau of Labor Statistics, 1986).
3. With the sizable oversupply of college graduates expected to continue well into the 1990s, career guidance professionals have a clear

responsibility to include an emphasis on alternative career planning for those whose college degrees are not directly useful in the labor market. This topic must be included in counseling.

4. There is clearly a need for career guidance professionals to increase their emphasis on helping persons consider postsecondary educational opportunities at the subbaccalaureate level, particularly in technical education.
5. In discussing educational plans with clients, career guidance professionals must emphasize more than the goal of education as preparation for paid employment. As high technology continues to influence occupational change, it becomes more and more important that career guidance professionals help clients see work as an integral part of a total lifestyle. There is a need to broaden the perspective provided to clients in career counseling.
6. The fact that more workers received the specific training needed for their jobs through on-the-job (OJT) training than through any form of schooling is significant here. The growing presence of training provided by the employer is important for career guidance professionals to convey to those they counsel.

The "Declining Middle?"

A considerable number of experts have projected that in the future U.S. occupational society a relatively small number of highly skilled workers and a somewhat larger number of poorly skilled workers will find the "middle" of the occupational society occupied by robots and other forms of automation (Kuttner, 1983; Leven, 1983; Schwartz & Neikirk, 1984). Others have stated that predictions of such a two-tier work force seem plausible only if efforts to meet training needs of the displaced, the underemployed, and the unemployed are insufficient (Harris, 1985). The logic of this argument is undeniable; that is, it is not difficult to envision conditions in which machines of various kinds do most of the work, leaving many persons with, in effect, no productive societal contributions to make in the occupational society.

Opponents of this point of view also present formidable arguments. Samuelson (1983) provided data indicating that the relative percentages of total income distributed among various quintiles of employed workers has remained remarkably steady over several decades. Kirkland (1985) contended that the concept of the *declining middle* is a statistical fluke caused by a U.S. Census Bureau effort to improve measurement of family income distribution. At the same time, he hinted that the continuation of middle-income families may be largely due to the rise in two-income households and that, if this condition did not exist, statistics might, indeed, show a declining middle.

The most compelling data, in my opinion, are those presented by Rosenthal (1985), showing that between 1973 and 1982 the percentage of total employment in the one-third middle earnings category actually increased. Additionally, Rosenthal has produced data demonstrating that one of the expected outcomes of moving to high-tech industries is to increase, not decrease, the growth of middle-income jobs. Furthermore, his data are based on occupational, not family-income, statistics (Rosenthal, 1985).

The implications for career guidance professionals of this argument and of the data on both sides of the issue include:

1. The declining middle phenomenon, although commonly discussed in today's popular literature, cannot, at present, be well validated with firm data. It would not be advisable to counsel persons today as though an occupational society with a declining middle is something they can expect soon.
2. It may well be that the declining middle phenomenon will come into existence 20 to 30 years from now. Thus, it is a topic that should be a part of today's career guidance conversations. Career guidance professionals will not be fair to their clients if they pretend that the possibility of the declining middle does not exist.
3. To whatever extent any given worker at the lower skill levels of the occupational society finds the declining middle to be a reality for him or her, career guidance must include discussion of how such workers can continue to maintain positive self-concepts and feelings of self-worth in their total life-style.

Conclusion

The impact of high technology on the occupational structure clearly varies—and will continue to vary—from nation to nation. Thus, the special problems in career guidance posed by such technology must also vary from nation to nation. In this article I have approached the problem only from the standpoint of the United States.

In the United States, it it clear that high technology is having an impact on the occupational society and thus on the challenges for change in vocational guidance. It is equally clear that neither the magnitude nor the rapidity of change brought about by technology is as great as some writers seem to suggest. The rate of change is, to be sure, more rapid than in the past and, as high technology emerges, the rate of change will increase still more. Yet in viewing the U.S. occupational structure as a whole, it seems unlikely that high technology will have great impact on the basic nature of the occupational society at least up to the year 2000.

This observation, of course, does not mean that the individual jobs of many workers will be unaffected by high technology. That simply is not true. High technology will require many workers to adapt to new tools and new procedures even while remaining in the same job and in the same occupation. The adjustment problems associated with such change pose significant challenges for vocational guidance.

The major challenge to career guidance being posed by high technology is that of finding ways of helping clients retain a basic commitment to work as an important part of their total system of personal values. At the same time, counselors must also help clients fit the concept of work into clients' total lifestyles in a meaningful and satisfying manner. This includes helping persons plan for productive use of work as part of leisure time.

References

Aspen Institute for Humanistic Studies. (1982). The hopes and fears of the information revolution. *Communications and Society Report-in-Brief,* No. 82–1.

Borchard, D. (1984, August). New choices: Career planning in a changing world. *The Futurist,* pp. 26–27.

Bridges, L. (1983, September). Brave new work. *Success,* pp. 22–26.

Clapp, D. (1983, May 30). Robot boom could lead to disaster or discovery. *Infoworld,* p. 14.

Cook, J. (1983, April). You mean we've been speaking prose all these years? *Forbes,* pp. 142–149.

Edgerton, R. (1983, June). A college education up to beating the Japanese. *AAHE Bulletin,* pp. 3–7.

Feingold, N. (1984, February). Emerging careers: Occupations for post industrial society. *The Futurist,* pp. 9–16.

Harris, P. R. (1985). Future work. *Personnel Journal, 64*(6), 52–58.

Honig, B. (1985, May 29). Jobs and education. *Education Week,* p. 23.

Hunt, H. A., & Hunt, T. L. (1983). *Human resource implications of robotics.* Kalamazoo, MI: W. E. Upjohn Institute for Employment Research.

Kirkland, R. I., Jr. (1985, June). Are service jobs good jobs? *Fortune,* pp. 38–43.

Kuttner, B. (1983, July). The declining middle. *Atlantic,* pp. 60–72.

Leven, H. M. (1983). The workplace: Employment and business interventions. In E. Seidman (Ed.), *Handbook of social intervention* (pp. 499–521). Beverly Hills, CA: Sage.

Main, J. (1982, June). Work won't be the same again. *Fortune*, pp. 58–65.
Morris, W. (1975). *Work and your future: Living poorer, working harder.* Reston, VA: Reston Publishing.
Naisbitt, J. (1982). *Megatrends: Ten new directions transforming our lives.* New York: Warner.
Reich, R. B. (1983, April). The next American frontier. *Atlantic*, pp. 97–108.
Rosenthal, N. H. (1985, March). *Tomorrow's jobs.* Unpublished paper presented at the annual meeting of the American Association for Counseling and Development, New York.
Rumberger, R. W. (1984). The growing imbalance between education and work. *Phi Delta Kappan, 65*, 342–346.
Rumberger, R. W., & Leven, H. M. (1984). *Forecasting the impact of new technologies on the future job market.* Palo Alto, CA: Stanford University, School of Education, Institute for Research on Educational Finance and Governance.
Samuelson, R. J. (1983, December). Middle-class media myth. *National Journal*, pp. 2673–2678.
Schwartz, G., & Neikirk, W. (1984). *The work revolution.* New York: Rawson Associates.
U.S. Bureau of Labor Statistics. (1986). *Occupational projections and training data* (Bulletin 225). Washington DC: U.S. Department of Labor.
U.S. Department of Labor. (1986). *Occupational outlook handbook: 1986-87.* Washington, DC: U.S. Government Printing Office.
U.S. Small Business Administration. (1984). *The state of small business: A report of the President.* Washington, DC: U.S. Government Printing Office.

Using Books to Enhance Career Awareness

Nancy K. Staley
John N. Mangieri

Career education has had an important place in our elementary schools. In the early 1970s Sidney P. Marland, then Undersecretary of Health, Education, and Welfare, established career education "to be the number one priority in America's schools." It was envisioned by the U.S. Office of Education "to be a comprehensive curriculum-related effort which attempts to meld diverse instructional materials and various teaching strategies into a sequential K–12+ program" (Marland, 1971, p. 22).

Although career education no longer occupies such a prominent national position, it should be an important area of concern for both elementary school teachers and school counselors. It is widely acknowledged that children begin to formulate career decisions at a relatively young age. Hoppock (1967) advised that, with rare exceptions, children in the early grades are not ready for concentrated doses of occupational information or formal coursework in careers. Yet he believed that they become aware of many occupations that were unknown to them before. They acquire impressions of the work people do in these occupations, the kinds of people employed, the compensations offered, and the abilities that are required for acceptable performance. On the basis of these impressions, they enthusiastically embrace some occupations as possible careers for themselves and absolutely remove others from either present or future consideration. (Hoppock, 1967)

It is ironic that at a time when the fourth edition of the *Dictionary of Occupational Titles* (U.S. Department of Labor, Employment, and Training Administration, 1977) gives information on some 20,000 jobs, many children have so little awareness of career options. A children's librarian reported that the results of a casual survey that she conducted with first and second graders showed that their responses to the age-old question—"What do you want to be when you grow up?"—differed little from those of previous generations. Most of the children's answers fell into the doctor-teacher-fireman category (Ridenour, 1980). Surveys such as this remind us that one of the major goals of adults who work with children must be to broaden children's awareness of job possibilities.

There are a variety of strategies and activities that are appropriate for helping boys and girls learn about career options. Hoppock (1967) suggested that the teacher be a good listener and let children talk about their occupational choices. He also advised encouraging children to fantasize about possible careers: "From kindergarten to third grade let the child dream. The child-development people tell us that these are the ages during which fantasy is a good thing . . . " (p. 363).

A wide assortment of children's books will provide children with vicarious experiences and the necessary background for dreaming and fantasizing about career options. Trade books can be used in a variety of ways. In some classrooms they will be a supplement to other activities, such as discussions, field trips, units of work. In other situations, books will form the nucleus for learning about career awareness.

Many elementary school teachers have book corners or classroom libraries, and most elementary schools provide libraries or media centers so that books are readily accessible to children and faculty. It is important that books about career awareness be included in these collections. Children should be given the opportunity to read both informational books that offer facts about many kinds of occupations and fiction that portrays positive role models. Counselors, teachers, and librarians should provide children with the best of the many books that are available about career awareness. An effort should be made to select books that portray men and women who have equal opportunities, and illustrations should reflect sexual as well as racial balance.

Suggested Readings to Enhance Career Awareness

The bibliography presented below will be helpful to teachers and counselors. Many books and book reviews were read in the process of compiling it. An attempt was made to choose books that were both culturally and sexually unbiased. Reading levels are indicated as a grade level span to suggest a time period during which children would probably be interested in reading these particular books.

Book reviewers and publishers usually designate in some way the appropriate age or interest level for which the book is intended. For uniformity, in this bibliography this information is organized as follows:

Grades K–3: P (primary), ages 5 to 9
Grades 4–6: I (intermediate), ages 10 to 12
Grades 7–9: A (advanced), ages 13 to 15

These designations are not meant to be applied rigidly. If, for example, a book is recommended for use with children in grades 4 through 6, it would probably be enjoyed by children in grades 4, 5, and 6. Younger children might enjoy it if it were read aloud to them, and accelerated readers in the second or third grades might like reading it independently. It is important to note that more than chronological age or grade in school is important in matching an appropriate book with a child. According to Huck (1979), "the readability level of a book is not as important as its content in relation to the reader's actual interest in a subject" (p. 528). Cullinan (1981) pointed out that "the developmental level of the reader is a major factor in the equation when selecting a good book" (p. 7).

The books in this bibliography are assigned to one of the 15 career categories that were established by the U.S. Office of Education or to a category termed *career options*. The names of the publishers are in abbreviated form; their complete names and addresses can be found in a standard reference work such as *Literary Market Place* (1982).

Agribusiness and Natural Resources

Benson, C. *Careers in agriculture*. Lerner, 1979. (Grades K–6)
Benson, C. *Careers in animal care*. Lerner, 1979. (Grades K–6)
Clymer, E. *Me and the eggman*. Dutton, 1972. (Grades 4–6)
Demuth, P. *Joel: Growing up a farm man*. Dodd, 1982. (Grades 4–6)
Facklam, M. *Wild animals, gentle women*. Harcourt, 1978. (Grades 7–9)
Garner, A. *Granny Reardun*. Collins/World, 1978. (Grades 4–6)
Hall, L. *Careers for dog lovers*. Follett, 1978. (Grades 4–6)
Krementz, J. *A very young rider*. Knopf, 1977. (Grades 4–6)
Lerner, M. *Careers in a zoo*. Lerner, 1980. (Grades K–6)
O'Conner, K. *Maybe you belong in a zoo! Zoo and aquarium careers*. Dodd, 1982. (Grades 4–6)

Business and Office

McHugh, M. *Law and the new woman*. Watts, 1975. (Grades 4–6)
Ray, J. A. *Careers in computers*. Lerner, 1979. (Grades K–6)

Communications and Media

Bendrick, J., & Bendrick, R. *Finding out about jobs: T.V. reporting*. Parents Magazine Press, 1976. (Grades 4–6)
Davis, M. *Careers in printing*. Lerner, 1979. (Grades K–6)
Davis, M. *Careers with a telephone company*. Lerner, 1979. (Grades K–6)
Duncan, L. *Chapters: My growth as a writer*. Little, Brown, 1982. (Grades 4–6)
Edmonds, I. G. *Broadcasting for beginners*. Hoal, 1981. (Grades 4–6)

Construction

Adkins, J. *How a house happens*. Walker, 1972. (Grades 4–6)
Berger, M. *Building construction*. Watts, 1978. (Grades 4–9)

Harmon, C. *Skyscraper goes up*. Random House, 1973. (Grades 4–6)
Kelly, J. E. *Tunnel builders*. Addison-Wesley, 1976. (Grades K–3)
Lieber, A. *You can be a carpenter.* Lothrop, Lee & Shepard, 1974. (Grades 6–9)
Ramos, G. *Careers in construction*. Lerner, 1979. (Grades K–6)
Sobol, H. L. *Pete's house*. Macmillan, 1978. (Grades K–6)

Consumer and Homemaker Operations

Lerner, M. *Careers in a supermarket*. Lerner, 1979. (Grades K–6)
Miles, B. *The real me*. Knopf, distributed by Random House, 1974. (Grades 3 and up)
Perl, L. *That crazy April*. Seabury, 1974. (Grades 4–9)
Rabe, B. *Naomi*. Thomas Nelson, 1975. (Grades 6–9)
Vestly, A. *Hello, Aurora*. Crowell, 1974. (Grades 4–6)

Environment

Benson, C. *Careers in conservation*. Lerner, 1979. (Grades K–6)
Bergaust, E. *Next 50 years on the moon*. Putnam, 1974. (Grades 4–6)
Berger, M. *Jobs that save our environment*. Lothrop, Lee & Shepard, 1973. (Grades 4 and up)
Chester, M. *Let's go to the moon*. Putnam, 1974. (Grades 4–6)
Cobb, V. *Supersuits*. Lippincott, 1975. (Grades 4–6)
Fodor, R. V. *What does a geologist do?* Dodd, 1977. (Grades 4–6)

Hospitality and Recreation

Adler, D. A. *You think it's fun to be a clown?* Doubleday, 1981. (Grades K–3)
Babcock, D., & Boyd, P. *Careers in the theater*. Lerner, 1980. (Grades K–6)
Cook, S. *The Alvin Ailey American Dance Theater.* William Morrow, 1978. (Grades 4–6)
Davis, M. *Careers in baseball*. Lerner, 1979. (Grades K–6)
Dean, K. S. *Maggie Adams, dancer.* Avon Books, 1980. (Grades 4–6)
Gross, R. B. *If you were a ballet dancer.* Scholastic Book Services, 1979. (Grades K–6)
Hancock, S. *Bill Pickett: First Black rodeo star.* Harcourt, 1978. (Grades 4–6)
Kelly, K. *Careers with the circus*. Lerner, 1979. (Grades K–6)
Klein, D. *On the way up*. Messner, 1978. (Grades 4–6)
Krementz, J. *A very young dancer.* Knopf, 1976. (Grades 4–9)
Krementz, J. *A very young gymnast*. Knopf, 1978. (Grades 4–9)
Lerner, M. *Careers in a restaurant*. Lerner, 1979. (Grades K–6)
Lerner, M. *Careers in hotels and motels*. Lerner, 1979. (Grades K–6)

Palladian, A. *Careers in soccer.* Lerner, 1979. (Grades K–6)
Peck, R. H. *Hotel and motel careers.* Watts. (Grades 4–6)
Ray, J. A. *Careers in football.* Lerner, 1979. (Grades K–6)
Ray, J. A. *Careers in hockey.* Lerner, 1979. (Grades K–6)
Streatfield, N. *Thursday's child.* Random House, 1971. (Grades 4–6)

Manufacturing

Cooke, D. C. *How books are made.* Dodd, Mead, 1963. (Grades 4–6)
Langer, H. *Who puts the print on the page.* Random House, 1976. (Grades 4–6)
Lerner, M. *Careers in auto manufacturing.* Lerner, 1979. (Grades K–6)
Lerner, M. *Careers in shipping.* Lerner, 1980. (Grades K–6)
Lerner, M. *Careers in toy making.* Lerner, 1980. (Grades K–6)
Lieber, A. *You can be a machinist.* Lothrop, Lee & Shepard, 1975. (Grades 7–9)
Lieber, A. *You can be a mechanic.* Lothrop, Lee & Shepard, 1975. (Grades 7–9)
Lieber, A. *You can be a printer.* Lothrop, Lee & Shepard, 1975. (Grades 7–9)
Lieber, A. *You can be a welder.* Lothrop, Lee & Shepard, 1977. (Grades 7–9)

Marine Science

Berger, M. *Oceanography lab.* Day, 1973. (Grades 4–6)
L'Engle, M. *A ring of endless light.* Farrar, Straus & Giroux, 1980. (Grades 7–9)

Marketing and Distribution

Asch, F. *Good lemonade.* Watts, 1976. (Grades K–6)
Bulla, C. R. *Shoeshine girl.* Crowell, 1975. (Grades 4–6)
Krantz, H. *100 pounds of popcorn.* Vanguard Press, 1961. (Grades 4–6)
Merrill, J. *The toothpaste millionaire.* Houghton Mifflin, 1974. (Grades K–6)
Pfeffer, S. B. *Kid power.* Watts, 1977. (Grades 4–6)
Williams, B. *I know a salesperson.* G. P. Putnam's Sons, 1978. (Grades K–3)

Personal Service

Beam, R. *What happens to garbage?* Messner, 1975. (Grades 4–6)
Bunting, E. *Barney the beard.* Four Winds, 1975. (Grades K–3)
Criner, B. & Criner, C. *Jobs in personal services.* Lothrop, Lee & Shepard, 1974. (Grades K–6)
Goldreich, G., & Goldreich, E. *What can she be? A newscaster.* Lothrop, 1972. (Grades 2–5)
Jahn, M. *How to make a hit record.* Westminister, 1975. (Grades 4–6)

Jeness, A. *The bakery factory: Who puts the bread on your table?* Crowell, 1978. (Grades 4–6)
Klever, A. *Women in television.* Westminister, 1975. (Grades 4–6)
Lerner, M. *Careers in beauty and grooming.* Lerner, 1979. (Grades K–6)
Lerner, M. *Careers with a newspaper.* Lerner, 1979. (Grades K–6)
Lieber, A. *You can be a plumber.* Lothrop, Lee & Shepard, 1974. (Grades 7–9)
Lieber, A. *You can be a professional driver.* Lothrop, Lee & Shepard, 1974. (Grades 7–9)
McGonagle, B. & McGonagle, M. *Prepare for a career in radio and television announcing.* Lothrop, Lee & Shepard, 1974. (Grades 4–9)
Pelta, K. *What does a lifeguard do?* Dodd, 1977. (Grades 4–6)
Pompian, R. O. *Advertising.* Watts, 1970. (Grades 7–9)
Ray, J. *Careers with a television station.* Lerner, 1979. (Grades K–6)
Steinberg, B. *Who keeps America clean?* Random House, 1976. (Grades 4–6)
Steinberg, B. *Who puts the news on television?* Random House, 1976. (Grades 4–6)

Public Service

Benson, C. *Careers in education.* Lerner, 1979. (Grades K–6)
Benson, C. *Careers with the city.* Lerner, 1979. (Grades K–6)
Criner, B., & Criner, C. *Jobs in public service.* Lothrop, Lee & Shepard, 1974. (Grades K–6)
Palladian, A. *Careers in the air force.* Lerner, 1979. (Grades K–6)
Palladian, A. *Careers in the army.* Lerner, 1979. (Grades K–6)
Palladian, A. *Careers in the navy.* Lerner, 1979. (Grades K–6)
Peterson, J. *Careers with a fire department.* Lerner, 1979. (Grades K–6)
Peterson, J. *Careers with the postal service.* Lerner, 1979. (Grades K–6)
Ray, J. A. *Careers with a police department.* Lerner, 1979. (Grades K–6)
Shuttlesworth, D. E. *Zoos in the making.* Dutton, 1977. (Grades 4–9)

Transportation

Dean, J. B. *Careers with an airline.* Lerner, 1979. (Grades K–6)
Gray, G. *Jobs in transportation.* Lothrop, Lee & Shepard, 1973. (Grades 4–6)
Lerner, M. *Careers in trucking.* Lerner, 1980. (Grades K–6)
Meade, C. *Careers with a railroad.* Lerner, 1979. (Grades K–6)

Fine Arts and Humanities

Berger, M. *Jobs in fine arts and humanities.* Lothrop, Lee & Shepard. (Grades 4–6)

Blumfield, M. J. *Careers in photography.* Lerner, 1980. (Grades K–6)
Busnar, G. *Careers in music.* Mesner, 1982. (Grades 4–9)
Cost, L. *The young ballet dancer.* Stein and Day, 1979. (Grades 4–6)
Cretan, G. Y. *All except Sammy.* Little, 1966. (Grades K–3)
Edmonds, E. G. *The mysteries of Troy.* Nelson, 1978. (Grades 4–6)
Goffstein, M. B. *Two piano tuners.* Farrar, 1977. (Grades 4–6)
Shapiro, I. *Darwin and the enchanted isles.* Coward, 1978. (Grades 4–6)
Smith, B. C. *Breakthrough: Women in religion.* Walker, 1978. (Grades 4–6)
Thomson, P. *Museum people: Collectors and keepers at the Smithsonian.* Prentice-Hall, 1977. (Grades 4–6)

Health

Berger, M. *Animal hospital.* John Day, 1973. (Grades 4–6)
Berger, M. *Medical center lab.* John Day, 1976. (Grades 7–9)
Bowman, K. *New women in medicine.* Creative Education/Children's Press, 1976. (Grades 4–6)
Buchenholtz, B. *Doctor in the zoo.* Viking Press, 1974. (Grades 4–9)
Dodge, B. S. *The story of nursing.* Little, Brown, 1965. (Grades 4–6)
Englebardt, S. L. *Jobs in health care.* Lothrop, Lee & Shepard, 1973. (Grades K–9)
Feather, J. H. *Sawtooth Harbor Bay.* Nelson, 1973. (Grades 4–6)
Iritani, C. A. *I know an animal doctor.* Putnam, 1970. (Grades K–3)
Lee, M. P. *The team that runs your hospital.* Westminister, 1981. (Grades 4–6)
McPhee, R. *Rounds with a country vet.* Dodd, 1977. (Grades 4–6)
Rockwell, H. *My doctor.* Macmillan, 1973. (Grades K–3)
Shay, A. *What it's like to be a doctor.* Regnery, 1971. (Grades 4–6)
Smith, D. B. *Kick a stone home.* Crowell, 1974. (Grades 7–9)

Career Options

Alexander, S. *Finding your first job.* Dutton, 1981. (Grades 4–6)
Ancona, G. *What do you do? A book about people and their work.* Dutton, 1976. (Grades 4–6)
Cleary, B. *Ramona and her father.* Morrow, 1977. (Grades 4–6)
Cole, S. *Working kids on working.* Lothrop, Lee & Shepard, 1981. (Grades 4–6)
Cowles, K. *What will I be?* Golden Press, 1979. (Grades K–3)
English, B. L. *Women at their work.* Dial, 1977. (Grades K–9)
Faber, N. *I found them in the yellow pages.* Little, Brown, 1973. (Grades K–3)
Fitzhugh, L. *Nobody's family is going to change.* Dell, 1975. (Grades 4–6)
Harper, A. *How we work.* Harper, 1977. (Grades K–3)

Hart, C. *Delilah*. Harper, 1973. (Grades K–6)
Horn, Y. *Dozens of ways to make money*. Harcourt, 1977. (Grades 4–6)
Johnston, T. *Odd jobs*. Putnam, 1977. (Grades K–3)
Kraus, R. *Owliver*. Windmill Press, 1974. (Grades K–3)
Lisker, S. O. *I am*. Hastings House, 1975. (Grades K–3)
Ott, J., & Stroer, R. *Work as you like it: A look at unusual jobs*. Messner, 1979. (Grades 4–6)
Saul, W. *Butcher, baker, cabinetmaker: Photographs of women at work*. Crowell, 1978. (Grades K–3)
Scarry, R. *Richard Scarry's busiest people ever*. Random House, 1976. (Grades K–6)
Seed, S. *Saturday's child: 36 women talk about their jobs*. O'Hara, 1973. (Grades 7–9)

Four Strategies for Using the Bibliography

Choosing Books

In selecting appropriate books from the bibliography, it is important to remember that children at a particular grade level are not all alike. There will be a wide range of reading abilities and interest levels among the children in a class. Therefore, when selecting books for a group of children, it is a good idea to choose many titles that appeal to both younger children and older ones. If possible, choose multiple copies of some books so that children can read together in small groups or with partners.

Read Aloud

It is recommended that some books be selected that will appeal to the entire class and that these be read aloud to the class. The selection may also include a difficult book that will stretch the children's imaginations. If a counselor is working with the teacher in a classroom situation, it may be possible for one of the adults to read to a small group of children or even to an individual child. Reading aloud to children is important throughout the elementary school years; it should not be limited to small children. Older children need to be introduced to good books that may be too difficult for them to read but that they can understand and enjoy if someone else reads to them. The reading aloud period should be followed by questions and discussion. Hearing these books read can provide students with vicarious experiences that they talk about, write about, and think about.

Sustained Silent Reading (SSR)

Children will enjoy reading many of these books silently. Blocks of time should be allocated for independent reading activities. One strategy that works well is Sustained Silent Reading (SSR). In many classrooms all members of the class (including the teacher) voluntarily read books of their choice for a predetermined time period. Students in the early grades may start with a 15-minute period that stretches to 30 minutes later in the year. Older children read silently for longer periods. The emphasis does not have to be on silence. Children might read with partners. The teacher might read with individual children at times; at other times they would read silently to themselves.

One may wonder how beginning readers cope with the decoding of words they encounter in their independent reading. Psycholinguistic theory supports the idea that even beginning readers read for meaning (Smith, 1973). As they try to make sense of the story and reconstruct the author's message, they deal with the words and sentences in context; they do not gain comprehension by looking at each word in isolation. It is helpful if the unknown word is explained so they can continue their efforts to understand the meaning of the passage. During SSR or other free reading periods, there will be times when the teacher is unavailable to explain new words. When the teacher is busy, he or she may assign this responsibility to some of the more able readers, who will be "word helpers." Because there is normally a wide range of reading abilities within one classroom, word helpers probably can be chosen from class members. When children read together with partners, they should be encouraged to help one another with unknown words.

Career Awareness Units

Teachers and counselors can work together to present a unit or theme that emphasizes career awareness. In the early grades the emphasis may be on community workers such as the druggist, dentist, grocer, and librarian. In the upper grades, a more sophisticated approach should be used. Children might explore more complex issues such as supply and demand, requirements for entry into occupations, and the effect of change on the future of occupations. Trade books can be a valuable source of information for the implementation of these career awareness units.

The preceding are not, of course, the only strategies in which counselors and teachers can use trade books to integrate career awareness in the elementary school curriculum. Other comparable measures can be used successfully to accomplish this goal. What we are advocating is the employment of trade books to enlarge the career awareness of children.

References

Cullinan, B. E. (1981). *Literature and the child.* New York: Harcourt Brace Jovanovich.

Hoppock, R. (1967). *Occupational information.* New York: McGraw-Hill.

Huck, C. S. (1979). *Children's literature in the elementary school.* New York: Holt, Rinehart and Winston.

Literary market place: The directory of American book publishing. (1982). New York: R. R. Bowker.

Marland, S. B. (1971). Career education. *Today's Education, 60,* 22–25.

Ridenour, S. C. (1980, February). Doctor-teacher-fireman: Career books for children. *School Library Journal,* pp. 32–33.

Smith, F. (1973). *Understanding reading.* New York: Holt, Rinehart and Winston.

U.S. Department of Labor, Employment and Training Administration. (1977). *Dictionary of occupational titles.* Washington, DC: U.S. Government Printing Office.

The Art of Career Exploration: Occupational Sex-Role Stereotyping Among Elementary School Children

Mary Bowe Hageman
Samuel T. Gladding

There has been considerable research in recent years on occupational sex-role stereotyping (Farmer, 1978; Navin & Sears, 1980; Remer & O'Neill, 1980; Wolleat, 1979; Worell, 1980). Much of this research has demonstrated that children think certain traditional vocations are definitely for men and others are for women (Schlossberg & Goodman, 1972) unless a concerted effort is made to change their perception.

Of the investigations into occupational sex-role stereotyping, many have focused on females and how to effectively change their attitudes. For example, Cramer, Wise, and Colburn (1977) reported positive results in a study of the effectiveness for eighth grade girls of a short "mini-course" designed to modify some of their stereotyped attitudes about vocations and make them more informed about career choices. Another study involving female high school students (Burlin, 1976) indicated that girls were aware of innovative occupations, but they did not feel free to pursue them. Significant others in the girl's lives, especially parents and boyfriends, were a very strong inhibiting influence. It was concluded that, unless these others changed their attitudes, very little actual change would take place for the girls themselves.

With elementary school children, indications have been mixed concerning a decline in occupational sex-role stereotyping. For example, Gregg and Dobson (1980), in a study of first and sixth graders, found that children accepted both men and women working in a variety of occupations. They found no significant difference between boys and girls in assigning occupational roles to either men or women. They did, however, find that girls, when asked to state their own interest in specific careers, chose traditionally female occupations, even though they had been willing to accept females in nontraditional jobs. It seems that even young girls still have a conflict between traditional feminine behavior and the active pursuit of a career. Patterson (1973) has indicated that many girls feel they have a choice between marriage and a career. Most of them, however, will work outside the home at some point in their lives (Conger, 1981).

The purpose of this study was to obtain further information in the field of occupational sex-role stereotyping among elementary school children. New data was gathered on children's willingness to accept men and women in various occupations and on their own willingness to aspire to a nontraditional occupation. The study was unique because of its incorporation of art as a concrete adjunct means of examining career aspirations in children. Children's socioeconomic backgrounds, grade level, and gender prejudices regarding specific careers were also considered.

Method

Participants

The participants were 90 sixth graders (47 females, 43 males) and 84 third graders (39 females, 45 males) in two elementary schools in Fairfield County, Connecticut. Socioeconomic differences existed between the children in the two schools: In one school a majority of the children came from upper-middle and lower-upper class families, while the other school's children were from upper-lower and lower-middle class backgrounds. Both schools, however, were located in suburban settings.

Instrument

Using as a guide the annual averages of employed persons that were published in January 1981 by the Bureau of Labor Statistics, U.S. Department of Labor (*Employment and Earnings*, 1981), the researchers compiled a checklist of 50 occupations. The Department of Labor breaks all occupations down into four major categories (with various subgroups under each): (a) white-collar workers, (b) blue-collar workers, (c) service workers, and (d) farm workers. The same annual table lists the percentages of females in each occupation.

We attempted to incorporate into our list occupations from each category, with emphasis on those occupations that would be familiar to children in the age group surveyed. We also attempted to use occupations that are considered traditional and nontraditional for women. The Labor Department defines an occupation as nontraditional if it has few, if any, female workers. A stricter interpretation classifies an occupation as nontraditional for women if 75% of the workers in that occupation are men (Bucknell & Gray, 1981). In our list 22 occupations met the latter definition of a nontraditional occupation for women, 23 were traditional by this standard, and 5 were "unclassified" because of a lack of government data on the percentage of women employed in them.

The percentage of females employed in a particular occupation was deleted from the list before it was given to the children. In its place were instructions asking the children to check after each occupation whether the occupation should be done by a man, a woman, both, or that it made no difference. The emphasis was on the word *should* rather that *could* so the actual prejudices of the children would come out. At the end of the list, there were two fill-in-the-blank statements: (a) "Career you would *most like* to have ________," and (b) "Career you think you *will have* ________."

Procedure

The same procedure was followed at both schools. Children were given the survey during their art classes. Each job title was read aloud to each class to ensure that there were no titles with which the children were unfamiliar.

The children were asked in filling in the first blank at the end of the list to think of the career they would follow if there were no obstacles of any kind (i.e., they could be whatever they wanted to be). For the second statement, the children were asked to try and be realistic (i.e., stating what they thought they really would do). The children were told the two answers could be the same or different. They were then given crayons and drawing paper and asked to draw themselves in the occupation they would most likely have.

Statistical Analysis

The data were analyzed by percentage of response according to gender, grade level, and socioeconomic differences. A 60% concurrence level was designated *a priori* to the research as a cutoff standard for "agreement" between groups. This figure was a compromise by the researchers between the Labor Department's definition of a nontraditional occupation for women as one in which its work force was 75% men and the Shepard and Hess (1975) use of 50% or more agreement to designate a liberal or conservative attitude toward occupational sex role stereotyping. Significant statistical differences at the 0.01 and 0.05 level were noted through chi-square analysis.

Results

In terms of actual percentage, third graders were in agreement on three times as many occupations appropriate for both sexes as sixth graders. Third graders agreed that men and women were equally suited to be writers, elementary teachers, school principals, pharmacists, musicians, artists, cashiers, salespersons, high school teachers, bank tellers, reporters, and cooks. Sixth graders had a 60% or better agreement only for the occupations of writer, elementary teacher, musician, and artist as appropriate for either gender.

The two grade levels agreed that males were still preferred for some predominantly male-dominated vocations. Sixth graders agreed that males were best suited to be television repairpersons, auto mechanics, engineers, park rangers, plumbers, cabinetmakers, construction workers, soldiers, fire fighters, or carpenters. The third graders agreed that men should be employed as television repairpersons, farmers, auto mechanics, surveyors, astronauts, electricians, plumbers, construction workers, truck drivers, soldiers, fire fighters, and carpenters.

The list of agreed-upon occupations for women was much smaller for both grades. Sixth graders concurred that women should be employed as secretaries, nurses, telephone operators, librarians, and sewing machine operators. The third graders only agreed on the occupations of secretary, nurse, and sewing machine operator.

Chi-square analysis showed a number of significant differences between the various groups. Sixth-grade girls were very willing to accept both men and women in sixteen traditionally male occupations; sixth-grade boys differed significantly as a group from the girls and thought only males should be employed in the occupations of: auto mechanic, architect, electrician, carpenter, doctor, school principal, astronaut, pilot, pharmacist, professional athlete, lawyer, dentist, truck driver, police officer, radio announcer, and reporter. Sixth grade boys also differed significantly from sixth-grade girls by indicating that the occupations of dental assistant and cleaner/servant should be "for women only."

For third graders the only significant differences between males and females were in the occupations of doctor, professional athlete, astronaut, and park ranger. Girls were more liberal than boys in checking who should work in these occupations.

When young girls were compared to older girls, there was only one occupation, lawyer, in which there was a significant difference. The older girls were more willing to accept both men and women as lawyers.

When the third-grade boys were compared to the sixth-grade boys, there were significant differences in seven occupations: waiting on tables, cashier, radio announcer, librarian, salesperson, cleaner/servant, and reporter. In each case, the older boys were more traditional and conservative in their choices.

In another aspect of the survey, the third-grade males all chose as their career choices traditionally male occupations. There was no difference for these boys in their choice of occupations they would most like to have and those they thought they would later have.

Approximately 25% of the third-grade girls listed nontraditional female jobs as the occupations they would most like to have. Half of these girls, however, changed their answers to traditionally female or neutral occupations when asked what occupation they thought they would have later.

A similar pattern occurred with sixth-grade students. Boys either chose a very traditional male job or an occupation connected with the arts. In contrast, more than 40% of sixth-grade females chose nontraditional jobs. Of these girls, 26% changed their choice to a more feminine-oriented occupation as the occupation they would eventually have. It is significant that even though one-fourth of the sixth-grade girls changed their minds about what occupation they would eventually have, nontraditional occupations were the final choices of 30% of these girls, a much larger figure than that for third-grade girls (13%).

Because the schools were different in their socioeconomic composition, it was possible to examine the differences that background might have. Looking first at the percentages, sixth graders in both schools felt that men and women were equally suited to be writers, pharmacists, and musicians. There was also agreement that men should be television repairpersons, electricians, members of the clergy, plumbers, construction workers, soldiers, fire fighters, and carpenters. Students in both schools concurred that women should be secretaries, nurses, phone operators, librarians, and sewing machine operators.

Third graders in both schools agreed that both men and women could become writers, elementary school teachers, pharmacists, musicians, artists, cashiers, salespersons, high school teachers, and reporters. Third graders in both schools also agreed that men should be television repairpersons, farmers, auto mechanics, surveyors, astronauts, engineers, electricians, plumbers, construction workers, truck drivers, soldiers, fire fighters, and carpenters. There was further agreement that women should be secretaries and nurses. Chi-square analysis revealed only one significant difference between the third graders in the two schools. This was for the career of school principal. The children from lower socioeconomic backgrounds believed this was a male-only occupation.

There were eight significant differences between the sixth graders of the two schools. The children from lower socioeconomic backgrounds were generally more conservative and preferred males in the occupations of doctor, engineer, chef, carpenter, school principal, scientist, astronaut, and elementary teacher.

Discussion

Several of the findings observed in this study merit further elaboration. First, the large number of differences between sixth-grade males and females over whether females should engage in sixteen traditional male occupations is noteworthy. The finding that sixth-grade males, in contrast to sixth-grade females, did not agree that females should work in these occupations seems to contradict the findings of Schlossberg and Goodman (1972) and Gregg and Dobson (1980), in which very few differences were found between the sexes over occupational roles. The discrepancy between this study and previous studies may be explained, however, by the very wide choice of occupations in this study, many of them purposely very traditionally male or female oriented. The influence of a different region and population could also be important factors.

The greater willingness of third-grade boys than sixth-grade boys to accept men and women in more occupations deserves some comment. By the sixth grade, boys are beginning to move into adolescence. Associated with this move is a search for identity and peer pressure to distinguish gender roles. This pressure possibly influences boys not only to close off avenues of career exploration for themselves, but mentally to limit girls, too.

Regarding the girls in this study, it is significant that sixth-grade girls chose nontraditional jobs as occupations they would most like to have considerably more often than third-grade girls (i.e., 40% versus 25%). It may well be that as girls become aware of the world of work, they feel freer to explore it mentally. The discouraging part of this finding is that so many girls resigned themselves to having a traditionally female or neutral occupation (i.e., 60% of sixth graders and 75% of third graders). While it is encouraging to realize that some of the girls are considering nontraditional alternatives, the findings of this research concur basically with Burlin's (1976) conclusion that most girls do not feel free to pursue a nontraditional career.

An unexpected finding of this study was the importance of role models and career consideration, a discovery revealed in the significant difference between opinions of third graders in the two schools over the career of school principal. One school had just replaced a male principal with a new female principal. The other school had had a male principal for over 10 years. The change in gender was probably responsible for the difference noted between schools. Whereas role models may not encourage children to consider an occupation, they do make such explorations possible.

Finally, the discovery that children from lower socioeconomic backgrounds were more conservative is not surprising. This finding is in line with research reported by Mussen, Conger, and Kagan (1979) on the effects of social class, sex, and peer group influences on the choice of vocations. A finding of this nature emphasizes the continued need to work more intensely with children from lower socioeconomic backgrounds in exploring career options.

Recommendations

There are no pat solutions to the problem of overcoming occupational sex-role stereotyping. The results of this study, however, suggest several directions that elementary school counselors and educators may take in working with children on career awareness.

1. One of the most obvious ways of working with children of this age is through play. As we have suggested, art may be incorporated as an adjunct technique to help boys and girls get more in touch with their vocational aspirations. Art is viewed in most schools as a type of creative play. When children express themselves in their art work, especially about vocations, they are leaving a paper trail that the counselor may use with the child in career exploration. By examining collected art work on careers, the counselor helps make an art as well as a discipline out of this important aspect of counseling. Other art forms (e.g., poetry, music, drama) may also be used by the counselor to help elementary school children become more in touch with themselves and the world of work.
2. Another facet of career exploration, which requires both an artistic and a diplomatic touch by the school counselor, is helping to eliminate subtle or blatant occupational prejudices in teachers and other school personnel. During in-service workshops the artistic works of children drawn or composed in career exploration classes can be displayed and discussed, giving teachers and other personnel an opportunity to examine their own biases.
3. A third recommendation that this study suggests is to work artistically with groups of all boys or all girls in exploring career fantasies. Female groups may be used to help girls reinforce one another on career aspirations. In a similar manner, boys, especially boys from lower socioeconomic groups, may benefit greatly by interacting with visiting tailors, chefs, or designers invited in by the counselor. These careers can be examined by boys who may have traditionally not explored such occupations because of peer or family pressure.
4. Finally, counselors can help make career exploration an art by forming committees within the school setting of parents, teachers, and other interested personnel who can make suggestions on the career exploration aspect of the counseling program. Just as most artists use a variety of brushes and colors on their canvases to create works of art, so the counselor may be equally artistic by using a variety of interested personnel to help children explore careers. New ideas and the reshaping of old ideas may result in a blending of talent that not only benefits the children, but the counselor and the school as well.

Conclusion

To truly effect change, the child's whole school environment must be involved. Support personnel must be included, as well as administrators, teachers, and counselors. There must be careful planning and a system of regular follow-up. The planning and work involved are worth the effort, however, when the alternative is considered. With occupational sex stereotyping, both sexes lose. We need scientists with "polished nails" if they choose. Girls need to know they can achieve and still wear gardenias in their hair. We need strong men teaching gentleness to children. Boys need to know they can be caring and still drive trucks if they choose. The keyword is *choice*.

As this study shows, some children of both sexes still have less choice than others because of socialization patterns associated with gender, socioeconomic class, and age. There is still a long way to go before most occupations will be considered "sex-free." However, by incorporating art, as well as other artistic awareness techniques (e.g., role play) (Schmidt, 1976), into career guidance curriculums, it is hoped that children of both sexes may feel freer to choose vocations of interest to them and in the process become more completely human.

References

Burlin, F. (1976). Sex-role stereotyping: Occupational aspirations of female high school students. *School Counselor, 24*, 102–108.

Bucknell, S., & Gray, F. (Eds.). (1981). *Nontraditional jobs for women: A resource guide for Connecticut women and career counselors.* Hartford, CT: Permanent Commission on the Status of Women.

Conger, J. J. (1981). Freedom and commitment: Families, youth, and social change. *American Psychologist, 36*, 1475-1484.

Cramer, S., Wise, P., & Colburn, E. (1977). An evaluation of a treatment to expand the career perceptions of junior high school girls. *School Counselor, 25*, 124–129.

Bureau of Labor Statistics. (1981). *Employment and Earnings.* Washington, DC: U.S. Department of Labor.

Farmer, H. S. (1978). Why women choose careers below their potential. In L. S. Hansen & R. S. Rapoza (Eds.), *Career development and counseling of women.* Springfield, IL: Charles C Thomas.

Gregg, C., & Dobson, K. (1980). Occupational sex stereotyping and occupational interests in children. *Elementary School Guidance and Counseling, 15*, 66–74.

Mussen, P. H., Conger, J. J., & Kagan, J. (1979). *Child development and personality.* New York: Harper & Row.

Navin, S. L., & Sears, S. J. (1980). Parental roles in elementary career guidance. *Elementary School Guidance and Counseling, 14*, 269-277.

Patterson, L. (1973). Girl's career—Expression of identity. *Vocational Guidance Quarterly, 21*, 268–274.

Remer, P., & O'Neill, C. (1980). Clients as change agents: What color could my parachute be? *Personnel and Guidance Journal, 58*, 425–429.

Schlossberg, N., & Goodman, J. (1972). A woman's place: Children's sex stereotyping of occupations. *Vocational Guidance Quarterly, 20*, 266–270.
Schmidt, J. A. (1976). Career guidance in the elementary school. *Elementary School Guidance and Counseling, 11*, 149–153.
Shepard, W. D., & Hess, D. T. (1975). Attitudes in four age groups toward sex role division in adult occupations and activities. *Journal of Vocational Behavior, 6*, 27–39.
Wolleat, P. L. (1979). School-age girls. *Counseling Psychologist, 8*, 22–23.
Worell, J. (1980). Psychological sex roles: Significance and change. In J. Worell (Ed.), *Psychological development in the elementary years*. New York: Academic Press.

Chapter 7

Counseling Issues in a Changing World of Work

Issues for elementary school counselors to consider about a changing world of work:

1. Create several classroom activities that will help students develop career awareness. Discuss the importance of increasing career awareness among elementary school children.
2. How can counselors reduce occupational sex-role stereotyping among elementary school children?
3. What might elementary school counselors do to help teachers incorporate career awareness activities into regular school subjects?
4. Discuss the pros and cons of having a career day in elementary schools?
5. Discuss the following statement: "Teachers need to concentrate on the basic subjects and don't have time for extras such as career education."
6. What kinds of career awareness activities can be used with children in kindergarten and first grade?
7. How can computers and other forms of technology be incorporated into career education programs at the elementary school level?
8. How can parents be involved in classroom programs of career education? What might parents gain from their participation in such programs?
9. What ways can elementary school counselors use to assess the effectiveness of career education programs?
10. How might activities for improving self-concept be incorporated into career education programs? What theoretical support is available for incorporating self-concept activities into career education?

CHAPTER 8

LEARNING IN A CHANGING WORLD

American society has placed emphasis on the need for children to learn basic academic skills. Parents throughout the country complain that children are not learning to read, write, and perform basic mathematics. Governmental and private commissions have studied the poor academic achievement of children and are asking educators to account for the failure of our schools in this important area. If elementary school counselors are to fulfill their mission in schools, they must collaborate with teachers, parents, and school administrators in an effort to improve children's achievement. This chapter discusses the matter of "back to the basics" and offers programs to help elementary school counselors promote academic achievement among students.

Chapter 8 begins with a study of the "Succeeding in School" program of classroom guidance. This ten-session program includes lessons on role-models for succeeding in school, being comfortable in school, being responsible in school, listening in school, asking for help in school, ways to improve school work, cooperating with peers at school, cooperating with teachers, discovering the bright side of school, and exploring the wonders of self. Other articles in the chapter cover such topics as:

1. Counseling with parents to improve the attitudes and achievement of remedial readers
2. Changing the attitudes and work habits of children who procrastinate with school work
3. Motivating children to attend school through multimodal friendship groups

Chapter 8 concludes with a review of the research published in the *Elementary School Guidance and Counseling* journal from 1974 to 1984. This review addresses the critical question, "Do elementary school counselors contribute to children's learning? The review establishes that elementary school counseling programs have positive influences on the affective, behavioral, and interpersonal domains of children's lives and, in turn, have significant effects on children's academic success. This research review provides counselors with evidence they can use to obtain increased support from parents, teachers, and school administrators.

Educational goals have fluctuated considerably throughout the 20th Century in the United States. In the 1950s schools were concerned about children's achievement in math and science, largely due to the launching of Sputnik by the U.S.S.R. The social unrest of the 1960s and 1970s brought children's emotional and social needs to the attention of educators. Education is now back to a period of increased interest in children's achievement in basic skills. This interest in "back to the basics" appears destined to continue into the 1990s. Elementary school counselors, therefore, must continue to demonstrate their contributions to children's willingness and readiness to achieve success in academic subject areas. Chapter 8 helps counselors work toward this end.

The Effects of Classroom Guidance on Children's Success in School

Edwin R. Gerler, Jr.
Ronald F. Anderson

During the 1970s classroom guidance was a high priority activity for school counselors, particularly at the elementary school level. The counselor's need for visibility in the school was an important argument for classroom guidance, along with the needs for preventing psychological problems among children and for promoting psychological maturity in children. Although these needs still exist, classroom guidance seems to be losing ground in some school districts where teachers and parents want less time for ancillary programs and more time for basic skills programs.

The results of studies on classroom guidance suggest that school systems should evaluate such programs thoroughly before abandoning them. Research indicates that group guidance may positively influence children's classroom behavior, attitudes toward school, and ultimately their academic success. For instance, Cobb and Richards (1983) found that classroom guidance in association with other counseling strategies significantly reduced behavioral problems among fourth- and fifth-grade children. Gerler, Kinney, and Anderson (1985) found that group guidance used with other behavior change techniques significantly improved the language arts and math grades of underachieving children. Downing (1977) discovered that group work designed to modify children's behavior had the additional benefit of improving achievement significantly. Other researchers (Deffenbacher & Kemper, 1974; Wirth, 1977) noted further positive changes in behavior and academic performance among children involved in various forms of group guidance.

In addition to the findings about the positive effects of group guidance on behavior, there is research indicating that children's attitudes toward school may improve from participation in classroom guidance activities. Day and Griffin (1980) reported data showing that children's increased enjoyment of school was attributable to participation in classroom guidance. Gerler (1980) found that children's school attendance increased significantly because of their involvement in classroom guidance, an indication that students' attitudes toward school had improved dramatically. Miller's (1973) report on psychological education research also showed childrens' attitudes toward school improving from participation in group guidance programs. These findings indicate the potential value of classroom guidance in children's education.

Unfortunately, many studies of classroom guidance programs have been limited to a single school or a single school district and have involved relatively few children. The studies have also typically employed only one or two measures of the programs' effects. There simply have not been enough studies examining multiple effects of classroom guidance on large numbers of children from varying social and economic environments.

The discussion to follow is of a large-scale, experimental study of classroom guidance in North Carolina. The study was an attempt to fill a gap in the counseling literature by (a) exposing large numbers of children to systematic classroom guidance and (b) by examining multiple effects of classroom guidance. The effects of group guidance on children's attitudes toward school, classroom behavior, and achievement in academic subjects were specifically examined. These variables were chosen because they are important aspects of children's schooling and because previous research (already cited here) has suggested that classroom guidance influences these variables positively.

Method

Participants

This study involved 896 fourth- and fifth-grade children from 18 different schools in virtually every geographic region of North Carolina. The participants included children from varying economic, social, and cultural environments. A total of 18 elementary school counselors volunteered to conduct classroom guidance sessions for the study.

Procedure

Elementary school counselors throughout North Carolina were sent information about conducting classroom guidance studies in their schools. The 18 counselors who volunteered to participate received packets of study materials that included (a) directions for implementing the study, (b) a 10-session classroom guidance unit titled "Succeeding in School," (c) instruments to measure the effects of the unit and directions for scoring the instruments, and (d) forms for recording the data collected.

Counselor's directions for implementing the study. Counselors received careful written instructions for implementing the classroom guidance study in their schools. The instructions identified the purpose of the study and outlined specific steps for counselors to follow in carrying out the study. Counselors were instructed to (a) explain to school principals the purpose of the study and assure principals that all data collected would be kept confidential and that no student would be identified individually to anyone outside the school, (b) discuss the nature of the study with fourth- and fifth-grade teachers and then assign classrooms randomly to treatment and control groups, (c) conduct the classroom guidance unit "Succeeding in School" twice a week for 5 weeks with the children in the treatment group (the children in the control group received the same unit after the study was completed), (d) administer the Attitude Toward School instrument (Miller, 1973) to each student during the week before and the week after the classroom guidance unit was presented, and (e) have teachers complete the Elementary Guidance Behavior Rating Scale (EGBRS) for each student and record students' conduct grades, language grades, and math grades immediately before and after the guidance unit.

The classroom guidance unit. The classroom guidance unit, "Succeeding in School," which counselors conducted with the treatment group children, was composed of 10 sessions of 30 to 40 minutes each. Session 1, Success in School, provided students with the ground rules for discussion and with the rationale for a classroom guidance unit on school success. Session 2, Being Comfortable in School, introduced the topic of relaxation and offered students an opportunity to practice some relaxation methods. Session 3, Being Responsible in School, had students discuss the meaning of responsibility and gave them an opportunity to discuss times that they had behaved responsibly at school. Session 4, Listening in School, had students discuss the importance of listening in school and allowed them to practice listening skills. Also, they shared personal experiences about the benefits of good listening. Session 5, Asking for Help in School, involved students in games designed to improve their skills in listening to teachers and in asking teachers for help. Session 6, How to Improve at School, asked students to identify a subject they would like to improve in and to discuss how they might work toward improving. Students discussed improvements they had already made in their school work. Session 7, Cooperating with Peers at School, included role playing activities to help students practice cooperation. Students also discussed the benefits of cooperating with peers. Session 8, Cooperating with Teachers, had students discuss several unfinished statements such as, "If I were teacher for a day, I'd. . . ." and "I would like to get along better with my teacher, but my problem is. . . ." Session 9, The Bright Side of School, had students identify and discuss positive happenings at school. They also thought of ways to change negative aspects of school. Session 10, The Bright Side of Me, allowed students to discuss their personal strengths and to receive positive feedback from one another. (A detailed outline of the classroom guidance unit is available from the senior author.)

Instrumentation and data collection. Counselors used the following five measures to assess students' progress resulting from participation in the classroom guidance unit.

1. *Ratings of student behavior.* Teachers completed the EGBRS for each child in the treatment and control groups during the week before and the week after counselors led the classroom guidance unit. The EGBRS, which was designed by a team of counselors, counselor educators, and education consultants and used in two previous elementary school guidance studies (Anderson, Kinney, & Gerler, 1984; Gerler, Kinney, & Anderson, 1985), consists of 20 items in which teachers rate negative classroom behaviors on a Likert scale ranging from *behavior observed constantly* (5) to *behavior observed never* (1). The highest total score possible on the scale is 100 and the lowest possible is 20, with lower scores indicating preferred classroom behavior. The EGBRS includes questions such as, "How often does a child interfere with the activities of others, fail to give attention to the task at hand, or use available time unwisely?" No data on reliability or validity are available on this instrument.

2. *Students' conduct grades.* Teachers recorded classroom conduct grades for treatment and control group children before and after the classroom guidance unit. Conduct grades were based on a 12-point scale, from A+ (12) through F (1). The pretreatment grades were regular classroom conduct grades averaged from the grading period immediately before the guidance unit. The posttreatment grades were regular classroom conduct grades averaged from the grading period during which the guidance unit was implemented.

3. *Students' attitudes toward school.* Children in the treatment and control groups completed a modified version of the Attitude Toward School instrument during the week before and the week after the guidance unit. This instrument has been used by the Minnesota Department of Education to assess the effects of psychological education activities. It consists of 25 multiple-choice sentence completion items in which children's attitudes toward such matters as teaching, subject matter, and homework are assessed. Each item offers four choices to students, with the first choice indicating the most negative attitude toward school and the fourth choice indicating the most positive attitude. The highest total score possible on the scale is 100 and the lowest possible is 25, with higher scores indicating more positive attitudes toward school. No data on reliability or validity are available on this instrument.

4. *Students' achievement in language arts.* Teachers recorded language arts grades for treatment and control group children before and after the classroom guidance unit. Again, grades were based on a 12-point scale, from A+ (12) through F (1). The pretreatment grades were regular classroom language grades averaged from the grading period immediately before the guidance unit. The

posttreatment grades were regular classroom language grades averaged from the grading period during which the guidance unit was implemented.

5. *Students' achievement in mathematics.* Teachers recorded math grades for treatment and control group children before and after the classroom guidance unit. The grades were based on a 12-point scale, from A+ (12) through F (1). The pretreatment grades were regular classroom math grades averaged from the grading period immediately before the guidance unit. The posttreatment grades were regular classroom math grades averaged from the grading period during which the guidance unit was implemented.

Results

Table 1 shows the changes in the five dependent measures from pretreatment to posttreatment for students in the treatment and control groups. The data were analyzed using an analysis of variance (ANOVA) on the change scores from pretreatment to posttreatment.

The treatment group's scores on the EGBRS declined (mean change of –3.52), whereas the control group's scores increased (mean change of 1.46). The difference in score changes between the groups was significant, $F(1, 894) = 61.60$, $p < .001$. Because lower scores on the EGBRS indicate preferred classroom behavior, the treatment group's behavior improved significantly over the control group's on this measure of classroom behavior.

Analysis of the changes in conduct grades indicates that the treatment group outperformed the control group. The treatment group's conduct grades improved slightly (mean change of 0.52), whereas the control group's conduct grades did not (mean change of –0.20). This difference in conduct grade changes between the groups was significant, $F(1, 894) = 27.00$, $p < .001$.

The treatment group's scores on the Attitude Toward School instrument increased (mean change of 1.51), whereas the control group's scores decreased (mean change of –1.21). This difference in score changes was significant, $F(1, 866) = 18.37$, $p < .001$. Because higher scores on this instrument indicate more positive attitudes toward school, the school attitude of the treatment group improved significantly over that of the control group. (The degree of freedom within groups on this measure is slightly smaller than on the other measures because some students were absent when the attitude instrument was administered.)

The treatment group's language grades increased slightly (mean change of 0.31), whereas the control group's language grades did not change (mean change of 0.00). This difference in language grade changes between the groups approached significance, $F(1, 894) = 3.12$, $p < .10$. It is not possible to

Table 1
ANOVA on Mean Changes in Dependent Measures from Pretreatment to Posttreatment

Groups	Pretreatment		Posttreatment		Change		ANOVA	
	M	*SD*	*M*	*SD*	*M*	*SD*	*F*	*p*
Behavior ratings								
Treatment ($n = 453$)	46.32	9.90	42.80	10.43	–3.52	10.27	61.60	<.001
Control ($n = 443$)	46.41	8.43	47.87	8.73	1.46	8.62		
Conduct grades								
Treatment ($n = 453$)	7.88	2.12	8.40	1.63	0.52	1.87	27.00	<.001
Control ($n = 443$)	7.93	3.10	7.73	2.11	–0.20	2.26		
School attitude scores								
Treatment ($n = 436$)	76.12	9.94	77.63	9.60	1.51	9.73	18.37	<.001
Control ($n = 432$)	76.00	8.91	74.79	8.73	–1.21	8.96		
Language grades								
Treatment ($n = 453$)	7.36	2.92	7.67	1.93	0.31	2.37	3.12	<.10
Control ($n = 443$)	7.31	2.31	7.31	2.98	–0.00	2.92		
Math grades								
Treatment ($n = 453$)	7.85	2.77	7.68	2.48	–0.17	2.63	0.98	NS
Control ($n = 443$)	7.87	2.65	7.88	2.79	0.01	2.78		

Note. Behavior ratings ranged from 20 to 100, with lower ratings indicating preferred classroom behavior. School attitude scores ranged from 25 to 100, with higher scores indicating positive attitudes toward school. The conduct, language, and math grades were based on a 12-point scale, with A = 12 through F = 1.

conclude, however, that the treatment group's performance in language arts improved significantly over that of the control group's.

Analysis of the changes in math grades shows no change in either the treatment group's grades (mean change of –0.17) or the control group's grades (mean change of 0.01). The difference in math grade changes between the groups was not statistically significant, $F(1, 894) = 0.98$, n.s.

Discussion

The results of the study show that elementary school counselors can use classroom guidance to influence children's classroom behavior positively. Several other studies (Kern & Hankins, 1977; Kern, Kelley, & Downey, 1973; Moracco & Kazandkian, 1977; West, Sonstegard, & Hagerman, 1980) have shown that counselors can use alternative approaches to change children's behavior, but the use of classroom guidance offers benefits that differ from other behavior change strategies. Prevention of classroom behavior problems may be among the benefits. In this study, for instance, the control group children's behavior did not simply remain stable; it became worse. The treatment group's behavior improved. This improvement probably occurred because children in the treatment group became more aware of the benefits of certain behaviors and because counselors reinforced appropriate behaviors during classroom guidance sessions.

A second outcome of this study further supports the notion that classroom guidance can prevent problems. The children who did not participate in the classroom guidance unit offered in this study became less positive about school. In contrast, the treatment group children's attitudes toward school improved. This improvement may be accounted for by the children's group discussions of positive school experiences, by their discussions about how to change negative school experiences, and by their enjoyment of the classroom guidance sessions. If classroom guidance influences children's attitudes positively, as indicated here, it may also prevent such persistent problems as truancy and dropping out of school. In fact, a previous longitudinal study (Gerler, 1980) showed that guidance strategies of this kind have positive effects on school attendance.

The other results of this study—those related directly to academic achievement—also seem promising. The changes in language grades that favored the treatment group at a level approaching statistical significance should encourage further, long-term studies of classroom guidance. Such studies might show whether the verbal give and take in classroom guidance improves children's language skills significantly. That academic grades did not decline significantly for the treatment group indicates that classroom guidance does not detract from basic skills areas, as some teachers and parents have argued (Gerler, 1982).

The outcomes of this study must be viewed cautiously. To begin with, the teachers and counselors who participated in the study knew the group assignments of the student participants. The possibility exists that this knowledge biased the results of the study in favor of the treatment group. Also, because the measurement instruments used in the study—the EGBRS and the Attitude Toward School measure—have undetermined reliability and validity, the scores collected from the instruments cannot be viewed with complete confidence. It is encouraging, however, that the scores on the EGBRS, which favored the treatment group children over the control group children, were corroborated by the conduct grades received by each group.

Some caution is also necessary regarding the assignment of students to the treatment and control groups. Because of practical considerations, counselors could not randomly assign individual students to the two groups but instead randomly assigned whole classrooms to the experimental groups. Analysis of pretest data, however, showed no significant differences between the groups, thus providing reasonable assurance that random assignment was effective.

Another limitation of the study was the lack of a placebo group. (Critelli and Neumann [1984] have argued persuasively in favor of using placebos in studies of psychological interventions.) The lack of a placebo creates the possibility that other factors, including the novelty or perhaps the intensity of the experience, caused the observed changes. Virtually all the children involved in the study, however, had previously experienced classroom guidance (albeit not as systematically as in this study). It seems likely, therefore, that the content of the guidance sessions rather than the novelty of the experience contributed to the treatment group's progress. An alternative research design might have reduced the need for a placebo group, but the simplicity of the design used was helpful for the larger population studied.

There is one other limitation of this study worth noting: Because of the study's size and the wide geographic distances separating schools involved in the study, researchers had difficulty monitoring whether counselors conducted the guidance sessions as prescribed. The lack of time and funds for travel made it impossible for the researchers to have regular, on-site visits with counselors who conducted the classroom guidance units. If, however, the number and types of phone calls received by the researchers during the study indicated the desire of counselors to carry out this study correctly, then this limitation can be disregarded.

This study has numerous implications for practitioners and researchers alike. First, the results indicate the potential of classroom guidance for meeting important educational needs, namely, improving classroom behavior, preventing problem behavior, and encouraging positive attitudes toward school. Furthermore, the results encourage additional research related to the effects of counseling on children's achievement.

A component that could have been included in this study and probably should be included in future studies of this kind is a premeasure, postmeasure of psychosocial development. Even though it is heartening to observe that classroom guidance helps prevent problem behaviors, it would be equally valuable to learn more about the developmental significance of classroom guidance.

Perhaps the most important benefit of this study is in the realization that researchers and counselors can cooperate to carry out large-scale experimental studies of counseling services. Although counselors can and do evaluate their own work, they get a better perspective on the effects of guidance and counseling when results are pooled, as in this study. Small-scale studies by individual counselors, although important, carry little hope of statistically significant findings.

In conclusion, the type of study described here has considerable potential for evaluating counseling services. The American Association for Counseling and Development (AACD) is, in fact, already seeking research funds from private foundations to carry out a similar study on a national scale. Research efforts of this kind should help counselors better understand the nature and value of their services and should demonstrate their contributions to the national goal of educational excellence.

References

Anderson, R. F., Kinney, J., & Gerler, E. R. (1984). The effects of divorce groups on children's classroom behavior and attitude toward divorce. *Elementary School Guidance & Counseling, 19,* 70-76.

Cobb, H. C., & Richards, H. C. (1983). Efficacy of counseling services in decreasing behavior problems of elementary school children. *Elementary School Guidance & Counseling, 17,* 180–187.

Critelli, J. W., & Neumann, K. F. (1984). The placebo: Conceptual analysis of a construct in transition. *American Psychologist, 39,* 32–39.

Day, R. W., & Griffin, R. E. (1980). Children's attitudes toward the magic circle. *Elementary School Guidance & Counseling, 15,* 136–146.

Deffenbacher, J. L., & Kemper, C. C. (1974). Counseling test-anxious sixth graders. *Elementary School Guidance & Counseling, 9,* 22–29.

Downing, C. J. (1977). Teaching children behavior change techniques. *Elementary School Guidance & Counseling, 11,* 277–283.

Gerler, E. R. (1980). A longitudinal study of multimodal approaches to small group psychological education. *School Counselor, 27,* 184–190.

Gerler, E. R. (1982). *Counseling the young learner.* Englewood Cliffs, NJ: Prentice-Hall.

Gerler, E. R., Kinney, J., & Anderson, R. F. (1985). The effects of counseling on classroom performance. *Journal of Humanistic Education and Development, 23,* 155–165.

Kern, R. M., & Hankins, G. (1977). Adlerian group counseling with contracted homework. *Elementary School Guidance & Counseling, 11*, 284–290.

Kern, R. M., Kelley, J. D., & Downey, M. (1973). Group counseling versus halo consultation. *Elementary School Guidance & Counseling, 8*, 68–70.

Miller, G. D. (1973). *Additional studies in elementary school guidance: Psychological education activities evaluated.* St. Paul: Minnesota Department of Education.

Moracco, J., & Kazandkian, A. (1977). Effectiveness of behavior counseling and counseling with non-western elementary school children. *Elementary School Guidance & Counseling, 11*, 244–251.

West, J., Sonstegard, M., & Hagerman, H. (1980). A study of counseling and consulting in Appalachia. *Elementary School Guidance & Counseling, 15*, 5–13.

Wirth, S. (1977). Effects of a multifaceted reading program on self-concept. *Elementary School Guidance & Counseling, 12*, 33–40.

Working With Young Procrastinators: Elementary School Students Who Do Not Complete School Assignments

Linda A. Morse

John just doesn't turn in his work!
Sue hasn't had recess in weeks, yet she still doesn't turn in her language!

Sound familiar? Many procrastinating students are referred to counselors each school year. In the past, the methods used to assist procrastinators involved behavior management plans as well as instruction on good homework habits and study skills. Yet, there are always some students for whom nothing seems to work. When every approach has been tried and regression rather than improvement occurs, counselors, students, teachers, and parents share in the frustration and discouragement. Because procrastination seems to be negatively related to achievement (Broadus, 1983), few adults are willing to give up on these procrastinating students.

Broadus (1984) described procrastinating students as those who:

1. Have good intentions of doing their homework and make such statements as, "I'll do it. Let me turn it in tomorrow or later today."
2. Focus on what they have not done rather than on what they have accomplished. Statements such as, "I can't do my math," may be made when there is only one part of a math assignment that they do not understand.
3. Seldom use low grades or teacher comments to improve performance. Bad papers are quickly thrown away.
4. Have a short attention span.
5. Believe they work better under pressure.
6. Frequently say, "I don't understand," or "I can't do this," when asked why they are not working.
7. Resent being reminded that homework is still not done.
8. Say that they can do better and then do not follow through to hand in the next assignment.

Because Broadus's characteristics of procrastinators so vividly fit many elementary-age students, I began to study the topic of procrastination and to apply the ideas from the literature on procrastination in counseling interventions with young children.

Literature Review

As a general term, procrastination has received little attention in the professional literature (Ottens, 1982), although some research and theory have focused on its specific components. Of the 16 causes and characteristics of procrastinators described by Broadus (1983), 7 seem especially related to elementary-age children. The seven factors of procrastination—self-concept, perfection, fear of failure, fear of success, rebellion against authority, internal locus of control, and lack of skill—are described below. Additionally, the interventions common to four programs (Broadus, 1983; Burka & Yuen, 1982; Ottens, 1982; Zinger, 1983) are described. Finally, the importance of a multimodal intervention is reported.

Factors of Procrastination

Burka and Yuen (1983), Beery (1975), and Ottens (1982) defined procrastination as a way of coping so as not to reveal one's weakness by completely testing one's ability. Broadus (1983) considered procrastination a general way of relating to people, managing tasks, and " . . . habitually postponing doing tasks that you feel ought to be done immediately" (p. 15).

Self-concept. Some authors link low academic achievement with low self-concept (Kanoy, Johnson, & Kanoy, 1980; Skaalvik, 1983), whereas others (Beery, 1975; Broadus, 1983; Burka & Yuen, 1983; Deci, 1975; Ellis & Harper, 1975; Ellis & Knaus, 1977; Raphael, 1983; Zinger, 1983) go a step further in establishing a relationship between procrastination, achievement, and self-concept. Beery (1975) and Burka and Yuen (1983) described how some people see their self-worth only in terms of their ability and performance: They are worthy people only when they have performed well. Thus, by procrastinating one has put forth no effort to perform a task and the established self-image is not threatened.

Fear of failure. Many authors (Beery, 1975; Broadus, 1983; Burka & Yuen, 1983; Deci, 1975; Dye, 1984; Ellis & Harper, 1975) have described the fear of failure as having unrealistic attitudes and expectations for performance. The procrastinating behaviors allow a person to avoid the risk of failure and protect the self-esteem.

Perfection. Closely related to the fear of failure is the need for perfection. If one cannot complete a task perfectly, then there is no point in starting the task. A person with this belief seems to have no appreciation for progress toward the goal, only for the goal itself.

Fear of success. Sometimes procrastinators perceive that success leads to negative outcomes. The more one accomplishes, the more one must do; the competition to beat one's previous record is constant. Parents and teachers often make statements such as "I know you can do better," intended as encouragement, whereas the procrastinating student perceives them as pressure (Broadus, 1983; Burka & Yuen, 1983; Dye, 1984).

Rebellion against authority. Sometimes the only way procrastinators believe that they have control over others is by not doing what is expected or requested. Procrastination then becomes a way of expressing anger and hostility toward those in authority (Ellis & Kraus, 1977) or a way of rebelling against authority (Broadus, 1983).

Locus of control. Another characteristic of procrastinators is the feeling of being overwhelmed. Procrastinators frequently see themselves as having so much to do and not knowing where to begin; therefore, they never start. Often they wait for someone to rescue them by either doing the task for them or saying it does not need to be done. Burka and Yuen (1983) reported that because the family often does not encourage children to have a sense of mastery and control over their own lives, children become discouraged at an early age. Beery (1975) proposed that procrastinators must learn to focus more on making choices related to increasing their own sense of self-esteem and fulfillment and less on meeting the expectations of others.

Thus, if students learn to be more internally controlled, they will be more likely to take action and procrastinate less. Learning to attribute failures to external control and success to internal control may also have a positive effect on procrastination (Bar-Tal, Goldberg, & Knaani, 1984; Kaneko, 1984; Rotter, 1982).

Lack of skill. Those procrastinators who have not learned the skills to approach and complete tasks in a more organized way are more likely to leave a task unfinished and be overcome by feelings of frustration, failure, and low self-esteem (Dobson, Campbell, & Dobson, 1982; Ottens, 1982; Zinger, 1983). Broadus (1983) pointed out, however, that teaching problem-solving, goal-setting, and time management skills is a necessary, but not sufficient, intervention for treating procrastinators. Interventions must also address the fears and negative feelings and attitudes of procrastinators.

Reported treatment interventions. The four intervention programs of Broadus (1983), Burka and Yuen (1982), Ottens (1982), and Zinger (1983) have several common intervention strategies: (a) becoming aware of procrastination's causes and behaviors, (b) changing internal dialogue or reframing, and (c) building self-esteem. All four programs use the strategy of goal setting. The four programs varied in length from 5 to 12 weekly sessions that lasted 1 to 2 1/2 hours each session. The researchers, however, reported limited empirical research on the effects of treatment for procrastinators, and none conducted studies with elementary-age students.

In contrast to the programs mentioned above, Lazarus (1979) believed that interventions must be broader based and include that aspect of the personality that "is made up of behaviors, affect, sensation, imagery, cognition, interpersonal responses, and our own biological substrate" (p. 8). Similarly, Keat (1978) proposed that this multimodal approach will produce faster and longer lasting results where behavior change is the goal. In this instance, the intervention strategy would address the multidimensional nature of personality and include activities that focused on developing awareness of procrastinating behaviors and causes, skills in time management, and realistic goal setting.

A Multimodal Intervention

The purpose of the multimodal group counseling intervention (Lazarus, 1978; Keat, 1978) was to assist procrastinating students in grades 3–6 in the completion of their school tasks. It was expected that the intervention would result in a greater percentage of school assignments being completed by those procrastinating students who participated in multimodal group counseling when compared to a similar group who did not participate.

Following consultation with teachers, I used the term *procrastinator* to refer to students turning in less than 75% of their work. Because students were given work compatible with their ability level, I assumed that the procrastination was not attributable to an inability to do the work, and in fact all identified procrastinators fell within the normal range of intelligence.

Students in grades 3–6 who turned in less than 75% of the assigned class work during a 2-week period before treatments were considered for the study. More specifically, I tabulated assignments for each student in each subject and then found the total number of assignments assigned and the total number of assignments completed. The total number of assignments completed during this time period was divided by the total number assigned. Because the number of assigned tasks varied from student to student, it was necessary to find a method of standardization. The calculation that resulted from dividing the number of completed assignments by the number of assigned tasks was multiplied by 10, thus converting the number of completed tasks to a base of 10. This converted score represented the homework completion rate.

Using this method, 31 students in the four grades were identified as procrastinators. By grade levels there were 4 students in grade 3, 7 in grade 4, 7 in grade 5, and 13 in grade 6. Because of developmental needs all of the identified third graders participated in the multimodal group counseling, whereas the remaining 27 students were randomly assigned to the treatment group or were placed on a waiting list. To facilitate the treatment process, students were grouped by grade level.

Multimodal Group Counseling

I conducted the three groups that were assigned to that school. There were 29 sessions of approximately 25 minutes each. When possible, groups met three times each week until the last 3 weeks, during which they met twice a week. The use of a dated checklist ensured that all activities were completed by each of the three treatment groups. A summary outline of sessions in the multimodal treatment plan is included in Table 1.

The causes of procrastination addressed in each group were low self-esteem, fear of failure, perfectionism, fear of success, rebellion against authority, lack of problem-solving skills, and locus of control (Broadus, 1983). The treatment strategies were developed from the modes of personality described by Keat (1978), which include health (H); emotions-feelings (E); learning-school (L); personal relationships (P); imagination (I); need to know (N); and guidance (G) of acts, behavior, and consequences (HELPING). Thus, treatment strategies included discussion of feelings, completion of worksheets on procrastination behaviors, verbal expression of feelings, guided imagery, and role plays on decision making.

Although goal setting was an important component, the goal-setting emphasis was on learning new skills and information about oneself rather than on achieving one's established goals. There was no punishment or negative consequence when a student reported that a goal was not met. Rather, the counselor offered help in determining what was difficult about meeting that goal and expressed confidence that there would be another goal that would be met.

Assessment and Results

During the 2 weeks immediately following the last group session, data on the total number of assignments given and the total number of assignments completed were tabulated for each student as was done before group participation. The resulting homework submission rate was used as the unit of comparison between students who participated in the multimodal group counseling and those on the waiting list. A t test was used to determine whether any difference existed between these two groups in their homework submission rate 2 weeks after the completion of group activities.

Two weeks after the groups were terminated, the mean converted homework completion score for students who participated in the multimodal group was 7.96 ($SD = 1.53$); the mean converted score of the students on the waiting list was 6.74 ($SD = 1.25$). The difference between the means was compared by a t test yielding a t of -2.26 ($p < .05$). The difference between the means of the control group before treatment ($M = 5.51$, $SD = 1.46$) and the treatment group before treatment ($M = 6.27$, $SD = 1.14$) was not significant ($t = 1.50$, $p > .05$).

Table 1
Multimodal Group Intervention

Mode	Group activities	Procrastinator characteristics
*H*ealth	Participated in relaxation exercises.	Locus of control
*E*motions	Brainstormed & discussed feeling words.	Fear of failure; fear of success
	Shared common fears.	Fear of failure; fear of success
	Discussed and shared feelings of frustration.	Perfection
	Discussed power and the power one feels.	Locus of control
*L*earning/school	Shared feelings about school, favorite subjects, performance levels.	Self-concept
	Discussed problems in completing assignments.	Rebellion against authority; fear of failure; fear of success
	Completed worksheet "Getting Work Done Survey."	Perfection; fear of failure
*P*eople/personal relationships	Shared feelings about family & friends	Rebellion against authority
	Discussed relationships with class-mates and the ability to function in the classroom group.	Rebellion against authority; locus of control
	Practiced communication skills.	Lack of skill
*I*magery/interests	Discussed strengths and weaknesses.	Fear of failure; Self-concept
	Shared likes and dislikes.	Self-concept
	Showed the filmstrip *Vultures* (Simon, 1977).	Self-concept
	Discussed self put-downs.	Fear of failure; Self-concept
	Participated in guided imagery to develop positive self-image.	Self-concept

(continued)

Table 1 (*Continued*)

Mode	Group activities	Procrastinator characteristics
*N*eed to Know	Discussed differences between thoughts & feelings.	Self-concept; rebellion against authority
	Identified thoughts & feelings under positive or negative categories.	Self-concept; rebellion against authority
	Practiced positive self-talk.	Self-concept
	Role-played positive & negative aspects of putdowns.	Self-concept
	Discussed how choices are made.	Lack of skill; locus of control
	Listed choices students make during their day.	Locus of control
*G*uidance of actions	Identified "putting-off" behaviors.	Perfection; fear of failure; fear of success
	Discussed ways time is wasted and saved.	Lack of skill
	Listed activities to be done in a day and time required to accomplish them.	Lack of skill
	Set priorities for completing tasks.	Lack of skill
	Wrote short-term goals & implementation strategies.	Lack of skill
	Recorded progress toward goals.	Lack of skill
	Wrote long-term goals (1, 5, & 10 year) & implementation strategies.	Lack of skill

Note. This research was gathered while the author was a counselor at Millcreek Elementary School, Lexington, KY.

Discussion

I observed students making progress in goal setting, attitude and behavior changes, and report card grades. Initially, students had great difficulty writing one goal with an implementation plan. Eventually, they were able to write three goals quickly so that there was time to continue with another activity during the same session. At the onset, one fifth-grade boy was noted for his loud disruptive comments in response to another student's comments ("Man, that SUCKS!" was his favorite saying.) By the end of the last session he was no longer saying those words or making other loud interruptive comments. One of the sixth-grade girls expressed excitement about getting a history project completed on time. When report cards were issued near midtreatment, half of the students brought them to show me the improvements they had made in many subjects.

In response to evaluation questions during the last session, several students mentioned that they had learned how to feel better about themselves as well as how to get their work done on time. Thus, both students' self-reports and quantitative analysis indicated that procrastinating students who participated in the multimodal group improved their homework completion score to a greater degree than did those procrastinating students on a waiting list.

Implications

When procrastinating students do not respond to problem-solving and time management skills and to a behavior modification—social reinforcement program, it may be helpful for the counselor to consider the problem in a broader sense. The positive changes in the homework completion rate of the students in this study suggests that a multimodal approach (Keat, 1977), although time consuming, may prove successful in working with this type of student. As a result, counselors might consider an intervention that emphasizes the acquisition of new skills and information about oneself as an alternative to more traditional strategies.

References

Bar-Tal, D., Goldberg, M., & Knaani, A. (1984). Causes of success and failure and their dimensions as a function of sex and gender: A phenomenological analysis. *British Journal of Educational Psychology, 54*, 51–56.

Beery, R. (1975). Fear of failure in the student experience. *Personnel and Guidance Journal, 54*, 191–203.

Broadus, L. (1983). *How to stop procrastinating and start living*. Minneapolis: Augsburg.

Burka, J., & Yuen, L. (1982, January). Mindgames procrastinators play. *Psychology Today*, pp. 32–37.

Burka, J., & Yuen, L. (1983). *Procrastination*. Reading, MA: Addison-Wesley.

Deci, E. (1975). *Intrinsic motivation*. New York: Plenum.

Dobson, J., Campbell, N., & Dobson, R. (1982). The relationship between children's self-concepts, perceptions of school, and life changes. *Elementary School Guidance & Counseling, 17,* 100–107.

Dye, G. (1984, Fall). Breaking the procrastination habit. *Newsletter of East Comprehensive Care Center,* p. 3.

Ellis, A., & Harper, R. (1975). *A new guide to rational living.* Englewood Cliffs, NJ: Prentice-Hall.

Ellis, A., & Knaus, W. (1977). *Overcoming procrastination.* New York: Institute for Rational Living.

Kaneko, C. (1984, Fall). Children's belief of controlling their circumstances. *Internationally Speaking,* p. 12.

Kanoy, R., Johnson, B., & Kanoy, K. (1980). Locus of control and self-concept in achieving and underachieving bright elementary students. *Psychology in the Schools, 17,* 395–399.

Keat, D. B. II. (1978). Multimodal evolution. *Elementary School Guidance & Counseling, 13,* 12–15.

Lazarus, A. A. (1978). What is multimodal therapy? A brief overview. *Elementary School Guidance & Counseling, 13,* 6–11.

Ottens, A. (1982). A guaranteed scheduling technique to manage students' procrastination. *College Student Personnel Journal, 16,* 371–376.

Raphael, B. (1983, November). My victory over procrastination. *Glamour,* p. 304.

Rotter, J. (1982). *The development and application of social learning theory.* New York: Praeger.

Simon, S. (Author). (1977). *Vultures* [film]. Niles, IL: Argus Communication.

Skaalvik, E. (1983). Academic achievement, self-esteem and valuing of school—some sex differences. *British Journal of Educational Psychology, 53,* 299–305.

Zinger, D. (1983). Procrastination: To do or not to do? *School Guidance Worker, 39,* 9–15.

Editor's note. A detailed description of treatment activities, including worksheets used, is available from Linda A. Morse, Cumberland Elementary School, 600 Cumberland Avenue, West Lafayette, IN 47096.

Multimodal Counseling: Motivating Children to Attend School Through Friendship Groups

Donald B. Keat II
Kathy L. Metzgar
Deborah Raykovitz
James McDonald

> *Happiness! It is useless to seek it elsewhere than in this warmth of human relations*. (Saint Exupery, 1939, p. 32)

Where can children find the joy of human relationships in a setting where many persons gather? The school, of course, can provide such a place. Unfortunately, for many children, school is a place to be avoided. This article focuses on using a friendship group to create a setting in which children can experience themselves in positive ways. As they learn to feel more positively about themselves, the children will feel better about coming to school, at least on the day of the group meeting. But affiliations within the groups should generalize so that the children can experience more satisfying interpersonal relationships in a broader range of settings.

This article illustrates how to approach the humanistic goal of improved personal relationships by multimodal means. In the multimodal approach, Keat (1979) has proposed the HELPING (health, emotions, learning, personal relationships, imagery, need to know, guidance of ABCs) model as an alternative to the BASIC ID (behavior, affect, sensation, imagery, cognition, interpersonal relations, drugs) (Lazarus, 1976, 1981). Gerler has focused on the particular modes of drugs and diet (1979, 1980a), the interpersonal domain (1980b), and imagery (1980c, 1984).

In this article we provide a second-order analysis of one of the seven modes. That is, analysis of the HELPING approach has presented us with a concern: motivation of children to attend school. We believe one of the best ways to motivate children to attend school is to formulate some reason for them to come to school. Focusing on the personal relationship domain, therefore, we concentrated on this mode and performed a second-order analysis (Keat, 1979). The results of this procedure can be seen in Table 1. Using friendship (P) as a focus (Keat, 1982), we have outlined in the table what can take place to foster positive interpersonal relationships. Our group meetings covered the topics listed in six of the seven zones (see "Modality" heading in Table 1). Health was the only area not systematically covered, although some counselors (e.g., Carlson, 1982) do use the health mode alone as a focus for counseling efforts.

Table 1
HELPING Children with Friendship (Second-Order Analysis)

Modality	Task, skill, concern	Training
*H*ealth	Overweight	Dieting and exercise (Mason, 1975)
	Cleanliness	Contracting (Keat & Guerney, 1980)
*E*motions-feelings	Feelings expression	Increase vocabulary Feelings thermometer
	Concerns	Anxiety management (Keat, 1977)
*L*earning-school	Getting to school Learning about others	Motivation to be in group I-learned statements
*P*ersonal relationships	Getting acquainted	Communication training I-messages (Gordon, 1970) Feelings bingo
	Getting along	Friendship training (Keat, 1980)
*I*magery interests	Low self-esteem	Overcoming Charlie Brown syndrome Question of the day
*N*eed to know	Decision making Mistaken thinking	Problem-solving practice Corrective self-talk
*G*uidance of ABCs	Getting along in group Group behavior	Rules Behavior management system

Program Design

The following is a session-by-session outline of what to do in each group meeting. The group on which these procedures were used was composed of five boys in the third grade. The activities were designed by Deborah Raykovitz and implemented by Kathy Metzgar. Each of the 10 sessions lasted approximately 30 minutes.

Session 1: Personal Relationships (P)

The purposes of Session 1 are to help the children become better acquainted with the other group members and to encourage good listening. The target behaviors are attending the group and verbal participation in asking questions.

The session begins by introducing yourself and having each group member do the same. Second, present the children with group details: (a) length per day (30 minutes), (b) number of sessions (*n* = 10), (c) focus of group (friendship), and (d) points earned for specific behaviors (e.g., targeted behaviors earned 1 point for sessions 1–6, each child got 1 point for attending the group, and 75 points gave a child the right to bring a friend to an additional group meeting). Third, explain that one way people get acquainted is by asking questions. Have children brainstorm questions. Emphasize things the children have in common and good listening techniques by using "Making a New Friend" (McElmurry & Tom, 1981). In this exercise, ask participants to find a partner and discuss questions such as family likes and dislikes about school, then tell the group about one of the most important things learned. Fourth, have members share one "I learned" statement about the asking questions exercise (e.g., "I learned that Joe has two horses"). Finally, inform students that the next session will be devoted to group rules; therefore, they need to think about what group rules they want.

Session 2: Guidance of ABCs

The purpose of Session 2 is to determine important rules for group discussion. The target behaviors are attending the group, coming prepared, and sharing the question of the day.

First, review some questions and answers from the previous week. Second, brainstorm rules and consequences for group discussion. The group rule suggestion list is as follows:

1. You have the right to pass.
2. Only one person talks at a time.
3. Raise your hand to speak.
4. Listen carefully.
5. Feelings shared are top secret.

The consequences for breaking the rules are as follows:

1. Receive a warning.
2. Take a time-out or lose points.
3. Return to the classroom for that group session.

Third, introduce Behavior Management System cards. Green cards indicate a warning and red cards indicate a time-out. Place the time-out rules on a poster in front of the time-out chairs so the children can read the rules while they take a time-out. The time-out rules state:

1. Sit in chair with all four chair legs on floor.
2. Sit quietly.
3. Face away from the group.
4. Set timer for 3 minutes—touch timer only once.
5. When time is up, you may join the group. . . . WELCOME BACK!

Fourth, introduce the question of the day to reemphasize that questions can help people get to know each other better. The following is a sample list of questions of the day:

1. Ask another player: What's your favorite thing to do?
2. Pretend to be an animal and ask the group to guess what you are.
3. Ask another player: If you had one wish, what would you wish for?
4. It's okay to feel jealous. When was a time you felt jealous?
5. What do you think is the color of love? Why?
6. Tell about a time you felt sad.
7. If you could be anyone else, who would that be? Why?
8. What time of the day do you like best?
9. If you were moving and could take only three things with you, what would they be?
10. Name three things that make a family happy.
11. What do you think of when you think of grandmother?
12. What is your favorite room in the house? Why?
13. What do you say to yourself when you're having a hard time learning something new?
14. Tell me something that happened with a teacher in school that you'll never forget.
15. What do you think is the difference between a friend and a best friend?

Finally, inform group members that the next meeting will be devoted to naming the group, and then ask them to think of possible suggestions.

Session 3: Need to Know

The purpose of the third session is to have each child understand and practice group problem solving. The target behaviors are (a) sharing a feeling (the second activity in the session), (b) answering the question of the day, and (c) participating in group problem solving (see the fourth activity of the fourth session).

First, review group rules and consequences. Second, pick a child to ask the other group members if there is anything they would like to share with the group before it gets started. The third activity is the question of the day.

Finally, introduce the steps to problem solving: name the problem, brainstorm, evaluate, choose, and try it out. Inform the group members that sometimes it will be their job to solve problems together and that their first effort will be in naming the group.

Session 4: Emotions and Personal Relationships

The purpose of the fourth session is to increase the student's feeling vocabulary. The target behaviors are to brainstorm feeling words and to use "I-messages." First, review the previous week. Second, brainstorm feeling words. Third, introduce I-messages—"I feel __________ today because __________."

Finally, play "Feelings Bingo" using I-messages. Feelings Bingo is similar to regular bingo, but with the following exceptions. The caller asks a group member to share an I-message after each feeling is called. The winner becomes the new caller and determines the criteria for winning (e.g., horizontal, diagonal, four corners). The board can be any facsimile of what appears in the boxed material.

Feelings Bingo Game

Happy	Afraid	Worried	Free space
Sad	Timid	Mad	Lonely
Joyful	Excited	Scared	Smart
Angry	Tired	Good	Overwhelmed

Session 5: Learning and School

The purpose of the fifth session is to increase the student's awareness of hidden verbal messages and nonverbal cues. The target behavior is to role play reading between the lines. First, review the previous week (good listening and brainstorming). Second, introduce the concept of reading between the lines. Third, role play reading between the lines by having the leader read the questions. The manner in which they are read and enunciated can have various connotations. Hypothetical items for reading between the lines are the following:

1. I'm going to Florida next week.
2. Slam door, sit down—I'll never talk to him again!
3. My dog died last night.
4. I'm just learning how to shoot pool!
5. You have an Atari?
6. I can spell supercalifragilisticexpealidocious!
7. I just love living in Pennsylvania.

The final activity is the question of the day.

Session 6: Emotions and Feelings

The purpose of the sixth session is to help each child understand that feelings can come in degrees and in feeling families (i.e., groups of similar feelings such as frustration and anger). The target behaviors are using the feelings thermometer (Green, 1978) and sharing a feeling and the degree to which it is felt.

First, review the previous week (reading between the lines). The second activity is the question of the day. Third, look at the feelings brainstormed in Session 4 and discuss feeling families and degrees of families. Finally, use the feelings thermometer (Green, 1978).

Session 7: Emotions and Guidance of ABCs

The first purpose of the seventh session is to have all students work as part of a group effort to earn points. The group goal was to earn 200 points. The first target behavior (see below) was worth 15 points, and the second target behavior was worth 10 points. The first session was 10 activity points and the fifth was 15 points. The goal was 50 points per session. Each counselor should work out a point system that fits the desired goals. The second purpose of the session is to determine what concerns the students have.

The target behaviors are (a) comparisons between honest feelings of group members and (b) group members giving friendly advice to each other. The first activity is the question of the day. Second, review the previous week and hand out the feelings thermometer. The third activity is honest discussion about feelings. Fourth, introduce feeling of worry (i.e., "What do you worry about?"). Finally, brainstorm what people worry about.

Session 8: Need to Know

The eighth session's purpose is to increase the student's awareness about self-talk. The target behavior is to collect group points by discussing worry and using corrective self-talk (e.g., "Everything is going to be all right.").

The first activity is the question of the day. Second, review last week (what people worry about). Third, introduce self-talk. Fourth, practice self-talk using Charlie Brown handout (a picture of Charlie with cartoon-like balloons to be filled in with thoughts). Group members are to write their fears in the circles and a corrective self-talk statement outside each.

Session 9: Need to Know, Imagery

The purpose of the ninth session is to help the students understand that it is okay to make mistakes. The target behaviors are self-talk and making mistakes. The first activity is the question of the day. Second, return their Charlie Brown handouts and review self-talk. Third, complete the handout. Finally, discuss individual handouts with the group.

Session 10: Multimodal Summary

The purposes of the last session are to evaluate the group and to review everything accomplished in the sessions. The target behavior is evaluative and integrative thinking. The three activities are the question of the day, reviewing major points of sessions, and evaluation.

Results

To determine any effects of the group meetings, we compared the attendance records of the five boys from February 1983 with their attendance records of February 1984. If attendance improved overall, the group may have had some impact on the five male members. This does not mean that the group was solely responsible for the improved attendance; rather, it may have played a role in the increased daily attendance while the group was in session. If this was the case, then conducting similar groups in the future would certainly be an option for guidance counselors. The results can be seen in Table 2.

According to the table, four of the participants improved their daily attendance from 1983 to 1984. The fifth boy showed no difference in attendance. In 1983, the group was absent an average of 6 days; in 1984, the average dropped to less than 1 day.

In addition to the main goal of increased attendance, the other goals of learning to cooperate with peers were reached. The goal for Session 1 was to help group members become acquainted with one another and to encourage good listening. Both verbal behaviors (talking) and nonverbal behaviors (smiling, looking at each other) of the group indicated that the subgoals of friendship were being achieved.

Table 2
Attendance Results

Days Absent	February 1983	February 1984
Subject one	2	0
Subject two	6	1
Subject three	14	0
Subject four	5	1
Subject five	3	3

The purpose for Session 2 was to determine important rules for group discussion. By having the group work together, we achieved a sense of group cohesion. Both of these goals were achieved in Session 2. The five boys devised their own adequate list of group rules. Also, they worked well together and seemed to enjoy each other's company.

The goal of Session 3 was to have each child understand and practice group problem solving. The five boys all did this well by actively participating in solving the problem confronting them: naming the group.

In Session 4, the children's goal was to increase their feelings vocabulary. Everyone brainstormed feeling words and shared at least one I-message with the group. This sharing conveyed a sense of trust and cohesion.

Session 5's goal was to increase the student's awareness of hidden verbal messages and nonverbal cues through the use of role playing. Only one participant had problems with reading between the lines. Other group members tried to help him understand the concept, but by the end of the session, he still did not understand it.

The purpose of Session 6 was to convey the idea that feelings can be grouped by families and can be measured in degrees. This point was well accepted by the children; they used the same feelings on their thermometers but colored in different degrees. The target of 75 points was reached by the end of Session 6. Thus, the boys earned their special activity of bringing a friend to the group.

Session 7's goals were to give the children the opportunity to work together for a group effort and to introduce the feeling of worry. The first goal was achieved from the beginning of this session until the group terminated. The boys earned points for working together through brainstorming and a discussion. Everyone participated well, thus earning group points for self-disclosure. This discussion related to the second goal because all group members talked about why they were currently worried. The session was productive.

The purpose of Session 8 was to increase the boys' awareness of self-talk, but the boys had another goal. They wanted to discuss how a person could tell when someone else was worried. Thus, although the session's original goal was not attained, the boys' personal goal was.

Session 9 was designed to aid the children in understanding that everyone makes mistakes. Because the children had already shared what worried them, they decided to brainstorm ways of dealing with worry. All group members understood that everyone makes mistakes and decided it would be beneficial to devise a way to deal with worry resulting from errors. All group members contributed various ways of dealing with worry.

The final session was held to evaluate the group and to discuss important points from the previous sessions. All group members completed an anonymous evaluation form, and we openly discussed all activities. The second goal of 200 points was not attained by the group; thus, they were not able to participate in the final special activity. During a follow-up meeting, however, the boys' group efforts were recognized when they were permitted to play "Feelings Twister," a game based on the commercial game "Twister." In the boys' game, feelings were substituted for the colors used in the regular Twister game. All other procedures were similar. The feelings used on the large floor gameboard were happy, sad, worried, glad, jealous, and mad. Once one of the six feelings was indicated on the game spinner, the children were instructed to place either a foot or a hand on that feeling. The game ended when a player lost his balance.

Summary

Five third-grade boys were chosen to participate in a friendship group with the objective of increasing their daily attendance at school. Participation in the group seemed to be a factor in increasing the daily attendance of four of the five children; the fifth boy's daily attendance remained the same.

Components of friendship training were also used in the group through skill learning (i.e., problem solving, determining rules). One of the obvious outcomes—group cohesiveness—was displayed over and over.

Other guidance counselors may wish to try a similar program in their school. Modifications to accommodate individual situations are open to counselor creativity.

References

Carlson, J. (1982). The multimodal effect of physical exercise. *Elementary School Guidance & Counseling, 16*, 304–309.
Gerler, E. R., Jr. (1979). The evolving "D" in "BASIC ID." *Personnel and Guidance Journal, 57*, 540–542.
Gerler, E. R., Jr. (1980a). Physical exercise and multimodal counseling groups. *Journal for Specialists in Group Work, 5*, 157–162.
Gerler, E. R., Jr. (1980b). The interpersonal domain in multimodal teacher groups. *Journal for Specialists in Group Work, 5*, 107–112.
Gerler, E. R., Jr. (1980c). Mental imagery in multimodal career education. *Vocational Guidance Quarterly, 28*, 306–312.
Gerler, E. R., Jr. (1984). The imagery in BASIC ID: A factor in education. *Journal of Humanistic Education and Development, 22*, 115–122.
Gordon, T. (1970). *Parent effectiveness training.* New York: Wyden.
Green, B. J. (1978). HELPING children of divorce: A multimodal approach. *Elementary School Guidance & Counseling, 13*, 31–45.
Keat, D. B. (Author and speaker). (1977). *Self-relaxation for children* [Cassette Recording No. C–600]. Harrisburg, PA: Professional Associates.
Keat, D. B. (1979). *Multimodal therapy with children.* New York: Pergamon.
Keat, D. B. (Author and speaker). (1980). *Friendship training for children* [Cassette Recording No. C–590]. Harrisburg, PA: Professional Associates.
Keat, D. B. (1982). Personal reflections: HELPING children with friendship. *Elementary School Guidance & Counseling, 16*, 253–256.
Keat, D. B., & Guerney, L. B. (1980). *HELPING your child.* Falls Church, VA: American Personnel and Guidance Association.
Lazarus, A. A. (Ed.). (1976). *Multimodal behavior therapy.* New York: Springer.
Lazarus, A. A. (1981). *The practice of multimodal therapy.* New York: McGraw-Hill.
Mason, G. (1975). *Help your child lose weight and keep it off.* New York: Grosset & Dunlap.
McElmurry, M. A., & Tom, D. N. (1981). *Feelings: Understanding our feelings of sadness, happiness, love and loneliness.* Carthage, IL: Good Apple.
Saint Exupery, A. de (1939). *Wind, sand and stars.* New York: Harcourt Brace Jovanovich.

Elementary School Counseling Research and the Classroom Learning Environment

Edwin R. Gerler, Jr.

Do elementary school counselors contribute to children's learning? Some studies in the *Elementary School Guidance & Counseling* journal have shown that counselors can improve children's learning and cognitive functioning. Costar's study (1980), for example, measured the effects of a program on test-taking skills with fourth graders and found small gains in reading test scores among the students. Another study (Harris, 1976) demonstrated a counseling program's positive effects on thinking skills among fifth and sixth graders. Other studies (Deutsch & Wolleat, 1981; Quatrano & Bergland, 1974) have found positive effects of elementary school counseling on children's cognitive skills in career-related areas.

Despite the limited research on elementary school counseling that deals with the cognitive domain, elementary school counselors can make a strong case for their contributions to the classroom learning environment. Considerable research evidence outside the counseling literature indicates that children's learning and cognitive development depend on how children behave in school (Hoge & Luce, 1979), how children feel about themselves (Braun, 1976), how children function socially (Cartledge & Milburn, 1978), and how children use their senses (Richardson, DiBenedetto, & Bradley, 1977) and their mental images (Pressley, 1977). These areas are, of course, important components of elementary school counseling programs designed to promote children's learning (see Gerler, Kinney, & Anderson, 1985, for an extensive review of research on various domains important to children's learning).

In this article, I review the research published in *ESG&C* from 1974 to 1984. This review explores research evidence of elementary school counselors' effectiveness in helping children to improve classroom behavior, to explore feelings, to improve socially, and to enhance sensory awareness and mental imagery. This review is intended to help counselors know what research indicates about the nature and extent of their contributions to the learning environment in elementary schools. Elementary school counselors should be able to use this evidence for demonstrating the importance of their work to school policy makers.

Elementary School Counseling Research: 1974–1984

Does Counseling Improve Children's Behavior?

Research has examined various strategies for behavior change used by elementary school counselors to encourage the classroom behaviors necessary for academic success. Table 1 summarizes the research on behavior change published in *ESG&C* from 1974 to 1984. Several of these studies focused on counselors' consulting practices with teachers. Cobb and Richards (1983), for instance, studied teacher consultation in combination with classroom guidance and group counseling and found a significant reduction in behavior problems among fourth and fifth graders. Lewin, Nelson, and Tollefson (1983) studied consultation with groups of student teachers and found significant positive changes in children's behavior as reported by the student teachers. (The researchers, however, found no change in the student teachers' negative attitudes toward the children whose behavior was reportedly changed.) Moracco and Kazandkian (1977) examined consulting strategies with teachers of first, second, and third graders and found improved classroom behavior as measured by a behavior rating scale. Hansen and Himes (1977) also reported promising results from consulting with teachers about students' classroom behavior.

Researchers have examined behavior change methods other than consultation with teachers. Thomas (1974) found that videotape modeling (a videotape of appropriate attentiveness in the classroom) significantly increased the attentiveness of first graders. Bleck and Bleck (1982) used play group counseling with disruptive third graders to raise self-esteem scores and behavior rating scores significantly. Other researchers of elementary school counseling have found that promising behavior change results from reinforcement programs (Hosford & Bowles, 1974), from behavior contracts (Thompson, Prater, & Poppen, 1974), and from various group counseling and group guidance approaches (Kern & Hankings, 1977; Kern, Kelley, & Downey, 1973; West, Sonstegard, & Hagerman, 1980). Finally, and perhaps most encouraging, Downing (1977) found that group counseling designed to modify the behavior of sixth-grade children had the additional benefit of significantly improving achievement.

Thus, elementary school counselors have used various techniques to modify children's classroom behavior successfully. Consultation with teachers seems a particularly useful approach to improving children's behavior. Also promising is Downing's (1977) finding that programs to promote behavior change may result in improved academic performance in the classroom. Elementary school counselors should share this evidence with school administrators and other decision makers in the schools.

Table 1
Behavior Change Research in ESG&C (1974–1984)

Study	Participants	Outcome	Significance
Bleck & Bleck (1982)	73 3rd graders	Improved behavior	.05
Cobb & Richards (1983)	90 4th and 5th graders	Improved behavior	.05
Downing (1977)	33 6th graders	Improved PIAT scores	.05
Hansen & Hines (1977)	45 teachers	No reported behavior changes in children	NS
Hosford & Bowles (1974)	136 4th–6th graders	Improved attendance	NS
Kern & Hankins (1977)	63 4th & 5th graders	Improved behavior	.05
Kern, Kelley, & Downey (1973)	54 4th–6th graders	Improved behavior	.05
Lewin, Nelson, & Tollefson (1983)	35 student teachers	Improved child behavior	.05
Moracco & Kazandkian (1977)	60 1st–3rd graders	Improved behavior	.05–.01
Thomas (1974)	69 1st graders	Improved attending behavior	.01
Thompson, Prater, & Poppen (1974)	71 2nd–5th graders	Improved behavior	NS
West, Sonstegard, & Hagerman (1980)	Ages and numbers varied	Improved behavior and academic performance	.05–.01

Does Affective Education Work?

In the late 1960s and throughout most of the 1970s, elementary school counselors devoted much of their time to conducting affective education programs to raise children's levels of self-esteem. Table 2 summarizes the affective

Table 2
Affective Education Research in ESG&C (1974–1984)

Study	Participants	Outcome	Significance
Buffington & Stilwell (1980)	190 4th & 5th graders	Improved self-control	NS
Calsyn, Pennell, & Harter (1984)	44 6th graders	Improved self-esteem	NS
Day & Griffin (1980)	187 2nd, 4th, & 6th graders	Positive attitudes	NS
Deffenbacher & Kemper (1974)	21 6th graders	Improved GPA	.001
Edmondson (1979)	165 4th graders	Improved self-concept	NS
Kaiser & Sillin (1977)	184 6th graders	Improved self-concept	.05
Wirth (1977)	184 3rd–6th graders	Improved achievement responsibility	.05–.01

education research published in *ESG&C* from 1974 to 1984. This literature reported improved scores on self-esteem measures as a result of the popular Magic Circle program (a small-group program designed to help children learn listening skills) (Edmondson, 1979) and because of other affective classroom guidance activities (Calsyn, Pennell, & Harter, 1984; Kaiser & Sillin, 1977). Additional research found slight improvements in children's self-control as a result of affective education (Buffington & Stilwell, 1980) and found considerable enthusiasm among children for participation in affective guidance programs such as the Magic Circle program (Day & Griffin, 1980).

It was hoped that these programs would improve children's achievement as a result of improving their self-esteem, increasing their sense of self-control, and increasing their enthusiasm for school. That hope has been realized in part. Wirth (1977), for example, reported significantly higher scores among fifth and sixth graders on an achievement responsibility scale when an affective education component was added to the school's regular reading program. Deffenbacher and Kemper (1974) reported significantly improved grade point averages among sixth graders involved in a program to decrease test anxiety.

Elementary school counselors need to present this research evidence to teachers and others in schools. As one counselor stated:

> Teachers keep telling me that they don't have time to do Magic Circles and other things like that because they need to teach reading and math. I need to work harder at showing them that children who practice listening in Magic Circles will do better at reading and math. (Gerler, 1982, p. 139)

This counselor's positive approach is exemplary. Counselors can use the affective education research cited here to help more professionals in the schools see the value of exploring feelings in the classroom.

Do Counseling Activities Help Children Socially?

Another aspect of research on elementary school counseling has focused on children's relationships with peers, parents, and teachers. Table 3 summarizes the research on training to develop interpersonal skills that was published in *ESG&C* from 1974 to 1984. The research on counselors' work to improve relationships among children has been particularly encouraging. Vogelsong's (1978) communication skills training with fifth graders significantly improved the children's scores on a test of empathy, and a similar program studied by Calsyn, Quicke, and Harris (1980) produced significantly higher scores among fourth and fifth graders on a communication skills instrument. Keelin and Keelin (1976) found promising effects on interpersonal behavior among children who participated in the Magic Circle program, and Kameen and Brown (1978) found increased peer acceptance among students receiving individual and group counseling.

Another important area of elementary school counselor's work—training parents to communicate better with children—also has produced positive research results. Giannotti and Doyle (1982) found that parent effectiveness training improved parents' attitudes toward parenting and improved children's scores on behavior rating scales and self-concept measures. Summerlin and Ward (1981) also indicated that parenting groups improved parents' attitudes toward parenting. Studies by Hayes, Cunningham, and Robinson (1977) and by Wantz and Recor (1984) found that parent effectiveness groups and children's counseling groups improved scores for children on measures of motivation, anxiety, and self-esteem. A study by Frazier and Matthes (1974), which compared Adlerian and behavioral parent education programs, found the Adlerian approach resulted in improved scores among parents on a child-rearing practices scale. Furthermore, Hudgins and Shoudt (1977) indicated improved responses and communication skills among participants in a parent education program.

Table 3
Research on Interpersonal Skills Training in ESG&C (1974–1984)

Study	Participants	Outcome	Significance
Asbury (1984)	9 teachers & 9 children	Improved child behavior	Baseline data showed change
Brown & Kameen (1975)	19 teachers	Improved professional competence	.002–.001
Calsyn, Quicke, & Harris (1980)	178 4th & 5th graders	Improved communication skills	.001
Frazier & Matthes (1975)	74 parents	Improved parenting skills	.05
Giannotti & Doyle (1982)	92 parents, 46 children	Improved parent attitude, improved child behavior, & improved child self-concept	.01
Hayes, Cunningham, & Robinson (1977)	92 5th & 6th graders	Improved motivation & self-esteem, reduced anxiety	.05–.01
Hudgins & Shoudt (1977)	10 parents	Improved communication skills	.001
Kameen & Brown (1978)	714 K–7 students & 22 teachers	Improved self-perception & peer acceptance among children, no changes in teachers	NS
Keelin (1976)	20 4-year-olds	Improved interpersonal behavior	NS
Shelton & Dobson (1974)	60 disadvantaged children	Improved attendance & GPA	.05–.01
Summerlin & Ward (1981)	50 parents	Improved parenting attitudes	.001
Vogelsong (1978)	16 5th graders	Improved empathy	.001
Wantz & Recor (1984)	11 parents & 9 children	Improved child behavior	.05
Zirges (1981)	Teachers (Unspecified number)	Improved student self-esteem & reading	.025–.001

Research on groups of teachers that is related to counselors' work in the interpersonal domain also has produced encouraging results. Brown and Kameen (1975) studied inservice groups for teachers designed to improve teaching behaviors. The study found improved ratings of professional competence for the participants. Asbury's (1984) study showed that empathy training for teachers may result in improved student behavior. Even more promising were Shelton and Dobson's (1974) findings of significantly improved school attendance and grade point averages among children whose teachers had participated in communication training. In addition, Zirges' (1981) study found that teacher communication training resulted in improved student self-esteem and reading performance as well as improved job satisfaction among teachers.

Together, these studies provide impressive evidence that elementary school counseling programs designed to improve relations at school and at home can have positive effects including improved academic performance among students. It is important for counselors to inform parents, teachers, and school administrators of the important role counselors play in the school's social environment. The research reviewed here should help counselors speak convincingly about the importance of their human relations programs.

Are Mental Imagery and Sensory Awareness Activities Effective?

In keeping with Will Rogers' statement that "schools ain't what they used to be and never was," some innovative elementary school counseling programs have developed imagery and sensory guidance activities to relieve high levels of stress among children. These kinds of activities are not well understood by many parents and teachers and, in fact, some counselors shy away from work in these areas. One counselor commented: "Mental imagery work scares me a little, though what I've read about it makes it seem relatively harmless. I still wonder how much good it actually is. I guess I need some training in mental imagery" (Gerler, 1982, p. 142).

The research on elementary school counselors' use of imagery and sensory activities is promising, although not extensive (see Table 4). The research deals primarily with relaxation training. Some studies (Gumaer & Voorneveld, 1975; Vacc & Greenleaf, 1980), for instance, have found indications that relaxation training (involving sensory and imagery activities) reduces anxiety, improves behavior, increases self-esteem, and improves social status among fourth and fifth graders. Omizo (1981) found that relaxation training for hyperactive boys resulted in improved behavior ratings from teachers and parents. In addition, Danielson (1984) found some increases on achievement test scores resulting from relaxation and imagery training with children. Most of the other literature

Table 4
Research on Imagery and Sensory Training in ESG&C (1974–1984)

Study	Participants	Outcome	Significance
Danielson (1984)	5th graders (Unspecified number)	Improved achievement scores	.05–.01
Gumaer & Voorneveld (1975)	20 4th & 5th graders	Increased self-esteem & social status, reduced anxiety	NS
Omizo (1981)	30 hyperactive boys	Improved behavior	.03
Vacc & Greenleaf (1980)	28 emotionally handicapped children	Improved behavior & reduced anxiety	NS

related to elementary school counselors' use of imagery and sensory activities has described model programs with little discussion of research or evaluation of the model programs.

Because some parents and teachers (and even some counselors) are unclear about the value of mental imagery and sensory awareness activities, counselors should increase their efforts to understand the research in this area and to communicate research results to parents and teachers. Only then will this important aspect of counselors' work be properly recognized in schools.

Conclusion

This review of more than a decade of research on elementary school counseling establishes that counseling programs can positively influence the affective, behavioral, and interpersonal domains of children's lives and, as a result, can affect children's achievement positively. The research also holds promise for the direct intervention of counselors in the imagery and sensory domains.

Counselors and researchers should note that many published studies of elementary school counseling have serious weaknesses. For instance, although most studies presented in this review used control groups, few of them included placebos. Critelli and Neumann (1984) argued persuasively in favor of using placebos in studies of psychological interventions. Further studies of elementary school counseling programs should take this argument into consideration.

Another important weakness of research on elementary school counseling has been the lack of detailed information about the participants. Authors of future studies should take special care in describing research participants.

This research review provides counselors with evidence of their importance to the school's learning climate. There is some experimental research published outside the *ESG&C* journal that further demonstrates the improvement in children's academic performance following elementary school counseling. Gerler, Kinney, and Anderson (1985), for instance, found that elementary school counselors can significantly improve the academic progress of underachieving children. Gerler and Locke (1980) also proved the positive effects of elementary school counseling on children's school achievement. These additional studies further support the importance of counselors in the learning climate of elementary schools.

If counselors use the available research evidence, they are likely to find increased support for their programs from teachers, parents, and school administrators. For example, counselors can use the tables or other sections of this article in presentations at parent-teacher meetings and at school board meetings to provide evidence that well conceived counseling programs have positive effects on classroom learning environments. This evidence is powerful because the majority of studies cited have results at the .05 level of statistical significance or better. Even the studies listed in Tables 1 through 4 with nonsignificant (NS) findings offer positive comments on counselors' work. In short, the past decade of research on elementary counseling holds considerable promise for counselors and the schools they serve.

References

Asbury, F. R. (1984). The empathy treatment. *Elementary School Guidance & Counseling, 18*, 181–187.

Bleck, R. T., & Bleck, B. L. (1982). The disruptive child's play group. *Elementary School Guidance & Counseling, 17*, 137–141.

Braun, C. (1976). Teacher expectation: Sociopsychological dynamics. *Review of Educational Research, 46*, 185–213.

Brown, J., & Kameen, M. (1975). Focused videotape feedback: A consultation approach with teachers. *Elementary School Guidance & Counseling, 10*, 4–12.

Buffington, P. W., & Stilwell, W. E. (1980). Self-control and affective education: A case of omission. *Elementary School Guidance & Counseling, 15*, 152–156.

Calsyn, R. J., Pennell, C., & Harter, M. (1984). Are affective education programs more effective with girls than with boys? *Elementary School Guidance & Counseling, 19*, 132–140.

Calsyn, R. J., Quickie, J., & Harris, S. (1980). Do improved communication skills lead to increased self-esteem? *Elementary School Guidance & Counseling, 15*, 48–55.

Cartledge, G., & Milburn, J. F. (1978). The case for teaching social skills in the classroom: A review. *Review of Educational Research, 48*, 133–156.

Cobb, H. C., & Richards, H. C. (1983). Efficacy of counseling services in decreasing behavior problems of elementary school children. *Elementary School Guidance & Counseling, 17*, 180–187.

Costar, E. (1980). Scoring high in reading: The effectiveness of teaching achievement test-taking behaviors. *Elementary School Guidance & Counseling, 15*, 157–159.

Critelli, J. W., & Neumann, K. F. (1984). The placebo: Conceptual analysis of a construct in transition. *American Psychologist, 39*, 32–39.

Danielson, H. A. (1984). The quieting reflex and success imagery. *Elementary School Guidance & Counseling, 19*, 152–155.

Day, R. W., & Griffin, R. E. (1980). Children's attitudes toward the magic circle. *Elementary School Guidance & Counseling, 15*, 136–146.

Deffenbacher, J. L., & Kemper, C. C. (1974). Counseling test-anxious sixth graders. *Elementary School Guidance & Counseling, 9*, 22–29.

Deutsch, R., & Wolleat, P. L. (1981). Dispelling the forced-choice myth. *Elementary School Guidance & Counseling, 16*, 112–120.

Downing, C. J. (1977). Teaching children behavior change techniques. *Elementary School Guidance & Counseling, 11*, 277–283.

Edmondson, R. J. (1979). Utilization of H.D.P. and T.A. programs to enhance self-esteem. *Elementary School Guidance & Counseling, 13*, 299–301.

Frazier, F., & Matthes, W. A. (1975). Parent education: A comparison of Adlerian and behavioral approaches. *Elementary School Guidance & Counseling, 10*, 31–38.

Gerler, E. R. (1982). *Counseling the young learner*. Englewood Cliffs, NJ: Prentice-Hall.

Gerler, E. R., Kinney, J., & Anderson, R. F. (1985). The effects of counseling on classroom performance. *Journal of Humanistic Education and Development, 23*, 155–165.

Gerler, E. R, & Locke, D. C. (1980). Multimodal education: A model with promise. *Phi Delta Kappan, 62*, 214–215.

Giannotti, T. J., & Doyle, R. E. (1982). The effectiveness of parental training on learning disabled children and their parents. *Elementary School Guidance & Counseling, 17*, 131–136.

Gumaer, J., & Voorneveld, R. (1975) . Affective education with gifted children. *Elementary School Guidance & Counseling, 10*, 86–94.

Hansen, J., & Himes, B. (1977). Critical incidents in consultation. *Elementary School Guidance & Counseling, 11*, 291–295.

Harris, S. R. (1976). Rational-emotive education and the human development program: A guidance study. *Elementary School Guidance & Counseling, 11*, 113–122.

Hayes, E. J., Cunningham, G. K., & Robinson, J. B. (1977). Counseling focus: Are parents necessary? *Elementary School Guidance & Counseling, 12*, 8–14.

Hoge, R. D., & Luce, S. (1979). Predicting academic achievement from classroom behavior. *Review of Educational Research, 49*, 479–496.

Hosford, R. E., & Bowles, S. A. (1974). Determining culturally appropriate reinforcers for Anglo and Chicano students. *Elementary School Guidance & Counseling, 8*, 290–300.

Hudgins, A. L., & Shoudt, J. T. (1977). HRD technology and parent training groups. *Elementary School Guidance & Counseling, 12*, 59–61.

Kaiser, H., & Sillin, P. C. (1977). Guidance effectiveness in the elementary school. *Elementary School Guidance & Counseling, 12*, 61–64.

Kameen, M. C., & Brown, J. A. (1978). Teacher esprit and intimacy and pupil personal competence perceptions. *Elementary School Guidance & Counseling, 12*, 180–283.

Keelin, P. W., & Keelin, M. S. (1976). The effects of magic circles on the interpersonal communication of 4-year-old children. *Elementary School Guidance & Counseling, 11*, 138–140.

Kern, R. M., & Hankins, G. (1977). Adlerian group counseling with contracted homework. *Elementary School Guidance & Counseling, 11*, 284–290.

Kern, R. M., Kelley, J. D., & Downey, M. (1973). Group counseling versus halo consultation. *Elementary School Guidance & Counseling, 8*, 68–70.

Lewin, P., Nelson, R. E., & Tollefson, N. (1983). Teacher attitudes toward disruptive children. *Elementary School Guidance & Counseling, 17*, 188–193.

Moracco, J., & Kazandkian, A. (1977). Effectiveness of behavior counseling and counseling with non-western elementary school children. *Elementary School Guidance & Counseling, 11*, 244–251.

Omizo, M. M. (1981). Relaxation training and biofeedback with hyperactive elementary school children. *Elementary School Guidance & Counseling, 15*, 329–332.

Pressley, M. (1977). Imagery and children's learning: Putting the picture in developmental perspective. *Review of Educational Research, 47*, 585–622.

Quatrano, L. A., & Bergland, B. W. (1974). Group experiences in building planning strategies. *Elementary School Guidance & Counseling, 8*, 173–181.

Richardson, E., DiBenedetto, B., & Bradley, C. M. (1977). The relationship of sound blending to reading achievement. *Review of Educational Research, 47*, 319–334.

Shelton, J. E., & Dobson, R. L. (1974). Family-teacher involvement: A counselor's key. *Elementary School Guidance & Counseling, 8*, 190–196.

Summerlin, M. L., & Ward, G. R. (1981). The effect of parent group participation. *Elementary School Guidance & Counseling, 16*, 133–136.

Thomas, G. M. (1974). Using videotaped modeling to increase attending behavior. *Elementary School Guidance & Counseling, 9*, 35–40.

Thompson, C. L., Prater, A. R., & Poppen, W. A. (1974). One more time: How do you motivate students? *Elementary School Guidance & Counseling, 9*, 30–34.

Vacc, N. A., & Greenleaf, S. (1980). Relaxation training and covert positive reinforcement with elementary school children. *Elementary School Guidance & Counseling, 14*, 232–235.

Vogelsong, E. L. (1978). Relationship enhancement training for children. *Elementary School Guidance & Counseling, 12*, 272–279.

Wantz, R. A., & Recor, R. D. (1984). Simultaneous parent-child group intervention. *Elementary School Guidance & Counseling, 19*, 126–131.

West, J., Sonstegard, M., & Hagerman, H. (1980). A study of counseling and consulting in Appalachia. *Elementary School Guidance & Counseling, 15*, 5–13.

Wirth, S. (1977). Effects of a multifaceted reading program on self-concept. *Elementary School Guidance & Counseling, 12*, 33–40.

Zirges, J. D. (1981). The guidance counselor as program developer. *Elementary School Guidance & Counseling, 16*, 83–90.

Chapter 8

Counseling Issues Related to Learning in a Changing World

Issues for elementary school counselors to consider about learning in a changing world:

1. Many people assume that the teacher's primary area of concern is the cognitive domain while the counselor's concern is the affective domain. How do the two areas complement each other?
2. Standardized achievement test results from your elementary school indicate that students are falling behind in math and language skills. Describe several intervention strategies that you as an elementary school counselor might use to help these students improve their math and language skills.
3. Develop an inservice program to help teachers incorporate career education activities into the teaching of basic subjects. How might these activities improve student performance in basic subjects?
4. How might elementary school counselors help children overcome procrastination with school work?
5. How can elementary school counselors collaborate with teachers to improve the learning environment in classrooms?
6. How might peer helpers be used to assist underachievers to improve their work at school? How would peer helpers benefit from this experience?
7. Classroom guidance has had positive effects on children's success in school. Develop several group guidance activities that you can use to improve the level of academic achievement among students.
8. How can elementary school counselors encourage parents to become more involved in children's learning?
9. Discuss this statement: "Reducing class size is more important to children's success in school than is hiring additional elementary school counselors."
10. What is the single most important contribution elementary school counselors make to children's learning?

CHAPTER 9

CHILDREN'S BEHAVIOR IN A CHANGING WORLD

Children's behavior, both in and out of school, is an important concern of parents and educators. The popular media has documented seemingly widespread school absenteeism and delinquency among our nation's youth. How to change children's misbehavior and to foster productive behavior are concerns of elementary school counselors. The techniques available to parents, teachers, and elementary school counselors for managing children's behavior are numerous. The techniques include modeling, positive reinforcement, behavior contracting, and desensitization. These behavioral change procedures have been thoroughly tested. Although the application of these methods is often difficult, the collaborative efforts of educators and parents in applying behavioral techniques eases some of the difficulties and increases the chances of success. This chapter presents counseling procedures that will continue to be used in the 1990s to help make needed changes in children's behavior.

Chapter 9 begins with the useful study, "Changing Student Attitudes and Behavior Through Group Counseling." Results of the study showed that 5th- and 6th-grade students improved their attitudes toward school from participation in a structured counseling group and consequently, behaved in ways that resulted in improved academic achievement.

The next article, "Project Explore: An Activity-Based Counseling Group," illustrates the usefulness of another type of counseling group to improve children's behavior. The authors describe creative group activities with such intriguing titles as "People Pyramids," "Yurt Circle," "Carabiner Walk," "Reach for the Sky," and "Blindfold Soccer." The authors report that this 9-week activity group was fun, well received by clients, and effective in improving behaviors related to problem solving, communications, and group cooperation.

The third article in this chapter examines a series of interventions elementary school counselors can implement to decrease behavior problems of children. These interventions include classroom guidance sessions, small group counseling sessions, and consultation with teachers. The authors found that students who received a combination of these treatment procedures improved their scores on a behavior problem checklist.

The effects of classroom meetings on students' behavior at school is the topic of the final article in Chapter 9. The authors concluded from their 20-week study that "classroom meetings have potential not only as a treatment technique for children with behavioral problems but also as a technique in the prevention of problem behavior."

Changing Student Attitudes and Behavior Through Group Counseling

Robert D. Myrick
R. Wiley Dixon

Students with positive school attitudes tend to obtain higher school grades. Attitudes toward school also influence performance on standardized achievement tests (Brodie, 1964; Gable, Roberts, & Owen, 1977; Neale, Gill, & Tismer, 1970; Williams, 1970). In contrast, students who have negative attitudes about themselves and school often have problems learning. They perform poorly in class and on standardized tests. In addition, they frequently disrupt or distract others from learning effectively and become discipline referrals.

A review of the professional literature, including articles published in a variety of journals, indicates that counselor intervention with students who have negative attitudes has been a neglected topic for several years. The few studies on the topic lacked adequate experimental designs and provided little evidence that counselors were effective in altering negative attitudes and related behaviors. For example, Gutsch and Bellamy (1966) attempted to show that counselors, through group sessions, could help change behavior. Their study, however, was inconclusive because it involved only 16 students, 8 each in a control group and an experimental group. Some of their conclusions were based on subgroups of 4 students each, and this created problems in the analysis of the data. Petty (1965) described some ideas for improving attitude and citizenship in school but provided no supporting data. Lodato, Sokoloff, and Schwartz (1964) studied four elementary and two junior high school groups and concluded that group counseling could modify attitudes in slow learners. Yet, they also provided no supporting data.

Group counseling apparently affected student attitudes and grade point averages (GPAs) in one study (Benson & Blocher, 1967), but the group process was not clearly described. In a similar study (Wittmer, 1969), a combination of tutoring and counseling was used with 18 underachieving seventh grade students. There was no control group, however, and it was not possible to tell whether counseling or tutoring was the contributing factor for improved attitudes and GPAs. In a later study, Hallwell, Musella, and Silvino (1970) found only slight improvement in attitudes and no significant change in GPAs. Krivatsy-O'Hara, Reed, and Davenport (1978) reported that group counseling could be effective with potential high school dropouts. There was no control group. Their conclusions were based on anonymous questionnaires from 51 students, and they did not provide details about the counseling sessions.

There is a need for more counselors to report data regarding their effectiveness with students who have negative attitudes about school. There is also a need for these data to come from carefully designed experimental studies. Finally, there is a need for counselors to describe the counseling procedures they have used.

Counselors Working Together

Thirteen school counselors in Orange County, Florida, were concerned about students who had negative school attitudes. They noted that school achievement was low among these students and that teachers frequently asked for assistance in bringing about some kind of change. With university and county staff assisting them during after-school meetings, the counselors developed a group counseling strategy and an instrument for measuring behavior change. They agreed to work together in a collaborative study.

During their first meeting, the counselors listed observable behaviors of students who had negative attitudes about school. How can one tell whether a student has a negative attitude? A list of classroom behaviors related to negative attitude was obtained, and the items were rank ordered in terms of their effect on school achievement. This resulted in six behaviors, which were placed on a checklist so that teachers could report student behavior. Subsequent planning meetings focused on (a) identifying and selecting target students for counseling and study, (b) developing some structured group counseling sessions, (c) discussing and role-playing group leadership skills, and (d) planning the collection of data for the study.

Experimental Procedures

Population and Sample

After reviewing school records and consulting with teachers, the counselors identified 12 students (grades 5–6), in their respective schools, whose attitudes needed improvement. Of these, 6 were randomly assigned to participate in a series of group counseling sessions. The other 6 served as a comparison group and received counseling at a later date. The two groups in each of the schools enabled counselors to assess the effectiveness of group counseling.

The Counselor Intervention

A series of six small-group counseling sessions was carefully outlined and practiced in the counselor meetings so that all counselors would use the same activities and similar leadership skills. In general, the group sessions lasted about 30–45 minutes and consisted of the following:

Session 1: Feelings About School. After explaining that the purpose of the group was to help students think more about themselves and school, counselors used a handmade set of cards with feeling words written on them to help members disclose their ideas and feelings. Cards were distributed randomly, and the students discussed the meanings of the words—for example: "What does the word *disappointment* mean to you?" "Is that a pleasant or unpleasant feeling?" "How can you tell whether a person feels that way?" "Have you ever seen someone who felt that way?" "Have you ever felt that way?" The feeling words were also listed on a large piece of paper and used later for reference. Other words were added as they came up in following sessions.

Session 2: Illustrated Tee Shirt. In this session, the students drew symbols on a picture of a "tee shirt" that was divided into five sections. "Draw a little picture or symbol that . . . (a) tells something about this school, (b) represents something you would like to change about school, (c) tells what you like about school, and (d) shows one thing about yourself that you would like to change or improve on, and write three words that teachers might use to describe you." This activity encouraged group members to continue voicing their opinions and feelings about school. It also gave counselors an opportunity to help group members understand how feelings are related to behaviors in school. For instance, when the students discussed how teachers might describe them, the counselors asked: "What do you do that makes them see you that way?" "If you wanted to be described differently, what would you have to do?"

Session 3: Dear Abby. The group activity began when a counselor stated:

> Think of a problem that you are having in school . . . or perhaps a problem that someone you know is having . . . or maybe a problem that students your age have in school that might be interesting to discuss. Write them down on these small pieces of paper and do not sign your name. I will collect them, and then we will discuss some of them in our group.

After reading a problem aloud, the counselor stated, "If you had a problem like this, how would you feel?" Later, "Well, if you had these feelings, how might you behave?" Still later, "What could a person do in a situation like this?"

Group members learned that they were not alone in their feelings about school. This session also led to discussions about the consequences of behavior and alternative actions. At this point, however, primary attention was on how feelings and behaviors are related to school problems.

Session 4: Giving and Receiving Feedback. Group members learned a three-step feedback model: (a) be specific about the behavior you see or hear, (b) tell how it makes you feel, and (c) tell what your feelings make you want to do (Myrick & Erney, 1978). The students first practiced by thinking of examples and talking to an empty chair. Then, each identified a teacher or classmate to whom positive feedback might be given during the coming week. This session encouraged a positive focus in school and helped the students act positively in the school environment.

Session 5: Some First Steps. First, reports of how the feedback model worked outside the group were heard, and each member identified "one thing about myself that I want to improve." Second, each described a first step that might be taken, as group members listened and offered other suggestions as to how a person might get started. The students were encouraged to begin their first step that week.

Session 6: Being Positive. The session began with students describing what happened to them during the week when they tried to take their first steps. During the second part of the session, the group members, including the counselor, took a turn in the "cool seat," where they received compliments from others. The members were to say aloud anything positive that came to mind about a student who was sitting in the cool seat chair. This helped the group end on a positive note.

The Criterion Measures

All students in the study were rated by their teachers on a classroom behavior checklist. It consisted of six items on a 5-point Likert-type scale (from "Strongly Agree" to "Strongly Disagree"). These items were those identified by the counselors as behaviors related to attitudes about the school that affected achievement: (a) contributes to discussion, (b) starts assignments, (c) follows directions and school rules, (d) completes assignments, (e) has materials ready to work, and (f) accepts helpful corrections and suggestions. The instrument was administered prior to and after group counseling.

A second instrument was given only to those students who participated in group counseling. They reported their perceptions of the experience on a Likert-type scale by responding to six items. The group experience (a) increased my understanding of others, (b) affected my behavior outside the group, (c) increased my understanding of self, and (d) helped me like school better. They were also asked (e) if they would recommend the group to others and (f) if they disliked being in the group.

The Findings

Ten of the counselors provided data for the study. Data were complete on 59 students who received counseling and 59 students who did not ($N = 118$). To statistically control for any initial between-group differences, an analysis of covariance procedure (ANCOVA), with the premeasure used as a covariate, was used to examine the data. It was hypothesized that group counseling would make a difference and that those receiving counseling would make significant gains in their classroom behavior.

The Classroom Behavior Checklist

The statistical analysis of classroom behavior, as rated by teachers, showed a significant difference (.05 level of confidence) between the two comparison groups of students in the study. Those students who received group counseling improved their classroom behavior significantly more than those who did not receive group counseling ($F = 8.48$, $p < .001$). The analysis also showed that group counseling was effective across sex of student and schools, suggesting that both boys and girls benefited regardless of school or counselor.

Student Perceptions

An analysis was also made with a follow-up instrument that was administered to students who participated in the group counseling sessions. Data were received from 42 students. Of these, 72% reported that the group increased their understanding of themselves, and 86% said it helped them gain a better understanding of others. In addition, 62% indicated that the experience helped change their behavior outside the group, and 60% said that they liked school better as a result of the group. Approximately 81% recommended a similar group to other students. Finally, the students also expressed their ideas by writing what they liked best and least about the group, what they would say about the group, and what they had learned. This information is provided in the boxed material.

It can be seen that in general, the students liked the opportunity to share their ideas and feelings. They liked learning about themselves and others through the group. The group enabled them to disclose feelings about themselves, others, and school. It also helped them obtain feedback from others. It

Student Likes and Dislikes

What I Liked Best (the group sessions):

They helped me with my work
I liked the activities we did and hope we can meet again
Getting out of class
Being allowed to talk
Talking together
Giving feedback to each other
Making more friends
Getting to understand things better
Getting to know some of my friends in the group a little better

I Learned:

That I hardly ever get feedback
How to control my temper
Showed me that you can get more friends by being nice
How to ask and give people information
How to control my attitude
To be kind to others and nice
To think positive about school
To be considerate of others
To go to school and to be a better student

What I Liked Least:

Only staying 20 minutes
Writing things
Nothing, I liked everything
The time we met
Leaving the group
Didn't have enough time together
When the group was over
When we all acted up

What I Would Say About Our Group:

It is a happy group
I liked it and if you ever have a chance to go, then go
You learn to understand things better
It was fun and we had a good teacher
This class is real fun

encouraged them to think about their behavior in school, including something on which they could improve.

Not everyone liked being in the group (10%). Some disliked their group because of a particular person. As expected, these students not only have negative attitudes about school but about themselves and others. Yet, the things students disliked most tended to focus on the operational procedures needed to bring the group together. "There wasn't enough time" and "The group is ending" were the two most expressed dislikes, which is in reality a positive vote for the group experience.

Conclusion

Principals, teachers, and parents often view school adjustment and discipline as one of the most important goals of a school guidance program. Positive attitudes about school and about achieving behaviors in the classroom are seen as essential if students are to learn effectively and efficiently. Thus, it is surprising that so little attention in the counseling literature has been directed to such an important issue as working with students who have negative school attitudes. What are counselors doing to assist students who are performing poorly in school because of their attitudes?

This study demonstrated that counselors can help. The structured series of group sessions was effective. Students liked the experience, and they were aware of positive changes in themselves. Teachers reported differences in student classroom behavior, especially those related to achievement.

In addition, the counselors in this study enjoyed working together on a counselor project. They shared ideas, pooled information, practiced skills, and planned an accountability study in which they could all participate. They felt more energized and enthusiastic about their work. Collaborating together helped them focus on a special population that needed attention and that benefited from counselor intervention.

References

Benson, R. L., & Blocher, D. H. (1967). Evaluation of developmental counseling with groups of low achievers in a high school setting. *The School Counselor, 14*, 215–220.

Brodie, T. A. (1964). Attitude toward school and academic achievement. *The Personnel and Guidance Journal, 43*, 375–378.

Gable, R. K., Roberts, R. D., & Owen, S. V. (1977). Affective and cognitive correlates of classroom achievement. *Educational and Psychological Measurement, 37*, 977–986.

Gutsch, K., & Bellamy, W. (1966). Effectiveness of an attitudinal group approach as a behavior determinant. *The School Counselor, 14*, 40–43.

Hallwell, J. W., Musella, D. F., & Silvino, P. J. (1970). Effects of counseling on attitudes and grades with intermediate grade pupils designated as having poor attitudes. *Elementary School Guidance & Counseling, 5*, 113–123.

Krivatsy-O'Hara, S., Reed, P., & Davenport, J. (1978). Group counseling with potential high school dropouts. *The Personnel and Guidance Journal, 56*, 510–512.

Lodato, F. J., Sokoloff, M. A., & Schwartz, L. J. (1964). Group counseling as a method of modifying attitudes in slow learners. *The School Counselor, 12*, 27–33.

Myrick, R. D., & Erney, T. A. (1978). *Caring and sharing*. Minneapolis: Educational Media.

Neale, D. C., Gill, N., & Tismer, R. (1970). Relationship between attitudes toward school and their achievement. *Journal of Educational Research, 63*, 232–239.

Petty, M. (1965). Improving citizenship and attitudes. *The School Counselor, 13*, 94–99.

Williams, R. L. (1970). Personality, ability, and achievement correlates of scholastic attitudes. *Journal of Educational Research, 63*, 401–403.

Wittmer, J. (1969). The effects of counseling and tutoring on the attitudes and achievement of seventh grade underachievers. *The School Counselor, 16*, 287–290.

Project Explore: An Activity-Based Counseling Group

Kevin Duncan
David L. Beck
Richard A. Granum

Children referred to school counselors often exhibit problem behaviors, such as acting out, underachieving, or being withdrawn. A look beyond the symptoms reveals that poorly developed skills in problem solving, communication, and cooperation exacerbate their problems and impede efforts to remediate the difficulties. These skill deficits must be eliminated, because students need to develop the basic tools for coping in society (Goldstein, Sprafkin, Gershaw, & Klein, 1980). Traditional individual and group counseling interventions are often ineffective when dealing with these skill problems (Goldstein et al., 1980). Innovative approaches to counseling need to be developed to help overcome these impediments (Anderson & Otto, 1984). The development of these basic skills may enhance the likelihood that future counseling will be successful. We designed an action-oriented group process that would engage children physically, cognitively, and emotionally to develop their basic skills.

The group process has been used with handicapped students at Saint Joseph's Children's Home, a residential treatment center, and at Torrington Middle School, Torrington, Wyoming, with both handicapped and nonhandicapped students. Participants have been boys and girls between the ages of 8 and 14. Group size has varied from a low of 6 to a high of 22 participants. The group-format activities and processing techniques have undergone four successive modifications over a 2-year period.

The purpose of this article is to share the activities and processing format as they currently exist and discuss the student outcomes that have been observed.

Format

A five-step procedure is used to direct each activity and the group processing. First, the counselor describes the nature of the activity to be attempted and provides a demonstration when appropriate. Second, the students engage in the activity while the counselor observes the interactions within the group. Third, after allowing a few trials, the facilitator stops the actions and begins a processing segment. Initially, the processing is directed toward discussing how the clients attempted to complete the task. Communication styles and participant roles are discussed.

After this processing phase, the counselor asks each student to make a commitment to a specific behavior leading to the successful completion of the task. Fourth, the clients again attempt to complete the task, and fifth, the action is stopped and discussion resumes. Comparisons are made between the students' first and second attempts to solve the problem (Steps 2 & 4), and particular emphasis is placed on their emotional responses. Parallels are then drawn between current emotions and other life experiences in which they experienced similar emotions. At this point, either the group concludes, or a second activity is presented and the group continues, following the same format.

Videotaping was used in some group sessions. It provided an opportunity for peers to identify roles and behavior patterns. The students seemed to enjoy seeing themselves. We found this to be a valuable source of feedback for the group and a means of processing the group dynamics.

Activities

This group is based on activities. Space and equipment requirements must be considered. Some activities dictate that a large open space be available such as a gymnasium or outdoor play area, but other activities can be done in a small room. Props are generally objects readily found in a school setting, but certain activities necessitate a minimal amount of simple construction. Caution must be exercised to limit risk of injury during these activities. The removal of eyeglasses, watches, and even shoes may be prudent, as is the use of spotters or crash mats.

Described below is a representative sample of activities used. The number of activities needed per session depends on the nature of the activity and the amount of time available for the group. The verbal abilities of clients will affect the amount of time spent in processing. If meetings are held once per week for 1 hour, approximately 15 activities are needed during a 9-week quarter.

Bump. Select either bean bags or foam balls and divide the participants into groups of three. One client tosses the object and the other two catch it while holding their hands behind their backs. Once they catch the object, they must carry it a predetermined distance. The counselor can vary the activity by placing the catchers in different positions, e.g., back to back. (Rohnke, 1977).

Lap Ball. All players sit in a very close circle, shoulder to shoulder. The object of the game is to pass a ball from lap to lap without the use of hands (Sobel, 1983).

All Aboard. This requires a small platform or sturdy table not quite big enough to accommodate the group. Tell all group members to get on the platform and stay on it for 5 seconds (Rohnke, 1977).

People Pyramids. The object is to build pyramids. Traditional triangle shapes and circular shapes should be attempted (Fluegelman, 1976).

Four Pointers. The object is to get the group to move from point A to point B with only six supporting points (feet, arms, or knees) touching the ground. Distance to be traveled, number of supporting points, and number of contestants can be varied depending on the size or skill level of the group (Rohnke, 1977).

Yurt Circle. An even number of players forms a tight, shoulder-to-shoulder circle while holding hands. Every other person is designated as an "in" or an "out." On command, the "ins" lean inward, and the "outs" lean outward simultaneously. Once they are stable in this position, on command, the "ins" and "outs" simultaneously lean in opposite directions (Fluegelman, 1981).

Carabiner Walk. While standing, participants gather together in a bunch and are then encircled by a length of soft rope. Working together, they move to a particular location. Have the participants learn something new about another person in the group as they do this (Rohnke, 1977).

Pass and Catch. Have the players line up in two parallel lines, each facing the other, about 10 feet apart. The first person in one line throws a ball to the person directly opposite him or her, then runs to the end of his or her respective line. Repeat until all have had a turn. A variation involves repeating the process until the line moves from one point to another (Sobel, 1983).

Reach for the Sky. Group members form a human ladder and place a chalk mark as high as they can on a wall or tall tree. This can be done with pairs, groups of three, or the entire group (Rohnke, 1977).

Stand Up. Players sit back-to-back with a partner with their elbows interlocked; both have their knees bent. The object is to stand up. Variations include accomplishing the same task with three, four, or five players (Fluegelman, 1976).

Trolley. Four participants glide from point A to B, each using two 8-foot 2 x 4's as skis and eight 4-foot lengths of rope attached at 2-foot intervals as ski poles. Doing this backwards is even harder (Rohnke, 1977).

Willow in the Wind. A group of six to eight players forms a tight circle around a person standing in the center. The person in the center stands with eyes closed and arms crossed over the chest. The players forming the circle gently push the person back and forth so the person in the center sways in the breeze but is not blown over (Fluegelman, 1981).

Leaning Tower. Using 10 to 50 styrofoam cups, the group tries to create the largest tower possible. The students can take turns adding one cup at a time, or they can designate a crew chief to direct the design of the construction from a blueprint, with his or her back to the group.

I Like You Because. All group members sit on chairs in a circle except one, who stands in the middle. The person in the middle touches a person in the circle and says "I like you because. . . ." (and names an attribute of the person, e.g., kindness, sense of humor) "and because. . . ." (names something else tangible, e.g., you are wearing a sweater), at which time all who are wearing sweaters and the person in the middle scramble for another chair. The person left without a chair repeats the process.

Cooperation by Design. This exercise takes only a few hundred feet of rope or string, a large area, and a group to hold the rope or string. The players try to create various shapes and emotions without talking.

Almost Infinite Circle. Using two lengths of yarn, pairs of participants are interlocked by tying the ends of the yarn to each person's wrists. They try to free themselves without cutting the yarn or breaking it (Rohnke, 1977).

Blindfold Soccer. This is just a simple game of soccer, except that players are in pairs and one is blindfolded. The sighted player directs the blindfolded player, who kicks the ball. The activity can be varied by having the player kick the ball to a specific point (Rohnke, 1977).

Old Faithfuls. Trust walks and trust falls remain two well-liked activities.

Co-Kicks. The game is traditional soccer, with one minor exception. All players are paired with a teammate, and the two are tied together at the ankle with a length of strong string or rope (Sobel, 1983).

Python Pentathlon. All group members are seated on the floor in a line, and each student puts his or her legs around the waist of the person in front. The group is then instructed to move to a predetermined point (Rohnke, 1977).

Art of Listening. Participants are seated in pairs, back to back. One is given a pencil and a blank sheet of paper and the other a piece of paper with a geometric design. This individual then instructs the other in re-creating the design. The person receiving instructions is not allowed to ask questions.

Knots. All players stand in a circle, shoulder to shoulder, and then grasp the hands of two others, one with each hand. Players are not to grasp the hands of the persons next to them. Now, untie the knot. Pivoting of hands without breaking the grasp is permissible (Fluegelman, 1976).

The Circles. Group members stand in a circle, facing each other's backs. They place their arms around the person in front of them and their hands on the waist of the person in front of that person. First they all try to walk, then each sits on the knees of the person behind without breaking the circle. To make it easier, have the first person sit on a chair and build the circle from there.

The Clock. Participants form a circle facing inwards and join hands. Shuffle or side-step clockwise or counterclockwise until one person is at a predetermined point. Speed is critical, as is maintaining the circle. Have the participants face outward to vary this activity (Rohnke, 1977).

Discussion

Though no formal measures were used to evaluate the group, some notable outcomes were observed. As the group progressed, participants became more skillful and successful in completing assigned tasks. Children were actively involved in the group, seemed eager to participate, and often requested permission to re-do activities at the end of sessions. Less arguing and blaming behaviors were noted as the group progressed. Processing became more personal and there was more self-disclosure with each session.

The processing component of the group, of course, was the most crucial element. The predetermined discussion format was instrumental in leading this group. A clear emphasis on the dynamics involved in problem solving, as opposed to success and competition, was essential in producing meaningful processing. Participants shared points of view as a way to model appropriate cooperation and communication skills. Clients were asked to state what they would do differently during the next attempt to complete the task, thus helping to establish a pattern that would be useful for dealing with problems in everyday life. Clients were engaged in a problem-solving sequence, which could be generalized to other problems. Children assessed, took ownership of their contribution, committed themselves to an alternative course of action, and applied it in the succeeding round. When done verbally, this process helped to establish communication skills and lent support and encouragement, which fostered cooperation.

The second round of processing (Step 5) allowed the group to find parallel group solutions to other problems the students faced. On one occasion, when using the carabiner walk, the group decided to exclude an uncooperative member from the activity. Their solution was similar to divorce or sending a child to the other parent, because they could not resolve the problem. After discussing this theme, the group reintegrated the excluded child and completed the task with greater ease.

We found a group size of 8 to 10 students ideal for discussion purposes. When the group size was smaller, there was a paucity of ideas and perceptions for discussion because of absences. When used with larger groups (up to 22 students), the processing suffered because the facilitator was unable to engage each student in depth and tend to all participants in timely fashion.

In summary, this 9-week activity group—designed to improve client problem solving, communications, and cooperation skills—was fun, well received by clients, and effective in improving skills.

References

Anderson, W. P., & Otto, R. L. (1984). Designing groups for use with special populations: A case history. *Journal for Specialists in Group Work, 9,* 179–185.

Fluegelman, A. (1976). *The new games book.* Garden City, NY: Dolphin Books/Doubleday.

Fluegelman, A. (1981). *More new games.* Garden City, NY: Dolphin Books/Doubleday.

Goldstein, A. P., Sprafkin, R. P., Gershaw, N. J., & Klein, P. (1980). *Skillstreaming the adolescent: A structured learning approach to teaching prosocial skills.* Champaign, IL: Research Press.

Rohnke, K. (1977). *Cowtails and cobras.* Hamilton, MA: Project Adventure, Inc.

Sobel, J. (1983). *Everybody wins.* New York: Walker and Co.

Efficacy of Counseling Services in Decreasing Behavior Problems of Elementary School Children

Harriet C. Cobb
Herbert C. Richards

The maintenance of discipline in the classroom has always been a high priority for most school administrators and teachers, and recent Gallup Poll statistics reveal a nationwide "back to basics" movement that has reduced everyone's tolerance for classroom disruption (Brodinsky, 1977). The development of reading, writing, and arithmetic competence is incompatible with a chaotic classroom. Parents have now joined the ranks of those concerned about creating a more "studious" classroom environment, and any professional who can help teachers with their discipline problems would be a welcome addition to the school program. Although part of the answer can be found in training teachers to be better classroom managers, the elementary school counselor should be a natural ally in the teacher's struggle with behavior problems; such problems for many children extend well beyond the classroom.

A variety of counseling and consultation interventions have been found to have a measurable impact on teacher-assessed behavior problems (Fortune, 1975; Lewis, 1970; Marchant, 1972; Palmo, 1972; Sugar, 1975). It should be noted, however, that in most intervention studies, teachers, who must necessarily be aware of treatment onset, are also called on to judge subsequent behaviors. The position that we have taken is that teacher judgments are probably more useful in deciding the efficacy of an intervention than those made by an external observer (although their awareness of intervention may contaminate judgments); such judgments should be cross-checked by ratings made by a naive classroom observer for their objectivity.

The purpose of the present study is to assess the effectiveness of a program intended to improve classroom climate and conduct. To assess program impact, both teachers and an observer (who was unaware of any intervention) rated classroom behavior problems before and after program implementation.

Method

Participants

The participants were 90 fourth and fifth graders, 43 boys and 47 girls, who were attending four self-contained classes of a rural elementary school in the extreme western portion of Virginia. The children were almost exclusively from lower or lower-middle class homes, and all but two were White.

Measures

Thirty-five items were selected from the *Behavior Problem Checklist* (Quay & Peterson, 1967) to measure the prevalence of behavior problems before and following intervention. This instrument, when used in its entirety, requires raters to judge the presence and severity of 55 commonly observed behavior problems (i.e., symptoms) typical of some school-age children. The problems are scaled on 3-point Likert continua, and ratings on each can range from zero (problem is absent for the child under observation) to two (item constitutes a severe problem). The rated symptoms tend to group themselves into three factor analytically distinct categories of disturbance: conduct disorders, such as disruptiveness or tantrums (Factor I); personality problems, such as hypersensitivity or anxiety (Factor II); and behaviors suggesting immaturity or inadequacy, such as attention-seeking (Factor III). The reliability of the checklist and its factor pattern have been repeatedly demonstrated in the literature (e.g., Grieger & Richards, 1975). Scores on each of the three factors are obtained by summing the ratings across the factorially homogenous individual scales.

The items selected for the present study were those that could be readily observed in the classroom setting. They included 14 conduct disorders, 13 personality problems, and 8 immaturity-inadequacy symptoms. Because the observations were made by two observers (a classroom teacher and an independent observer) on three occasions (a pretest and two posttests), two kinds of reliability estimates were obtained—objectivity and stability. The objectivity estimates were made for each factor and occasion by correlating the scores obtained from teacher judgments with those from the independent observer. Because the teacher and observer scores were eventually averaged, these reliability estimates were corrected according to the Spearman-Brown formula. Cross-time stability estimates were obtained by correlating the averaged ratings on one occasion with those obtained on another. The resulting reliability figures for the revised 35-item checklist were computed and can be obtained from the senior author.

Procedure

Data collection. Four female classroom teachers, two at the fourth- and two at the fifth-grade level, agreed to participate in the study. Each was informed about the purpose of the investigation and the intervention plan, and each was trained to use the *Behavior Problem Checklist.* A female classroom observer who was unaware of the intervention plan was also trained to use the checklist. The independent observer was only told that the purpose of the observations was to help collect information about the prevalence of problem behaviors in fourth and fifth graders over a 4-month period. Teachers were cautioned not to inform the observer about any interventions that might be taking place in the interim periods.

Observations were made in all four classrooms on three separate occasions—a pretest and two posttests (i.e., posttest 1 and posttest 2). One fourth- and one fifth-grade class were randomly assigned to treatment group 1, a group that underwent intervention in the 8-week period immediately following the pretest observations; no intervention took place in the remaining classes (treatment group 2) until after the 8-week period following pretest 1 observations.

The counselor and teacher mutually agreed on which children (a subgroup of the class referred to as the Target Group) were to participate in additional small group counseling sessions. Their selection was based primarily on the results of the pretest observations and teacher judgments about children who could best work together. Those children with a number of severe problem behaviors were considered to be in need of more intensive intervention. Thirteen Group 1 and 15 Group 2 children were targeted in this manner.

Treatment

The classroom guidance sessions—(counselor led). The eight classroom guidance sessions led by the counselor during the intervention period were focused around the theme "Learning About Ourselves and Others." The general format was planned by the counselor in collaboration with the teachers in the study. The primary objective of the guidance unit was to increase student self-awareness and increase understanding of others' unique characteristics. Each session was approximately a half hour in length, and the teacher remained in the classroom during the activity. The teacher was encouraged to point out situations relevant to the guidance unit as they occurred during the school day.

Session One: The first session was spent focusing on having each child identify his or her strengths or accomplishments, and sharing with the others in a group discussion period.

Session Two: The second session dealt with identifying the student's individual interests. Checklists were given to the students who were asked to respond to items such as:

1. I like to read.
2. I would rather play a quiet game inside than baseball outside.
3. I like working in a group on a project more than working alone.

Children's responses were discussed and the characteristics of several occupations were matched with general interests expressed.

Session Three: The third session was composed of a values clarification activity. Several objects representing specific values (encyclopedia: knowledge; aspirin: health; heart: friendship; picture of home: family) were placed on a table in front of the class. The children took turns arranging the objects in an order reflecting their hierarchy of values. The reasons for the relationship were discussed as well as possible differences between their rankings and what their parents' rankings may have been.

Session Four: During this session students were introduced to the concept of goal setting as a means of self-improvement (the students in the small group sessions were "experts" on goal setting and had several helpful hints to offer to the rest of the class). The idea of reducing broad goals into smaller objectives was discussed, and each student was asked to set one goal for himself or herself, to be discussed the following week.

Session Five: This session was spent following up on the previous week's "goal setting." The students' progress toward their goals was shared, and ways to increase success were discussed.

Session Six: The fable from the Transactional Analysis Program about being kind to others with "warm fuzzies" and "cold pricklies" was told to the students. Their reactions to the story and related examples in their own lives were shared.

Session Seven: "Parent–Adult–Child" communication unit from the Transactional Analysis Program was represented to the students. They took turns role playing the different styles of communication and rehearsed the "Adult" response to the different situations presented.

Session Eight: The final session was devoted to discussing ways of using what they had learned in the previous sessions in order to increase positive feelings about themselves and others. Each child was asked to draw a picture illustrating something they learned in the past 8 weeks of guidance sessions.

Classroom guidance sessions—(teacher led). Each teacher spent a minimum of 40 minutes per week involving the class in selected guidance activities. Although space does not permit a detailed description of these activities, the interested reader is referred to Canfield and Wells (1976) *100 Ways to Enhance*

Self-Concept in the Classroom. Further information may also be obtained by writing the senior author.

Small group counseling sessions. The small group counseling sessions for each group followed a similar pattern. A modified version of Silverman's (1976) "Achievement Motivation" groups was used. Each child selected for the program was interviewed individually by the counselor before being entered into the program. The child was informed of the purpose of the program: to help children do their best in school by learning and practicing new ways of behaving. Each child was given the choice of whether to participate; all children interviewed remained in the program throughout the intervention period. In addition, a note was sent home to their parents describing the program and asking for their cooperation.

Groups composed of five to eight children met twice weekly for approximately 30 minutes each session for a total of 8 weeks. During the first session, the children were given a simple checklist on which teachers would indicate whether the daily goals were met. The form listed 11 specific goals common to all the children (e.g., take-home assignments, books, and notebooks needed) and provided space for one additional personal goal. The first three goals were to be checked off by the parents, and the remaining nine items were to be checked off by the teacher on a daily basis as having been met or not met. At that time each child, with the help of the counselor and the other students, selected a personal goal. These personal goals reflected one or more major problem behaviors noted on the *Behavior Problem Checklist.* The other goals were selected by the teacher and counselor as being desirable for all children in the classroom. The items on the Daily Progress Report were checked off at the end of each day by the teacher and the reason for zeroes was to be clearly explained to the student.

Each week a goal for a specified number of check marks to be accumulated by each member was established by the group. Each child who reached the goal was allowed to participate in a reward session during the last half of the Friday group meeting. The rewards chosen by the students included playing indoor–outdoor games, viewing films, listening to music, or preparing some type of snack, such as popcorn. Children who did not achieve the appropriate number of points remained in their classroom during the reward session.

Most of the group time was spent discussing ways to achieve the goals. Role playing and behavior rehearsal were used frequently as techniques for practicing skills. These major themes emerged during the sessions: developing good school work habits, learning appropriate assertive behavior, and dealing with conflicts. Children in one of the groups practiced relaxation procedures under the supervision of the counselor in separate sessions. The children were also encouraged to support each other in their efforts to achieve their goals.

Consultation with teachers. The counselor met with each teacher at least twice weekly during the intervention period. Problems and issues such as handling disruptive behavior and increasing on-task behavior were discussed. Alternatives such as changing seating arrangements or rearranging class assignments were presented. The progress of the child in the small group sessions was monitored, and modifications were made when necessary.

Results and Discussion

Mean scores for all 90 participants broken down according to treatment group and *Behavior Problem Checklist* factor are shown as a function of measurement occasion in Figure 1. Similar means for the 28 target participants are presented in Figure 2. Both figures suggest that behavior problem scores declined markedly over time on all three factors. Moreover, the most obvious decreases occurred for each group following intervention (for Group 1, intervention occurred between the Pretest and Posttest 1; for Group 2, between Posttest 1 and Posttest 2). This pattern is particularly evident for the target participants depicted in Figure 2.

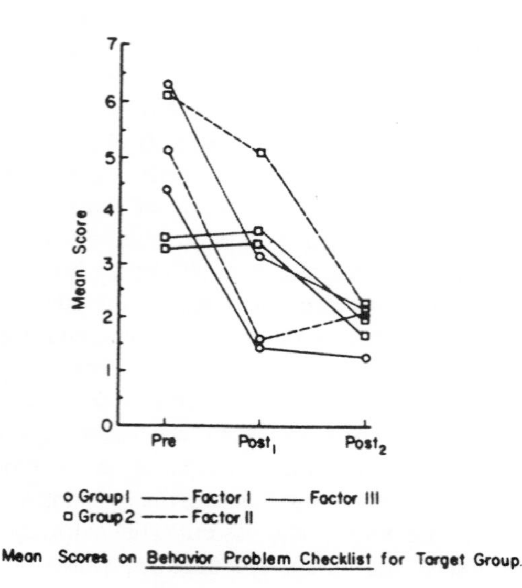

Mean Scores on Behavior Problem Checklist for Target Group.

Figure 1

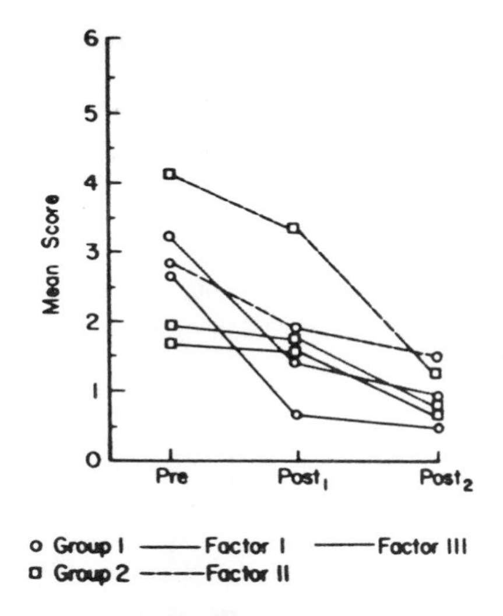

Mean Scores on the Behavior Problem Checklist for Total Sample.

Figure 2

A series of analyses were conducted to assess the statistical significance of the trends indicated in Figures 1 and 2. The pattern of significant ($p < .05$) gain scores was entirely consistent with the hypothesis that improvement in behavior on all three factors occurred after, and only after, treatment was instituted. Only the change on Factor I from Posttest 1 to Posttest 2 for the nontarget participants of Group 2 failed the significance test. A technical write-up of the actual analyses performed and tabled results can be obtained from the junior author on request.

Taken together, the results of the present study support the belief that counselor-consultation intervention can be successful in reducing the behavior problems of elementary school children. More specifically, the combination of group guidance, small group counseling, and teacher consultation seems to be a very effective method of intervention. Not only were major decreases in conduct, personality, and immaturity problem behaviors observed over the course of the study (see Figures 1 and 2), but also these decreases were statistically significant only when observations (i.e., testings) spanned treatment. In this respect, the data unambiguously support the efficacy of the intervention model.

A word of caution is in order, however, because as in previous studies the direct participation of teachers may have influenced the observations. We have reason to believe that teacher–observers wanted the program to succeed, and their enthusiasm may have exaggerated the actual effects of the treatment. But the importance of the caution must not be overemphasized. The objectivity of teacher judgments, as cross-checked by classroom observers who were unaware of treatment onset, remained high throughout the study, at least as far as Factors I and II were concerned. Contamination effects, if there were any, probably were confined to Factor III. It should also be noted that the independent observer ratings, ratings that by design could not be contaminated, were averaged with those made by teachers.

Contaminated observations or not, a favorable outcome was perceived by the teachers themselves. Perhaps this result alone is worthwhile. Not only have these teachers had a positive experience with elementary guidance but also they have new skills for coping with behavior problems—skills that they can continue to apply in their classrooms. An important implication for all elementary school counselors is the desirability of being able to help reduce behavior problems in the classroom in light of the current "back to basics" movement. It seems that a worthwhile endeavor for counselors would be to improve and refine their own skills in this area, so that they can effectively provide this highly valued service. One systematic method that counselors can use to aid teachers in meeting their disciplinary objectives has been described in this report; the results of the empirical inquiry suggest that this approach is effective.

References

Brodinsky, B. (1977). Back to the basics: The movement and its meaning. *Phi Delta Kappan, 58,* 522–526.

Canfield, J., & Wells, H. C. (1976). *100 ways to enhance self-concept in the classroom.* Englewood Cliffs, NJ: Prentice-Hall.

Fortune, L. A. (1975). The effects of multidimensional elementary school counseling on the self-concepts and classroom behavior of alienated elementary school children. (Doctoral dissertation, Washington State University, 1975). *Dissertation Abstracts International, 36,* 704A.

Grieger, R. M., & Richards, H. C. (1975). Prevalance and structure of behavior symptoms among children in special education and regular classroom settings. *Journal of School Psychology, 14,* 27–38.

Lewis, M. D. (1970). Elementary school counseling and consultation: Their effects on teachers' perceptions. *School Counselor, 18,* 49–53.

Marchant, W. C. (1972). Counseling and/or consultation: A test of the educational model in the elementary school. *Elementary School Guidance and Counseling, 7,* 4–8.

Palmo, A. J. (1971). The effect of group counseling and parent-teacher consultations on the classroom behavior of elementary school children. (Doctoral dissertation, West Virginia University, 1971). *Dissertation Abstracts International, 32,* 1863A.

Quay, H. C., & Peterson, D. R. (1979). *Manual for the behavior problem checklist.* Miami: Authors.

Silverman, M. (1976). The achievement motivation group: A counselor directed approach. *Elementary School Guidance and Counseling, 11,* 100–107.

Sugar, M. S. (1974). Case analysis: Consultation and counseling. *Elementary School Guidance & Counseling, 9,* 58–67.

The Effects of Classroom Meetings on Self-Concept and Behavior

Sandra N. Sorsdahl
Robert P. Sanche

During the 1970s, teachers in regular classrooms observed a steady increase in the number of children with personal, social, and behavioral problems in the schools (Gearheart & Weishahn, 1980). An undetermined portion of the increase may be attributed to the passage in 1975 of Public Law 94-142 (Education for all Handicapped Act of 1975), which required that children with special needs be placed in regular classrooms. Various other reasons for placing children with special needs in regular classrooms have been presented in the literature. The pervasiveness of the problem is well documented because 13 of the 14 annual Gallup Polls on the public's attitudes toward public schools (Gallup, 1982) have identified discipline as the most important problem in education in the United States. Although the nature of the problem is important, a more critical factor is the manner in which school systems provide needed support services for teachers and counseling services for children.

Traditionally, school administrators have responded to the increase in the numbers of behavioral problems in the schools by providing more specialized personnel who can give corrective or therapeutic services directly to individual children (Newcomer, 1980). As the need for more support services increases, there is pressure to provide counseling as a preventive measure in addition to providing traditional counseling to meet the therapeutic needs of children (Gazda, 1969; Purkey, 1970). Administrators increasingly expect that regular classroom teachers are the professionals who can best provide preventive or *developmental* (Newcomer, 1980) counseling as a supplement to therapeutic counseling.

In the socialization of children, the peer group plays a crucial role, not only in helping the development of the child's self-concept and social adjustment but also in acting as the most powerful agent affecting positive changes in the behavior of children (Gazda, 1969; Schmuck & Schmuck, 1971). Although clear evidence exists of the influence that both the teacher and the peer group can have on the behavior of individual students, it remains unclear precisely what structure and what process are most effective in preventing problematic behavior in the classroom. This study examined one specific group structure that can potentially influence the socialization of children—classroom meetings

(Glasser, 1969). These meetings involve entire classes and their teachers for the purpose of problem solving or discussion.

Classroom meetings have some distinct advantages over both individual treatment and other group counseling methods. Problem behavior occurs in the classroom and in the child's interpersonal relationships. Classroom meetings provide an intervention that addresses the problem in the social setting in which it occurs. In this setting, the teacher can ensure that problem behavior is treated with the caring, assistance, and support of the social peer group. In addition, intervention in the classroom can increase the child's feelings of being included in a supportive, accepting group rather than increasing his or her feelings of being singled out and excluded from the classroom group to receive counseling. The number of children receiving support can be increased, and professional counseling personnel then are able to concentrate on children with the most serious needs.

Dougherty (1980) stated that "classroom meetings are an important way to meet the [demand] . . . that guidance and counseling 'is for all kids, not a select few'" (p. 131). Certainly, as Hillman, Penezar, and Barr (1975) pointed out, "students who do not have serious problems can profit by learning how to make decisions, accept responsibility, get along with others, and . . . become adequate adults" (p. 761). Classroom meetings can provide the teacher with a method of assisting students in developing their own problem-solving skills and with a viable behavior management technique.

Research has indicated that group counseling is beneficial to elementary school children (Dinkmeyer, 1970; Kelly & Matthews, 1971). This study was intended to investigate the efficacy of providing preventive group counseling to entire classes of children through classroom meetings. A secondary purpose was to determine whether children's self-concepts would improve as a result of classroom meetings.

Method

Participants

The study involved 91 elementary school children in Saskatoon, Saskatchewan, Canada. One fourth-grade class in each of four schools was used, with two classes serving as experimental groups and two classes as control groups. Because classroom meetings, by definition, require intact classes of children and their regular teachers, random selection of children and random assignment of teachers to classes were not possible.

Selection of schools involved determining those that were comparable in size and were in communities with similar socioeconomic mixes. From this group, four schools were chosen in which fourth-grade teachers were judged to be using democratic principles in the classroom, to be generally accepting and nonjudgmental of students, and to be interested in participating in the study.

Instruments

Two measurement instruments, the Pupil Behavior Rating Scale (PBRS) (Lambert, Hartsough, & Bower, 1979) and the Piers-Harris Children's Self-Concept Scale (P-H) (Piers, 1969), were completed as pretest and posttest measures of behavior and self-concept, respectively, for the 91 children in both the experimental and control groups. Two rating scales, the Classroom Meeting Behaviour Rating Scale (CMB) and the Classroom Meeting Self-Concept Rating Scale (CMSC), were developed for the study. The CMB is a measure of interpersonal behavior during classroom meetings. It consists of 10 items that allow teachers to rate children on classroom meeting behaviors such as attentiveness, tolerance for the views of others, tact and manners, participation, obedience to rules, and ability to achieve or participate in the consensus of the meeting. Each item is scored on a 5-point scale ranging from *almost always* to *almost never.* Sample items include "refuses to agree, prevents consensus," "tactless, rude, socially inappropriate," and "behavior often requires a review of rules or removal from the meeting."

The CMSC is a measure of classroom meeting self-concept; that is, children's perceptions of their value, status, role, and membership in the meeting groups. Examples of items from CMSC are "confident, able to make responses in opposition to the majority," "makes aggressive or angry comments," and "tends to lead discussions, offers comments that lead to further discussion." Teachers rate each child's behavior on a 5-point scale ranging from *almost never* to *almost always.* The split-half reliability coefficient is .88 for the CMB and .93 for the CMSC, both well beyond the .60 that Salvia and Ysseldyke (1981) considered a minimum standard. These instruments were also completed by the teachers as pretests and posttests for the 45 children in the experimental groups.

Procedures

Teachers in the experimental groups were given 5 hours of instruction in the theory and techniques of classroom meetings. Instruction included the use of videotaped demonstrations of both general discussion and problem-solving classroom meetings. Ample time was provided for experimental teachers to ask questions and clarify procedures for classroom meetings.

Experimental groups participated in classroom meetings twice a week for 20 weeks. The control groups were given special activity periods involving the same amount of time that was spent on classroom meetings by the experimental groups. Although the activities provided during this time were regular school activities, the teachers presented these time periods to the control group as special times, to control for any possible Hawthorne effect. Thus, any relative changes found in the experimental group should have been the result of involvement in classroom meetings rather than the result of participation in a "special program."

Classroom Meetings

Classroom meetings were developed according to the guidelines established by Dreikurs (1957) and Glasser (1969) and as described by Dinkmeyer, McKay, and Dinkmeyer (1980), Dreikurs and Cassel (1972), and Dreikurs, Grunwald, and Pepper (1971). Two types of meetings were used: general discussion and problem solving.

Initially, all meetings were discussion oriented and involved such topics as feelings, friends, or subjects requiring imaginative thinking. Topics included "you are establishing a new city," "dreams," "you witness a UFO landing," and "you are moving to a new school and can choose your teacher."

After 4 weeks of meetings, both experimental groups seemed comfortable with discussions, and mutual respect among students seemed to have been established. Problem-solving meetings were introduced in the 5th week. They dealt with subjects that presented real problems to students or to the class. Topics included "gum chewing," "missing pencils," "rough behavior," and "lateness in returning to class after recess."

During the remainder of the treatment period, one discussion meeting and one problem-solving meeting were scheduled each week. The following procedures were used during classroom meetings:

1. Students were seated in a tight circle, and the teacher was part of that circle.
2. Children indicated that they wished to speak by raising their hands, and only one child spoke at a time.
3. Mutual respect and empathy were stressed. Children were expected to listen to others and to show respect for the contributions of others.
4. The leaders taught and acted as models by focusing on the positive and by using encouragement and feedback.

5. Skills such as good listening and attentiveness, speaking directly to the person being addressed, using eye contact and personal names, paraphrasing, and active and reflective listening were encouraged.
6. Although the teachers were initially quite directive, they attempted to be nonjudgmental and to offer opinions sparingly. It was stressed that there were no right or wrong answers.
7. Questions were directed only to those who raised their hands. At various points in each meeting, a question was presented to which each child in turn could respond or pass (not answer).
8. Children were taught to summarize at the end of general discussions. In problem-solving meetings, they were encouraged to explore various problem solutions before committing themselves to specific plans of action.
9. Solutions were chosen by consensus so that all members had agreed to try a solution before it was accepted. Solutions were reviewed to ensure that they were successful; if they did not work satisfactorily, another meeting was held.
10. Time guidelines were adhered to in order to conclude meetings while interest was high. Problem-solving topics were continued at the next meeting if consensus on a solution was not reached.

Data Analysis and Results

The intent of the study was to determine whether classroom meetings, as a form of group counseling, could be used to improve the behaviors and self-concepts of fourth-grade students. Before analyzing the data from the study, scores for the two experimental and two control groups were combined to form one group of 45 experimental participants and one group of 46 control participants. Because it was not possible to establish equivalent groups through random assignment of students, one-way analyses of variance (ANOVAs) were completed to determine whether the two groups differed on pretest PBRS and P-H means.

The groups did not differ significantly on pretest P-H means but they did differ significantly on PBRS means ($F = 7.71$, $df = 1, 89$, $p < .05$). An analysis of covariance was used to test for posttest differences between the experimental and control groups on the PBRS. Pretest PBRS scores were used as the covariate. Because no significant pretest differences in P-H means were found, the posttest P-H means were compared by a one-way ANOVA. Pretest to posttest means for behavior (CMB) and self-concept (CMSC) for the experimental group in classroom meetings were tested by one-way ANOVAs.

There was a significant difference ($F = 11.86$, $df = 1, 86$, $p < .05$) on posttest PBRS means in favor of the experimental group; that is, when adjustments were made for pretest differences between the groups, the posttest mean for the experimental group was significantly better after treatment. The students who participated in classroom meetings improved their behavior significantly more than did those in the control group. The students in the experimental group also showed significant improvement in behavior (CMB) during classroom meetings ($F = 116.07$, $df = 1, 86$, $p < .05$).

The experimental and control groups did not differ significantly on posttest P-H self-concept scores. The experimental group did show a significant improvement on pretest to posttest self-concept (CMSC) during classroom meetings ($F = 52.98$, $df = 1, 86$, $p < .05$). The experimental group did not improve on a measure of general self-concept (P-H), but they did improve significantly on a measure of self-concept during classroom meetings.

Discussion

Behavior

Experimental and control groups differed significantly, with the experimental group having higher scores on classroom behavior (PBRS). Children participating in meetings improved significantly in ratings of classroom behavior. In addition, significant improvement in teacher ratings of behavior in classroom meetings (CMB) was found. The results indicated that classroom meetings were effective in improving children's behavior in meetings. The results also indicated that improvement in behavior was carried over from classroom meetings to the larger classroom setting.

Because the teachers who conducted the classroom meetings also administered the CMB, CMSC, and PBRS, bias in their ratings was possible. The treatment in this study—the classroom meeting—made it necessary to use intact groups of children and their teachers. In future studies, provisions should be made for a second teacher or counselor to participate in the classroom meetings and to rate the children independently on the three scales.

Teacher observations suggested that children in the control groups did react to the presentation of a special time by displaying anticipation and excitement. Because both the control and experimental groups had the perception of involvement in a special activity, the improved behavior observed can be considered a result of classroom meetings rather than a result of participation in a special program.

Self-Concept

Self-concept, as measured by the P-H, did not differ significantly between experimental and control groups and did not increase significantly for the experimental group after treatment. Self-concept, however, in the classroom meeting (CMSC) did increase significantly after participation in meetings.

It is possible that the multifaceted nature of self-concept (Coopersmith, 1967; Purkey, 1970) may have accounted for the lack of change in general self-concept as measured by the P-H. Because overall self-concept is generally considered to comprise situation-specific aspects, "global measures may not be valid when applied to more specific facets of self-concept" (Boersma, Chapman, & Battle, 1979, p. 433). A general measure of self-concept, such as the P-H, may have been too broad to reflect changes resulting from the classroom meeting intervention because changes in several situation-specific aspects would be necessary before changes in measured, general self-concept became evident. This possibility is also supported by the finding that the measure of self-concept in the classroom meeting (CMSC), which is situation-specific to the study, significantly increased, whereas the measure of general self-concept (P-H) did not. Furthermore, a longer period of treatment may have been necessary for increases in specific aspects of self-concept to be apparent in global self-concept.

Implications

The results of this study suggest that classroom meetings have potential not only as a treatment technique for children with behavioral problems but also as a technique in the prevention of problem behavior. Komechak (1971) stated that is is "vital that the teacher follow up on gains made [in counseling] by helping the child transfer these learnings [to classroom living]" (p. 14). This extension of counseling to the classroom can be encouraged by the involvement of the teacher and the peer group in both processes. Classroom meetings also seem to be effective means of providing preventive counseling to entire classes of children by enhancing their problem-solving skills, their decision-making skills, their acceptance of responsibility, and their interpersonal skills.

Classroom meetings seem to be a cost-efficient approach to providing more preventive counseling for children. Some counseling techniques presently offered through individual or small-group approaches could be provided in larger groups, resulting in the need for fewer group leaders. Intervention to diminish problem behavior could be provided more often at an earlier stage, reducing the need for subsequent expensive special placements. Furthermore, the professional counselors' time could be reserved for children with more pressing needs. Such an approach would allow counselors to use their skills to work with more seriously disturbed children and to train and support teachers in implementing classroom meetings. Classroom meetings seem to have significant potential for providing preventive counseling services to large numbers of children through their regular classroom teachers.

References

Boersma, F. J., Chapman, J. W., & Battle, J. (1979). Academic self-concept change in special education students: Some suggestions for interpreting self-concept scores. *Journal of Special Education, 13,* 433–441.

Coopersmith, S. (1967). *The antecedents of self-esteem.* San Francisco: Freeman.

Dinkmeyer, D. (1970). Developmental group counseling. *Elementary School Guidance & Counseling, 4,* 267–272.

Dinkmeyer, D., McKay, G., & Dinkmeyer, D. (1980). *Systematic training for effective teaching.* Circle Pines, MN: American Guidance Service.

Dougherty, A. M. (1980). Designing classroom meetings for the middle school child. *School Counselor, 28,* 127–132.

Dreikurs, R. (1957). *Psychology in the classroom.* New York: Harper & Row.

Dreikurs, R., & Cassel, P. (1972). *Discipline without tears.* New York: Hawthorn Books.

Dreikurs, R., Grunwald, B., & Pepper, F. (1971). *Maintaining sanity in the classroom.* New York: Harper & Row.

Gallup, G. H. (1982). The 14th annual gallup poll of the public's attitudes toward the public schools. *Phi Delta Kappan, 64,* 37–50.

Gazda, G. M. (Ed.). (1969). *Theories and methods of group counseling in the schools.* Springfield, IL: Charles C Thomas.

Gearheart, B. R., & Weishahn, M. W. (1980). *The handicapped student in the regular classroom.* St. Louis: C. V. Mosby.

Glasser, W. (1969). *Schools without failure.* New York: Harper & Row.

Hillman, B. W., Penezar, J. T., & Barr, R. (1975). Activity group guidance: A developmental approach. *Personnel and Guidance Journal, 53,* 761–767.

Kelly, E. W., & Matthews, D. B. (1971). Group counseling with discipline-problem children at the elementary school level. *School Counselor, 18,* 273–278.

Komechak, M. G. (1971). The activity-interaction group: A process for short-term counseling with elementary school children. *Elementary School Guidance & Counseling, 6,* 13–20.

Lambert, N. M., Hartsough, C. S., & Bower, E. M. (1979). *A process for the assessment of effective student functioning: Administration and use manual.* Monterey, CA: Publishers Test Service.

Newcomer, P. L. (1980). *Understanding and teaching emotionally disturbed children.* Boston: Allyn & Bacon.

Piers, E. V. (1969). *Manual for the Piers-Harris Children's Self-Concept Scale.* Nashville: Counselor Recordings and Tests.

Purkey, W. W. (1970). *Self-concept and school achievement.* Englewood Cliffs, NJ: Prentice-Hall.

Salvia, J., & Ysseldyke, J. E. (1981). *Assessment in special and remedial education* (2nd ed.). Boston: Houghton Mifflin.

Schmuck, R. A., & Schmuck, P. A. (1971). *Group processes in the classroom.* Dubuque, IA: Brown.

Chapter 9

Counseling Issues Related to Children's Behavior in a Changing World

Issues for elementary school counselors to consider about children's behavior in a changing world:

1. Discuss how school environment effects student behavior. What changes in the school environment might create positive changes in student behavior?
2. How can elementary school counselors use group counseling to improve student behavior in the classroom?
3. Elementary school counselors often use behavior management techniques to help children with behavior problems. Discuss the advantages and disadvantages of using behavior management techniques with children.
4. Several parents have informed you that they are having difficulty handling the misbehavior of their children at home. How would you help these parents to improve the behavior of their children?
5. What are some activities elementary school counselors might include as part of teacher and parent group sessions on improving children's behavior?
6. Why is it difficult for an elementary school counselor to change children's classroom behavior through individual counseling in the counselor's office?
7. How would you respond to a teacher who says, "Children's behavior is getting worse and worse. I'm getting out of teaching as soon as I can?"
8. How can elementary school counselors use video technology to improve children's behavior in the classroom?
9. Develop an inservice training program that is intended to help teachers reduce behavior problems in the classroom. How do you feel about elementary school counselors involving themselves in this kind of inservice training?

CHAPTER 10

HUMAN RELATIONS IN A CHANGING WORLD

Children need to support each other in a world filled with conflict. They must learn and practice the interpersonal skills necessary for their present lives and also for the demands of peer pressure in adolescence. Elementary school counselors must find ways both to challenge and support youngsters in the area of human relations. Chapter 10 describes ways that counselors can build positive relationships among children and between children and adults.

The topics covered in this chapter are as follows:

1. The effects of the DUSO program on children's social skills
2. Peer counseling programs to foster interpersonal relations
3. Use of children's books to foster social development

Each of the procedures discussed in Chapter 10 offer counselors and teachers ways to improve human relation skills in children. As Mary Trepanier and Jane Romatowski note in their article on using books to promote social development,

> The elementary classroom is a busy marketplace where ideas and values are constantly exchanged. In this marketplace the teacher has the opportunity to use the interactions of children with peers, with adults, and with the curriculum for promoting cognitive and social growth. The creative use of such interactions and of the curriculum can increase children's awareness of the perspective of others and promote more altruistic behavior.

The main goal of this chapter is to show that elementary school counselors play a major part in developing and maintaining a healthy social climate for children. This aspect of counselors' work is important in part because children's relations with teachers, peers, and family affect learning and achievement. In addition, counselors who strive to improve children's interpersonal skills are helping to insure that the 1990s and beyond will be years in which society will move forward on the basis of cooperative efforts among the nation's citizens. Finally, the work of elementary school counselors in this area will likely help to produce citizens who strive for productive relations across cultures and nations.

Effects of DUSO-2 and DUSO-2-Revised on Children's Social Skills and Self-Esteem

Carol Lynn Morse
Jerry Bockoven
Alex Bettesworth

With the 1970s came the ubiquitous affective education programs for children. Some, like the Developing Understanding of Self and Others (DUSO) program (Dinkmeyer, 1970) have been revised (DUSO-R) for the 1980s (Dinkmeyer & Dinkmeyer, 1982) and widely disseminated. More than 150,000 DUSO kits were sold during a 10-year period (American Guidance Service, 1982). The few empirical studies on DUSO-2 and DUSO-2-Revised provide some evidence of their effectiveness and shed some light on the question, "Do these programs provide anything of value for children?" There are no follow-up studies, however, evaluating the long-lasting (i.e., temporal) effects of the DUSO-2 and DUSO-2-Revised programs even though the need for such studies is recognized as important in the literature (Elardo & Elardo, 1976). Counselors and teachers who are investing precious time and resources in DUSO-type programs would benefit from such studies by using the results to guide their use as well as their expectations of the materials.

We undertook this study as an attempt to remedy the deficiency of follow-up information in the literature by examining the temporal effects of DUSO-2 and DUSO-2-Revised, both of which are designed for second- through sixth-grade students (DUSO-1 and DUSO-1-Revised are intended for kindergarten through second-grade students). Specifically, the question we addressed was: What are the effects of DUSO-2 and DUSO-2-Revised treatment on children's self-esteem and social skill levels, 6 months following exposure to these programs?

DUSO-2 and DUSO-2-Revised

DUSO-2 and DUSO-2-Revised have been compared in detail by Bockover and Morse (1986). Essentially, both versions have similar goals for helping children: (a) to understand themselves better, (b) to develop positive self-images, (c) to enhance awareness of the relationship between themselves and others, and (d) to recognize their own goals and needs (Dinkmeyer & Dinkmeyer, 1982). The changes in DUSO-2-Revised are considerable and involve all aspects of the kit—teachers manuals, audiocassettes of songs and stories, discussion pictures, activity suggestions, role-playing activities, career activities, puppet activities, and discussion guide cards. These revisions may rest more on impressions of those who have used the program, important though such feedback may be, than on empirical evidence.

Previous Research

Several authors have provided summaries of empirical studies investigating the effectiveness of the original and revised DUSO programs (Bockover & Morse, 1986; Elardo & Elardo, 1976; Medway & Smith, 1978; Morse & Bockover, 1987). In general, this research has indicated the positive effects of DUSO-type training on measures of affect (Eldridge, Barcikowski, & Witmer, 1973), self-reliance and feelings of belonging (Koval & Hales, 1972), self-concept (Stacey & Rust, 1986), and behavior (Wantz & Recor, 1984). These encouraging findings are moderated, however, by a number of other studies that failed to discover results in favor of DUSO (Allen, 1976; Marshall, 1973; McGoran, 1976; Quain, 1976; Terry, 1976).

Oregon DUSO-2 Research Studies Series

Because the previous studies on DUSO-2 and DUSO-2-Revised had addressed only the most basic research questions, we designed the Oregon DUSO-2 Research Studies Series to explore the effects of these affective education curricula in more detail. We hoped that by investigating these programs systematically and sequentially, information about their short-term and long-range effects could be provided for consumers. The initial study in this series (Bockover & Morse, 1986) was designed to compare the effects of DUSO-2, DUSO-2-Revised, and attention-only control groups on measures of self-esteem (Battle, 1981) and social skills (Thorpe, Clark, & Tiegs, 1953). The results of this investigation indicated that following an 8-week treatment period (3 hours per week), children exposed to DUSO-2-Revised made significantly greater gains with respect to general, social, and total self-esteem than did those given mere attention via entertainment activities such as art, crafts, and stories. Furthermore, it was found that children assigned to the DUSO-2 group made significantly greater gains in terms of their awareness of expected social standards than did children in the attention-only group. In this article we provide the results of a second research project of the Oregon DUSO-2-Revised Research Studies Series.

Method

Procedures

We attempted to contact the 26 children, aged 7 to 9 years, included in the initial investigation 6 months after their involvement. We were unable to contact 2 of these children, but the remaining 24 agreed (via their parents) to participate in this study and complete the same instruments under similar testing conditions as the original study.

Instruments

As in the original study, the social adjustment section of the California Test of Personality (CTP) (Thorpe et al., 1953) and the Culture Free Self-Esteem Inventory (CFSEI) (Battle, 1981) were used in the follow-up study. Both are established as valid and reliable instruments (Battle, 1977, 1980, 1981; Coopersmith, 1967; Thorpe et al., 1953). The social adjustment section of the CTP includes 6 subunits: Social Standards, Social Skills, Freedom from Antisocial Tendencies, Family Relations, School Relations, and Community Relations (Thorpe et al., 1953). The total self-esteem score of the CFSEI is subdivided into four categories: General, Social, Academic, and Parental. The CFSEI also includes a lie scale, which purports to measure the child's tendency to respond to the questionnaire in socially desirable ways (Battle, 1981).

Data Analysis and Hypothesis

The results of the initial study in the Oregon DUSO-2-Revised Research Studies Series were obtained by comparing the average gain scores (pretest to posttest) for the three randomly assigned groups (i.e., DUSO-2, DUSO-2-Revised, attention only). In this second-phase study, these three groups were compared using the average gain scores measured from pretest to follow-up testing (i.e., 6 months later). This procedure made it possible to compare the two studies and organize the results into three categories of temporal effects: (a) maintenance effects—significant group differences observed in the initial study that were maintained in the follow-up study, (b) latent effects—group differences not observed in the initial study that emerged as significant in the follow-up study, and (c) diminished effects—significant group differences observed in the initial study that were not obtained in the results of the follow-up study. We hypothesized that differences among these three kinds of temporal effects would be found in the present study.

Because this is the first follow-up study of its kind on the DUSO-2 or DUSO-2-Revised programs and because the sample size was somewhat small

($N = 24$), we decided to relax the traditional .05 significance level to .10 for the three group comparisons. (Support for this procedure has been documented by Howell, 1982.) The criteria for significance for two-group (post hoc) comparisons using Fisher's least significant difference method (Fisher, 1949) was kept at the .05 level, however.

Results and Discussion

The overall results of this study yielded three latent and maintenance effects and one diminished effect (see Table 1). These findings support this type of categorization and in this way corroborate the hypothesis.

Table 1
Significant Group Differences on Gains Made Pretest to Posttest Compared to Gains Made Pretest to Follow-Up

Dependent Measure	Gains Made Pretest To Posttest[a]	Gains Made Pretest To Follow-Up[b]	Temporal Effect
CTP Social Standards subscale	DUSO-2 Attention-only	DUSO-2 Attention-only	Maintenance
CFSEI Total Self-Esteem score	DUSO-2-Revised Attention-only	DUSO-2 and DUSO-2-Revised Attention-only	Maintenance and latent
CFSEI General Self-Esteem subscale	DUSO-2-Revised Attention-only	No significant results	Diminished
CFSEI Social Self-Esteem subscale	DUSO-2-Revised Attention-only	DUSO-2-Revised Attention-only	Maintenance
CTP Total Social Adjustment score	No significant results	DUSO-2 Attention-only	Latent
CFSEI Lie subscale[c]	No significant results	Attention-only > DUSO-2-Revised	Latent

Note. Findings based on post-hoc analysis using Fisher's (1949) least significant difference method, $p < .05$.
[a]Initial study.
[b]Present study.
[c]Higher scores on the CFSEI Lie Scale indicate a greater tendency to answer test items in a socially desirable way.

Maintenance effects were evident for the DUSO-2 group in relation to changes in the child's knowledge of socially acceptable standards. In addition, the DUSO-2-Revised group "maintained" significantly higher change scores than the attention-only control group in terms of overall self-esteem and the child's feelings of confidence in social settings (CFSEI Social Self-Esteem). Taken by themselves, these results suggest a distinction between the two kits. The maintenance effects of the DUSO-2-Revised curriculum seems to display a penchant toward influencing the affective component of a child's functioning (i.e., feelings of confidence and self-esteem), whereas the DUSO-2 kit's effects tend toward the cognitive aspect (i.e., "knowledge" of social standards [Thorpe et al., 1953]).

Only one diminished effect was found; it involved the CFSEI General Self-Esteem subscale (defined as the child's feeling of confidence not attached to any particular situation [Battle, 1981]). The significantly higher gain scores of the DUSO-2-Revised group over the attention-only group found in the initial study were not found in the pretest to follow-up period. This result may indicate that the initial effects either disappeared or that these vague feelings of confidence attached themselves to a specific situational context (i.e., social self-esteem). Whatever the case, these results raise the question of the difference between the Total Self-Esteem score (which is the aggregate of the subscales) and the CFSEI General Self-Esteem subscale. Clearly there is no difference in effects, however, the author of the CFSEI is unclear (if not silent) as to the specific distinction between these two scores. Future research in this area (i.e., factor analysis of the subscales and total scores on this measure) would promote further understanding of the effects of DUSO-2-Revised.

Latency effects were evident for both kits. The DUSO-2-Revised group gain scores were significantly lower than the attention-only control group's gain scores on the CFSEI Lie scale in the pretest to follow-up period. A lower score on this subscale indicates that the child is answering the questionnaire in an "honest" fashion and is not yielding to the perceived socially desirable answers. This result would suggest that the DUSO-2-Revised group developed a greater sense of self-autonomy and independence over time than the attention-only control group. Again, it seems that the DUSO-2-Revised kit tends to yield higher scores on the measures that include an affective component.

The DUSO-2 group's latency effects surfaced on the CFSEI Total Self-Esteem subscale and the CTP Social Adjustment Total score. The Social Adjustment scale on the CTP may be categorized as a self-report behavioral measure, whereas the CFSEI Self-Esteem subscale is clearly in the affective camp. This would suggest that although the original DUSO-2 curriculum may be seen as more effective in terms of changes in the cognitive-behavioral realm of social functioning, it does include some degree of affective efficacy.

One additional data treatment procedure involved subtracting the posttest score obtained for each subject from the scores obtained at the time of follow-up. This procedure yielded a gain score (posttest to follow-up) for each participant. No significant differences were found, however, among groups, thus indicating that none of the groups made significant gains or losses in terms of self-esteem or social skill levels between the posttest and follow-up period.

Conclusion

Given the findings of this study, it is somewhat lamentable that previous studies of the 1970 DUSO curriculum did not include follow-up designs such as this one. If the authors of DUSO-R had the advantage of such information when considering whether to retain, expand, or exclude components of the DUSO curriculum, they might have enhanced the likelihood of creating a package that could have influenced all three of the vital components of social functioning (i.e., cognitive, behavioral, affective). As it stands, however, the DUSO-2-Revised curriculum seems to focus primarily on the affective realm, which in and of itself is an important factor in helping children develop into healthy and happy adults.

These findings further suggest that present consumers of the DUSO-2 and DUSO-2-Revised programs may do well to alter their group guidance practices in order to adjust for the weaknesses that may be inherent in either kit. This study points to the possibility that the DUSO-type programs may be imperfect tools for building a complete cognitive, affective, and behavioral structure for developing self-esteem and social skills with children. Counselors and teachers who are informed of the use, as well as the limitations, of these tools can use them more effectively in conjunction with other resources in helping children.

Specifically, consumers of the DUSO-2 and DUSO-2-Revised kits may enhance the impact of these programs by providing supplemental resources designed to help children put the lessons into behavioral practice. In addition, those who exclusively use the DUSO-2-Revised curriculum may need to bolster areas of functioning related to children's beliefs and self-talk (i.e., cognitions) about themselves and others, whereas DUSO-2 users would do well to supplement areas related to their students' awareness and understanding of feelings. Possibilities for implementing these suggestions include using additional materials from other sources or created by the user, as well as using spontaneous comments tailored to help the students generalize the lessons to specific areas of functioning (i.e., cognitive, affective, behavioral). Also, because both kits offer a wide variety of program choices for each session, consumers may wish to focus on selecting the lessons that would balance the respective weaknesses of each program.

Finally, because of the latent effects found in this study, consumers would do well to caution themselves against making immediate judgments as to the effectiveness of the DUSO-2 and DUSO-2-Revised programs. It would seem that some aspects of these kits take time to influence students. Further studies assessing these latent effects would be a helpful contribution to the present understanding of these curricula.

References

Allen, R. (1976). The effects of DUSO upon the reported self-esteem of selected fifth grade subjects (Doctoral dissertation, University of South Carolina, 1976). *Dissertation Abstracts International, 27,* 2066A.

American Guidance Service. (1982). *Developing understanding of self and others—revised.* Circle Pines, MN: Author.

Battle, J. (1977). A comparison of two self-report inventories. *Psychological Reports, 41,* 159–160.

Battle, J. (1980). The relationship between self-esteem and depression among high school students. *Perceptual and Motor Skills, 51,* 157–158.

Battle, J. (1981). *Culture Free Self-Esteem Inventory.* Seattle: Special Child Publications.

Bockoven, J., & Morse, C. (1986). A comparative study of the efficacy of the DUSO and DUSO-R on children's social skills and self-esteem. *Elementary School Guidance & Counseling, 20,* 290–296.

Coopersmith, S. (1967). *The antecedents of self-esteem.* San Francisco: Freeman.

Dinkmeyer, D. (1970). *Developing understanding of self and others.* Circle Pines, MN: American Guidance Service.

Dinkmeyer, D., & Dinkmeyer, D., Jr. (1982). *Developing understanding of self and others, D-2* (rev. ed.). Circle Pines, MN: American Guidance Service.

Elardo, P., & Elardo, R. (1976). A critical analysis of social development programs in elementary education. *Journal of School Psychology, 14,* 118–130.

Eldridge, M., Barcikowski, R., & Witmer, J. (1973). Effects of DUSO on the self-concepts of second-grade students. *Elementary School Guidance & Counseling, 7,* 256–260.

Fisher, R. (1949). *The design of experiments.* Edinburgh, Scotland: Oliver & Boyd.

Howell, D. (1982). *Statistical methods for psychology.* Boston: Duxbury Press.

Koval, C., & Hales, L. (1972). The effects of DUSO guidance program and self-concepts on primary school children. *Child Study Journal, 2,* 57–61.

Marshall, P. (1973). Effective counselor uses of DUSO guidance materials. *Guidelines for Pupil Services, 12,* 20–23.

McGoran, S. (1976). *The effects of the DUSO I program on the self-concepts of first grade children.* Unpublished master's thesis, University of Washington, Kent.

Medway, F., & Smith, R. (1978). An examination of contemporary elementary schools affective education programs. *Psychology in Schools, 15*, 260–268.

Morse, C., & Bockoven, J. (1987). The Oregon DUSO-R Research Studies Series: Integrating a children's social skills curriculum in a family education/counseling center. *Individual Psychology, 43*, 101–114.

Quain, J. (1976). Affective education: Teacher training for affective education; change in self-concept and affectivity in kindergarten children (Doctoral dissertation, St. Louis University, 1976). *Dissertation Abstracts International, 37*, 7604A.

Stacey, S., & Rust, J. (1986). Evaluating the effectiveness of the DUSO-1 (revised). *Elementary School Guidance & Counseling, 20*, 84–90.

Terry, B. (1976). The effects of the implementation of the DUSO kit on self concept and self achievement of third grade students (Doctoral dissertation, University of South Carolina, 1976). *Dissertation Abstracts International, 37*, 2088A.

Thorpe, L., Clark, W., & Tiegs, E. (1953). *California Test of Personality.* Monterey, CA: McGraw-Hill.

Wantz, R., & Recor, R. (1984). Simultaneous parent-child group intervention. *Elementary School Guidance & Counseling, 19*, 126–131.

Editor's Note: Readers may want to review *Elementary School Guidance & Counseling*, (1986), *20*, 290–296 for additional information on this research study.

Peer Counseling: More on an Emerging Strategy

Alan G. Downe
H. A. Altmann
Ione Nysetvold

Recently counselors at all levels of the helping profession have begun to use a relatively new concept known as *peer facilitation* or *peer counseling*. The proliferation of community self-help groups, client-to-client counseling programs within correctional and rehabilitative centers, and the vast array of burgeoning volunteer crisis-counseling programs testify to the overwhelming support accorded to strategies using lay counselors in lieu of professional practitioners. Brown (1974) attributed this growth in popularity to the rapid increase in demand for counseling services among contemporary North Americans and the shortage of professionally trained personnel available to render such services within the community.

Nowhere has the demand for counseling outstripped the supply of helping services to a greater degree than in the elementary school system, where professional counselors have often found themselves relegated to the level of traveling psychometricians and agents of occasional intervention. A strategy that offers the teacher, school counselor, or educational social worker an opportunity to increase accessibility of counseling services for students is needed. One such strategy is to train students to carry on a formal helping function within the school environment as peer counselors. In this article we examine directions in the "peer-helper" movement with special emphasis on its potential role in the elementary school.

Peer counseling is a process in which trained, supervised students are selected to help in the systematic facilitation of affective growth and the development of effective coping skills among other students. Of course, the notion of a student-to-student helping relationship in school settings is not new. Peer tutors have been employed extensively to facilitate academic performance throughout the history of education in the Western world (Anderson, 1976). It is a relatively recent phenomenon, however, that peer influence has been directed toward affective education and the provision of nonacademic, interpersonal helping activities. Since the mid-1970s, the principle of peer facilitation has become accepted as a valuable human resource for school counseling services.

Peer counseling strategies have been rather slow to catch on at the elementary school level, although in the elementary school counseling literature interest has fluctuated for about 10 years. In an attempt to uncover some of the reasons for the low incidence of such programming in the elementary school setting, Jacobs, Masson, and Vass (1975) surveyed counselors in the state of West Virginia and asked them why they had been reluctant to implement programs that used the peer-helper approach. Four explanations were given by counselors for their reticence: (a) they did not know enough about it; (b) they lacked the time to train and supervise student counselors; (c) they thought they lacked skills needed to train and supervise; and (d) they did not have the support for such a program from teachers and administrators.

Despite the frequency and very real nature of these counselor's concerns, the incidence of peer counseling has continued to increase in elementary schools across North America. Inventive, insightful risk takers like Barbara Varenhorst (1974) and Jim Gumaer (1973, 1976) spurred the early development of this approach and demonstrated its validity in both secondary and elementary schools. Excellent new programs (Bowman & Myrick, 1980; Carr & Saunders, 1980; Myrick & Erney, 1978) for selecting, training, and involving peer counselors in helping activities have been made available for the schools. Attempts to evaluate peer counseling programs (McIntyre, Thomas, & Borgen, 1982) are providing validation for the success of the concept and building a reputation of respectability for the approach. As Donald Keat (1976) pointed out, "the age of peer help is now upon us" (p. 7).

Psychological Processes Involved in Interactions Among Peers

Before examining the specific applications of peer interaction to interpersonal helping relationships, school counselors may find it useful to look first at some of the psychological and behavioral processes considered to underlie the effectiveness of peer counselor activities. By understanding various aspects of the dynamic interplay between those psychological and behavioral factors that affect peer influence, it may be possible to achieve greater insight into the means through which effective peer helping relationships can be facilitated. Much of what occurs within a peer counseling relationship can be explained by the precepts of social learning theory.

Social Learning, Modeling, and the Interaction of Peers

Bandura's (1969, 1977) theory of social learning places special emphasis on the role played by vicarious processes inherent in much of a child's learned behavior. Drawing from Bandura's (1977) consideration of these processes, we suggest that the following four elements are involved in governing the learning by observation of children.

The child pays attention to the modeled behavior. For vicarious learning to occur, the attention of a child must be directed toward the behavioral stimulus and held there long enough for the behavior, its antecedents, and its consequences to be observed. Whether or not attention is paid to the stimulus can depend on its distinctiveness, the kind of affective reaction associated with it, and the child's perception of the functional value of the modeled behavior. Sensory and arousal characteristics of the observer will also influence the degree to which the stimulus is attended.

The child mentally retains the modeled behavior. After attending to the behavior stimulus, the child needs to maintain a cognitive representation of the modeled behavior. The degree to which retention occurs is influenced by the way the modeled behavior is coded and organized in the child's memory, as well as whether there has been an adequate opportunity for rehearsal of the behavior.

The child has the perceptual-motor capacity to reproduce the modeled behavior. Not all children can perform all the same behaviors. If a child attends to and retains a behavioral stimulus that cannot be imitated because of developmental or physical deficits, then vicarious learning cannot occur.

The child is motivated to reproduce the modeled behavior. An observed behavior will be performed by a child if the behavior is reinforced.

Each of these elements of the social learning process has its own special applicability to the relationship between peer counselors and the fellow students they try to help. The qualities of distinctiveness, positive affective valence, and functional valence are frequently present in the behavioral performance of valued peers so that conditions that facilitate attention to a modeling stimulus are readily provided by a peer-to-peer relationship. Cognitive coding and organization of behavior may be easiest to interpret when it is shared between persons of the same age, thereby increasing the likelihood that behavior performed by a peer will be retained and that vicarious learning can occur. The rehearsal of new behaviors, also important to the retention process, may often be carried out with less threat of inhibition in the presence of a trusted peer.

A third element of the social learning model requires the observer to have sufficient motor skills to be able to reproduce the remembered behavior at an appropriate time. Because the participants in peer-interactive relationships are more than likely at approximately equivalent levels of social, physical, and cognitive development, the potential for copying a model of the same age will probably be greater than if the behavior were to be performed by an adult with several more years of developmental experience and a more advanced repertoire of communicative and other skill behaviors. Finally, the desire to attain levels of status displayed by the peer model and to experience observed reinforcers provides the incentives and motivations inherent in the social learning process.

The relating of one peer to another thus provides all of the elements present in social learning. Because Bandura (1969) suggested that "an observer becomes empathetically aroused as a result of intuiting the experiences and affective states of another person" (p. 171), a relationship with an effective peer facilitator might direct empathic arousal toward appropriate and increasingly capable forms of behavioral change. We suggest that the dynamic effects of the peer helping process can be largely explained within the cognitive-behavioral framework advanced by social learning theory. The use of a social learning framework as a theoretical base for future research into the dynamics and outcomes of peer counseling relationships is recommended.

Roles for Peer Counselors

The trend in most elementary school peer counseling programs has been toward involving the students in a remedial, treatment-oriented model for the delivery of helping services. Whereas the trend among many high school peer-helper programs has been toward the development of individual counseling skills, most elementary school programs that we reviewed focus on training students to function in group settings, often as aides to the professional counselor or teacher who acts as a group leader.

Many problems have been addressed using this approach. Academic failure (Dineen, Clark, & Risley, 1977), low self-esteem (Carr & Saunders, 1980), and shyness (McCann, 1975) have been common targets for the elementary school peer counselor and are particularly appropriate because of their high degree of relevance to the learning process. Ethnic and race relations have also been dealt with effectively by numerous programs based on the concept of peer-to-peer helping relationships (Gumaer, 1973; Hoffman, 1976). Peer counseling has also been shown to be effective in addressing problems such as the transfer of students to a new school (Bogat, Jones, & Jason, 1980).

It is clear that peers are extremely well suited for filling a modeling role, and this concept has been applied to a wide range of classroom situations. Hoffman (1976), Edwards (1976), and Strom and Engelbrecht (1974), particularly, have emphasized the influence of peer facilitators in programs in which pupils served as models for effective communication behaviors, basic academic and social skills, and creative play. Children in these studies have proved to be effective role models for peers. In addition, because this modeling takes place in such a way that students are allowed the opportunity to observe and practice alternative behaviors under lifelike conditions, transfer of this learning to natural situations is also greatly enhanced.

Peer helpers also have an important role as a resource for interpersonal support. Varenhorst (1974) summarized the parameters of this supportive capacity when she pointed out that

> As a psychologist, I can care genuinely for Ralph (an isolated, alienated junior high school student), but I can't be his buddy, eat his lunch with him, walk home from school with him, or shoot baskets in his backyard. I know students as friends, but I can't go to class with them, walk in the hall with them, or be a close friend to all of them. These students need their peers, who will be their friends or be friendly or help them learn the skills to build their own friendship group. (p. 271)

Programs striving to achieve these goals in elementary schools have attempted to foster such sharing by placing peers in group counseling situations (Gumaer, 1976; Hoffman, 1976), recommending "buddy system" pairings (Varenhorst, 1974), establishing student-operated "drop-in centers" in the school (McCann, 1975), and providing orientation aids (Mastroianni & Dinkmeyer, 1980).

Some argument exists about the most appropriate term to use when describing the pupil-to-pupil helping process. Because the term *counselor* tends to conjure images of professional help, often with a specific treatment model, Anderson (1976) has favored using the term *peer facilitator* to avoid confusing parents and school administrators with inaccuracies about the helping process being used. For the same reasons, Jacobs et al. (1976) suggested terms such as *student aide, student helper,* and *peer helper*. We argue that the label attached to the individual trained for interpersonal helping is less important than the actual work performed, and that maintaining open lines of communication with administrators, teachers, and parents about the rationale and role of a peer counselor program will do more to guard against misunderstandings than will any particular terminology.

Selection of Peer Counselors

As a general rule, many peer counselor program coordinators have taken a rather cavalier attitude toward the identification and selection of prospective peer counselors in the elementary school classroom. Three commonly used criteria for choosing participants for peer counseling training include (a) similarity to targeted students, (b) the recommendation of a teacher or principal, and (c) psychometric assessment. No single criterion may be adequate for accurate selection in all situations; thus, certain features of each of these criteria must be considered.

The idea that simply because an individual is similar to others he or she can serve as a useful helping resource for them is not necessarily supported by some of the empirical evidence currently available. Bachman's (1975) research indicated that "similarity to subject" (p. 106) may be relatively inconsequential in terms of helper characteristics sought after by children needing help. More specifically, of the participants in Bachman's study who preferred to take their problems to peers, fewer than 10% did so because they believed that their friends were similar to them. Thus, choosing peer counselors simply because they are the same age as or at the same grade level as the targeted participant may be somewhat inadequate for providing consistently helpful resources for elementary school children.

Similarly, problems arise when the recommendations of adults are used as the sole criteria for choosing those best suited for training and involvement as peer facilitators. Although pupils selected as peer counselors on the basis of referrals from teachers and other school personnel often do make excellent helpers, this approach is sometimes confounded by the failure of the intuitive perceptions of helpfulness held by these adults to coincide with the facilitative qualities that appeal to members of the class. In trying to determine the individual most likely to be an adequate helper, teachers may equate helpfulness with prestige status within a classroom clique or subgroup, with academic achievement, or with high levels of appropriate child-adult behavior. These characteristics may not be highly valued by the student clientele.

What seems to be needed most is an assessment device that will aid in identifying those with the potential for making successful peer counselors. Not enough is now known, however, about the functional qualities of helpfulness in the elementary school or the means by which younger children perceive the helping relationship. Although an attempt has been made to construct a scale to measure facilitativeness, efforts have been directed toward standardizing it for populations of high school students only, and few field data are yet available as to concomitant levels of reliability and validity.

Sociometry as an Aid in the Selection Process

Techniques using a sociometric approach for the analysis of classroom social structure have acquired credibility in a wide range of applications (Northway & Weld, 1957). Basically, sociometric analysis involves the collection of data from participants regarding their preference for others with whom they would like to perform an important task. Such approaches might be particularly useful when applied to the selection of students capable of filling roles as peer counselors.

Lippitt and Gold (1959) examined the social structure of the classroom and its effect on the mental health of pupils. They found a very definite social power structure characterized not only by consensus about who belongs where in the social hierarchy, but also by high structural stability throughout the school year. Furthermore, they demonstrated that the same children were not at the top and bottom of all social substructures, suggesting that just because a child stands out in one area, he or she cannot necessarily be considered as a class leader in others.

Gumaer (1973) applied sociometric methods to the selection of candidates for peer facilitator training. He suggested that by asking members of the class to indicate classmates to whom they would go with a personal problem it would be possible to tap the social structure for some indication of which individuals were perceived by their peers as being intrinsically helpful. In doing so, it would become possible to select prospectively successful peer counselors without having to resort to the opinion of a third party.

A practical example of Gumaer's techniques was supplied by McCann (1975), who selected candidates for peer counselor training and work at her elementary school. McCann asked children in a sixth-grade class to think of their classmates and write down the name of the one with whom they would feel most comfortable discussing a problem, to underline that name, and to write their own names on the same sheet of paper. The papers were collected and a tally was made of the number of selections received by each child in the class. A sociogram was constructed, with vectors pointing from each child to the classmate he or she had chosen. Prospective peer counselors were indicated as those who had been chosen by the greatest number of students and were thus central to a cluster of vectors on the sociogram.

Importance of Selection Procedures

Despite the rather cavalier attitude sometimes taken in choosing whom to train for peer-helper rules, the selection process is perhaps the most important determinant in the overall success of a program of peer help. Although sociogrammatic analyses have been used infrequently for the selection of elementary school peer counselors, as Gumaer (1976) suggested, they are a promising strategy for future applications in the classroom. Input from teachers and parents can be used to supplement classmates' perceptions of potentially helpful peers and to assess the capacity of prospective peer counselors to cope with additional stresses encountered in their role.

Training for Peer Counselors

Whereas the selection process is important, the training process is critical. Although we have long believed that too much attention is often paid to training novice counselors in individual skills (Mahon & Altmann, 1977), there is much evidence to indicate the importance of a structured program for training persons for a formal helping role.

Of the peer counselor programs in the elementary schools that we have reviewed, all placed a fairly strong emphasis on the skill-training components of the program, although a wide range of training procedures was used. In most cases, training tended to be conducted in a small group that met with the professional counselor-coordinator on several occasions to discuss and practice specific helping skills.

The length of training and the number of skill-training sessions varied considerably from program to program. McCann (1975) met with her trainees for eight 1-hour weekly sessions, whereas Edwards (1976) held training sessions once daily during lunch recess for 10 days, and Hoffman (1976) engaged prospective peer group models in ten 1-hour sessions held on a weekly basis. Weekend retreats and workshop formats have been used with some success, especially with older children (Pyle, 1977). In one program reviewed, skill development was initiated in a single training session, but more advanced levels of performance were attained by meeting with peer facilitators immediately before and after each session with the target group (Weise, 1976).

In general, considerable variety seems to characterize the length and intensity of peer-counselor training in the elementary schools and seems closely related to the actual skills being taught, the purposes of the program, and the priorities of the program coordinator. Many peer-counselor training programs tend to be developed in a rather piecemeal fashion according to the biases of the person designing the program and the nature of the specific problems being addressed.

There is also considerable variety in the types of skills regularly imparted during training. Most programs seem to emphasize listening skills, with attending behavior stressed most strongly. In the peer-counselor training programs we reviewed, most curricula are designed to teach students how to reflect and paraphrase responses, as well as various means of describing and comparing affective feelings. Skills involving action-oriented strategies such as setting goals, giving advice, and contracting have been largely absent from many of the peer-counseling programs at the elementary school level. The absence of such skills suggests that peer counselors are intended to function largely as cathartic supports and effective listeners. Strategies engendering behavioral change are often left to the professional counselor or educator to design and implement.

One concern is the dearth of curricular provision for instructing helpers at the elementary school level in ethical considerations inherent in the paraprofessional helping process. Certainly the concept of filling facilitator roles with individuals incognizant of principles pertaining to confidentiality and other ethical issues is one that ought to create some trepidation for anyone initiating and coordinating a program of peer-mediated help. Yet only Hoffman (1976) and a few other program designers seem to have included formal instruction on the ethics of counselors. We strongly recommend that students receiving peer-counselor training be exposed to concepts and dilemmas related to the maintenance of confidentiality, as well as to other ethical issues relevant to their roles in the general counseling program at their school.

Evaluation

Any new intervention suffers from inadequate evaluation, and peer counseling has been no exception. Those developing some peer programs have failed to conduct a needs assessment before implementation, thus using subjective comments as the main means of evaluation. We believe that three essential aspects of peer counseling are assessment of the self as helper (Brammer, 1979; Egan, 1975; Myrick & Erney, 1978), assessment of knowledge and skills used in the process (Myrick & Erney, 1978), and assessment of outcome (McIntyre et al., 1982). Although standardized instruments are often appropriate for evaluation, we support the notion of first identifying the needs in a specific setting and then developing instruments to determine whether the program has met those needs.

Evaluation of a peer counseling program can be simple and straightforward. Moreover, evaluation is necessary for the accountability and survival of peer counseling programs.

Peer Counseling: Promise in an Emerging Strategy

Although peer counseling is still a relatively new approach to helping in school settings, it offers some definite benefits for students and school professionals. The development of an effective peer-counseling program can provide a school with a cost-effective vehicle for broadening the range and variety of helping formats offered in a guidance or social work program. Furthermore, the additional support provided for the helping professional in the school setting, in terms of the roles adopted by peer counselors, allows the professional to focus on problems requiring his or her attention. Also, the use of peer-counselor programming allows a guidance service to address problems that would be less effectively handled in adult-child helping relationships.

Some definite benefits exist for the young person who becomes involved as a peer counselor. A sense of self-esteem, arising possibly from the prestige of being selected and the satisfaction of personal investment in the needs of others, has been reported by students who act as peer counselors (Bowman & Myrick, 1980; Carr & Saunders, 1980; Keat, 1976). The child who experiences peer-counselor training develops not only an array of interpersonal skills that may transfer to other situations but also an awareness of the personal benefits from being a helper. A structured opportunity to broaden his or her social contacts in the school environment through involvement in peer counseling allows a student to experience an enriched and extensive extracurricular activity in addition to special attention from adults.

Of course, benefits are also realized by the students who constitute the target population addressed by a particular peer-counseling program. The opportunity to share experiences, feelings, and outlook with a peer helper whose similarity in age may allow for greater understanding is a valuable component of the developmental guidance required by any student. The presence of an effective and valued role model, as well as the added element of social support in informal situations, also contributes significantly to the promotion of personal growth.

Peer counseling approaches are particularly well suited to the elementary school. This view is based on the notion that the elementary school child is uniquely different from junior and senior high school students. Some of these differences produce distinctive needs that can be met through a peer relationship. Muro and Dinkmeyer (1977) discussed numerous reasons why elementary school children require the attention of special helpers. One of the ideas they cited is the very nature of the child. The elementary school child has limited freedom at home and school, where adults are mainly in control and directing. Experiences of the child in these settings can be quite stressful and require a source for disclosure.

Egocentricity dominates and characterizes the thinking process of a child (Muro & Dinkmeyer, 1977). Adult logic and simply lack of time produce frustration and lead to limited and ineffective communication between children and adults. Children possess the skills to communicate effectively, but the recipient of disclosure must be able to comprehend the world of the child. For many students only another peer will be available to take the time, to try to understand, and maybe help.

References

Anderson, R. (1976). Peer facilitation: History and issues. *Elementary School Guidance & Counseling, 11*, 16–33.

Bachman, R. (1975). Elementary school children's perception of helpers and their characteristics. *Elementary School Guidance & Counseling, 10*, 103–109.

Bandura, A. (1969). *Principles of behavior modification*. New York: Holt, Rinehart and Winston.
Bandura, A. (1977). *Social learning theory*. Englewood Cliffs, NJ: Prentice-Hall.
Bogat, A. G., Jones, J. W., & Jason, L. A. (1980). School transitions: Preventive intervention following an elementary school closing. *Journal of Community Psychology, 8*, 343–352.
Bowman, R. P., & Myrick, R. D. (1980). I'm a junior counselor having lots of fun. *School Counselor, 28*, 31–33.
Brammer, L. (1979). *The helping relationship: Process and skills*. Englewood Cliffs, NJ: Prentice-Hall.
Brown, W. (1974). Effectiveness of paraprofessionals: The evidence. *Personnel and Guidance Journal, 53*, 257–263.
Carr, R. A., & Saunders, G. (1980). *Peer counseling starter kit*. Victoria, B.C.: University of Victoria.
Dineen, J. P., Clark, H. B., & Risley, T. R. (1977). Peer tutoring among elementary students: Educational benefits to the tutor. *Journal of Applied Behavior Analysis, 10*, 231–238.
Edwards, S. (1976). Student helpers: A multilevel facilitation program. *Elementary School Guidance & Counseling, 11*, 53–58.
Egan, G. (1975). *The skilled helper: A model for systematic helping and interpersonal relating*. Monterey, CA: Brooks/Cole.
Gumaer, J. (1973). Peer-facilitated groups. *Elementary School Guidance & Counseling, 8*, 4–11.
Gumaer, J. (1976). Training peer facilitators. *Elementary School Guidance & Counseling, 11*, 27–36.
Hoffman, L. (1976). Peers as group counseling models. *Elementary School Guidance & Counseling, 11*, 37–44.
Jacobs, E., Masson, R., & Vass, M. (1975). *A peer counseling training model* (pamphlet). Martinsburg, WV: Berkeley County School District.
Jacobs, E., Masson, R., & Vass, M. (1976). Peer helpers: An easy way to get started. *Elementary School Guidance & Counseling, 11*, 68–71.
Keat, D. (1976). Training as multimodal treatment for peers. *Elementary School Guidance & Counseling, 11*, 7–13.
Lippitt, R., & Gold, M. (1959). Classroom social structure as a mental health problem. *Journal of Social Issues, 15*, 40–49.
Mastroianni, M., & Dinkmeyer, D. (1980). Developing an interest in others through peer facilitation. *Elementary School Guidance & Counseling, 14*, 214–221.
Mahon, B., & Altmann, H. (1977). Skill training: Cautions and recommendations. *Counselor Education and Supervision, 17*, 42–50.
McCann, B. (1975). Peer counseling: An approach to psychological education. *Elementary School Guidance & Counseling, 9*, 180–187.
McIntyre, D. L., Thomas, G. H., & Borgen, W. A. (1982). A peer counselling model for use in secondary schools. *Canadian Counsellor, 17*, 29–36.

Muro, J. J., & Dinkmeyer, C. D. (1977). *Counseling in the elementary and middle schools*. Dubuque, IA: Brown.

Myrick, R., & Erney, T. (1978). *Caring and sharing: Becoming a peer facilitator.* Minneapolis: Educational Media Corp.

Northway, M. L., & Weld, L. (1957). *Sociometric testing*. Toronto: University of Toronto Press.

Pyle, K. (1977). Developing a teen-peer facilitator program. *School Counselor, 24*, 278–282.

Strom, R., & Engelbrecht, C. (1974). Creative peer teaching. *Journal of Creative Behaviour, 8*, 93–100.

Varenhorst, B. (1974). Training adolescents as peer counselors. *Personnel and Guidance Journal, 53*, 271–275.

Weise, R. (1976). Diary of a peer facilitator program. *Elementary School Guidance & Counseling, 11*, 62–66.

Successful Training for Elementary and Middle School Peer Helpers

Chari Campbell

Perhaps the most critical component in any peer helper program is training. The procedures chosen to train students can make a difference between a successful program and an unsuccessful one. Although a number of peer programs were launched in the 1970s, some that lacked planning and organization soon floundered and then disappeared. In others, however, the planners ensured success and support for their programs by being more systematic in their approach, defining the training programs in detail, and selecting the peer projects and tasks carefully (Myrick & Bowman, 1981). A growing body of research indicates that a more systematic approach to teaching helping skills will lead to more successful interventions (Bowman & Myrick, 1980; Briskin & Anderson, 1973; Kern & Kirby, 1971; Kum & Gal, 1976; McCann, 1975; Vogelsong, 1978). Gains in self-esteem, classroom behavior, and academic achievement are reported for peer helpers and their helpees in programs that have carefully defined goals and objectives of training (Myrick & Bowman, 1981).

What are the characteristics of successful peer helper programs? An examination of such programs reveals that the length and number of training sessions is a matter of individual preference. Some helping projects seem to require more preparation than others. Depending on the counselor's schedule and faculty support, training can vary in length from four 1/2-hour sessions to over twenty 45-minute training sessions.

Depending on the counselor's orientation, training programs may vary in their theoretical bases from Adlerian or Rogerian to behavioral. In addition, the perceived or assessed needs of the school will determine whether the training focuses on techniques for working with targeted students with problems or on skills for leading developmental guidance activities with small or large groups.

Tailored to the Setting

Peer helper programs should reflect schools in which they are established. More specifically, the needs, attitudes, and values of the students and the teachers determine the types of projects in which the peer helpers will participate. It is wise to solicit faculty and administrative input before determining the goals and objectives of a training program. After the needs of the school have been assessed, a training program may be designed that specifically addresses those needs. This approach of tailoring the program to the particular demands of the setting will help to ensure support for the program.

Tailored to the Task

Peer helpers can be trained to work in various helping roles. Myrick and Bowman (1981) categorized the helping roles into four groups: student, assistants, tutors, special friends, and small-group leaders.

Student assistants work indirectly with other students by assisting teachers, librarians, or office personnel with specific tasks. Some student assistants, such as school safety patrol leaders, help to supervise other children. Student tutors work directly with other students, either individually or in small groups. Tutors build and reinforce basic skills in academic subject areas. Special friends are assigned on a one-to-one basis to help students with special needs. For example, a special friend may help to draw out a shy child, motivate an underachiever, or help a new child feel more comfortable in the school. Small-group leaders direct or codirect such activities as small-group discussions, role-playing activities, or puppet activities.

Although some basic helping skills can be useful for students involved in any of these roles, other skills and concepts may also be needed for specific projects. Thus, the content of training sessions may vary from project to project. For example, Myrick and Bowman (1981) described a training model that focuses upon basic relationship and communication skills during the first phase of training and then gives students the opportunity to practice for specific helping projects using role playing and other techniques.

Additionally, the Myrick and Bowman model suggested that training be arranged so that students can participate in some structured beginning projects after initial training. Then, after further training, students may become involved in more sophisticated projects. These authors emphasized that it is the training and the projects themselves that characterize most programs as either beginning, intermediate, or advanced.

Tailored to the Counselor's Style

There are many possible directions a peer helper program can take. The types of helping projects that can be performed by children helping children seem limited only by the program leader's creativity. Rockwell and Dustin (1979) pointed out that no single program can include every option and that counselors must select from several choices.

A program should be tailored to the personal and professional style of its coordinator. The leader's preferences for certain counseling theories will be reflected in the peer training program. Because most peer program leaders are counselors, they should also be aware of their own strengths as professional helpers. They can also include some of their favorite counseling activities in the program. This personalization of the peer training will give strength and energy to the program. Some counselors have discovered that their own skills become sharpened and polished as they become involved in training students. This is one of the many benefits for the counselor of a well-planned peer training program.

Selection of Students

The selection of students is an integral part of training. A review of the literature suggests a wide variance in approach to the selection process. Bowman (1980) selected a variety of students for different purposes, including those with: (a) high academic achievement—they needed and wanted a challenge; (b) high motivation—they especially expressed interest in the program; (c) low self-concept—they needed more success experiences; (d) negative school attitude—they needed to be involved in a positive school experience; and (e) ability to reach out—they cared about others.

Others found the use of sociograms helpful (e.g., Gumaer, 1973; Kern & Kirby, 1971; McCann, 1975). Some used teacher input for the selection of peer helpers (e.g., Briskin & Anderson, 1973; Gumaer, 1973). Rockwell and Dustin (1979) suggested using self-selection, teacher and student input, counselor recommendations, and some objective criteria for student selection. Hoffman (1976) selected students on the basis of leadership abilities observed by the counselor in informal settings around the school. Some counselors, however, reported successful peer programs without systematic selection of trainees (e.g., Delworth, Moore, Mullich, & Leone, 1974; Golin & Safferstone, 1971; Gray & Tindall, 1974; Varenhorst, 1973).

Regardless of the selection process used, however, the effectiveness of the peer programs seems to depend on the thoroughness of the training. A systematic approach to preparing students for specific tasks builds program success.

Some Successful Programs

Many training programs have been described in the literature. The following descriptions of programs are not intended to provide a comprehensive list but illustrate the variety of approaches to peer training that have been used successfully. The programs described use three approaches to peer training: preparing students to work with individuals, with small groups, and with whole classrooms.

Working with Individuals

There are many valuable projects for which peer helpers can be trained to assist other students on a one-to-one basis. These projects include helping with new student orientation, being available for students who need a friend to talk to, reinforcing students' completion of academic assignments, and tutoring in an academic subject. Training for these projects must be designed to prepare students for the particular task. It is suggested that peer helpers be trained in groups even when their projects may involve working with students on a one-to-one basis.

In one case, McCann (1975) developed a training program to prepare sixth graders to work individually with other students in a school drop-in center. The program consisted of eight 1-hour sessions that focused on listening skills, nonverbal communication, self-disclosure, reflective listening, and developing alternative courses of action when faced with a problem. The center was open to fifth-grade students twice a week during recess or lunch. Kum and Gal (1976) cited a similar program in which sixth-grade students were trained in ten 1-hour sessions, focusing on constructive communication and decision-making skills.

In another example, Briskin and Anderson (1973) developed a program to teach behavioral principles to peer helpers. The training program consisted of six 1/2-hour sessions and included such topics as recognizing targeted behavior, administering a time-out procedure, and giving positive reinforcement for appropriate behavior. After the training sessions were completed, the sixth-grade peer helpers were assigned to work as contingency managers for two disruptive third graders. Each of the six peer helpers spent 1/2 hour each day in the third-grade classroom. When they observed one of the targeted behaviors, the time-out procedure was implemented by briefly removing the misbehaving child from the classroom. Appropriate behavior, however, was reinforced with compliments. The data collected throughout the 18-day program suggested that peer helpers can be trained to be highly successful in using contingency management procedures.

Working as Small-Group Facilitators

Following an Adlerian approach, Kern and Kirby (1971) trained fifth- and sixth-grade students to work as peer helpers. Their training program, which consisted of three 1-hour sessions, focused on developing the skill to encourage positive behavior in other students, identifying the goals of misbehavior, and exploring more effective ways of behaving. After completing training, the peer helpers assisted the counselor with group counseling for poorly adjusted peers.

Gumaer (1973) described a nine-session training program that prepared fifth-grade students to facilitate small-group discussions with second graders. Training focused on developing communication skills. More specifically, students were taught to clarify, reflect, and give feedback. After practicing these skills for several weeks, the students were asked to explore topics such as minority groups, stereotypes, and prejudice. The peer helpers then led small-group discussions with second graders.

Hoffman's program (1976) also emphasized preparing students to work as small-group facilitators. Ten 1-hour training sessions included such topics as helping others talk, giving respect, accepting others, listening for feelings, being aware of one's own feelings, words, and actions, and supporting student efforts at behavioral change within and outside the group.

Leading Class Discussions

Some counselors have trained peer helpers to lead or assist with guidance activities in the classroom. Such a project should include very structured activities such as those provided in published guidance materials. Training for this kind of peer involvement might first include rehearsal of the activities. Then peers might practice leading the activities with a small group of children. After this training the same activities can be used with more confidence in an entire classroom of students.

Another way to train peers systematically to lead classroom guidance activities is to divide up the activity and allow three or four peers to share responsibility for the various tasks. For example, one peer helper could read a guidance story, a second might then lead a discussion, and a third peer could present a role-playing activity on the topic. Familiarity with the guidance materials allow for a more smooth delivery in the large group.

Conclusion

The peer helper movement is no longer in its infancy. In the past decade a growing number of elementary and middle school counselors have been involved in training of peer helpers. With greater experience in teaching children helping skills, their training programs have expanded, evolved, and gained wider acceptance.

As the peer helper movement has gained momentum more presentations on this topic have been appearing on programs at state and national guidance conferences each year. Beginning in March 1983, a periodical devoted entirely to peer helper programs, the *Peer Facilitator Quarterly* (Bowman, 1983), became available. As counselors find their own ways to train students systematically in helping skills and develop their own peer helper programs, they will find their guidance more effectively extended to all students in their schools.

References

Bowman, R. P. (1980). The peer facilitator movement: Its impact on our schools. *Florida Personnel and Guidance Association Guidelines, 25*, 2.

Bowman, R. P. (1983). *Peer Facilitator Quarterly, 1*, 1–16.

Bowman, R. P., & Myrick, R. D. (1980). I'm a junior counselor, having lots of fun. *School Counselor, 28*, 31–38.

Briskin, A. S., & Anderson, E. M. (1973). Students as contingency managers. *Elementary School Guidance & Counseling, 7*, 262–268.

Delworth, J., Moore, M., Mullich, J., & Leone, P. (1974). Training student volunteers. *Personnel and Guidance Journal, 53*, 57–60.

Golin, N., & Safferstone, M. (1971). *Peer group counseling: A manual for trainers*. Miami: Dade County Public Schools.

Gray, H. D., & Tindall, J. (1974). Communication training study: A model for training junior high school counselors. *School Counselor, 22*, 107–112.

Gumaer, J. (1973). Peer facilitated groups. *Elementary School Guidance & Counseling, 8*, 4–11.

Hoffman, L. R. (1976). Peers as group counseling models. *Elementary School Guidance & Counseling, 11*, 37–44.

Kern, R., & Kirby, J. (1971). Utilizing peer helper influence in group counseling. *Elementary School Guidance & Counseling, 6*, 70–75.

Kum, W., & Gal, E. (1976). Programs in practice. *Elementary School Guidance & Counseling, 11*, 74.

McCann, B. G. (1975). Peer counseling: An approach to psychological education. *Elementary School Guidance & Counseling, 9*, 180–187.

Myrick, R. D., & Bowman, R. P. (1981). *Children helping children: Teaching students to become friendly helpers*. Minneapolis: Educational Media Corporation.

Rockwell, L. K., & Dustin, R. (1979). Building a model for training peer counselors. *School Counselor, 26*, 311–316.

Varenhorst, B. (1973). Middle/junior high school counselor's corner. *Elementary School Guidance & Counseling, 8*, 54–57.

Vogelsong, E. L. (1978). Relationship enhancement training for children. *Elementary School Guidance & Counseling, 12*, 272–279.

Classroom Use of Selected Children's Books: Prosocial Development in Young Children

Mary L. Trepanier
Jane A. Romatowski

The elementary classroom is a busy marketplace where ideas and values are constantly exchanged. In this marketplace the teacher has the opportunity to use the interactions of children with peers, with adults, and with the curriculum for promoting cognitive and social growth. The creative use of such interactions and of the curriculum can increase children's awareness of the perspective of others and promote more altruistic behavior. Since cognitive and social skills are emergent in young children, positive experiences during the elementary school years are critical for their full development.

Psychological theory and past research supports the belief that prosocial development and altruistic behavior is emerging during the elementary school years. Altruistic behavior, such as sharing, requires the ability to take the perspective of another (perspective-taking and role-taking), to understand others' feelings and emotions (empathy), and to evaluate others' needs and decide on an appropriate action (critical thinking) (Mussen & Eisenberg-Berg, 1977). Several studies report that perspective-taking, role-taking, reasoning, and empathy, are positively related to altruistic behavior (Buckley, Siegel, & Nell, 1979; Levine & Hoffman, 1975; Marcus, Telleen, & Roke, 1979; Rubin & Schneider, 1973). According to Piaget (1926) these cognitive and social skills generally develop during the period of concrete operations (7–12 years). With increasing age, children become less egocentric and able to attend to a perspective other than their own. This heightening of awareness about others is possible through the use of selected children's books. Therefore, the purpose of this research was to investigate whether a classroom-oriented intervention technique using selected children's books could effect a positive change in the prosocial development of young children, age 5–7.

The specific intervention technique in this study consisted of reading selected children's books and using planned critical thinking questions by kindergarten and first-grade classroom teachers during regularly scheduled story-telling times. All the books focused directly on sharing or an interpersonal conflict that was successfully resolved through sharing. The planned critical thinking questions throughout the story focused the children's attention on: (a) the interpersonal conflict, (b) the feelings of each character, (c) the cause of the feelings, (d) the resolution of the conflict by sharing, and (e) the change in the feelings of the characters as a result of sharing. Following the reading of the story, the teachers emphasized the importance of sharing and its role in resolving interpersonal conflicts.

This training technique was chosen because it is directly applicable to classroom settings and because its essential components have been identified by prior research as significant for the development of altruism. These components are specified below:

1. Stories and questions should direct the child's attention to the feelings and emotions of the characters and elicit empathy and altruism (Howard & Barnett, 1979; Iannoti, 1978; Staub, 1971).
2. The perspective-taking tasks should be within the developmental capabilities of 5- to 7-year-old children (Urberg & Docherty, 1976).
3. The questioning should encourage children to use hypothesis-testing and reasoning skills to solve a social conflict (Rubin & Schneider, 1973).
4. The conflict resolution through sharing and the verbal reinforcement of this by the teacher should present an appropriate model of prosocial behavior to the children (Bryan, 1975).

We anticipated that through such a classroom training technique children's development of sharing could be positively influenced. Those children in the experimental group receiving training would show a change in performance from pretesting to posttesting. This change would be measured by analyzing the responses to two-conflict-situation pictures and accompanying story dilemmas. Those children in the control group receiving parallel story experiences that did not focus on sharing were not expected to show a pretest to posttest change.

Method

Participants

Initially, 99 children in one kindergarten and three first-grade classrooms were pretested for base level of perspective-taking and sharing. These children were drawn from three inner-city schools located in a large metropolitan area. Those children scoring high on sharing (i.e., giving a sharing response as a first response both times) were not included in the study. Of the remaining 64 children, 33 were chosen for the control group and 31 for the experimental group. Of the respondents, there were 39 boys and 25 girls ranging in age from 5.2 years to 7.5 years with a mean of 6.7 years.

Procedure

Pretesting and Posttesting. The participants in the experimental and control groups were pretested and posttested by the researchers to determine the participants' levels on sharing and perspective-taking. Testing of each participant was conducted in a room separate from the classroom.

The tasks involved the use of two conflict-situation pictures with accompanying stories. Picture 1 and its story concerned a conflict between a bigger boy (Todd) and smaller boy (Billy) playing ball on the playground. The picture depicted the bigger boy holding the ball out of reach of the smaller boy. Picture 2 and its story involved a girl (Shirley) holding a double popsicle and noticing her friend (Tommy) looking at it.

For each task, participants were shown the picture, told a story about the picture, and then asked the following questions:

1. How do you think (Potential Receiver [the character in the picture-story who could be the recipient of a sharing act]) feels?
2. Why does (Potential Receiver) feel that way?
3. How can you tell (Potential Receiver) feels that way?
4. How do you think (Potential Sharer [the character in the picture-story who could be the sharing agent]) feels?
5. Why does (Potential Sharer) feel that way?
6. How can you tell (Potential Sharer) feels that way?
7. What do you think will happen next?
8. What else could (Potential Sharer) have done?
9. What else could have (Potential Receiver) done?

Care was taken by the experimenters to describe all the situations in a neutral tone without suggestion of feelings or solutions.

Training of Teachers. Three participating teachers were trained in the use of the intervention technique for the experimental group and in the parallel story experience for the control group. This training consisted of listening to an audiotape of a sample story, discussing story guidelines for each story, and identifying the parallel story experiences for the control group.

Intervention Technique. During the intervention technique, the experimental group heard a total of 9 selected books focusing on sharing over a 3-week period (3 books per week). Each story was interrupted at preselected critical intervals to permit the participants to label the feelings of story characters, identify the causes for feelings and behaviors, solve the conflict situation, and explain the successful resolution of the conflict. At the end of each story, the teacher emphasized the role that sharing played in the story or in resolving the conflict.

Control Group Experience. The parallel experiences for the control group included the reading of 9 stories that did not focus on sharing over a 3-week period (3 books per week). Further, the stories were interrupted for questions and discussion of story events only.

Materials. For the intervention, 9 readily accessible children's books were selected by the researchers. Criteria for selection were: age-appropriate; story characters with easily identifiable feelings; a clear statement of the conflict; and a successful resolution of the conflict through sharing. Titles of books used in the study appear in the Appendix. In addition, 9 books not focusing on sharing were selected for the control group.

Results

Responses to Pictures 1 and 2 were scored using the same taxonomy for each picture. After two scorers independently scored the protocols, the researchers found the interrater agreement on the questions was 93%. Disagreements were resolved by consensus.

Chi square analysis of pretest responses for each question suggested that there was no significant relationship between group membership (experimental or control) and response. Therefore, the groups were essentially equivalent on the pretest.

Posttest responses were also analyzed using the chi square technique. Because the questions and the scoring taxonomy were identical for Pictures 1 and 2, the analysis for each question reflects a summary of the data across both pictures. The scoring taxonomy used for each question and the results follow.

When asked to label the feelings of the characters in Pictures 1 and 2 and to identify causes for the feelings, no relationship between the group and response was found. Both the experimental and the control groups were competent in identifying the characters' feelings and the causes for these feelings. This finding of no relationship on the posttest was not unexpected inasmuch as a high level of competency for both groups was demonstrated on the pretest. Posttest performance change was limited by this ceiling effect.

Next, participants were asked to identify the source of their information regarding the potential receiver's feelings and the potential sharer's feelings (How can you tell Potential Receiver and Potential Sharer felt that way?). Responses were categorized as appropriate or inappropriate references to facial expressions or bodily gestures. The analysis for the potential receiver question suggested a significant relationship between group membership and response category ($x^2(1) = 5.337, p < .05$). In order to determine which of the cells was contributing significantly to this relationship, cell chi squares were converted into a standardized residual with an associated probability level. The standardized residual can be interpreted in a manner similar to a z score with 0 as the mean and a standard deviation of 1 (Everitt, 1977). An examination of the standardized residuals suggested that the experimental group (residual = 2.32, $p < .05$) was significantly more accurate than the control group in identifying their source of information. While 48% of the control group correctly referred to the facial or bodily characteristics of the receiver, 71% of the experimental group correctly referred to facial characteristics. A similar trend was evident for the question regarding the source of information for the potential sharer's feelings. While 61% of the experimental group correctly referred to facial characteristics, only 48% of the control group correctly referred to facial characteristics.

Responses to the questions, What happened next? and What could have happened next?, were categorized as a sharing response, an aggressive response, or other (avoidance of problem, don't know response). Though chi squares were not statistically significant, it is interesting to note some differences between the groups. While 50% of the experimental group gave a sharing response to the What happened next? question, only 39% of the control group responded similarly. For the What could have happened next? question, a larger percentage of participants in the experimental group (21%) as compared to the control group (13%) moved from an aggressive response to a sharing response.

Discussion

The results of this study suggested that children's prosocial development can be facilitated through a classroom-oriented intervention technique. Although not dramatic, changes were evident in children's verbal sharing responses as a result of the teacher reading selected children's books and asking critical thinking questions. This was evident on the posttest because more children in the experimental group than in the control group verbally suggested sharing as a solution to interpersonal conflicts.

As anticipated, given previous research (Kurdek, 1977; Selman, 1971; Urberg & Docherty, 1976), these results also suggested that children between the ages of 5–7 years were very competent at labeling their feelings. Participants experienced more difficulty in identifying the source of their information regarding the feelings of others and citing the cause of these feelings of others, specifically in identifying facial expressions and bodily gestures. The intervention technique was very successful in facilitating development in this area. This seems quite reasonable given the training technique used. The critical questions designed for use with the books at preselected intervals in the story allowed for such development. Given the age of the participants and their transitional phase of development with respect to the identification of facial clues as a source of information about feelings (Shantz, 1975), it was not surprising that responses were qualitatively better after training.

Dealing with changes in social cognition in young children in a short period of time is, at best, difficult. Clearly, the topic is worthy of longer study, given the amount of success realized in this 3-week period. An expansion of the ideas encountered in the books into other activities, such as role-playing, sociodrama, language-experience stories, and others, may have enhanced the processing of relevant information.

Classroom teachers interested in encouraging prosocial development and altruistic behavior in young children will find this technique to be easily learned. The materials needed for replicating this study are readily accessible and easily incorporated into the curriculum. Adaptation of this technique to one's particular classroom setting will certainly result in a positive growth experience for children.

References

Bryan, J. H. (1975). Children's cooperation and helping behaviors. In M. Hetherington (Ed.), *Review of child development research: Vol. 5*. Chicago: University of Chicago Press.

Buckley, N., Siegel, L. S., & Ness, S. (1979). Egocentrism, empathy, and altruistic behavior in young children. *Developmental Psychology, 15*, 329–330.

Everitt, B. S. (1977). *The analysis of contingency tables*. New York: John Wiley & Sons.

Howard, J. A., & Barnett, M. A. (1979, May). *Arousal of empathy and subsequent generosity in young children*. Paper presented at the annual meeting of the Midwest Psychological Association, Chicago.

Iannotti, R. J. (1978). Effect of role-taking experiences on role taking, empathy, altruism, and aggression. *Developmental Psychology, 14*, 119–124.

Kurdek, L. A. (1977). Structural components and intellectual correlates of cognitive perspective-taking in first- through fourth-grade children. *Child Development, 48*, 1503–1511.

Levine, L. E., & Hoffman, M. L. (1975). Empathy and cooperation in 4-year-olds. *Developmental Psychology, 11*, 533–534.

Marcus, R. F., Telleen, S., & Roke, E. J. (1979). Relation between cooperation and empathy in young children. *Developmental Psychology, 15*, 346–347.

Mussen, P., & Eisenberg-Berg, N. (1977). *Roots of caring, sharing and helping*. San Francisco: W. H. Frieman.

Piaget, J. (1926). *The language and thought of the child*. New York: Harcourt Brace.

Rubin, K. H., & Schneider, F. W. (1973). The relationship between moral judgment, egocentrism and altruistic behavior. *Child Development, 44*, 661–665.
Selman, R. L. (1971). Taking another's perspective: Role-taking development in early childhood. *Child Development, 42*, 1721–1734.
Shantz, C. U. (1975). The development of social cognition. In M. Hetherington (Ed.), *Review of Child Development Research: Vol. 5*. Chicago: University of Chicago Press.
Staub, E. (1971). The use of role-playing and induction in children's learning of helping and sharing behavior. *Child Development, 42*, 805–816.
Urberg, K. A., & Docherty, E. M. (1976). Development of role-taking skills in young children. *Developmental Psychology, 12*, 198–203.

Appendix

Books Used in Study

Consall, B. (1964). *It's mine*. New York: Harper & Row.
Brennar, B., & Ungerer, T. (1966). *Mr. Tall and Mrs. Small*. Reading, MA: Addison-Wesley.
Cole, W. (1970). *Aunt Bella's umbrella*. New York: Doubleday.
Keats, E. J. (1967). *Peter's chair*. New York: Harper & Row.
Lionni, L. (1967). *Frederick*. New York: Random House.
Scott, A. H. (1972). *On mother's lap*. New York: McGraw Hill.
Silverstein, S. (1964). *The giving tree*. New York: Harper & Row.
Steig, W. (1971). *Amos and Boris*. New York: Farrar & Giroux.
Steptoe, J. (1969). *Stevie*. New York: Harper & Row.
Zolotow, C. (1958). *Do you know what I'll do?* New York: Harper & Row.

Chapter 10

Counseling Issues Related to Human Relations in a Changing World

Issues for elementary school counselors to consider about human relations in a changing world:

1. Discuss the following statement: "Learning how to get along with others is the most important part of education."
2. You are a counselor who is interested in developing a peer helping group in your school. Discuss how you would select and train students to become peer helpers. How would you get support from teachers and parents for your peer helping program? How would you evaluate the program?
3. How can elementary school counselors use programs such as *Developing Understanding of Self and Others (DUSO)* to improve human relations at school?
4. How might counselors use video technology to improve relationships between children and adults?
5. How can elementary school counselors use children's drawings as part of a human relations program in the school?
6. What role does self-esteem play in children's relationships?
7. Discuss the possible uses of books to improve children's social skills.